FOR Dummies™

BUSINESS AND
GENERAL
REFERENCE
BOOK SERIES
FROM IDG

Personal Finance For Dummies, 2nd Edition
by Eric Tyson

P9-DWH-995

Quick Reference Card

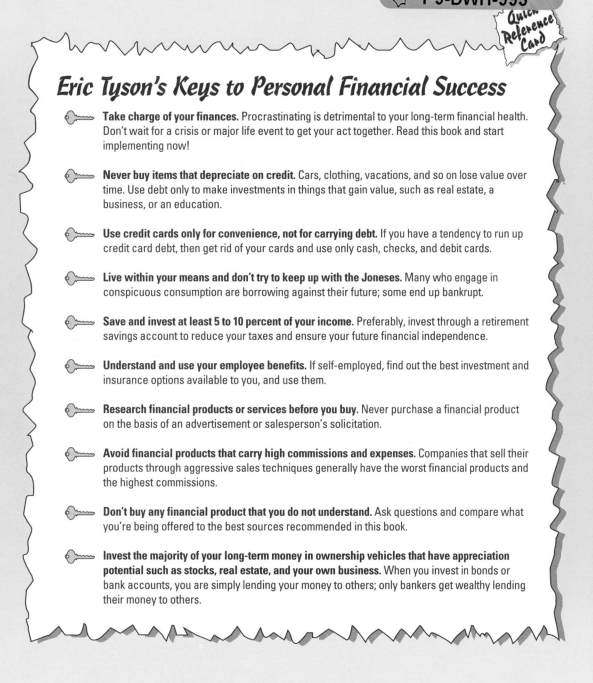

Eric Tyson's Keys to Personal Financial Success

- **Take charge of your finances.** Procrastinating is detrimental to your long-term financial health. Don't wait for a crisis or major life event to get your act together. Read this book and start implementing now!

- **Never buy items that depreciate on credit.** Cars, clothing, vacations, and so on lose value over time. Use debt only to make investments in things that gain value, such as real estate, a business, or an education.

- **Use credit cards only for convenience, not for carrying debt.** If you have a tendency to run up credit card debt, then get rid of your cards and use only cash, checks, and debit cards.

- **Live within your means and don't try to keep up with the Joneses.** Many who engage in conspicuous consumption are borrowing against their future; some end up bankrupt.

- **Save and invest at least 5 to 10 percent of your income.** Preferably, invest through a retirement savings account to reduce your taxes and ensure your future financial independence.

- **Understand and use your employee benefits.** If self-employed, find out the best investment and insurance options available to you, and use them.

- **Research financial products or services before you buy.** Never purchase a financial product on the basis of an advertisement or salesperson's solicitation.

- **Avoid financial products that carry high commissions and expenses.** Companies that sell their products through aggressive sales techniques generally have the worst financial products and the highest commissions.

- **Don't buy any financial product that you do not understand.** Ask questions and compare what you're being offered to the best sources recommended in this book.

- **Invest the majority of your long-term money in ownership vehicles that have appreciation potential such as stocks, real estate, and your own business.** When you invest in bonds or bank accounts, you are simply lending your money to others; only bankers get wealthy lending their money to others.

...For Dummies: Bestselling Book Series for Beginners

BUSINESS AND
GENERAL
REFERENCE
BOOK SERIES
FROM IDG

Personal Finance For Dummies, 2nd Edition
by Eric Tyson

Quick Reference Card

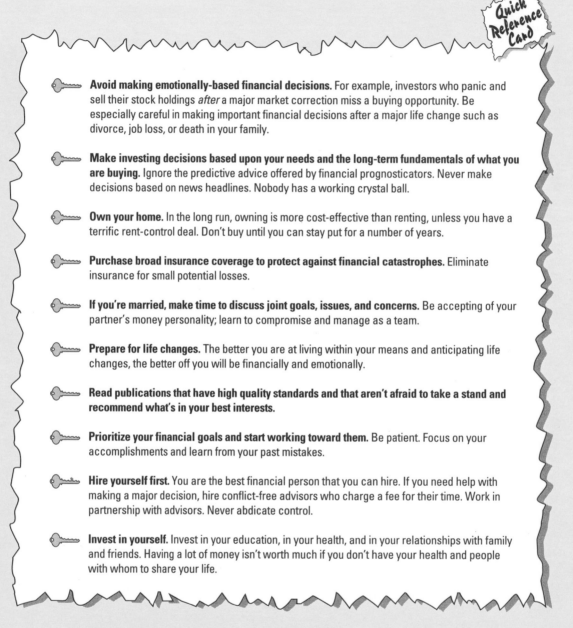

Avoid making emotionally-based financial decisions. For example, investors who panic and sell their stock holdings *after* a major market correction miss a buying opportunity. Be especially careful in making important financial decisions after a major life change such as divorce, job loss, or death in your family.

Make investing decisions based upon your needs and the long-term fundamentals of what you are buying. Ignore the predictive advice offered by financial prognosticators. Never make decisions based on news headlines. Nobody has a working crystal ball.

Own your home. In the long run, owning is more cost-effective than renting, unless you have a terrific rent-control deal. Don't buy until you can stay put for a number of years.

Purchase broad insurance coverage to protect against financial catastrophes. Eliminate insurance for small potential losses.

If you're married, make time to discuss joint goals, issues, and concerns. Be accepting of your partner's money personality; learn to compromise and manage as a team.

Prepare for life changes. The better you are at living within your means and anticipating life changes, the better off you will be financially and emotionally.

Read publications that have high quality standards and that aren't afraid to take a stand and recommend what's in your best interests.

Prioritize your financial goals and start working toward them. Be patient. Focus on your accomplishments and learn from your past mistakes.

Hire yourself first. You are the best financial person that you can hire. If you need help with making a major decision, hire conflict-free advisors who charge a fee for their time. Work in partnership with advisors. Never abdicate control.

Invest in yourself. Invest in your education, in your health, and in your relationships with family and friends. Having a lot of money isn't worth much if you don't have your health and people with whom to share your life.

Copyright © 1996 Eric Tyson.
All rights reserved.
Cheat Sheet $2.95 value. Item 5013-6.
For more information about IDG Books,
call 1-800-762-2974.

IDG
BOOKS
WORLDWIDE

...For Dummies: Bestselling Book Series for Beginners

Praise for Eric Tyson and This Book

Some nice things that people have said about Eric Tyson and this book:

"Eric Tyson is doing something important — namely, helping people at all income levels to take control of their financial futures. This book is a natural outgrowth of Tyson's vision that he has nurtured for years. Like Henry Ford, he wants to make something that was previously accessible only to the wealthy accessible to middle-income Americans. With Ford, it was automobiles; with Tyson, it is thoughtful financial planning. I am enthusiastic about his efforts and see this book as yet one more step down the path of turning his vision into practical reality."
> — James C. Collins, coauthor of the best-seller *Built to Last*

"Smart advice for dummies . . . skip the tomes . . . and buy *Personal Finance For Dummies,* which rewards your candor with advice and comfort."
> — Temma Ehrenfeld, *Newsweek*

"Worth getting. Scores of all-purpose money-management books reach bookstores every year, but only once every couple of years does a standout personal finance primer come along. *Personal Finance For Dummies,* by financial counselor and columnist Eric Tyson, provides detailed, action-oriented advice on everyday financial questions . . . Tyson's style is readable and unintimidating."
> — Kristin Davis, *Kiplinger's Personal Finance Magazine*

"*Personal Finance For Dummies* is the perfect book for people who feel guilty about inadequately managing their money but are intimidated by all of the publications out there. It's a painless way to learn how to take control. My college-aged daughters even enjoyed reading it!"
> — Karen Tofte, producer, National Public Radio's
> *Sound Money*

"Best new personal finance book."
> — Michael Pellecchia, Syndicated Columnist

"Eric Tyson . . . seems the perfect writer for a . . .*For Dummies* book. He doesn't tell you what to do or consider doing without explaining the why's and how's — and the booby traps to avoid — in plain English . . . it will lead you through the thickets of your own finances as painlessly as I can imagine."
> — Clarence Petersen, *Chicago Tribune*

"*Personal Finance For Dummies* is, by far, the best book I have read on financial planning. It is a simplified volume of information that provides tremendous insight and guidance into the world of investing and other money issues."
> — Althea Thompson, Producer, PBS *Nightly*
> *Business Report*

"This book provides easy-to-understand personal financial information and advice for those without great wealth or knowledge in this area. Practitioners like Eric Tyson, who care about the well-being of middle-income people, are rare in today's society."
> — Joel Hyatt, founder, Hyatt Legal Services, one of the
> nation's largest general-practice law firms providing
> personal legal services to families and individuals

"*Personal Finance For Dummies* is a sane and useful guide that will be of benefit to anyone seeking a careful and prudent method of managing their financial world.
— John Robbins, founder of EarthSave and author
of *May All Be Fed*

"Among my favorite financial guides are . . . Eric Tyson's *Personal Finance For Dummies.*"
— Jonathan Clements, *The Wall Street Journal*

"*Personal Finance For Dummies* offers a valuable guide for common misconceptions and major pitfalls. It's a no-nonsense, straightforward, easy-to-read personal finance book. . . . With this book, you can easily learn enough about finances to start thinking for yourself."
— Charles R. Schwab, Chairman and CEO,
The Charles Schwab Corporation

". . . easy and fun to read and chock full of good advice."
— Ann Perry, *The San Diego Union-Tribune*

"For those named in the title, such as myself, *Personal Finance For Dummies* is a godsend. It's bright, funny, and it can save you money, too."
— Jerome Crowe, reporter, *Los Angeles Times*

"Confused by finances and taxes? Eric Tyson has written *Personal Finance For Dummies,* a friendly, easy-to-follow guide to smart money strategies."
— Deb Lawler, anchor, WBZ radio,
Boston, Massachusetts

"This is a great book. It's understandable. Other financial books are too technical and this one really is different."
— Shad Johnson, Producer, Business Radio Network

"An invaluable, easy-to-read financial help book that should be in every family's library."
— *Stan Schaffer,* reporter, *The Morning Call,*
Allentown, Pennsylvania

". . . presents complicated issues with simplicity, clarity and a touch of humor."
— *The Times – Picayune,* New Orleans, LA

"If you're wondering where to start in becoming financially literate, may I recommend *Personal Finance For Dummies* by Eric Tyson."
— Peter McWilliams, *Worcester Telegram & Gazette,*
Worcester, MA.

" . . . straightforward, readable . . .Tyson is an authoritative writer . . ."
— *Orange County Register*

"As small-business owners, we were busy and overwhelmed by all the insurance sales pitches we were getting from agents until we met Eric Tyson. He showed us how to get better coverage and save nearly $2,500 on our life and disability insurance policies alone. It was actually hard to believe — we thought there was some kind of catch!"
— Nina Weisbord and Kyle Terres, interviewed on the
FOX-TV program *On the Money,* a weekly San Francisco
Bay Area business program. Tom Vacar, business
reporter for FOX-TV, said, "Tyson's advice was a godsend."

Praise for Eric Tyson's Other National Best-Sellers

Critical acclaim for Eric Tyson's other national best-sellers

"If reading financial information gives you a splitting headache, Eric Tyson's books are like a cold washcloth and a couple of aspirin. In *Investing for Dummies,* Tyson handily dispatches both the basics . . . and more complicated."
— Lisa M. Sodders, *The Capital-Journal*

"You don't have to be a novice to like *Mutual Funds For Dummies.* Despite the book's chatty, informal style, author Eric Tyson clearly has a mastery of his subject. He knows mutual funds, and he knows how to explain them in simple English."
— Steven T. Goldberg, *Kiplinger's Personal Finance Magazine*

"It can be overwhelming to keep up with the latest developments, which is why you might turn to the book *Mutual Funds For Dummies* by Eric Tyson. A light touch and the use of plenty of graphics help the pages fly by. This book is a primer for those who flinch when contemplating the 7,000 funds you can now buy."
— Brian Banmiller, Fox-TV

"Eric Tyson has brought his financial experience, investment knowledge, and down-to-earth writing style to create an *outstanding* book on mutual funds for all investors — and an essential book for new investors as they first consider the challenging task of investing. In short, a classic . . . "
— John C. Bogle, former CEO & founder, *The Vanguard Group*

"A book that should help investors be smarter . . . readable, comprehensive . . . Tyson's encyclopedic book is chockful of useful examples and advice for both new and experienced investors . . ."
— Kim Campbell, *Christian Science Monitor*

" . . . Smart ideas about mutual funds. The beauty of this book is that you don't have to read it from cover to cover. If you want a simple overview, focus on the highlights; if you want more depth, read the chapters that interest you."
— *The Times-Picayune*, New Orleans, LA

". . . injects common sense into the dizzying world of mutual funds . . ."
— Cliff Pletschet, *Oakland Tribune,* CA

"If you are considering buying a home, don't fail to read this excellent new book. The book is full of profitable "insider tips" which most real estate writers either don't know or are afraid to reveal. Try as I can, I can't find anything negative about this great home buying book . On my scale of 1 to 10, this book rates a 12."
— Robert J. Bruss, syndicated real estate columnist, on Tyson's *Home Buying For Dummies*

"A survival guide to buying or investing in real estate . . . "
— *Homes & Real Estate Magazine* on Tyson's
Home Buying for Dummies

"The new *Home Buying for Dummies* immediately earned a spot on my reference book shelf. . . ."
— Broderick Perkins, *San Jose Mercury News*

" . . . among tax advice books, is far and away the best. *Taxes for Dummies* is fun to read and teaches about the tax system. And it talks about fitting taxes into your daily financial planning. In other words, it's a book you can use after April 15th as well as before."
— Kathy M. Kristof, *The Los Angeles Times,* on
Taxes For Dummies by Eric Tyson and David J. Silverman

"Smart chapters — not just thumbnail sketches — for filling out tax forms."
— Susan Tompor, Gannett News Service on
Taxes For Dummies by Eric Tyson and David J. Silverman

 "It's hard to imagine a more accessible source."
— *The Orange County Register*

"*Mutual Fund$ for Dummie$* by Eric Tyson is an excellent source for not only the novice investor but also for someone looking to enhance their understanding of one of the fastest growing investment tools."
— Tarun Reddy, *Northwest Arkansas Times*

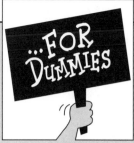

™

References for the Rest of Us!™

BUSINESS AND GENERAL REFERENCE BOOK SERIES FROM IDG

Do you find that traditional reference books are overloaded with technical details and advice you'll never use? Do you postpone important life decisions because you just don't want to deal with them? Then our *...For Dummies*™ business and general reference book series is for you.

...For Dummies business and general reference books are written for those frustrated and hard-working souls who know they aren't dumb, but find that the myriad of personal and business issues and the accompanying horror stories make them feel helpless. *...For Dummies* books use a lighthearted approach, a down-to-earth style, and even cartoons and humorous icons to diffuse fears and build confidence. Lighthearted but not lightweight, these books are perfect survival guides to solve your everyday personal and business problems.

> *"More than a publishing phenomenon, 'Dummies' is a sign of the times."*
> — The New York Times

> *". . . you won't go wrong buying them."*
> — Walter Mossberg, Wall Street Journal, on IDG's ...For Dummies™ books

> *"A world of detailed and authoritative information is packed into them..."*
> — U.S. News and World Report

Already, hundreds of thousands of satisfied readers agree. They have made *...For Dummies* the #1 introductory level computer book series and a best-selling business book series. They have written asking for more. So, if you're looking for the best and easiest way to learn about business and other general reference topics, look to *...For Dummies* to give you a helping hand.

™

IDG
BOOKS
WORLDWIDE

7/96r

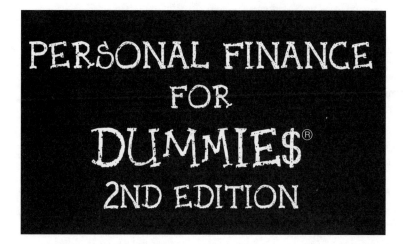

PERSONAL FINANCE FOR DUMMIE$® 2ND EDITION

by Eric Tyson

Financial Counselor, Syndicated Writer,
and author of ...*For Dummies* best-sellers on *Investing,
Mutual Funds, Home Buying,* and *Taxes*

IDG Books Worldwide, Inc.
An International Data Group Company

Foster City, CA ♦ Chicago, IL ♦ Indianapolis, IN ♦ Southlake, TX

Personal Finance For Dummies®, 2nd Edition

Published by
IDG Books Worldwide, Inc.
An International Data Group Company
919 E. Hillsdale Blvd.
Suite 400
Foster City, CA 94404
www.idgbooks.com (IDG Books Worldwide Web Site)
http://www.dummies.com (Dummies Press Web Site)

Copyright © Eric Tyson. All rights reserved. No part of this book, including interior design, cover design, and icons, may be reproduced or transmitted in any form, by any means (electronic, photocopying, recording, or otherwise) without the prior written permission of the publisher.

Library of Congress Catalog Card No.: 96-78140

ISBN: 0-7645-5013-6

Printed in the United States of America

10 9 8 7 6 5 4 3 2 1

2B/RQ/RQ/ZW/IN

Distributed in the United States by IDG Books Worldwide, Inc.

Distributed by Macmillan Canada for Canada; by Contemporanea de Ediciones for Venezuela; by Distribuidora Cuspide for Argentina; by CITEC for Brazil; by Ediciones ZETA S.C.R. Ltda. for Peru; by Editorial Limusa SA for Mexico; by Transworld Publishers Limited in the United Kingdom and Europe; by Academic Bookshop for Egypt; by Levant Distributors S.A.R.L. for Lebanon; by Al Jassim for Saudi Arabia; by Simron Pty. Ltd. for South Africa; by Pustak Mahal for India; by The Computer Bookshop for India; by Toppan Company Ltd. for Japan; by Addison Wesley Publishing Company for Korea; by Longman Singapore Publishers Ltd. for Singapore, Malaysia, Thailand, and Indonesia; by Unalis Corporation for Taiwan; by WS Computer Publishing Company, Inc. for the Philippines; by WoodsLane Pty. Ltd. for Australia; by WoodsLane Enterprises Ltd. for New Zealand. Authorized Sales Agent: Anthony Rudkin Associates for the Middle East and North Africa.

For general information on IDG Books Worldwide's books in the U.S., please call our Consumer Customer Service department at 800-762-2974. For reseller information, including discounts and premium sales, please call our Reseller Customer Service department at 800-434-3422.

For information on where to purchase IDG Books Worldwide's books outside the U.S., please contact our International Sales department at 415-655-3172 or fax 415-655-3295.

For information on foreign language translations, please contact our Foreign & Subsidiary Rights department at 415-655-3021 or fax 415-655-3281.

For sales inquiries and special prices for bulk quantities, please contact our Sales department at 415-655-3200 or write to the address above.

For information on using IDG Books Worldwide's books in the classroom or for ordering examination copies, please contact our Educational Sales department at 800-434-2086 or fax 817-251-8174.

For authorization to photocopy items for corporate, personal, or educational use, please contact Copyright Clearance Center, 222 Rosewood Drive, Danvers, MA 01923, or fax 508-750-4470.

LIMIT OF LIABILITY/DISCLAIMER OF WARRANTY: AUTHOR AND PUBLISHER HAVE USED THEIR BEST EFFORTS IN PREPARING THIS BOOK. IDG BOOKS WORLDWIDE, INC., AND AUTHOR MAKE NO REPRESENTATION OR WARRANTIES WITH RESPECT TO THE ACCURACY OR COMPLETENESS OF THE CONTENTS OF THIS BOOK AND SPECIFICALLY DISCLAIM ANY IMPLIED WARRANTIES OF MERCHANTABILITY OR FITNESS FOR ANY PARTICULAR PURPOSE AND SHALL IN NO EVENT BE LIABLE FOR ANY LOSS OF PROFIT OR ANY OTHER COMMERCIAL DAMAGE, INCLUDING BUT NOT LIMITED TO SPECIAL, INCIDENTAL, CONSEQUENTIAL, OR OTHER DAMAGES.

Note: This book is intended to offer general information on personal finance. The author and publisher are not engaged in rendering legal, tax, accounting, investment, real estate, or similar professional services. Although legal, tax, accounting, investment, real estate, and similar issues addressed by this book have been checked with sources believed to be reliable, some material may be affected by changes in the laws and/or interpretation of laws since the manuscript in this book was completed. Therefore, the accuracy and completeness of the information provided herein and the opinions that have been generated are not guaranteed or warranted to produce particular results, and the strategies outlined in this book may not be suitable for every individual. If legal, accounting, tax, investment, real estate, or other expert advice is needed or appropriate, the reader is strongly encouraged to obtain the services of a professional expert.

Trademarks: All brand names and product names used in this book are trade names, service marks, trademarks, or registered trademarks of their respective owners. IDG Books Worldwide is not associated with any product or vendor mentioned in this book.

 is a trademark under exclusive license to IDG Books Worldwide, Inc., from International Data Group, Inc.

About the Author

Eric Tyson, MBA

Eric Tyson first became interested in money matters more than two decades ago. After his father was laid off during the 1973 recession and received some retirement money from Philco-Ford, Eric worked with his dad to make investing decisions with the money.

A couple of years later, Eric won his high school's Science Fair with a project on what influences the stock market. Dr. Martin Zweig, who provided some guidance, awarded Eric a one-year subscription to the *Zweig Forecast,* now a famous investment newsletter. Therefore, Eric's project must have led to Dr. Zweig's current fame! Of course, Eric's mom and dad share the credit with Martin for Eric's victory.

After toiling away for a number of years as a management consultant to Fortune 500 financial-service firms, Eric finally figured out how to pursue his dream. He took his inside knowledge of the banking, investment, and insurance industries and committed himself to making personal financial management accessible to us all.

Today, Eric is a nationally recognized personal financial counselor, writer, and lecturer based in San Francisco. He has taught thousands of people from all income levels. So he knows the financial concerns and questions of real folks just like you. Despite being handicapped by an M.B.A. from Stanford, and a B.S. in Economics and Biology from Yale, Eric remains a master at "keeping it simple."

An accomplished freelance personal finance writer, his Investor's Guide syndicated column, distributed by King Features, is read by millions nationally.

He is author of five national best-selling financial books in the ...*For Dummies* series on Personal Finance, Investing, Mutual Funds, Home Buying, and Taxes. His work has been featured and quoted in numerous local and national publications including *Newsweek, The Wall Street Journal, Los Angeles Times, Chicago Tribune, Forbes, Kiplinger's Personal Finance Magazine, Parenting, Money, Bottom Line/Personal,* and on the NBC *Today Show*, ABC, CNBC, PBS Nightly Business Report, CNN, and FOX-TV, and on CBS national radio, NPR *Sound Money*, Bloomberg Business Radio, and Business Radio Network.

Eric also teaches the Bay Area's most highly attended personal financial management course, at the University of California, Berkeley.

ABOUT IDG BOOKS WORLDWIDE

WINNER
Eighth Annual
Computer Press
Awards ≥ 1992

WINNER
Ninth Annual
Computer Press
Awards ≥ 1993

IDG
BOOKS
WORLDWIDE

Welcome to the world of IDG Books Worldwide.

IDG Books Worldwide, Inc., is a subsidiary of International Data Group, the world's largest publisher of computer-related information and the leading global provider of information services on information technology. IDG was founded more than 25 years ago and now employs more than 8,500 people worldwide. IDG publishes more than 270 computer publications in over 75 countries (see listing below). More than 90 million people read one or more IDG publications each month.

Launched in 1990, IDG Books Worldwide is today the #1 publisher of best-selling computer books in the United States. We are proud to have received eight awards from the Computer Press Association in recognition of editorial excellence and three from *Computer Currents'* First Annual Readers' Choice Awards. Our best-selling *...For Dummies*® series has more than 25 million copies in print with translations in 30 languages. IDG Books Worldwide, through a joint venture with IDG's Hi-Tech Beijing, became the first U.S. publisher to publish a computer book in the People's Republic of China. In record time, IDG Books Worldwide has become the first choice for millions of readers around the world who want to learn how to better manage their businesses.

Our mission is simple: Every one of our books is designed to bring extra value and skill-building instructions to the reader. Our books are written by experts who understand and care about our readers. The knowledge base of our editorial staff comes from years of experience in publishing, education, and journalism — experience which we use to produce books for the '90s. In short, we care about books, so we attract the best people. We devote special attention to details such as audience, interior design, use of icons, and illustrations. And because we use an efficient process of authoring, editing, and desktop publishing our books electronically, we can spend more time ensuring superior content and spend less time on the technicalities of making books.

You can count on our commitment to deliver high-quality books at competitive prices on topics you want to read about. At IDG Books Worldwide, we continue in the IDG tradition of delivering quality for more than 25 years. You'll find no better book on a subject than one from IDG Books Worldwide.

John J. Kilcullen

John Kilcullen
President and CEO
IDG Books Worldwide, Inc.

IDG Books Worldwide, Inc., is a subsidiary of International Data Group, the world's largest publisher of computer-related information and the leading global provider of information services on information technology. International Data Group publishes over 276 computer publications in over 75 countries. Ninety million people read one or more International Data Group publications each month. International Data Group's publications include: **ARGENTINA:** Annuario de Informatica, Computerworld Argentina, PC World Argentina; **AUSTRALIA:** Australian Macworld, Client/Server Journal, Computer Living, Computerworld, Computerworld 100, Digital News, IT Casebook, Network World, On-line World Australia, PC World, Publishing Essentials, Reseller, WebMaster; **AUSTRIA:** Computerwelt Osterreich, Networks Austria, PC Tip; **BELARUS:** PC World Belarus; **BELGIUM:** Data News; **BRAZIL:** Annuário de Informática, Computerworld Brazil, Connections, Super Game Power, Macworld, PC Player, PC World Brazil, Publish Brazil, Reseller News; **BULGARIA:** Computerworld Bulgaria, Networkworld/Bulgaria, PC & MacWorld Bulgaria; **CANADA:** CIO Canada, Client/Server World, ComputerWorld Canada, InfoCanada, Network World Canada; **CHILE:** Computerworld Chile, PC World Chile; **COLOMBIA:** Computerworld Colombia, PC World Colombia; **COSTA RICA:** PC World Centro America; **THE CZECH AND SLOVAK REPUBLICS:** Computerworld Czechoslovakia, Elektronika Czechoslovakia, Macworld Czech Republic, PC World Czechoslovakia; **DENMARK:** Communications World, Computerworld Danmark, Macworld Danmark, PC Privat Danmark, PC World Danmark, PC World Danmark Supplements, TECH World; **DOMINICAN REPUBLIC:** PC World Republica Dominicana; **ECUADOR:** PC World Ecuador; **EGYPT:** Computerworld Middle East, PC World Middle East; **EL SALVADOR:** PC World Centro America; **FINLAND:** MikroPC, Tietoverkko, Tietoviikko; **FRANCE:** Distributique, Golden, Hebdo-Distributique, Info PC, Le Guide du Monde Informatique, Le Monde Informatique, Reseaux & Telecoms; **GERMANY:** Computer Partner, Computerwoche, Computerwoche Extra, Computerwoche Focus, I/M Information Management, Macwelt, PC Welt; **GREECE:** GamePro, Multimedia World; **GUATEMALA:** PC World Centro America; **HONDURAS:** PC World Centro America; **HONG KONG:** Computerworld Hong Kong, PCWorld Hong Kong, Publish in Asia; **HUNGARY:** ABCD CD-ROM, Computerworld Szamitastechnika, PC & Mac World Hungary, PC-X Magazine; **ICELAND:** Tolvuheimur/PC World Island; **INDIA:** Information Systems Computerworld, PC World India, Publish in Asia; **INDONESIA:** InfoKomputer PC World, Komputek Computerworld, Publish in Asia; **IRELAND:** ComputerScope, PC Live!; **ISRAEL:** People & Computers; **ITALY:** Computerworld Italia, Computerworld Italia Special Editions, Macworld Italia, Networking Italia, PC Shopping, PC World Italia, PC World/Walt Disney; **JAPAN:** DTP World, HP Open World Japan, Macworld Japan, Nikkei Personal Computing, Open World Japan, OS/2 World Japan, SunWorld Japan, Windows World Japan; **KENYA:** East African Computer News; **KOREA:** Hi-Tech Information/Computerworld, Macworld Korea, PC World Korea; **MACEDONIA:** PC World Macedonia; **MALAYSIA:** Computerworld Malaysia, PC World Malaysia, Publish in Asia; **MEXICO:** Computerworld Mexico, Macworld, PC World Mexico; **MYANMAR:** PC World Myanmar; **NETHERLANDS:** Computer! Totaal, LAN Magazine, LanWorld Buyers Guide, Macworld, Net Magazine, Totaal! Beurskrant; **NEW ZEALAND:** Absolute Beginner's Guide, Computer Buyer, Computer Industry Directory, Computerworld New Zealand, MTB, Network World, PC World New Zealand; **NICARAGUA:** PC World Centro America; **NIGERIA:** PC World Nigeria; **NORWAY:** Computerworld Norge, Computerworld Privat (Datamagasinet), CW Rapport Norge, IDG's KURSGUIDE, Macworld Norge, Multimediaworld, PC World Ekspress, PC World Nettverk, PC World Norge, PC World's Produktguide, Windows World Spesial; **PAKISTAN:** Computerworld Pakistan, PC World Pakistan; Panama: PC World Panama; **P. R. OF CHINA:** China Computer Users, China Computerworld, China Infoworld, China Telecom World Weekly, Computer & Communication, Electronic Design China, Electronics Today, Electronics Weekly, Game Camp, Game Soft, Network World China, PC World China, Popular Computer Weekly, Software Weekly, Software World, Telecom World; **PERU:** Computerworld Peru, PC World Profesional Peru, PC World Peru; **PHILIPPINES:** Computerworld Philippines, PC World Philippines, Publish in Asia; **POLAND:** Computerworld Poland, Computerworld Special Report, Macworld, Networld, PC World Komputer; **PORTUGAL:** Cerebro/PC World, Computerworld/Correio Informático, Dealer World Portugal, MacIn/PCIn, Multimedia World Portugal; **PUERTO RICO:** PC World Puerto Rico; **ROMANIA:** Computerworld Romania, PC World Romania, Telecom Romania; **RUSSIA:** Computerworld Russia, Mir PK, Sety; **SINGAPORE:** Computerworld Singapore, PC World Singapore, Publish in Asia; **SLOVENIA:** MONITOR; **SOUTH AFRICA:** Computing S.A., InfoWorld S.A., Network World S.A., Software World; **SPAIN:** Computerworld España, COMUNICACIONES WORLD, Dealer World, Macworld España, PC World España; **SWEDEN:** CAP&Design, Computer Sweden, Corporate Computing, MacWorld, Maxi Data, MikroDatorn, Nätverk & Kommunikation, PC/Aktiv, PC World, Windows World; **SWITZERLAND:** Computerworld Schweiz, Macworld Schweiz, PCtip; **TAIWAN:** Computerworld Taiwan, Macworld Taiwan, PC World Taiwan, Publish Taiwan, Windows World; **THAILAND:** Thai Computerworld, Publish in Asia; **TURKEY:** Computerworld Turkiye, MACWORLD Turkiye, PC World Turkiye; **UKRAINE:** Computerworld Kiev, Computers & Software, Multimedia World Ukraine, PC World Ukraine; **UNITED KINGDOM:** Acorn User, Amiga Action, Amiga Computing, Appletalk, Computing, GamePro, Macworld, Network News, Parents and Computers, PC Advisor, PC Home, PSX Pro UK, The WEB; **UNITED STATES:** Cable in the Classroom, CD Review, CIO Magazine, Computerworld, Computerworld Client/Server Journal, Digital Video Magazine, DOS World, Federal Computer Week, GamePro, InfoWorld, I-Way, JavaWorld, Macworld, Multimedia World, Netscape World Online, Network World, PC Entertainment, PC World, Publish, SunWorld Online, SWATPro Magazine, Video Event, WebMaster; **URUGUAY:** PC World Uruguay; **VENEZUELA:** Computerworld Venezuela, PC World Venezuela; and **VIETNAM:** PC World Vietnam.
7/16/96

Dedication

This book is hereby and irrevocably dedicated to my family and friends, as well as to my counseling clients and customers, who ultimately have taught me everything that I know about how to explain financial terms and strategies so that all of us may benefit.

Author's Acknowledgments

Being an entrepreneur involves endless challenges and without the support and input of my good friends and mentors Peter Mazonson, Jim Collins, and my best friend and wife, Judy, I couldn't have accomplished what I have.

I hold many people accountable for my perverse and maniacal interest in figuring out the financial services industry and money matters, but most of the blame falls on my loving parents, Charles and Paulina, who taught me most of what I know that's been of use in the real world.

I'd also like to thank Maggie McCall, David Ish, Paul Kozak, Chris Treadway, Sally St. Lawrence, K.T. Rabin, Will Hearst III, Ray Brown, Susan Wolf, Rich Caramella, Lisa Baker, Renn Vera, Maureen Taylor, Jerry Jacob, Robert Crum, Duc Nguyen, and Maria Carmicino and all the good folks at King Features for believing in and supporting my writing and teaching.

Many thanks to all the people who provided insightful comments on this book, especially tax and financial planning extraordinaire Barton Francis and Mike van den Akker, Gretchen Morgenson, Craig Litman, Gerri Detweiler, Mark White, Alan Bush, Nancy Coolidge, and Chris Jensen.

And thanks to all the wonderful people at IDG books on the front line and behind the scenes, especially John Kilcullen, who had the vision, foresight, and courage to do this book, Milissa Koloski, Kathy Welton, and Diane Steele. I'd especially like to thank my ever capable and talented project editor Kathy Cox and Suzanne Packer, my careful copy editor. I'd also like to thank Justin Wells and Judy Lee for other thoughtful suggestions and willingness to help me meet difficult deadlines.

Publisher's Acknowledgments

We're proud of this book; please send us your comments about it by using the Reader Response Card at the back of the book or by e-mailing us at feedback/dummies@idgbooks.com. Some of the people who helped bring this book to market include the following:

Acquisitions, Development, and Editorial

Project Editor: Kathleen M. Cox

Acquisitions Editor: Kathleen A. Welton, Vice President and Publisher

Permissions Editor: Joyce Pepple

Copy Editor: Suzanne Packer

Technical Editor: Barton Francis

Editorial Manager: Mary C. Corder

Editorial Assistant: Ann Miller

Special Help: Kristin A. Cocks

Indexer: Sherry Massey

Production

Project Coordinator: Sherry Gomoll

Layout and Graphics: Linda M. Boyer, Dominique DeFelice, Angela F. Hunckler, Todd Klemme, Jane Martin, Elizabeth Cardenás-Nelson, Anna Rohrer, Brent Savage, Gina Scott

Proofreaders: Michael Bolinger, Robert Springer, Carrie Voorhis, Ethel Winslow, Karen York

General & Administrative

IDG Books Worldwide, Inc.: John Kilcullen, President and CEO; Steven Berkowitz, COO and Publisher

Dummies, Inc.: Milissa Koloski, Executive Vice President and Publisher

Dummies Technology Press and Dummies Editorial: Diane Graves Steele, Associate Publisher; Judith A. Taylor, Brand Manager

Dummies Trade Press: Kathleen A. Welton, Vice President and Publisher; Stacy S. Collins, Brand Manager

IDG Books Production for Dummies Press: Beth Jenkins, Production Director; Cindy L. Phipps, Supervisor of Project Coordination; Kathie S. Schutte, Supervisor of Page Layout; Shelley Lea, Supervisor of Graphics and Design; Debbie J. Gates, Production Systems Specialist

Dummies Packaging and Book Design: Patti Sandez, Packaging Assistant; Kavish+Kavish, Cover Design

♦

The publisher would like to give special thanks to Patrick J. McGovern, without whom this book would not have been possible.

♦

Contents at a Glance

Introduction 1

Part I: Before You Begin Your Journey 7

Chapter 1: Potholes on the Road to Personal Financial Success 9
Chapter 2: Measuring Your Financial Health 21
Chapter 3: Hiring Financial Help: Truths and Consequences 33

Part II: Saving for a Purpose 53

Chapter 4: Your Money: Where Did It Go? 55
Chapter 5: Dealing with Debt and Credit Problems 69
Chapter 6: Reducing Your Spending 85
Chapter 7: Taking the Trauma Out of Taxes 107
Chapter 8: Saving for Specific Goals 131

Part III: Investing What You Save 153

Chapter 9: Important Investment Concepts 155
Chapter 10: Investment Vehicles 185
Chapter 11: Mutual Funds: Investments for All of Us 205
Chapter 12: Investing Money Inside Retirement Accounts 229
Chapter 13: Investing Money Outside Retirement Accounts 251
Chapter 14: Investing for Educational Expenses 269
Chapter 15: Real Estate 101 281

Part IV: Protecting What You've Got 323

Chapter 16: Insurance Basics 325
Chapter 17: Insurance on You 343
Chapter 18: Insuring Your Assets 365

Part V: The Part of Tens 377

Chapter 19: Ten Questions to Ask Financial Advisors *Before* You Hire Them 379
Chapter 20: Eric's Tips for Ten Life Changes 385
Chapter 21: Ten Tips for Using Your Computer for Your Personal Finances 401

Index 415

Reader Response Card .... Back of Book

Cartoons at a Glance

By Rich Tennant • Fax: 508-546-7747 • E-mail: the5wave@tiac.net

page 7

page 53

page 153

page 323

page 377

Table of Contents

Introduction 1

Why This Book 1
Uses for This Book 4
The Big Picture 4
    Part I: Before You Begin Your Journey 5
    Part II: Saving for a Purpose 5
    Part III: Investing What You Save 5
    Part IV: Protecting What You've Got 5
    Part V: The Part of Tens 6
Icons Used in This Book 6

Part I: Before You Begin Your Journey 7

Chapter 1: Potholes on the Road to Personal Financial Success 9

What You Don't Know CAN Hurt You 10
    Teaching personal finance in schools 12
    Talking money at home 13
    Illiteracy and conflicts in publishing and advising 14
You Can and You Must Just Do It! 19

Chapter 2: Measuring Your Financial Health 21

Bad Debt versus Good Debt 21
    How much bad debt is too much? 23
Your Financial Net Worth 24
    Financial assets 24
    Financial liabilities 25
    Your net worth calculation 25
    Interpreting your net worth results 27
Savings Analysis 28
How Are You at Investing? 30
How's Your Insurance Intelligence? 31

Chapter 3: Hiring Financial Help: Truths and Consequences 33

Alice in Financial-Planner Land 34
    Alice's adventures 34
    Lessons learned from Alice's trip to Financial-Planner Land 36
The Frustrations of Finding Good Financial Planners 38
    Regulatory problems 39

Letting the Big Bad Wolf guard the Three Little Pigs 39
Financial planners' top conflicts of interest 40
Financial Management Options 43
Doing nothing 44
Doing it yourself 44
Hiring financial help 45
Should You Hire a Financial Planner? 47
How a good financial planner can help 48
Not for everyone... 50
How to find a good financial planner 50
Caution: Savings at Risk...51

Part II: Saving for a Purpose 53

Chapter 4: Your Money: Where Did It Go? 55

Why You Overspend 56
You're just a consumption machine 56
Access to credit 56
Ten leading causes of overspending..................................57
Spending Analysis 61
Tracking your spending on paper 62
Tracking your spending on the computer 66
Spending less: the secret to growing rich on your income 68

Chapter 5: Dealing with Debt and Credit Problems 69

Using Savings to Reduce Your Debt 70
Decreasing Debt When You Lack Savings 71
Investigate lower interest rate credit cards 72
Cut 'em up, cut 'em all up 73
Debit cards: the best of both worlds 73
Filing Bankruptcy 76
Bankruptcy benefits 77
Bankruptcy drawbacks 77
Pick a number: 7 or 13... 79
Bankruptcy advice 79
Ending the Debt-and-Spend Cycle 81
Dealing with Credit Mistakes 83
Obtain a copy of your credit report 83
Get others to correct their mistakes 83
Tell your side of the story...84

Chapter 6: Reducing Your Spending 85

Four Keys to Successful Spending 85
Living within your means 86
Finding the best value 86

Eliminating fat 88
Avoid buying on credit 89
Strategies for Reducing Your Spending 89
Food 90
Shelter 93
Transportation 95
Clothing and accessories 99
Debt repayment 99
Stuff to make you and others happy 100
Personal business 103
Medical care 103
Insurance 104
Taxes 105
Costly addictions 106

Chapter 7: Taking the Trauma Out of Taxes 107

It's Not You — It's the System 108
The value of understanding the system 108
Your marginal income tax rate: the single
    most important tax number 110
Taxable income defined 111
How to Trim Taxes on Employment Income 112
Retirement plan contributions 112
Income shifting 113
Investment Income Reducing Techniques 113
Fill up those retirement accounts 114
Invest in tax-free money market funds and bonds 114
Select other tax-friendly investments 115
Strategies to Increase Your Deductions 116
Standard deductions 116
Itemized deductions 116
Purchasing real estate 117
Shifting or bunching deductions 118
Trading consumer debt for mortgage debt 118
Charitable contributions and expenses 119
Auto registration fees and state insurance 119
Deducting miscellaneous expenses 120
Self-employment expenses 121
Tax Preparation and Planning Options 124
Doing it yourself 124
Hiring help 126
Help, I Got an Audit Notice! 128
Audit preparation 129
The day of reckoning 129

Chapter 8: Saving for Specific Goals **131**

Prioritizing Your Savings Goals 132
    Only you know what's most important to you 132
    The advantages of retirement accounts 132
    Dealing with competing goals 133
Building Emergency Reserves 133
Saving to Buy a Home or Business 135
Saving for Children's Educational Expenses 136
Saving for Big Purchases 137
Preparing for Retirement 137
    What you need for retirement 139
    Retirement building blocks 140
    Social Security 141
    Personal savings/investments 144
    Pensions 144
    Retirement planning worksheet 145
    How to make up for lost time 147
    Common objections to saving in retirement accounts 150

Part III: Investing What You Save *153*

Chapter 9: Important Investment Concepts **155**

Common Investment Mistakes 156
Setting Your Goals 159
The Major Investment Flavors 160
    Lending investments 161
    Ownership investments 162
    Investing versus gambling 163
Investment Returns 164
Investment Risks 166
    Focus on the risks that you can control 168
    Low-risk, high-return investments 168
Diversification 168
    Asset allocation: spreading it around 169
    Allocating money for the long-term 171
Investment Firms Are Not Created Equal 172
    Where to focus 173
    Places to consider avoiding 174
Experts Who Predict the Future 178
    Investment newsletters 179
    Investment gurus 182

Chapter 10: Investment Vehicles 185

Lending Vehicles for Slow-Trip Money 185
    Transaction/checking accounts 186
    Savings and money market accounts 186
    Bonds 187
Ownership Vehicles to Build Wealth 189
    Stocks 189
    Real estate 195
    Investing in small business 200
Investment Odds and Ends 202
    Precious metals 203
    Annuities 203
    Collectibles 204
    Life insurance with a cash value 204

Chapter 11: Mutual Funds: Investments for All of Us 205

Mutual Fund Benefits 205
Fund Types 208
    Money market funds 208
    Bond funds 209
    Hybrid funds 209
    Stock funds 210
    U.S., international, and global funds 211
    Index funds 212
    Specialty (sector) funds 213
Selecting the Best Mutual Funds 214
    Cost 214
    Historic performance 217
    Fund manager and fund family reputation 218
    Tax-friendliness 218
    Your needs and goals 219
Best Places for Fund Investing 220
    Vanguard Group 220
    Fidelity Investments 221
    Charles Schwab & Company 222
    Jack White & Company 223
Tracking Fund Rankings and Performance 223
    Beware the worst sources 224
    Consider fund directories 225
    Understanding your fund's performance 226
    Following and selling your funds 228

Chapter 12: Investing Money Inside Retirement Accounts 229

Types of Retirement Accounts 230
    Employer-sponsored plans 230
    Self-employment plans 232

Individual Retirement Accounts (IRAs) 235
Annuities: an odd investment 236
Inappropriate Retirement Account Investments 238
Tax-free bonds 238
Annuities 239
Limited partnerships 239
Allocating Your Money in Retirement Plans 239
Prioritizing retirement contributions 240
Setting up a retirement account 240
Allocating money when your employer
    selects the investment options 240
Allocating money in plans that you design 243
Transferring Retirement Accounts 246
Moving Money from Your Employer's Retirement Account 249
Issues Unique to 403(b) Plans 249

Chapter 13: Investing Money Outside Retirement Accounts 251

Getting Started 252
Pay off high-interest debt...252
Contribute to retirement accounts 253
Taxes and Your Investments 253
Investing Your Savings/Emergency Reserve 254
Bank and credit union accounts 254
Money market mutual funds 255
Investing Money for the Longer-Term 258
Bond funds 260
U.S. Treasury bond funds 261
State-and-federal-tax-free bond funds 263
Federal-tax-free-only bond funds 265
Certificates of deposit (CDs) 265
Stock funds 266
Annuities 267
Real estate 267
Small-business investments 268

Chapter 14: Investing for Educational Expenses 269

The Big Mistake Nonwealthy Parents Make
    when Saving for Their Kids' Education 269
How the Financial Aid System Works 270
Treatment of retirement accounts 272
Treatment of money in the kids' names 272
Treatment of home equity and other assets 273
How Will I Pay for Educational Expenses? 274
Some tips: Loans, grants, and scholarships..............................274
The borrowing versus saving debate 276

What's college going to cost? 276

Setting realistic savings goals 277

Good and Bad Investments for Educational Funds 278

Good investments: no-load mutual funds 278

Bad investments 278

Overlooked investments: Time and attention 279

Chapter 15: Real Estate 101 .... **281**

To Buy or Continue Renting? 281

What's my timeline? 282

Can I afford it? 283

How much will lenders allow you to borrow? 284

What's more expensive: owning or renting? 285

Consider the long-term cost of renting 287

Mortgages: Side Effect of the American Dream 289

Fixed-rate mortgages 289

Adjustable-rate mortgages (ARMs) 290

Choosing between fixed- and adjustable-rate mortgages 291

How to buy with less money down 293

15-year versus 30-year mortgages 294

Selecting the best fixed-rate mortgage 296

Selecting an adjustable-rate mortgage 298

Finding the best lender 301

Increasing your approval chances 303

Finding the Right Property and Location 305

Condos, townhouses, co-ops or detached home? 305

Cast a broad net 306

Find out actual sale prices 307

Research the neighborhood and area 307

Working with Real Estate Agents 307

Real estate agents' top conflicts of interest 308

Qualities to look for in real estate agents 311

Putting Your Deal Together 313

Negotiating 101 313

Inspect, inspect, inspect 315

Title insurance and escrow fees 316

After You Buy 316

Refinancing your mortgage 317

Mortgage life insurance 318

Is getting a reverse mortgage a good idea? 319

Selling your house 320

Part IV: Protecting What You've Got *323*

Chapter 16: Insurance Basics **325**

Insurance: A Big, Inefficient Business 325
Eric's Three Laws of Buying Insurance 326
    Law I: Insure for the big stuff, don't sweat the small stuff 327
    Law II: Buy broad coverage 332
    Law III: Shop around and buy direct 333
Dealing with Insurance Problems 337
    Help! I've been denied coverage! 337
    Help! My insurer is hassling me about paying a claim 338

Chapter 17: Insurance on You **343**

Life Insurance 343
    How much do you need? 345
    Term versus cash value life insurance 346
    Buying term insurance 350
    How to get rid of cash value life insurance 351
    If you need cash value life insurance 352
Disability Insurance 352
    How much disability insurance do you need? 353
    Other features you need in disability insurance 354
    Where to buy disability insurance 355
Health Insurance 356
    Choosing the best health plan 357
    Buying health insurance 359
    If you're denied insurance 360
    Retiree medical care insurance 361
The Most Overlooked Form of Insurance 364

Chapter 18: Insuring Your Assets **365**

Homeowner's/Renter's Insurance 365
    Dwelling coverage: the cost to rebuild 366
    Personal property coverage 366
    Liability insurance 367
    Flood and earthquake insurance 367
    Deductibles 368
    Special discounts 369
    Where to buy homeowner's/renter's insurance 369
Auto Insurance 370
    Bodily injury/property damage liability 370
    Uninsured or underinsured motorist liability 370
    Deductibles 371
    Special discounts 371

Little stuff coverage to skip 372
Where to buy auto insurance 373
Umbrella Insurance 373
Estate Planning 374
Wills, living wills, and medical powers of attorney 374
Probate and living trusts 375
Estate planning to minimize estate taxes 376

Part V: The Part of Tens *377*

Chapter 19: Ten Questions to Ask Financial Advisors *Before* You Hire Them 379

Chapter 20: Eric's Tips for Ten Life Changes 385
Starting Out: Your First Job 386
Changing Jobs or Careers 387
Getting Married 388
Starting a Small Business 390
Buying a Home 391
Having Children 392
Caring for Aging Parents 394
Getting a Divorce 395
Receiving a Windfall 397
Retiring 398

Chapter 21: Ten Tips for Using Your Computer for Your Personal Finances 401
Focus on software 402
Tread carefully on the Web 403
Pay your bills and track your money 405
Plan for retirement 407
Prepare your taxes 408
Research investments 408
Tracking your investment returns often not worth the headache 411
Trading online 412
Reading and searching periodicals 413
Preparing legal documents 414

Index *415*

Reader Response Card .... *Back of Book*

Introduction

Welcome to *Personal Finance For Dummies,* 2nd Edition. For a number of years, I dreamed of writing a personal finance book that would be different. The book would describe in plain, readable English the most important concepts that you need to know in order to manage your personal finances. It would give specific answers to financial questions where it could, and where it couldn't give the answers, it would suggest the best resources to turn to.

As fate would have it, my path crossed that of IDG Books. As a computer dummy, I was overjoyed to finally find computer books that offered clear explanations and practical advice. The *...For Dummies* approach is how I had conceived my personal finance book; I just didn't know it at the time!

As you can see from the quotes in the front of this edition, readers and reviewers alike were pretty pleased with the first edition. However, I and the good folks at IDG don't rest on our laurels. So what you hold in your hands reflects more hard work to bring you the freshest and more material to address your personal financial quandaries.

Why This Book

Many Americans are financially illiterate. If you are, it's probably not your fault. Personal Finance 101 is not offered in our schools — not in high school, not even in the best colleges and graduate schools. It should be. (Of course, if it were, I wouldn't be able to write fun and useful books such as this — or maybe they would use this book in the course!)

There are some common financial problems and mistakes, and different people keep making those same mistakes over and over. This book, like a good friend, can whop you upside the head to keep you from falling into the same traps.

  ✔ **Not planning.** Human beings were born to procrastinate. That's why there are deadlines and extensions. With your finances, unfortunately, you have no deadlines and you think you have unlimited extensions! You can leave your money sitting in lousy investments for years. You can end up paying higher taxes, having gaps in your retirement and insurance coverage, and overpaying for financial products. Of course, planning your finances isn't as much fun as planning a vacation, but doing the former will help you take more of the latter.

✓ **Overspending.** The average American saves less than 5 percent of after-tax income (in contrast with the average Canadian who saves about 9 percent, French at 12 percent, German at 14 percent, and Japanese at 15 percent). It's simple arithmetic to determine that savings is the difference between what you earn minus what you spend (assuming you're not spending more than you're earning!). To increase your savings, you either have to work more (yuck!), know a wealthy family who wants to leave its fortune to you, or simply learn to spend less. For most of us, the thrifty approach is the key to building savings and wealth.

✓ **Buying on credit.** Even with the benefit of today's lower interest rates, carrying a balance month-to-month on your credit card or buying a car on credit means that even more of your future earnings are earmarked for debt repayment. Buying on credit encourages you to spend more than you can really afford.

✓ **Not saving soon enough for retirement.** Most people say they want to retire by their mid-60s or sooner. But in order to accomplish this financially, you need to save a reasonable chunk (around 10 percent) of your income starting sooner rather than later. The longer you wait to start saving for retirement, the harder it will be to reach your goal. And you'll pay much more in taxes to boot if you don't take advantage of the tax benefits of investing through particular retirement accounts.

✓ **Falling prey to financial sales pitches.** Great deals that can't wait for a little reflection or a second opinion are often disasters waiting to happen. A sucker may be born every minute, but a slick salesperson is born every second! Steer clear of those who pressure you to make decisions, promise high investment returns, and lack the proper training and experience to help you.

✓ **Not doing your homework.** To get the best financial deal, you need to shop around, read reviews, and get advice from disinterested, objective third parties. You need to check references and track records so you don't hire incompetent, self-serving, or fraudulent financial advisors. But with all the different financial products available, making informed financial decisions has become an overwhelming task. I've done a lot of the homework for you with the investment, insurance, credit, and other products I recommend in this book. Where I'm not able to give precise advice, I explain what additional research you need to do and how to go about doing it.

✓ **Making decisions based on emotion.** You are most vulnerable to making the wrong moves financially after a major life change (that is, job loss, divorce) or when you feel under pressure. Maybe your investments have plunged in value. Or a recent divorce has you fearing that you won't be able to afford to retire when you had planned, so you pour thousands of dollars into some newfangled financial product. Take your time and keep your emotions out of the picture. In Chapter 20, I discuss how to approach major life changes with an eye to determining what changes in your financial picture may need to be made.

✔ **Not separating the wheat from the chaff.** In any field in which you're not an expert, you run the danger of following the advice of someone who you think is an expert but really isn't. This book teaches you to separate the financial fluff from the financial facts. If you look in the mirror, you'll see the person who is best able to manage your personal finances. Educate that person and trust that person.

✔ **Exposure to catastrophic risk.** You're vulnerable if you or your family don't have insurance to pay for financially devastating losses. People without a savings reserve and support network can end up homeless. Many people lack sufficient insurance coverage to replace their income. Don't wait for a tragedy to strike to learn whether or not you have the right kind of insurance coverage.

✔ **Focusing too much on money.** Too much emphasis on making and saving money can warp your perspective on what's important in life. Money is not the first or even second priority in happy people's lives. Your health, your relationships with family and friends, career satisfaction, and fulfilling interests are all more important.

Unfair as it seems, many of these traps await you when you are actually seeking help. The world is filled with biased and bad financial advice; as a practicing financial counselor, I see and hear about the consequences of this bad advice every day. Of course, every profession has some bad apples, but too many people calling themselves "financial planners" have conflicts of interest.

All too often, financial advice today ignores the big picture and focuses narrowly on investing. You need to broaden your understanding of personal finance to include all areas of your financial life: spending, taxes, saving, insurance, and planning for major goals like education, buying a home, and retirement. Because money is not an end in itself but part of your whole life, this book helps connect your financial goals and problems to the rest of your life.

Even if you understand the financial basics, thinking about your finances in a holistic way can be difficult. Sometimes you're too close to the situation to be objective. Like the organization of your desk or files (or disorganization, as the case may be), your finances may reflect the history of your life more than they reflect a comprehensive plan for your future.

You are likely a busy person and don't have enough hours in your day to get things done. Thus, you want to know how to diagnose your financial situation quickly (and painlessly) and determine what you should do from there. Unfortunately, after figuring out which financial strategies make sense for you, choosing specific financial products in the marketplace can be a nightmare. You have literally thousands of investment, insurance, and loan options to choose from. Talk about information overload!

To complicate matters, you probably hear about most products through advertising that can be misleading if not downright false. Of course, some very ethical and useful firms advertise, but so do those that are more interested in converting your hard-earned income and savings into their profits. And they may not be here tomorrow when you need them.

You want to know the best places to go for your circumstances. That's why some people choose to hire someone like me as a financial counselor. As a result of their concerns, I've filled this book with specific, tried-and-proven product recommendations.

Uses for This Book

You can use this book in one of three ways:

- ✔ If you want to find out about a specific area, such as getting out of high-interest consumer debt or investing in mutual funds, you can flip to that section and get your answers quickly.

- ✔ If you want a crash course in personal finance, read it cover-to-cover. Reading the whole book helps to solidify major financial concepts and gets you thinking about your finances in a more comprehensive way.

- ✔ As a paper weight!

Seriously, though, this book is basic enough for a novice to get his or her arms around the thorniest of financial issues. But advanced readers will be challenged as well to think about their finances in a new way and identify areas for improvement. Check out the table of contents for a chapter-by-chapter run-down of what's in this book. You can also look up a specific topic in the index and then flip to the page it lists. Or you can turn the page and start at the beginning: Chapter 1.

The Big Picture

This book is organized into five parts, each covering a major area of your personal finances. The chapters within each part cover specific topics in detail. You can read each chapter and part without having to read what comes before, which is useful if you have better things to do with your free time. This book also makes for great reading anywhere you might be sitting for a length of time (perhaps the bathroom). You may be referred occasionally to somewhere else in the book for more detail on a particular subject. Here is a summary of what you find in each part.

Part I: Before You Begin Your Journey

This part reveals common causes of missing links in personal finance knowledge and explains how to diagnose your current financial health. You may want to hire someone to help, so in this part you learn more than you ever wanted to know about finding the right person and avoiding a lemon.

Part II: Saving for a Purpose

Most people don't have gobs of extra cash. Therefore, this part shows you how to figure where all your dollars are going and how to reduce your spending. Chapter 5 is solely devoted to solving the problem of getting out from under the burden of high-interest consumer debt, such as on credit cards. I also provide specifics for reducing your tax burden and figuring out how much you should be saving if you want to retire someday or for some other purpose.

Part III: Investing What You Save

Earning and saving money is hard work. So you want to be careful when it comes to investing what you have worked so hard to save (or waited so long to inherit!). Learning investment basics helps you to pick investments wisely and understand investment risks, returns, and a whole lot more. I explain all the major and best types of investment options including how to hire your own professional money manager through a mutual fund (don't worry if you don't have much to invest). I recommend specific strategies and investments for both inside and outside of tax-sheltered retirement accounts. I also discuss buying, selling, and investing in real estate as well as other wealth-building investments.

Part IV: Protecting What You've Got

Insurance is an important part of your financial life; unfortunately, for most people, it is a thoroughly overwhelming and dreadfully boring topic. But perhaps I can pique your interest in this esoteric topic when I tell you that you're probably paying more than you should for insurance and don't have the right coverages for your situation. This part tells you all you ever wanted to know (OK, fine, all you never wanted to know but probably should know anyway) about how to buy the right insurance at the best price.

Part V: The Part of Tens

I guess I'm still not sure whether IDG or David Letterman first came up with top ten lists. Although Dave's are just a bit funnier (only because he has a team of professional joke writers), these lists of tens can help you manage major life changes or keep you from getting in a jam if picking a financial advisor. In this part, you can also find top software to dazzle and delight your friends.

Icons Used in This Book

This nerdy guy (who is rumored to bear some resemblance to a senior official at IDG Books!) appears beside discussions that aren't critical if you just want to learn basic concepts and get answers to your financial questions. You can safely ignore these sections, but reading them will deepen and enhance your personal financial knowledge. This stuff can also come in handy if you're ever on a game show or find yourself stuck on an elevator with a financial geek.

This target flags strategy recommendations for making the most of your money (for example, pay off your credit card with your lottery winnings).

This icon highlights the best financial products in investment, insurance, and so on to implement strategy recommendations (for example, call Ethical Bank & Trust for low-interest rate loans).

This icon is a friendly reminder of information discussed elsewhere in the book or stuff you'll definitely want to remember.

This icon marks things to avoid and common mistakes people make in managing their finances.

This icon alerts you to scams and scoundrels that prey on the unsuspecting.

This icon highlights when you should consider doing some additional research. Don't worry, I explain what to look for and look out for.

Part I

Before You Begin Your Journey

The 5th Wave   By Rich Tennant

"That reminds me - I have to figure out how to save for retirement and send these two to college."

In this part . . .

You see the basic concepts that underlie sensible management of personal finances. You also find out why you didn't know these concepts before now (and whom to blame). Here, you'll undergo a (gentle) financial physical exam to diagnose your current economic health. You may discover that you need help, so I try to steer you toward those who can truly assist you and away from those who may have something else in mind.

Chapter 1

Potholes on the Road to Personal Financial Success

"*I*'ve made just about every financial mistake there is to make," lamented one of the students in my personal finance course, which I teach for the University of California at Berkeley. The student, who had an anxious yet depressed look, seemed to be asking me for forgiveness.

This is when it first dawned on me that as grown-up children — referred to as adults — we're not really allowed to make mistakes. Consider that if you mangle your car in an accident because you weren't paying attention or get fired from a job because of poor attendance and performance, you sure don't feel very good, and others around you are seldom encouraging.

With financial matters, however, the fact that you've made a mistake may not be as obvious as twisted metal or a pink slip and no more paycheck. Some mistakes take months, years, even decades to manifest themselves. Even then, some people don't realize the foolishness of their ways.

If you're young, congratulations for being so forward thinking as to realize the immense value of investing now in your personal financial education. You'll reap the rewards for many decades to come. But even if you're not so young, you surely have many years to make the most of what money you currently have and will earn (and may even inherit!) in the future.

Throughout our journey together, I hope to challenge and even change the way you think about money, about making important personal financial decisions — and heck — sometimes even about the meaning of life. No, I'm not a philosopher but I do know that money, for better but more often for worse, is connected to many other parts of our lives.

Few people like to be made to feel stupid or told that they're doing something wrong. And what you do with your money is a quite personal and confidential matter. I've endeavored not to be paternalistic in this book but to provide guidance and advice that is in your best interest. You don't have to take it all — pick what works best for you and understand the pros and cons of your options. But from this day forward, please don't make the easily avoidable mistakes that I document in this chapter and throughout this book.

What You Don't Know CAN Hurt You

No, you're not a dummy. We're barely acquainted, but I do know that you're not dumb. Real dummies don't read and educate themselves. And real dummies don't understand the value of investing in their education. Real dummies also can't deflate their egos enough to admit that they need help and guidance.

Here's what dumb is. Dumb is the man who walked into a Circle-K convenience store, put a $20 bill on the counter, and asked for change. When the cashier opened the register, the man pulled a gun and demanded all the cash. The crook took the loot — $15 — and fled, leaving his $20 bill on the counter. Or how about the criminal in Charleston, South Carolina, who robbed a person who lacked cash? The victim offered the assailant a check, which the assailant later attempted to cash at the bank, where — surprise, surprise — he was arrested.

So you are most definitely not dumb! But you may be financially illiterate. Sadly, most Americans don't know how to manage their personal finances because in most cases they were never taught how to do so. Nearly 100 percent of our high schools and colleges offer not a single course to teach this vital, lifelong-needed skill.

For the handful of schools that do offer a course remotely related to a personal finance class, the class is typically an economics course and an elective at that. "Archaic theory is being taught and it doesn't do anything for the students as far as preparing them for the real world," says one high school principal that I know. Having taken more than my fair share of economics courses in college, I whole-heartedly agree.

Lucky people learn the financial keys to success at home or from knowledgeable friends. Others never learn or learn the hard way: by making lots of costly mistakes. Lack of proficiency in personal financial management causes not only tremendous anxiety but also serious problems. Consider the following sobering statistics:

✔ Approximately one million personal bankruptcies are filed in the United States annually. That's about one in every one hundred households. So in the next ten years, nearly one in every ten households in the United States — the most affluent country in the world — will file bankruptcy.

✔ Studies show that fewer than 20 percent of baby boomers are saving adequately for retirement, and one-quarter of adults between the ages of 35 and 54 have not even *begun* to save for retirement.

✔ One in two marriages ends in divorce. Studies show that financial disagreement is one of the leading causes of marital discord. In a survey conducted by *Worth* magazine and the market research firm of Roper/Starch, couples admitted fighting about money more than anything else and more than three times more often than they fight about their sex lives. And a staggering 57 percent of those surveyed agreed with the statement, "In every marriage, money eventually becomes the most important concern."

✔ Fewer than 10 percent of American adults understand a 401(k) well enough to explain it to someone else. Fewer than one in four can explain what a municipal bond is.

✔ In a Princeton Survey Research Associates investing basics test, approximately a third of those quizzed answered fewer than 50 percent of the questions correctly. These results are all the more stunning when you consider that all of the questions only offered two or three multiple choice answers as options.

✔ Nearly 80 percent of consumers do not know how the grace period on a credit card works. An even greater percentage don't understand that interest starts accumulating *immediately* for new purchases on credit cards with outstanding debts.

✔ Fifty-three percent of people in a *Money*/Vanguard multiple choice quiz did not know that *total return* was the best overall measure of a mutual fund's performance.

The overall costs of personal financial illiteracy to our society are huge. The high rate of spending and low rate of saving in the United States lead to lower long-term economic growth and higher interest rates. Annually, billions of dollars are wasted through the purchase of inferior and inefficient financial products.

Uh-oh. Now I've *really* depressed you. You were probably feeling bad enough about your own financial situation, and here you are taking responsibility for the country's economic problems, too!

Teaching personal finance in schools

As part of her fifth grade math class, Nancy Donovan teaches personal finance as a way to illustrate how math can be used in the real world. "Students choose a career, find jobs, and figure out what their taxes and take home paychecks will be. They also have to rent apartments and figure out a monthly budget," says Donovan, adding, "Students like it and parents have commented to me how surprised they are with how much financial knowledge their kids can handle." Donovan also has her students invest $10,000 (play money) and track the performance of their investments.

To urge that our schools teach the basics of personal finance is just common sense. We should be teaching our children how to manage a household budget, about the importance of saving money for future goals, and about the consequences and dangers of overspending. Unfortunately, few schools offer classes like Nancy Donovan's. In most cases, the financial basics aren't taught at all.

Some people argue that it's the parents' job to teach their children the financial basics. However, this well-meant sentiment is what we rely on now, and, for all too many, it isn't working. In some families, financial illiteracy is passed on from generation to generation.

Some education professionals agree that schools should teach financial basics. If people aren't taught financial basics in schools, where do they learn them? But others say that schools would have to cut something vital out of the curriculum.

Giving due respect to schoolteachers who work hard and often don't earn the pay or respect of other professions, I believe that personal finance should *at a minimum* replace the least important subject that schools are teaching now. (Of course, the hard part would be getting people to agree on the least important subject.)

We must recognize that education takes place in the home, on the streets, *and* in the schools. Therefore, schools must bear some responsibility for teaching this very important life skill. And with more students holding down after-school jobs, teaching money-management know-how through the schools makes even more sense.

Lobby your schools! Make sure that financial basics are taught in schools at all levels. If you think you're powerless to change the situation, you're mistaken. Many changes to our education system have started at the grassroots level.

Talking money at home

I was fortunate that my parents taught and instilled in me the importance of personal financial management. Mom and Dad taught me a lot of things that have been invaluable throughout my life. In fact, in certain areas, I learned more from my folks than from supposedly more well-educated people with all sorts of fancy credentials after their names. Among the useful things my folks taught me were sound principles of earning, spending, and saving money. My parents had to know how to do these things because they were raising a family of three children on (usually) one modest income. They knew the importance of making the most of what you have and passing on that vital skill to the kids.

In many families, however, *money* is a taboo subject — parents don't level with their kids about the limitations, realities, and details of their budgets. Some parents I talk with believe that dealing with money is an adult issue that kids should be insulated from so that the kids can better enjoy being kids. Some studies have even shown that parents today are more likely to talk with their kids about sex than about financial matters! And you know how comfortable many parents feel when talking to their kids about sex, so you can imagine how few talk about money.

In many families, kids may hear about money *only* when disagreements and financial crises bubble to the surface. Thus begins the harmful cycle of children having negative associations with money and financial management.

In other cases, some parents, with the best of intentions, do pass on their money-management habits. Unfortunately, some of those habits are, of course, *bad* habits. Now, I'm not saying that you shouldn't listen to your parents. (You know how well I listened to mine.) But in personal finance, as in any other area, family advice can be problematic. Think about where your parents learned about money management and consider whether they had the time, energy, or inclination to research choices before making their decisions. For example, your parents may think that banks are the best places to invest money. Banks are **not** the best places to invest money — you can find where the better places are in Part III of this book.

In still other cases, mom and dad have the right approach, but the kids go to the other extreme out of rebellion. For example, if your parents spent money carefully and thoughtfully, you may tend to do the opposite, such as buying yourself gifts the moment any extra money comes your way.

Although you and I can't change what the educational system and your parents did or didn't teach you about personal finances, you have the ability to find out now what you need to know to manage your finances. And if you have children of your own, I'm sure you'll agree that kids really are amazing. Don't underestimate their potential or set them out into the world without the skills they need to be productive and happy adults. Buy them some good financial books when they head off to college or to their first jobs.

Illiteracy and conflicts in publishing and advising

Okay, you're smart enough to realize that you're probably not a financial genius. So you set out to take control of your finances by reading or consulting a financial advisor. Because the pitfalls are so numerous and the challenges are so mighty in choosing an advisor, I devote all of Chapter 3 to the financial planning business and what you need to know to avoid being fooled.

Reading is good. Reading is fundamental. But reading to learn about managing your money can be dangerous if you're a novice. Surprisingly, written misinformation can come from popular and seemingly reliable information sources.

Won't gurus make me rich?

One formerly best-selling personal finance book (*Wealth Without Risk* by Charles Givens) advises you to "Buy disability insurance only if you are in poor health or accident prone." Putting aside the minor detail that *no* insurance company (that's interested in making a profit) would issue you a disability policy *after* you fall into poor health, how do you know when you'll be accident prone? Because health problems and auto accidents cause many disabilities, unless you have a working crystal ball, you can't see them coming until it's too late!

That same book also purports to describe how to send your kids to college "free." A few months before your child begins college, you're supposed to buy a four-bedroom property a few miles from campus. Then you're advised to rent out the house to students. The idea is that while your kid is completing a four-year degree, the value of your rental property will appreciate dramatically because of the shortage of off-campus housing in almost every college campus area.

You realize, I'm sure, that college students will give your property the same love and attention that people give to rental cars. And, on the financial side, a modestly priced property would need to roughly *double in value over a four-year period* for this college-financing scheme to work. This is about as common as triplets (yes, it happens, but rarely).

Furthermore, this risky strategy is more likely to cost you money than to pay for college. Many real estate markets *drop* in value over a four-year time period, and if that were to happen, your already substantial college costs would be added to, not paid off. Then you need to factor in the hassles and expenses of locating, buying, and selling the property. And another minor detail: How many parents paying tuition bills also have piles of extra cash lying around available for the down payment on a property?

Don't the media act as watchdogs?

You may be asking how Charles Givens became so popular despite the obvious flaws in his advice? Thanks to his talent for working the media and great self-promotion through seminars. One of the problems of the mass media is that hucksters like Givens can get good coverage and publicity. Many members of the media are also financially illiterate. And they love a good story. So Givens got all sorts of free publicity, being quoted in the press and invited on a number of national programs such as *The Today Show, Oprah, Donahue,* and *Larry King Live.*

Thousands of people went to seminars conducted by Givens, partly because of the credibility Givens built through media appearances. As has now been well documented by some of those same media, many unsuspecting investors were sold commission-laden products, including risky limited partnerships, through his organization.

One example is the widely publicized case of Helen Giszczak, a 69-year-old retired secretary. She invested nearly two-thirds of her modest life savings in limited partnerships, which she said were described to her as "probably the most conservative investments we know of." But some of her limited partnerships ended up in bankruptcy, and the others lost much of their value.

Helen Giszczak appeared on the *Donahue* show with John Allen, a former investment broker-turned-securities lawyer who helped her sue Givens' organization to get her money back. After a lengthy dialogue with Giszczak and Allen, Phil Donahue asked Helen how a smart person like her could get sucked in like that. She replied, "He was on your show and Oprah's. You gave him credibility. You gave him free advertising."

Helen deserves praise for fighting back like she did, but it is unfortunate that she had to learn her lesson the hard way. Don't assume that someone with something to sell who is getting good press will take care of you. That "guru" could just be good at press relations and self-promotion. Certainly, talk shows and the media at-large can and do provide useful information on a variety of topics, but be aware that sometimes bad eggs turn up on them. And the bad eggs don't always smell up front.

Don't financial media know what's going to happen next?

Scores of widely read financial publications offer predictive advice and commentary about investment markets. But such commentary can often be wrong or misguided.

For example, on October 16, 1987, just three days before the U.S. stock market crashed, one of the most widely read daily business papers had this to say about the prior day's stock market decline: "But it is not yet time to pry the rubber seals out of the office windows . . . On September 22nd, it should be remembered, the market had a record 75-point one-day rise. The underlying economic news is mostly good, not bad."

On the next trading day — Monday, October 19 — the stock market plunged 508 points — nearly 23 percent!

Although most financial publications shy away from making predictions, many love to quote predictions made by the "experts." The monthly, weekly, and daily barrage of conflicting crystal ball visions causes many investors — perhaps even you — to be paralyzed and fearful. As you can clearly see in Part III of this book, you don't need a working crystal ball or a guru telling you when to buy and sell. The best investments for growth are not only easy to identify but, once bought, are generally best held for the long haul.

Don't writers know what they're writing about?

Writers are people too. Some good, some bad; some full of hot tips, some full of hot air. During the 1980s, one of the most widely read personal finance magazines ran a piece that purported to tell you where to get "safe, high yields." In addition to utility stocks and junk bonds, the article recommended real estate and oil and gas *limited partnerships* (LPs) sold through brokers. Such LPs are not safe investments. Over the past decade, most people who bought these problematic investment vehicles lost huge portions of their money.

Just as at the circus: oddities sell

Over recent years, I've done some work with different parts of the media and observed how and what the media follows and ignores. As anyone who followed the O.J. trial knows, some members of the media love an unusual story. The financial media, when at its worst, is no different than the news media that fawned all over the O.J. trial. The more bizarre and novel something is, the more attention it gets — never mind if it's good for the readers and viewers.

With financial "guru" Charles Givens, the appeal was that people believed they could get rich without taking risks. Recent years have seen a flood of "We Can Beat the Market" investing books written by a 17-year-old high school student, an investment club, and others. One such book was written by a couple of Generation Xers who, despite failing at publishing a print newsletter, soared to fame by claiming that, using the online world to research stocks, anybody can easily and with low-risk make 25 to 35+ percent per year. As you will see in Part III, such returns are unrealistic but they play well with some of the media.

Another popular business magazine ran an article that touted life insurance as one of the best investments. The piece advocated the purchase of *cash-value insurance* — which contains an investment account as well as life insurance protection. The article went on to claim that life insurance should be the first consideration in most responsible investment programs. As you see in Parts III and IV of this book, this advice is *wrong, wrong, wrong* for the vast majority of working people who need life insurance. (They should buy *term insurance,* which is pure life insurance protection.) Any number of investment options would make a better first consideration than buying cash-value insurance, but you wouldn't have learned that from reading the article.

More than a few writers and talk-show hosts claim to be personal finance experts but hardly ever address spending and debt issues. Instead, they focus almost exclusively on investments. For example, they may make you feel like an undisciplined failure for not saving through your employer's retirement savings program to reduce your taxes when other considerations may also apply.

Saving through your employer's retirement program is all well and good, but the truth is, many people live paycheck-to-paycheck. So unless you *first* learn how to reduce spending and get out from under high-cost consumer debt, the "experts" can talk until they're blue in the face about terrific investment strategies. If you don't have anything to invest in the first place, then they're not really helping you.

There are good writers and smart writers at most financial publications. But there are also some people who would have been better off covering politics. Come to think of it, some of them *do* also cover politics, and therein lies the problem — you're getting financial advice from people who don't focus on the field, have little if any training in it, and have no experience as a practitioner working with people like you.

Don't book publishers exercise due diligence?

Book publishers are businesses first, and like most businesses, their business practices vary. Some have a reputation for care and quality; some just want to push a product out the door with maximum hype and minimum effort.

For instance, you may think that book publishers check out an author before they sign him or her to write an entire book. Well, you may be surprised to learn that some publishers don't do their homework.

What most publishers care about first is how marketable an author is. Some authors are marketable because of their well-earned reputation for sound advice. Others are marketable because of stellar promotional campaigns built on smoke and mirrors. Still others may have the potential for marketability if a publisher takes a chance on them, but most publishers like a sure thing.

Warning signs of pandering to advertisers

Newspapers, magazines, online services, radio, television — you name it — thousands of publications and media outlets today are doling out personal financial advice and perspectives. Although many of these "service providers" collect revenue from you the subscriber, virtually all are dependent — in some cases, fully dependent — on advertising dollars.

Although advertising is a necessary part of capitalism, unfortunately and sadly, advertisers can taint and, in some cases, dictate the content of what you read, listen to, and view.

Consider this case from a nonfinancial publication — *Modern Bride* magazine. *Harper's* magazine got a hold of an apologetic letter, which it humorously entitled "To Love, Honor And Obey Our Advertisers," that *Bride's* fashion advertising director sent to its advertisers. Here's an excerpt:

> "*Bride's* recommends that its readers (your customers) 'negotiate price,' 'borrow a slip or petticoat,' and 'compare catalog shoe prices,' and tells its readers that 'the groom's tuxedo may be free.' It is difficult to understand why *Bride's* was compelled to publish this information. With 57 years of publishing experience and 'support' to the bridal industry, *Bride's* could and should have been more sensitive to the retailers that its purports to serve. All of us in the bridal business must concentrate on projecting full-service bridal retailing in a positive light."

I don't find it difficult to understand why the writer of the criticized *Bride's* article revealed cost-saving strategies to its readers — she was trying to give them useful information and advice! Now, revealing letters like this one are hard to come by, so how can you, a consumer of financial information, separate the good from the advertiser-biased publications?

I've developed some ideas on the subject from having written and worked for a number of publications and from observing the workings of even more.

First, consider how dependent a publication or media outlet is on advertising. I see the most conflicts of interest that involve pandering to advertisers done by "free" publications and radio and television, which derive all of their revenue from advertising. Much of what is on the Internet is advertiser-driven as well.

Next, as you read various publications, watch TV, or listen to radio, note how consumer-oriented they are. Do you get the feeling that they're looking out for your interests? Or are they primarily creating an advertiser-friendly broadcast or publication?

For example, if lots of auto manufacturers advertise, does the media outlet ever tell you how to save money when shopping for a car and the importance of buying a car within your means?

Even more troubling, in the many advice guides on the market, few publishers require that the books be technically reviewed for accuracy by an expert in the field other than the author, who sometimes may not be an expert. You the reader are expected to be your own technical reviewer. But do you have the expertise to do that? (Don't worry, this book has been checked for accuracy.)

As an author and a financial counselor, I know that financial ideas and strategies can differ considerably. Different is not necessarily wrong. But when a reviewer looks at my text and tells me another, better way is out there — I take a second look. Maybe I even see things a new way. That's not possible if I'm the only expert who sees my book before publication. How do you know if a book's been technically reviewed? Check the credits page or the author's acknowledgments.

Authors write books for many reasons other than to teach and educate. The most common reason financial book authors write books is to further their own business interests. That may not always be a bad thing, but it's not the best thing for you when trying to educate yourself and better manage your own finances. For example, some investment books are written by investment newsletter sellers. Rather than teaching you how to make good investments, the author makes the investment world sound complicated so that you'll feel the need to subscribe to his ongoing newsletter.

You Can and You Must Just Do It!

Once you learn the basic concepts and where to buy the best financial products when you need to buy them, you'll soon see that managing your personal finances well is not much harder than other things you do regularly like tying your shoelaces and getting to and from work each day.

Regardless of your income, you can make your dollars stretch farther if you learn good financial habits and avoid mistakes. In fact, the lower your income, the more important it is that you make the most of your income and savings (because you don't have the luxury of falling back on your next fat paycheck or dividends check to bail you out).

More and more industries are subject to global competition, and you need to be on your financial toes now more than ever. Job security is on the wane. Layoffs and retraining for new jobs are on the increase. Putting in 20 or 30 years for one company and retiring with the gold watch and lifetime pension are becoming as rare as never having computer problems.

Speaking of company pensions, odds are increasing that you work for an employer that has you save toward your own retirement. Not only do you need to save the money, you must also decide how to invest it.

Managing your personal finances involves much more than just managing and investing money. It also includes making all the pieces of your financial life fit together. It means lifting yourself out of financial illiteracy. Like planning a vacation, managing your personal finances means formulating a plan to make the best use of your limited time and dollars.

We're only human

Perhaps you know that you should be living within your means, buying and holding sound investments for the long-term, and securing proper insurance coverage. However, you can't bring yourself to do these things. Everywhere you turn lurks temptation to spend money. Ads show attractive and popular people enjoying the fruits of their labors — a new car, exotic vacation, and lavish home.

Maybe you felt deprived as a youngster by your tight-wad parents or you're bored with life and like the adventure of buying new things. If only you can hit it big on one or two investments, you think, you could get rich quick and do what you really want with your life. As for disasters and catastrophes — well — those things happen to *other* people, don't they? Not to you. Besides, you'll probably have advance warning of pending problems and can prepare accordingly.

Your emotions and temptations can get the better of you. Certainly part of successfully managing your finances involves coming to terms with your shortcomings and the consequences of your behaviors. If you don't, you may end up enslaved to a dead-end job to keep feeding your spending addiction. Or you can spend more time with your investments than you do with your family, risking divorce. And catastrophes can happen to anyone, even you, without warning or time to prepare.

Knowing the right answers isn't enough, you've got to *practice* good financial habits just as you practice other habits, such as brushing your teeth. Don't be overwhelmed. As you read this book, make a short list of your financial marching orders and then start chipping away. I also highlight ways to overcome temptations and keep control of your money rather than letting your emotions and money rule you.

Here are a few areas you likely need to tackle:

- ✔ **Tracking and reducing spending.** If, like most people, you're not saving sufficiently to meet your future financial goals, then sound financial management also involves tracking and reducing your spending. See Part II.

- ✔ **Investing what you save.** Investing your savings is, of course, an important part of your financial puzzle. So, too, are understanding and making the best use of tax incentives, tax breaks, and your employer's benefits.

- ✔ **Making informed real estate and insurance purchases.** You need to ensure that you invest in real estate intelligently, that you have the right types of insurance coverage, and that you're not paying more than necessary.

Intelligent, personal financial strategies have little to do with your gender, ethnicity, or marital status. We *all* need to do it. Some aspects of financial management become more or less important at different points in your life, but for the most part, the principles remain the same for all of us. Before you can take control, though, you first have to take stock. Turn to the next chapter to begin your financial physical exam. (Don't worry, I don't use rubber gloves or needles.)

Chapter 2

Measuring Your Financial Health

· ·

In This Chapter

▶ The difference between bad debt and good debt

▶ Figuring whether you have too much debt

▶ Assets, liabilities, and your (financial) net worth

▶ How much you really saved last year

▶ Investment and insurance checkups

· ·

*H*ow financially healthy are you? You may already know the bad news. Or perhaps things aren't quite as bad as they seem.

Like many medical problems, financial problems are best detected early (clean living doesn't hurt either). Most problems can be fixed over time and with changes in your behavior. That's what the rest of the book is all about.

This chapter puts you through a *financial physical* to help you detect problems with your current financial health. But don't get depressed and dwell on your "problems" — view them for what they are — opportunities to improve your financial situation. In fact, the more areas for improvement that you can identify, the greater the potential you have to build real wealth and accomplish your financial and personal goals.

Bad Debt versus Good Debt

Why do you borrow money? Usually, it's because you don't have enough money to buy something you want or need — like a college education. If you want to buy a four-year college education, you could easily spend $50,000 to $100,000, perhaps even more. Not too many people have that kind of spare cash lying around. So borrowing money to finance part of that cost enables you to buy the education.

How about a new car? A trip to your friendly local car dealer shows you that a new set of wheels will set you back around $15,000 or more. Although more people have the money to pay for that than, say, the college education, what if you don't? Should you finance the car the way you'd finance the education?

The auto dealers and bankers eager to make you an auto loan say you deserve to and can afford to drive a nice, new car so borrow away.

I say, *NO! NO! NO!*

Why do I disagree with the auto dealers and lenders? For starters, I'm not trying to sell you a car or loan from which I derive a profit! More importantly, there's a *big* difference between borrowing for something that represents a long-term investment and borrowing for consumption.

Take a vacation (no, I don't mean right now). If you spend, say, $1,500 on a vacation, the money is gone. Poof! You may have fond memories and even some Kodak moments, but you'll have no financial value to show for it. "But," you say, "vacations replenish my soul and make me more productive when I return. In fact, the vacation more than pays for itself!"

Great. I'm not saying don't take a vacation. By all means, take one, two, three, or as many as you can afford yearly. But that's the point — *what you can afford.* If you had to borrow money to take the vacation in the form of an outstanding balance on your credit card for many months, then you *could not afford* the vacation you took.

I refer to debt incurred for consumption as *bad debt.* Don't get me wrong — you're not a bad person for having the debt, but the debt is bad for your long-term financial health. Borrowing to purchase a car or clothing also impairs your long-term financial health. This is bad debt, too.

You'll be able to take many more vacations during your lifetime if you save the cash in advance to afford them. If you get into the habit of borrowing and paying all that interest for vacations, cars, clothing, and other consumer items, you'll spend more of your future income paying back the debt and interest. So you'll have *less* money available for vacations and all your other goals.

One of the reasons you'll have less money using bad debt is because of the relatively high interest rates banks and other lenders charge for such debt. Money borrowed on credit cards, auto loans, and through other types of consumer loans not only collects a relatively high interest rate but is also not tax-deductible. Good debt, such as for real estate and business, is available at lower interest rates and is generally tax-deductible. Thus, bad debt not only is bad for your long-term financial health but is also much *more expensive* than good debt.

I'm not saying never borrow money and that all debt is bad. To the contrary, borrowing to pay for educational expenses can make sense. Education is generally a good long-term investment. It should increase your earning potential. This is *good debt*. Likewise, taking on a reasonable amount of debt to buy or start a business or to purchase real estate can be good debt. If properly and smartly managed, these investments should also increase in value.

How much bad debt is too much?

A useful but perhaps painful way to size up your debt load is to calculate how much debt you have relative to your annual income. Ignore, for now, good debt — the loans you may owe on real estate, a business, education, and so on. I'm focusing on bad debt, the higher-interest stuff used to buy items that depreciate in value.

For example, suppose that you earn $30,000 per year. Between your credit cards and an auto loan, you have $15,000 of debt. In this case, your bad debt represents 50 percent of your annual income.

$$\frac{debt}{annual\ income} = \text{debt danger ratio}$$

The financially healthy amount of bad debt is zero.

When your *debt danger ratio* starts to push beyond 25 percent of your income, that can spell real trouble. High-interest debt on credit cards and auto loans is like cancer when it gets to those levels. As with cancer, the growth of the debt can snowball and get out of control unless something significant intervenes. If you have this much debt, turn to Chapter 5 to find out how to get out of debt.

Playing the float

I have credit cards and I use them — but I pay my balance in full each month by the due date. Besides the convenience credit cards offer me in not having to carry around extra cash and checks, I get another benefit. I have free use of the bank's money extended to me through my credit card charges.

When you charge on a credit card that does not have an outstanding balance carried over from the prior month, you typically have several weeks, known as the *grace period,* from the date of the charge to when you must pay your bill. Financial types call this *playing the float.* Had you paid for this purchase by cash or check, you would have had to shell out the money sooner.

If you have difficulty saving money and plastic tends to burn holes through your budget, forget the float game. You'd be better off not using your credit cards. The same applies for those who pay their bills in full but who spend more because it's so easy to do so with a piece of plastic.

How much good debt is acceptable? The answer varies. The key question is, are you able to save sufficiently to accomplish your goals? Later in this chapter, I help you to figure how much you are actually saving, and Chapter 8 assists you in determining what you should be saving to accomplish your goals. See also Chapter 15 for a discussion of deciding how much mortgage debt is appropriate to take on when buying a home.

Avoid borrowing money for consumption (bad debt) — for spending on things like cars, clothing, vacations, and so on that decrease in value and eventually become financially worthless. Borrow money only for investments (good debt) — for purchasing things that retain and hopefully increase in value over the long term, such as education, real estate, or your own business.

Your Financial Net Worth

Your financial net worth is an important barometer of your financial health. It indicates your capacity to accomplish major financial goals such as buying a home, retiring, and withstanding unexpected expenses or loss of income.

Before we crunch any numbers here, before you experience the thrill of bigness or the agony of nothingness or negativity, let's get one thing perfectly clear. Sit down. Take a deep breath. And repeat after me:

"My financial net worth has absolutely, positively *no* relationship to my worth as a human being."

This is not a test. You don't have to compare your number with your neighbor's. It's not the scorecard of life. So do we have an understanding? Good! I hate to see people get depressed about unimportant things that they have the power and ability to change.

Your *net worth* is your financial assets minus your financial liabilities.

Financial Assets – Financial Liabilities = Net Worth

Financial assets

A *financial asset* is worth real money or is something that you plan to convert to hard dollars that you can use to buy things now or in the future.

Financial assets generally include money in bank accounts, stocks, bonds, and mutual fund accounts (see Part III, which deals with investments). Also included is money that you have in retirement accounts, including those with your employer. You should also include the value of any business(es) or real estate that you own.

I generally recommend that you exclude your personal residence. Include your home *only* if you expect to someday sell it or otherwise live off the money you now have tied up in it. If you plan on selling your home, add that portion of the money from the sale that you expect to realize and use to your list of assets.

Assets also include your future expected Social Security benefits and pension payments if your employer has such a plan. These are usually quoted in dollars per month rather than in a lump sum value. I show you in a moment how to account for these monthly benefits when tallying your financial assets.

Personal property such as your car, clothing, stereo, wine glasses, and straight teeth do *not* count as financial assets. I know adding these things to your assets makes your assets *look* larger (and some financial software packages and publications encourage you to list these items as assets), but you can't live off them unless you hock them at a pawn shop or otherwise sell them to meet your financial goals. (Technically, your smile might be able to charm others, so your teeth may actually have some value, but you shouldn't count on it.)

Financial liabilities

Your *financial liabilities* must be subtracted from your assets to arrive at your financial net worth.

Liabilities include loans and debts outstanding, like credit card and auto loan debts. Include money you've borrowed from family and friends (unless you're not gonna pay it back — I won't tell). Include mortgage debt on your home as a liability *only* if you include the value of your home in your asset list. Be sure to include debt owed on other real estate no matter what.

Your net worth calculation

Ready? Table 2-1 provides a place for you to figure your financial assets. Go ahead and write in the spaces provided, unless you plan to lend this book to someone and you don't want to put your money situation on display.

Important Note: See Table 8-1 in Chapter 8 to estimate your Social Security benefits.

Table 2-1	Your Financial Assets
Account	**Value**
Savings and investment accounts (including retirement accounts):	
Example: Bank savings account	$ 5,000
_____	$ _____
_____	$ _____
_____	$ _____
_____	$ _____
_____	$ _____
_____	$ _____
Total =	$ _____
Benefits earned that pay a monthly retirement income:	
Employer's pensions	$ _____ / month
Social Security	$ _____ / month
	x 240*
Total =	$ _____
Total Financial Assets =	$ _____

*In Table 2-1, to convert benefits that will be paid to you monthly into a total dollar amount, I assume that you will live 20 years in retirement. (Ah, think of two decades of lollygagging around — vacationing, harassing the kids, spoiling the grandkids, starting another career, or maybe just living off the fat of the land.) As a shortcut, multiply the benefits that you'll collect monthly in retirement by 240 (12 months in a year times 20 years). Inflation may reduce the value of your employer's pension if it doesn't contain a cost-of-living increase each year in the same way that Social Security does. Don't sweat this now — we'll take care of it in the section on planning for retirement (see Chapter 8).

Now comes the potentially depressing part — your debts and loans in Table 2-2:

Table 2-2	Your Financial Liabilities
Loan	**Balance**
Example: Gouge 'Em Bank Credit Card	$ 4,000
_____	$ _____

Loan	Balance
_____	$ _____
_____	$ _____
_____	$ _____
_____	$ _____
_____	$ _____
Total Financial Liabilities =	$ _____

Now, you can subtract your liabilities from your assets to figure your net worth in Table 2-3:

Table 2-3	Your Net Worth
Find	*Write It Here*
Total Financial Assets (from Table 2-1)	$ _____
Minus	−
Total Financial Liabilities (from Table 2-2)	$ _____
Net Worth =	$ _____

Interpreting your net worth results

Your net worth is important and useful only to you and your unique situation and goals. What is a lot of money to a person with a simple lifestyle and expectations may seem like very little to another with desires for an opulent lifestyle and high expectations.

In Chapter 8, you need to crunch some more numbers to determine your financial status more precisely for such goals as retirement planning. In the meantime, here's a quick and dirty way to evaluate your net worth:

> ✔ **Your net worth is less than half your annual income or even negative.**
> You've got lots of company — in fact, you're in here with the majority of Americans. If you're in your 20s and just starting to work, this is less concerning. It's most important to get rid of your debts, the highest-interest ones first. Then you need to build a safety reserve equal to three to six months of living expenses. You should definitely learn more about getting out of debt, reducing your spending, and developing tax-wise ways to save and invest your future earnings.

✔ **Your net worth is more than half your annual income but less than a few years' annual income.** If you're younger than 40, and especially if you own a home, consider yourself in good shape at this point. If you're older and still renting, you may be in okay shape, but you probably need to reduce your spending and accelerate your savings if you want to buy a home and retire by your 60s.

✔ **Your net worth is more than a few years' annual income.** You're probably on track to meet reasonable financial goals and may actually be ahead of the game, especially if you haven't reached your 40s yet.

Savings Analysis

In the past year, how much money have you actually saved? By savings I mean, the amount of new money you have added to your nest egg, stash, or whatever you like to call it.

Most people don't know or have only a vague idea of the rate at which they are saving money. The answer may sober, terrify, or pleasantly surprise you. In order to calculate your savings over the past year, you need to calculate your net worth as of today *and* as of one year ago.

The amount you actually saved over the past year is equal to the change in your net worth over the past year — in other words, your net worth today minus your net worth from one year ago. I know it may be a pain to find statements showing what your savings and investments were worth a year ago but bear with me; it's a useful exercise.

If you own your home, ignore this in the calculations. And do not include personal property such as car, computer, clothing, and so on with your assets.

Okay, now you have your two figures. Go ahead and plug them into Step 1 of Table 2-4. You may be anticipating the exercise and are already subtracting your net worth of a year ago from what it is today in order to determine your rate of savings. Your instincts are correct, but the exercise is not quite that simple. I must ask you to do a few more calculations in Step 2 of Table 2-4. Why? Well, counting the appreciation of investments you owned over the past year as savings wouldn't be fair. Suppose that you bought 100 shares of a stock a year ago at $17/share and now the value is at $34/share. Your investment increased in value during the past year by $1,700. Although you would be the envy of your friends at the next party if you casually mentioned your investments, the $1,700 of increased value of your investment is not really savings. Instead, it represents appreciation on your investments, so you must remove this appreciation from the calculations.

Note: Just so you know, I'm not unfairly penalizing you for your shrewd invest-ments — you also get to add back the decline in value of your less-successful investments.

Table 2-4	Your Savings Rate over the Past Year		
Today		*One Year Ago*	
Step 1: Figuring your savings.			
Savings & investments	$_____	Savings & investments	$_____
– Loans & debts	$_____	– Loans & debts	$_____
= Net worth today	$_____	= Net worth 1 year ago	$_____
Step 2: Correcting for changes in value of investments you owned during the year.			
Net worth today	$_____		
– Net worth 1 year ago	$_____		
– Appreciation of investments (over past year)	$_____		
+ Depreciation of investments (over past year)	$_____		
= Savings rate	$_____		

If all this gives you a headache or you got stuck or if you just hate crunching numbers, try the intuitive, seat-of-the-pants approach: Do you save a regular portion of your monthly income? You may save it in a separate savings account, retirement account, and so on.

How much do you save in a typical month? Get out your statements for ac-counts that you contribute to or save money in monthly. It doesn't matter if it's a retirement account that you can't access. Money is money. Savings is savings.

Note: If you're able to save, say, $200 per month for a few months but then spend it all on auto repairs, you're not saving. If you contributed $2,000 to an *individual retirement account* (IRA), for example, but depleted money that you had from long ago (in other words, it wasn't saved during the past year), you should not count the $2,000 as savings.

As you'll see later, you very likely should be saving at least 5 to 10 percent of your annual income for longer-term financial goals such as retirement. If you're not, be sure to read Chapter 6 on how to reduce your spending so that you can increase your savings.

How Are You at Investing?

Congratulations! You've completed the hardest part of your financial physical. The physical is a whole lot easier from here on in!

Regardless of how much or how little money you have invested in bank, mutual fund, or other types of accounts, you, of course, want your money invested in the wisest way possible.

Knowing the rights and wrongs of investing is vital to your long-term financial well being. Few people have so much extra money that they can afford major or frequent investing mistakes. The following questions help you size up how much time you need to spend with Part III of this book, which focuses on investing.

Note: The more *No* answers you reluctantly scribbled, the more you need to learn about investing, and the faster you should turn to Part III.

_____ Do you understand the investments you're currently in? (Y/N)

_____ Is the money that you would need to tap in the event of a short-term emergency in an investment where the principal does not fluctuate in value? (Y/N)

_____ Do you know what income-tax bracket you're in, and do you factor that into which investments you choose? (Y/N)

_____ For money outside of retirement accounts, do you understand how those investments produce income and gains and whether these types of investments make the most sense from the stand-point of taxes? (Y/N)

_____ Do you have your money in different, diversified investments that aren't dependent on one or a few securities or one type of investment (that is, bonds, stocks, U.S. investments, and so on)? (Y/N)

_____ Is the money that you will need for a major expenditure in the next few years invested conservatively rather than in riskier investments such as stocks, real estate, or pork bellies? (Y/N)

_____ Is the money that you have earmarked for longer-term purposes (more than five years) invested to keep you well ahead of inflation? (Y/N)

_____ Is the bulk of your long-term money invested inside retirement accounts, and have you exhausted possibilities for directing more money into these tax-sheltered accounts? (Y/N)

_____ Is your longer-term money, particularly what is inside of retirement accounts, invested in quality, growth-oriented investments rather than preservation-of-principal-oriented investments? (Y/N)

_____ If you work with a financial advisor, is that person compensated in a way that eliminates potential conflicts of interest in the strategies and investments he or she recommends? (Y/N)

Making and saving money is not a guarantee of financial success but rather a prerequisite. If you don't know how to choose quality investments that meet your needs, you will more than likely throw money away, which leads to the same end result as never having earned and saved it in the first place. Worse still, you won't have derived any enjoyment from spending the lost money on items, which you perhaps needed or wanted. Learn the best ways to invest; otherwise, you'll just be spinning your wheels working and saving.

How's Your Insurance Intelligence?

Now we're in the home stretch of your financial physical. Last but not least, you must deal with the prickly subject of protecting your assets and yourself with *insurance.* If you're like most people, reviewing your insurance policies and coverages is about as much fun as a root canal. Open wide!

_____ On each policy that you have, do you understand the individual coverages and protection types and amounts? (Y/N)

_____ Does your *current* insurance protection make sense given your current financial situation (as opposed to when you bought the policies)? (Y/N)

_____ If you couldn't make it financially without your income, do you have adequate long-term disability insurance coverage? (Y/N)

_____ If you have family members who are dependent on your continued income, do you have adequate life insurance coverage to replace that income should you die? (Y/N)

_____ If you bought life insurance (and have a net worth of less than $2 million to $3 million), did you buy term insurance? (Y/N)

_____ Do you buy insurance through companies that sell directly to the public (bypassing agents) and through discount brokers and fee-for-service advisors? (Y/N)

_____ Do you carry enough liability insurance on your home, car (including umbrella/excess liability), and business to protect all your assets? (Y/N)

_____ Did you recently (last year or two) shop around for the best price on your insurance policies? (Y/N)

_____ Do you know if your insurance companies have good track records regarding paying claims and keeping their customers satisfied? (Y/N)

That wasn't so bad, was it? If you answered *No* more than once or twice, don't feel dumb — more than nine out of ten people make major mistakes when buying insurance. See Part IV for your salvation. If you answered *Yes* to all the preceding questions, you can spare yourself from reading Part IV, but bear in mind that most people need help in this area as much as they do in other areas of personal finance.

Well, you survived your financial physical! Just like health exams, they can make you a little uncomfortable. The good news is that now you know more about your current financial health. Now, read the rest of this book to improve on it!

Chapter 3

Hiring Financial Help: Truths and Consequences

In This Chapter

▶ Alice's mishaps in Financial-Planner Land

▶ Why it's hard to find good financial help

▶ Financial planners' conflicts of interest

▶ Your financial management options

▶ Deciding whether you need help and how to find it if you need it

"The financial planning business has two problems. One is credibility, and the other is conflict of interest."

— *Fortune* magazine

"When I was a child, my father told me to pick a field where you only need to be mediocre to be great. I chose personal financial planning."

— financial planner Jim Schwartz, as quoted in *The Wall Street Journal*

*1*f you've recovered from your financial physical, you may be considering hiring help to whip you back into shape. Hiring help may seem like a practical choice if you're busy or if you'd simply rather spend time on other things.

Hiring a competent, ethical, and unbiased financial planner or advisor to help you make and implement financial decisions *can* be money well spent. But if you pick a poor advisor or someone who really isn't a financial planner but a salesperson in disguise, things could get worse instead of better. So before we talk about the different types of help to hire, let's take a little journey with Alice to give you an idea of what you're up against in the land of financial planners.

Alice in Financial-Planner Land

Alice is a client who landed on my doorstep a few years ago. She struck out the first four times she sought financial help. Her story illustrates many of the pitfalls in finding a good financial planner.

Alice's adventures

First, on the recommendation of her accountant, Alice called a *financial consultant,* who was a *certified financial planner* (CFP) at a well-known brokerage firm. Although Alice explained that she wanted a conservative investment, the broker sold her a mutual fund that, unbeknowst to Alice, primarily held *aggressive growth* (volatile) stocks.

After buying the fund and getting her first account statement a few days later, Alice noticed that there were several thousand dollars less in the fund than she had invested. The broker had told her he earned a 4 percent commission but assured her that she need not concern herself with it because the fund paid him and it wouldn't affect her investment.

After a little investigation, Alice discovered that the fund had, in fact, paid the broker out of her investment — a hefty 6.5 percent commission. Thus, the broker had not only lied about where the commission dollars came from (all such commissions come from the investors' money), but he had also understated the size of his commission.

Understandably steamed, Alice called the Securities and Exchange Commission (SEC), and after she jumped through many hoops, the brokerage firm coughed up nearly $2,000 for the broker's lie about the commission amount.

Thinking that perhaps men and women simply don't communicate well, Alice next turned to a female financial planner on the recommendation of a friend. The planner told Alice: "Women need to stick together." Then she promptly tried to sell Alice a limited partnership that, the planner said, was *sure* to return upward of 20 to 40 percent per year.

Alice took a gander at the *prospectus* — a delightfully long document written by attorneys — and saw in black and white on page 2 that the partnership paid the selling broker a 10 percent sales commission (which, she now knew, would be deducted from her investment).

Because Alice is a conscientious investor, she did more research in financial books and magazines and learned that limited partnerships are also handicapped by high, ongoing management fees. Alice did not return the dozen or so follow-up calls ("to see how you are doing") from her "sister" financial planner and fortunately passed on the partnership.

Wanting to learn more before her next attempt to get help, Alice enrolled in an "adult education class" at a local college. Alice, a student eager to learn, attended all the classes but soon felt only more confused. The world of finance and investments, her teacher said, is *very, very complicated.* Unless, of course, you're a financial expert.

The teacher, a "certified financial planner," told the class that he was just such an expert. He offered a free, one-hour consultation to all his students at the end of his "course." During her free session, Alice was told that she should invest in an *annuity.* Investigation, however, revealed (you guessed it) high sales commissions and management fees.

Alice was also uncomfortable because planner number three hadn't inquired about other aspects of her situation and seemed intent only on selling her an annuity. Annuities did not make sense for her, she later learned, because she was nearly retired and was in a low tax bracket.

At this point, most people probably would have bought a good financial book or put their money in a mattress or the next best place — their local bank — but Alice really wanted to talk to someone about her money issues and ideas.

After listening to a financial planner on a radio call-in program, Alice had the planner mail his background materials to her. In addition to a certified financial-planning credential, *this* planner had a seemingly endless list of other, lofty-sounding credentials, such as RIA, BSCE, LLB, and MBA.

Quite wary of sales commissions by now, Alice also liked the sound of the planner's fee: $350 for his time to help with her investment decisions and to discuss her other financial questions. Part way through their two-hour, $350 consultation, however, planner number four tried to persuade Alice that what she really needed was to hire him as an ongoing manager of her money. For just $2,000 per year for the service (commissions and management fees were extra), he would trade her in and out of investments based on his economic analyses and expert prognostications.

That seemed like a lot of money to Alice, who had $150,000 to invest, and she did not like the thought of turning over her money to someone who could move it around among various investments without her approval. Besides, she was interested in learning more about finance, and this "planner" kept telling her how complicated it is to make investing and other financial decisions. Alice therefore declined planner number four's sales pitch for managing her investments, whereupon the moody planner stormed out of her house, complaining that she had wasted his time (for which he had his $350 check in hand for a mere two hours of his time!).

Lessons learned from Alice's trip to Financial-Planner Land

Alice's case highlights four major problems that people often encounter when hiring financial help:

✔ First, you absolutely, positively *must* do your homework before hiring any financial advisor. Just look at Alice: Despite enthusiastic recommendations from her accountant and another from a friend, Alice ended up with bad advice from biased advisors.

✔ Second, the financial planning and brokerage fields are mine fields for consumers. The fundamental problem is the enormous conflict of interest that is created when "advisors" sell products that earn them sales commissions to people who believe they are getting unbiased advice. Selling ongoing money management services, as Alice learned from the last "advisor," creates conflicts of interest as well.

As an analogy, imagine that you have flu symptoms. Would you be comfortable seeing a physician who didn't charge for office visits but made money only by selling you drugs? Maybe you don't *need* the drugs — or at least not so many expensive ones. Maybe what you really need is Mom's chicken soup and 16 hours of sleep.

In its review of the financial planning industry, *Consumer Reports* said, "Financial planners often end up being wolves in sheep's clothing with hidden agendas to sell mutual funds, for example, or life insurance." Respected financial columnist Jane Bryant Quinn of *Newsweek* says, "Planners are supposed to pull apart your finances and suggest better ways of meeting your goals. They purport to be objective. But they can't be if they work for brokerage firms or insurance companies or if their income depends on sales commissions from the products they sell."

✔ Third, financial advisors often like to make things far more complicated than need be, and they're generally not interested in educating you. As others have observed, financial planning is hardly the only occupation guilty of this. As author George Bernard Shaw put it, "All professions are conspiracies against the laity."

The more you know and the more you realize that investing and other financial decisions needn't be complicated, the more you'll realize you don't need to spend gobs of money, or any money at all, on financial planners and advisors. If you look in the mirror, you see the person who is most qualified to be your best financial advisor and who has your best interests at heart.

The credentialization of America: What credentials qualify a financial advisor?

It seems that everywhere I turn today, more and more people carry credentials after their names. We have certified lactation consultants, certified foot reflexologists, and registered dietitians.

Among sales people, especially in the financial services industry, the use of dubious credentials and self-anointed and misleading titles is on the increase. Stock brokers are no longer called stock brokers — they are "financial consultants" and "financial advisors." Some life insurance agents now call themselves "estate planning specialists." Next thing I know, when I visit an auto dealer, I'll speak with a certified transportation consultant, and when I buy my next home, it will be through a certified housing consultant rather than a real estate agent. It seems that everything today is *certified* — even the once "used car" is now referred to by some dealers as "certified pre-owned!"

Speaking of "certified," tens of thousands of people have earned the Certified Financial Planning credential. This is basically a home-study course that, unlike gaining entrance into medical, law, or business school, virtually anyone can undertake. The test itself isn't difficult to pass — an astounding 74 percent of people recently enrolled in the College for Financial Planning passed the CFP test. Gaining admission to a top professional school and becoming an architect, attorney, or doctor is exponentially more difficult and demanding.

The CFP Board of Standards, which licenses the CFP credential, claims that the combination of passing a test and meeting continuing education requirements ensures that their profession is doing the best that it can. To that, I and others who regularly observe CFP incompetence and conflicts of interest, politely say "bunk!"

✔ The CFP tests nothing of a planner's business ethics or how the planner earns income.

✔ The CFP exam covers arcane financial details, which are rarely encountered by consumer-oriented planners and could easily be contained in a handy reference book.

✔ The CFP curriculum has little practical information on the important topics of asset allocation and mutual fund selection.

✔ And the few individuals who don't pass the CFP exam on the first try are told what answers they got wrong so that they can focus their time memorizing the trivial details and pass the exam on the second try.

Boston Globe columnist Charles Jaffe took the CFP exam and concluded that ". . . financial planning is a long way from qualifying as a profession."

Unfortunately, the vast majority of people with CFPs work on commission and are employed by securities and insurance brokerage firms, so they're not really financial planners so much as salespeople with a "credential." Most of the rest sell ongoing money management services.

Meeting the CFP continuing education requirements is a sham. CFPs can attend what amounts to sales presentations by companies pitching financial products to earn continuing education credit hours. Another method is for CFPs to read financial planning journals, which have multiple choice and true-false questions in the back. The planner can take the test on his or her own time and even refer back to the relevant articles to find the answers!

If you are interested in hiring financial help, be sure to read Chapter 19, which details the ten questions you should ask a financial advisor before you hire, including how to make sense of all the credential gobbledygook.

> ✔ Fourth, don't place a whole lot of faith in credentials, especially the Certified Financial Planning (CFP) moniker, which *Forbes* magazine columnist Gretchen Morgensen called a "meaningless label," adding, "When picking a financial planner, pay a lot of attention to how the planner is compensated. Pay no attention to CFPs. . . ."

What's truly amazing about Alice's situation is that none of the so-called financial "planners" ever bothered to ask about her insurance and debt situation. As it turns out, I learned that Alice not only lacked adequate homeowner's insurance, but she also had no health insurance!

Alice also had some relatively high-interest consumer debt that none of the "planners" ever asked about, probably because paying off her debt would have diminished the funds that Alice would have available for investment. Alice could afford both the insurance and debt payoff. In short, no one had taken the time to explain to Alice the costs and risks of not getting her financial house in order.

Finally, in case you're wondering, Alice did happily invest her money in a nice portfolio of commission-free mutual funds (see Chapter 11), which have been performing just swimmingly for her over the years.

The Frustrations of Finding Good Financial Planners

Overwhelmed and undereducated consumers like Alice, especially those in low- and middle-income brackets, have few attractive options if they want to hire financial help. Over 90 percent of the people who call themselves *financial planners* and *financial consultants* sell products and work on commission, which, as Alice found in the previous section, creates enormous conflicts of interest. Those conflicts of interest stem from the fact that the broker has an incentive to recommend strategies and sell products that pay generous commissions and to ignore strategies and products that pay no or low commissions.

The few financial advisors who are *fee-only* make most of their fees from money-management services. (*Fee-only* or *fee-based* means that the advisors' fees are paid by their clients, not by companies whose products they recommend.) Thus fee-based advisors tend to focus on those who have already accumulated significant wealth. Fee-based advisors may also have conflicts of interest in that they gravitate toward strategies and recommendations that involve their ongoing management of your money and tend to ignore or dismiss tactics that diminish the pool of investment money that they can manage for you for an ongoing-fee.

Regulatory problems

A pretty basic problem of oversight afflicts the financial planning field: Oversight is minimal *at best.* In many states, anyone can hang out a shingle and call him- or herself a financial planner. The U.S. Securities and Exchange Commission (SEC) polices only those who provide investment advice; they must register with the SEC as registered investment advisors (RIAs). The SEC provides no oversight of non-investing advice provided.

Several studies have shown that, because the SEC has so few investigators to police so many RIAs, the typical RIA is investigated on the order of every 15 years or so. The SEC believes that the states should police the approximately 300,000 people who call themselves financial planners. But most states have done little to monitor planners and protect consumers. Thus, as the nonprofit Consumer Federation of America said in its assessment of the industry: "Today's investors go up against a deadly combination of abusive securities industry practices and regulatory inattentiveness when investing their money."

Financial planners *should* have to disclose in writing, prior to working with a client, how they are compensated. This would make it easier for people to know how the planner earns a living. And it would eliminate much of the need for more formal government regulation. Several bills with this sort of common-sense provision that were introduced in state and federal government have been squashed. Financial planners, insurance brokers, and others selling products with commissions that are hidden to the public have lobbied successfully (by spending and contributing money to politicians' campaigns) to kill such bills.

Letting the Big Bad Wolf guard the Three Little Pigs

The International Association of Financial Planners (IAFP) and the Institute of Certified Financial Planners (ICFP) are the two primary trade associations that represent most financial planners. Unfortunately, these organizations tend to promote the status quo in the industry because they *are* the industry. Their membership and leadership are policing themselves.

In an article entitled "Costly Counsel: The Best Financial Planner May Be No Planner at All," *Barrons'* noted: "There is no effective regulation of planners, no accepted standard for admission into their ranks — a dog got into one trade group. All anyone need do is hang up a shingle and start planning."

In fact, the associations have lobbied government to defeat laws aimed at regulation of their membership's sales practices rather than advocating what's ethical or best for the public. Other sources to be wary of are "educational" materials produced by the National Endowment for Financial Education, which is funded by the College for Financial Planning that grants CFPs.

Financial planners' top conflicts of interest

All professions have conflicts of interest. Some fields have more than others, and the financial planning field is one of those fields. Knowing where some of the land mines lie can certainly help. Here, then, are the most common reasons that planners may not have 20/20 vision when giving financial directions.

Selling and pushing products that pay commissions

If a financial planner isn't charging you a fee for his time, you can rest assured he is earning commissions on the products he'll try to sell you. In order to sell financial products, this planner must have a broker's license. A person who sells financial products and earns commissions from those products is a salesperson, *not* a financial planner. Financial planning involves taking an objective, holistic look at your financial puzzle to find the pieces that fit it well, something that brokers are neither trained nor financially motivated to do.

To make it even harder for you to discern planners' agendas, you can *not* assume that planners who do charge fees for their time don't also earn commissions selling products. Sadly for people seeking financial advice, compensation *double-dipping* is becoming more and more common.

Selling products that provide a commission tends to skew a planner's recommendations. Products that carry commissions mean that you have fewer of your dollars working in the investments and insurance you buy. Because a commission is earned only when a product is sold, such a product or service is inevitably more attractive in the planner's eyes than any other option. For example, if the planner sells disability insurance that you could obtain at a lower cost through your employer or a group trade association (see Chapter 17), he may overlook or criticize your most attractive option (buying through your employer) and focus on *his* most attractive option — selling you a higher cost disability policy on which he derives a commission.

Another danger of trusting the recommendation of a commission-based planner is that she may steer you toward the products that have the biggest payback for her. These products are among the *worst* for you because they siphon off even more of your money up front to pay the commission. They also tend to be among the costliest and riskiest financial products available.

Planners who are also commission-greedy may try to *churn* your investments. They encourage you to buy and sell at the drop of a hat, attributing the need to changes in the economy or the companies you've invested in. More trading means — big surprise — more commissions for the broker.

"Financial planning" in banks

Over the past couple of decades, banks have witnessed a gradual erosion of the money in their coffers and vaults. The reason is simple — increasing numbers of investors realized that banks are generally lousy places to build wealth. The highest yielding bank savings accounts and certificates of deposit barely keep an investor ahead of inflation. If you factor in both inflation and taxes, these bank "investments" provide no real growth on your investment dollars.

Increasingly, banks have "financial representatives" and "investment specialists" sitting in their branches waiting to pounce on bank customers with big balances. In many banks, these "financial planners" are simply brokers who are out to sell investments that pay them (and the bank) hefty sales commissions.

Although you may expect your bank account balances to be confidential and off limits to the eager eyes of investment salespeople in a bank, numerous studies have demonstrated that banks are betraying customer trust.

✔ First, many customers have no idea that these bank reps are earning commissions and that those commissions are being siphoned out of customers' investment dollars.

✔ Second, many customers are mistaken (partly due to the banks' and salespeople's' poor disclosure) in believing that these investments like bank savings accounts are FDIC insured and cannot lose value.

✔ Finally, many of the reps in banks are inexperienced and don't well understand what they are selling and what is suitable for particular customers.

Taking a narrow view

Because of the way they earn their money, many planners are biased in favor of certain strategies and products. As a result, they do not typically keep your overall financial needs in mind. For example, if you have a problem with accumulated credit card debts, some planners may never know (or care) because they're focused on selling you an investment product. Likewise, a planner who sells a lot of life insurance tends to develop recommendations that require its purchase.

Not recommending saving through your employer's retirement plan

One of your best financial options is to take advantage of saving through your employer's retirement savings plan(s). Although this method of saving may not be as exciting as risking your money in cattle futures, it's not as dull as watching paint dry — and, most importantly, it is tax-deductible. Planners are reluctant to recommend taking full advantage of this option: It doesn't leave much money for the purchase of their commission-laden investment products.

Selling ongoing money-management services

The vast majority of financial planners/advisors who don't work on commission make their money by managing your money for an ongoing fee percentage (typically 1 to 3 percent annually of your investment). Although this removes the incentive to *churn* your account (buy and sell repeatedly and rapidly) to run up more commissions, it's a service that you're unlikely to need.

An ongoing fee percentage still creates a conflict of interest; the financial planner will tend to steer you away from beneficial financial strategies that reduce the asset pool from which he derives his percentage. Maximizing contributions to your employer's retirement savings plan, paying off debts like your mortgage, investing in real estate or small business, and so on — these financial strategies may make the most sense for you but are rarely recommended by an advisor who works on a percentage of assets under management basis.

The latest rage, particularly among brokerage firms, is the *wrap account* (also known as the *managed account*). Wrap accounts can cost you upward of 3 percent of your assets annually. As I explain in Part III, you can hire *professional money managers* for 1 percent per year or less.

Ignoring debts

Sometimes, your best investment is to pay off outstanding loans, whether credit card, auto, or even mortgage debts. But most financial planners don't recommend this strategy because paying down debts depletes the capital with which you could otherwise buy investments — the investments that the broker may be trying to sell you to earn a commission or the advisor would like to manage for an ongoing fee.

Not recommending real estate and small business investments

Like paying off debts, investing in real estate and small business takes away from your interest and ability to invest elsewhere. Most planners won't help with these choices. They may even tell you tales of real-estate and small-business-investing disasters to give you cold feet.

Sure, the value of real estate can go down just like any other investment. But over the long haul, owning a home makes good financial sense for most people. With small business, the risks are higher, but so are the potential returns. Don't let a financial planner convince you that these options are foolish — in fact, if you do your homework and know what you're doing, you can make higher rates of returns investing in real estate and small business than you can in traditional securities such as stocks and bonds. See Part III to read more about your investing options.

Selling legal services

More and more planners are getting into the business of drawing up *trusts* and providing other estate planning services for their clients. Although these and other legal documents may be right for you, you may be able to draw them up yourself at far lower cost if your situation is not complicated (see Chapter 18).

If you want advice on whether you need these legal documents, do a little investigating: Do some additional reading or consult an advisor who won't actually perform the work. Legal matters are complex enough that the competence of someone who doesn't specialize in it full-time should be carefully scrutinized. If you do ultimately hire someone to perform estate planning services for you, hire someone who specializes and works at it full-time. Read the section in Chapter 18 to learn more about estate planning.

Scaring you unnecessarily

Some planners put together nifty computer-generated projections showing that you will need millions of dollars by the time you retire to maintain your standard of living. Or that tuition will cost hundreds of thousands of dollars by the time your two-year-old is ready for college.

Waking up a client to the realities of his or her financial situation is an important and difficult job for a good financial planner. But some unscrupulous planners take this task to an extreme, deliberately scaring you into buying what they're selling. They paint a bleak picture and imply that you can fix your problems only if you do what they say. Don't let them scare you — you've got *Personal Finance For Dummies* and Eric Tyson on your side! Don't worry; instead, read this book and get your financial life in order.

Creating dependency

Another conflict-of-interest issue: Financial planners have a tendency to create dependency, making things seem so complicated that their clients feel as though they could never manage their finances on their own. If your advisor is reluctant to tell you how you can educate yourself about personal finance, or if she advises you that your time would be better spent learning yoga, you've probably found a *self-perpetuating consultant.*

Financial Management Options

Everyone has three basic choices about how to approach managing money: You can do nothing, you can do it yourself, or you can hire someone to help you.

Doing nothing

The *do-nothing* approach has a large following (and you thought you were the only one!). People who fall into this category may be leading terribly exciting, interesting lives and are therefore too busy to attend to something so mundane as dealing with their personal finances. Or they may be leading terribly mundane lives but are too busy fantasizing about more appealing ways to spend their time. For both types, everything from a major UFO sighting to taking out the garbage captures the imagination more than thinking about financial management.

But the dangers of doing nothing are many. Problem areas, left to themselves, get worse. Putting off saving for retirement or ignoring your buildup of debt eventually comes back to haunt you. Not carrying adequate insurance can be devastating when an accident occurs. In the last several years, fires and earthquakes in California, flooding in the Midwest, and hurricanes in the South and East all show how precariously we live in paradise.

Even if the do-nothing approach has been yours all your life, you are now officially promoted out of it! You bought this book to learn more about personal finance and to make changes in your money matters, right? So take control and keep reading!

Doing it yourself

The do-it-yourselfers learn enough about financial topics to make informed decisions on their own. Doing anything yourself, of course, requires you to invest some of your time to learn the basic concepts and keep up with changes. For some, personal financial management becomes a challenging and absorbing interest. Others focus on what they need to do to get the job done quickly and efficiently.

It's a myth that, if you self-direct your finances and make your own decisions, you will spend endless hours doing so. The harder part for most people is catching up to where they should be and correcting past mistakes. After you get things in order, which you can easily do with this book as your companion, you should not need to spend more than an hour or two every few months on your personal finances (unless a major issue, like a real estate purchase, comes up).

Some in the financial advisory business like to make things seem so complicated that they compare what they do to brain surgery! Their argument goes, "You wouldn't perform brain surgery on yourself so why would you manage your money yourself." Well, to this I say, personal financial management *ain't* brain surgery — not even close. You can manage on your own and, in fact, you can do better than what most advisors can do for you. Why? Because, you're not subject to conflicts of interest, and you care the most about your money.

Hiring financial help

Realizing that you need to hire someone to help you make and implement financial decisions can be a valuable insight. Spending a few hours and several hundred dollars to hire a competent professional can be a good investment, even if you have a modest income or assets. But you need to know what your money is buying.

Financial planners or advisors make money in one of three ways:

✔ They earn commissions based on sales of financial products.

✔ They can charge a percentage of your assets that they are investing.

✔ They can charge by the hour.

As you can see from Alice's journey into this area at the beginning of this chapter, hiring financial assistance can be anything but a tea party.

Commission-based "planners"

Commission-based planners aren't really planners, advisors, or counselors at all — they are salespeople. Many *stock brokers* and *insurance brokers* of the 1970s and 1980s are now called *financial consultants* or *financial service repre-sentatives* in order to glamorize the profession and obscure how the planners are compensated. Ditto for insurance salespeople calling themselves *estate planning specialists*.

That's like a Honda dealer calling himself a *transportation consultant*. A Honda dealer is a salesperson who makes a living selling Hondas, period. He's defi-nitely not going to tell you nice things about Ford, Chrysler, or Toyota cars — unless, of course, he happens to sell those, too. He also has no interest in educating you about money-saving public transit possibilities.

As I discuss earlier in this chapter, salespeople and brokers masquerading as planners can have an enormous self-interest when they push certain products, particularly those products that pay generous commissions. Being paid on commission tends to skew their recommendations toward certain strategies (such as buying investment or life insurance products) and causes the sales-people to ignore or downplay other aspects of your finances. For example, they'll gladly sell you a Gee-whiz-bang investment product rather than convince you to pay off your high-cost debts or to save and invest through your employer's retirement plan, thereby reducing your taxes.

Table 3-1 gives you an idea of the commissions that a financial planner/salesper-son can earn through selling particular financial products.

Table 3-1	Financial Product Commissions
Product	*Commission*
Life Insurance ($250,000, age 45):	
Term Life	$140 to $565
Universal/Whole Life	$1,020 to $2,580
Disability Insurance:	
($4,000/month benefit, age 35)	$345 to $1,200
Investments ($20,000):	
Mutual Funds	$800 to $1,700
Limited Partnerships	$1,400 to $2,000
Annuities	$1,000 to $1,800

Percentage of assets under management advisors

A generally better choice than a commission-based planner is a financial advisor who charges a percentage of the assets that are being managed or invested. This compensation system removes the incentives to sell you products with high commissions and to churn your assets with lots of transactions to generate more of those commissions.

Although it is an improvement over product-pushers working on commission, the fee-based system has flaws, too. First off, suppose that you're trying to decide to invest in stocks, bonds, or real estate. A planner who earns her living managing your money likely won't recommend real estate because that would deplete your investment capital. The planner also won't recommend paying down your mortgage for the same reason — she'll claim that you can earn more investing your money (with her help, of course) than it will cost you to borrow.

Fee-based planners are also only interested in managing money for those who have already accumulated a fair amount of it — which rules out most people. According to the Boston Company, an economics research firm, the median household (*median* means half have more, half have less) headed by a person aged 35 to 49 has just $6,000 in financial assets — far below the six-figure minimums of most fee-based advisors.

If what you really do need is someone to manage your money (you lucky dog), mutual funds or private money managers (discussed in Chapter 11) are what you should look for, not a financial planner who also tries to manage money.

Hourly based advisors

Your best bet for professional help with your personal finances is an advisor who charges for his time. Because he doesn't sell any financial products, his objectivity is maintained. He doesn't perform money management, so he can help you make comprehensive financial decisions dealing with loans, retirement planning, and selecting good investments including real estate, mutual funds, and small business.

The primary risk in selecting an hourly-based planner is incompetence. You can address this by checking references and learning enough yourself to discern between good and bad financial advice. Another risk comes from not clearly defining the work to be done and the approximate total cost before you begin. You should also review some of the other key questions outlined in Chapter 20.

A drawback of an entirely different kind occurs when you don't follow through on the recommendations of your advisor. You paid for her work but didn't act on it, so you didn't capture its value. If part of the reason that you hired the planner in the first place was that you're too busy or not interested enough to make changes to your financial situation, then you should look for this support in the services you buy from the planner.

If you just need someone as a sounding board for ideas or to recommend a specific strategy or product, you can hire an hourly based planner for one or two sessions of advice. You save money doing the legwork and implementation on your own. Just make sure that the planner is willing to give you specific enough advice that you can implement on your own.

Should You Hire a Financial Planner?

Most people reading this book don't need to hire a financial planner. But just because you're financially savvy, you shouldn't be too quick to write off the value of hiring help.

Good reasons for hiring a financial planner can be the same reasons for hiring someone to clean your home or do your taxes. If you're too busy or don't enjoy doing it, that's a fine reason to hire help. If you're uncomfortable making decisions on your own, using a planner for a second opinion makes good sense. And if you shy away from numbers and bristle at the thought of long division, a good planner can help you.

How a good financial planner can help

The following gives you a run-down of some of the important things a competent financial planner can assist you with.

Identifying problems and goals

Many otherwise intelligent people have a hard time being objective about their financial problems. They may ignore their debts or have unrealistic goals and expectations given their financial situations and behaviors. And many are so busy with other aspects of their lives that they never take the time to think about what their financial goals are. A good financial planner can give you the objective look you need.

Surprisingly, some people are in better financial position than they thought in relation to their goals. Good counselors really enjoy this aspect of their jobs — good news is easier and much more fun to deliver.

Identifying strategies to reach your financial goals

If your mind is like mine, it's a jumble of various plans, ideas, and concerns, along with a cobweb or two. A good counselor can help you sort out and straighten your thoughts and can propose alternative strategies for you to consider in accomplishing your financial goals.

Setting priorities

You could be doing dozens of things to improve your financial situation, but making a few key changes could probably have the greatest value. Equally important is to identify the changes that fit your overall situation and that won't keep you awake at night fretting about them. Good planners help you prioritize.

Saving research time and hassle

Even if you know what major financial decisions are most important to you, doing the research can be time-consuming and frustrating if you don't know where to turn for good information and advice. A good planner does research to match your needs to the best available strategies and products. So much lousy information is out there on various financial topics that you can easily get lost, discouraged, sidetracked, or swindled. A good advisor can keep you from making a bad decision based on poor or insufficient information. Your free time is precious. (Does your car license plate holder say *I'D RATHER BE* . . .? If so, you may be a good candidate to hire a financial planner — unless, of course, it says *I'D RATHER BE MANAGING MY OWN MONEY.*)

Purchasing commission-free financial products

If you hire a planner who charges for her time, you can easily save hundreds or thousands of dollars by avoiding the cost of commissions in the financial products you buy. This commission-free situation is especially valuable when it comes to purchasing investments and insurance.

Avoiding lousy financial products and strategies

A good counselor can keep you from doing something really dumb — particularly if a commission-based salesperson is giving you the *hard sell.* A conflict-free planner can recommend what is in your best interests.

Providing an objective voice for major decisions

Deciding when to retire, how much to spend on a home purchase, and where to invest your money are big decisions. Getting swept up in the emotional upheaval of these issues can cloud your perspective and objectivity. A competent and sensitive advisor can cut through this cloud to raise issues and provide sound counsel.

Helping you to just do it

Deciding what you need to do is not enough — you have to actually do it, too. And although you can use a planner for advice and make all the changes on your own, a good counselor can help you follow through with your plan as well. After all, part of the reason you hired the counselor in the first place may be that you're too busy or uninterested to manage your finances. If the counselor merely produces a nice-looking report of recommendations and doesn't encourage you to implement them, all you're left with is part of a dead tree!

Mediating

If you have a spouse or partner, financial decisions can produce real fireworks, particularly with financial decisions involving the extended family. Although a counselor can't be a therapist, a good one can be sensitive to the different needs and concerns of each party and can try to find middle ground on the financial issues you're grappling with.

Making you money and allowing you peace of mind

The whole point of professional financial planning is to help you make the most of your money and help you plan for and attain your financial and personal goals. In the process, the financial planner should show you how to enhance your investment returns; reduce your spending, taxes, and insurance costs; increase your savings; improve your catastrophic insurance coverage; and achieve your financial independence goals. And last but not least: Putting your financial house in order should take some weight off your mind — like that clean, light-headed feeling after a haircut.

Not for everyone

Although some people can benefit from the advice of a knowledgeable and ethical financial planner, you should consider your personality type before you decide to hire help. My experience has been that some people (believe it or not) enjoy the research and number-crunching. If this is you or if you're not really comfortable taking advice, you'd be better off doing your own homework and creating your own plan.

Likewise, if you have a specific tax or legal matter, you're better off hiring a good professional who specializes in that field rather than a financial planner.

How to find a good financial planner

Locating a good financial planner who is willing to work with the not-yet-rich-and-famous and who doesn't have conflicts of interest can be like finding a needle in a haystack. Two methods that can serve as good starting points are personal referral and associations.

Personal referral

One of the best ways to find a good financial planner is to get a personal referral from a satisfied customer who is someone you trust. A referral from an accountant or an attorney whose judgment you've tested can help as well.

Word-of-mouth is how the best financial planners continue to build their practices. Satisfied customers are any professional's best and least costly marketers.

However, never *ever* take a recommendation from anyone as gospel. I don't care *who* is making the referral — even if it's your mother or the Pope. You must do your homework: Ask the planner the ten questions in Chapter 20. I've seen people get into real trouble because of blindly accepting someone else's recommendation. Remember: The person making the recommendation is (probably) not a personal finance expert. He or she could be just as bewildered as you are.

You may get referred to a planner or broker who returns the favor by sending business to the tax, legal, or real estate person who referred you. On more than a few occasions, professionals in other fields have made it clear that they would refer business to me if I referred business to them. I refused, of course. Good professionals don't do tit for tat. Hire professionals who make referrals to others based on their competence and ethics.

Associations

Associations of financial planners are more than happy to refer you to planners in your area. But as I discuss earlier in this chapter, the major trade associations are composed of planners who sell products and work on commission.

Two better places to start include the following:

> ✔ **The National Association of Personal Financial Advisors**
> **1130 Lake Cook Road**
> **Buffalo Grove, IL 60089**
>
> The NAPFA is made up of fee-only planners. Its members are not supposed to earn commissions from products they sell, so at least you don't have to worry about the planners selling products. However, most planners in this association earn their living by providing money-management services and charging a fee that is a percentage of assets under management.
>
> ✔ **The American Institute of Certified Public Accountants (AICPA)**
> **1211 Avenue of the Americas**
> **New York, NY 10036**
>
> The AICPA is the professional association of CPAs that can provide names of members who have completed the Institute's Personal Financial Specialist (PFS) program. Many, but certainly not all, of the CPAs who have completed the PFS program provide financial advice on a fee basis. Competent CPAs have the advantage of understanding the tax consequences of different choices, which are important components of any financial plan. On the other hand, it is hard for a professional to keep current in two broad fields.

Caution: Savings at Risk

You have no interest in becoming a financial planner (presumably), so why waste your time reading about the ways that planners of dubious distinction often cultivate their clients? Simple: The channel through which you hear of a planner may provide clues to a planner's integrity and way of doing business.

> ✔ **Cold calling.** You've just come home after a hard day. No sooner has your posterior hit the recliner to settle in for the night when the phone rings. It's Joe the financial planner, and he wants to help you achieve all your financial dreams. *Cold calling* (the salesperson calls you, without an appointment) is the most inefficient way a planner can get new clients. It's also intrusive and is typically used by aggressive salespeople who work on commission.

Keep a log beside your telephone. Record the date, time, name of organization, and name of caller every time you receive a cold call. Tell cold callers to never call you again. Then, if they do call you again, you can sue them for $500 in small claims court!

✔ **Adult education classes.** Here's what often happens at adult education classes given at local universities: You pay a reasonable fee for the course. You go to class giddy at the prospect of learning how to manage your finances. And then the instructor ends up being a broker or financial planner hungry for clients. He confuses more than he conveys. He's short on specifics. But he'll be more than happy to show you the way if you contact (and hire) him outside of class.

Instructors for these courses are paid to teach. They don't need to solicit clients in class, and, in fact it's unethical for them to do so. I should note, however, that part of the problem is that some universities take advantage of the fact that they know such "teachers" want to solicit business. So the universities set the pay at a low level, thinking, erroneously, that they'll save money. So, *never* assume that someone who is teaching a financial-planning course at a local college is ethical, competent, or looking out for your best interests. Although I may sound cynical in so saying, assume that these people are none of the above until they clearly prove otherwise.

Ethical instructors who are there to teach do *not* solicit clients and may actively discourage students from hiring them. Smart universities pay their instructors well and weed out the instructors who are more interested in building up their client base than teaching.

✔ **"Free" seminars.** This is a case of "you get what you pay for." Because you don't pay a fee to attend "free seminars," and the "teachers" don't get paid either, these events tend to be more clear-cut sales pitches. The "instructor" may share some information, but smart seminar leaders know that the goal of a successful seminar is to establish himself or herself as an expert and to whet the prospects' appetites.

Note: Be *especially* wary of seminars targeted at selected groups, such as special seminars for people who have received retirement plan distributions or those touting "Financial Planning for Women." Financial planning is not specific to gender, ethnicity, or marital status.

Don't assume that the financial planner giving a presentation at your employer's office is the right planner for you either. It's surprising how little investigation some corporate benefits departments conduct on the people they let in. In most cases, planners are accepted simply because they don't charge. One organization I'm familiar with gave preference to planners who, in addition to doing free presentations, also brought in a catered lunch! Guess what — this attracted lots of the brokers who sell commission-based products.

Part II
Saving for a Purpose

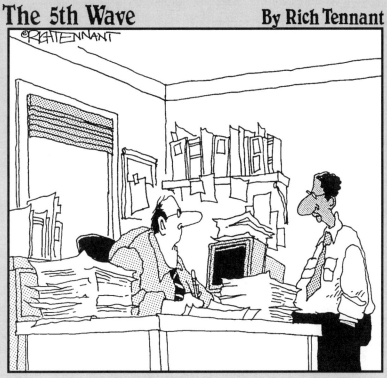

The 5th Wave   By Rich Tennant

"I've been working over 80 hours a week for the past two years preparing for retirement, and it hasn't bothered me OR my wife, whats-her-name."

In this part . . .

1 show you how to identify where your hard-earned dollars are going. I pinpoint numerous ways to make those dollars go toward helping you build up your savings instead of going to wasteful spending. What? You're buried in debt with little to show for it? Well, it's never too late to start digging out. Here you'll find out how to reduce your taxes and credit-card burden, how to save for retirement, how to get the best deal on a mortgage, and lots more.

Chapter 4

Your Money: Where Did It Go?

In This Chapter

▶ Who me? Overspend?

▶ Leading causes of overspending

▶ Analyzing your spending

▶ The road to salvation

Pay yourself first.

It's not what you make, it's what you keep.

A penny saved is a penny earned.

These little proverbs have been around for a long time; they offer good, common-sense advice.

Although I certainly cannot hope to compete with the eloquence of these nuggets of wisdom, allow me to add a little advice of my own: In order to accomplish your financial goals, you must live within your means.

To live within your means involves three steps:

1. **Spend less than you earn.**

2. **Save what you do not spend.**

3. **Invest what you save.**

For those of you who have a hard time living within your means, the first step is usually the hardest step: spending less than you earn. Many folks earn just enough to make ends meet. And some can't even do that; they simply spend more than they make. The result of such spending habits is, of course, accumulation of debt — witness the U.S. government and its five trillion-dollars worth of debt accumulation.

Whatever your financial dreams, you need to save and invest (unless you plan on winning the lottery or gaining a large inheritance). To put yourself in a position that allows you to start saving, you first need to take a close look at your spending habits.

Why You Overspend

America has become a spending disaster. Why? Simply because most of the influences on you in society are encouraging you to spend, and because credit is so widely and easily available.

You're just a consumption machine

Think about it. In the media and in the hallowed halls of our government, more often than not, you're referred to as a *consumer.*

Not a person, not a citizen, not a human being — but a c-o-n-s-u-m-e-r.

In fact, some people I've worked with feel unpatriotic or inadequate if they don't spend enough. "Saving too much and not spending enough could hurt the economy," they say. "People could be thrown out of work, and it could be a friend or family member. My favorite politician might not get reelected if I don't single-handedly prop up the economy by spending. I wouldn't be doing my part if I didn't consume by spending as much as possible."

Balderdash! Ultimately, you are the one who suffers the consequences of spending more than you can afford.

Access to credit

As you probably already know, spending your money is very easy to do. Thanks to innovations in technology like bank machines and credit cards, your money is always available for spending, 24 hours a day, 365 days a year (except during leap years, when your money is available 366 days a year). Every little outlet in the mall is pitching its own credit card, including the gas station across the street and the convenience store down the road. It certainly won't surprise me when those two little kids on my block start taking credit cards at their lemonade stand. I can hear it now: "We take Visa, Mr. Tyson, but we don't take American Express."

Sometimes, it may seem as though lenders are trying to give away money by making credit so easily available. But this is a dangerous illusion. When it comes to consumer debt (credit cards, auto loans, and the like), lenders aren't giving away anything except the opportunity for you to get in over your head, rack up high interest charges, and delay your progress toward your financial and personal goals.

Credit is most dangerous when you make consumption purchases that you couldn't afford in the first place.

Ten leading causes of overspending

Many people are tempted to live beyond their means. In America, the total amount of outstanding consumer installment debt that is on credit cards, auto loans, and other monthly lines of credit exceeds one — not million, not billion, but — *trillion* dollars.

Here are some of the adversaries you're up against as you attempt to control your spending. In Chapter 5, I explain detailed strategies for getting out of debt.

Using credit cards

The modern-day bank credit card was invented by Bank of America near the tail end of the baby boom. The credit industry has been booming along with the boomers ever since.

If you pay your bill in full every month, credit cards offer a convenient way to buy things with an interest-free, short-term loan. But if you carry your debt over month to month at high interest rates, credit cards encourage you to live beyond your means. Credit cards make spending money that you don't have easy and tempting.

If you have a knack for charging up a storm and spending more than you should with those little pieces of plastic, only one solution exists: Get rid of them. Put scissors to the plastic. Go cold turkey. You *can* function without them (see the next chapter for details if you think you can't live without credit cards).

Making minimum monthly payments

You'll *never* get your credit card debt paid off if you keep charging on your card and make only the minimum monthly payment. Interest continues to pile up on your outstanding debt. Paying only the minimum monthly payment is like using a Dixie cup to bail water from a sinking boat that has a basketball-sized hole in the bottom.

Taking out car loans

It's too easy to walk onto a car lot and go home with a new car that you could never afford if you had to pay cash. The dealer gets you thinking in terms of monthly payments that sound very small compared to what that four-wheeler is *really* gonna cost you. Auto loans are easy for just about anyone to get (except maybe a recently paroled felon).

Suppose that you're tired of driving around in the old clunker. The car is battlescarred and boring, and you don't like to be seen in it. Plus, the car is likely to only need more and more repairs in the months ahead. So off you go to your friendly local car dealer.

You start looking around at all the shiny, new cars and then — like the feeling you experience when spotting a water fountain on a scorching hot day — there it is: the replacement for your old clunker. It's sleek and clean and — oooh, look! — it has A/C, stereo, and power everything.

Before you have an opportunity to read the fine print on the sticker page on the side window, the salesperson moseys on up next to you. He gets you talking about how nice the car is, the weather, anything but the price of that car.

"How," you begin to think to yourself, "can this guy afford to spend time with me without knowing if I can afford this thing?" After taking you out for a test drive and talking more about the car, the weather, and your love life, or lack thereof, comes your moment of truth.

The salesperson, it seems, doesn't care about how much money you have. If, in fact, you have lots of money, that doesn't matter either. Either way, it's no problem!

The car is only $299 a month.

That's not bad, you think. Heck, you were expecting to hear that the car cost at least 15 to 20 grand. Before you know it, the dealer runs a credit report on you, has you sign a few papers, and minutes later you're driving home — the proud owner of a spanking new car.

See, the dealer wants you to think in terms of monthly payments because the cost *sounds* so cheap: $299 for a car. But, of course, that's $299 per month, every month, for many, many months. You're gonna be payin' forever — after all, you just bought a car that cost a huge chunk (perhaps 100 percent or more) of your yearly take-home income!

But it gets worse. What does the total sticker price come to when interest charges are added in? And how about insurance and registration and maintenance over the seven or so years that you'll own it? Now you're probably up to more than a *year's* worth of your income. Ouch! See Chapter 6 for how to spend what you afford on a car.

Bending to peer pressure

You go out with the guys or the gals (or both) to dinner, a movie, and then club-hopping. Try to remember the last time one of you said, "Let's go someplace cheaper. I can't afford to spend this much."

On the one hand, you don't want to be a stick in the mud. But on the other hand, some of your friends have more money than you do — and the ones who don't may be running up debt even faster than you are.

Spending to feel good

Life is full of stress, obligations, and demands. "I work hard," you say. "And darn it, I deserve to indulge!" Especially after your boss took the credit for your last great idea or blamed you for his last major screwup. So you buy something expensive or go to a fancy restaurant. Feel better? You won't when the bill arrives. And the more you spend, the less you save, and the longer you'll be stuck working and working for jerks like that!

Becoming addicted to spending

Just as people can become addicted to alcohol, tobacco, TV, and even love, some become addicted to the high they get from spending. A number of psychological causes can be identified for spending addiction, some of them dating back to how your family handled money and spending. (And you thought you'd identified all the problems you can blame on Mom and Dad!)

If your spending and debt problems are chronic, Debtors' Anonymous, a 12-step support group program patterned after Alcoholics Anonymous, can help. See Chapter 5 for more information.

Trying to keep current

You just have to see the latest hit movie or wear the latest designer clothes or get the new, superimproved, oversized tennis racquet with shock-absorbers, double-wishbone suspension, polyxylitol handgrips, and what not. All your friends are getting one, so you'd better get one, too. Right?

Wrong. Besides, many new technologies or products don't live up to their billing. Be smug and wait until a product is proven and until you can afford it.

Ignoring your financial goals when buying

When was the last time you heard someone say that he decided to forego a purchase because he was saving toward retirement or a home purchase? Doesn't happen very often does it? Just dealing with the here-and-now and forgetting your long-term needs and goals are very tempting. That's why people toil away for too many years in jobs they dislike.

Living for today has its virtues: Tomorrow *may* not come. But odds are very high that it will. Will you still feel the same way tomorrow about today's spending decisions? Or will you feel guilty that you again failed to stick to your goals?

Of course, this assumes that you have financial goals to stick to. Most people haven't yet set goals and don't know how much they should be saving to accomplish them. Chapter 8 helps you to kick-start that process.

Wanting only the best for your children

For children, many of the best things in life are free, just as they are for you. Junior *can* live without the latest $100 sneakers. Later on in life, your children will thank you: Better to pass on sound judgment and wise thriftiness than the worship of material goods.

Education can cost good money, I know. However, education experts — and my wife is one of them — are the first to dissuade you of the assumption that you're doing the best for your children if you spend lots of money to live in a town with a supposedly top-of-the-line school district or to fund the tuition of a private school education from pre-school through high school if you can't be home enough to take care of your children's other wants and needs.

Education begins in and is best done in the home. Some parents I see spend so much time running around working, working, working to afford all the supposedly best things for their kids that they neglect to spend *time* with their kids — the most important ingredient to their children's long-term happiness and success.

Thinking that money can buy happiness

Recall the handful of moments in your life that you wouldn't trade for anything. Odds are, those moments don't include the time you bought a car or found a sweater that you liked for 50 percent off at your favorite retailer. The old saying is true: The most enjoyable and precious things of value in your life can't be bought.

What I am about to say should go without saying, but I must say it because many people act as if it weren't so: Money can't buy happiness. It is tempting to think that if you could make only 10 or 20 percent more money, you'd be happier and less stressed out over your bills. You'd have more money to travel, eat out, and buy that new car you've been eyeing, right? Not so fast. A great deal of thoughtful research suggests that little relationship exists between money and happiness.

TECHNICAL STUFF

Being happy with what you have

Americans — even those who have not had an "easy" life — should be able to come up with things to be happy about and grateful for: A family who loves them; friends who laugh at their stupid jokes; the freedom to catch a movie or play or read a good book; a great singing voice, sense of humor, or full head of hair; the fact that they live in a country not at war with any other country.

And financially speaking, we Americans are pretty spoiled. Two-thirds of the people in the world have a standard of living that is a mere 20 percent of the U.S. average. Think about that. In other words, the average American is five times better off financially than two out of every three people in the world.

Be happy with what you have and content with the things that you can't change. I know financially wealthy people who have all the material goods they want yet are emotionally poor. Likewise, I know people who are struggling financially and are quite happy, contented, and emotionally wealthy.

"Wealth is like health: Although its absence can breed misery, having it is no guarantee of happiness," summarizes Dr. David Myers, professor of psychology at Michigan's Hope College, in his book *The Pursuit of Happiness: Who Is Happy and Why.* (This guy has it good! Imagine studying happiness for a living.)

Despite cheap air travel, VCRs, compact discs, microwaves, computers, voice mail, and all the other stuff that's supposed to make our lives easier and more enjoyable, Americans aren't any happier than they were three decades ago. According to research conducted by the National Opinion Research Center, 35 percent of Americans in 1957 said that they were "very happy," whereas in the 1990s, fewer said the same. These unexpected results occurred even though incomes, after adjusting for inflation, more than doubled during that time.

As Dr. Myers observes in *The Pursuit of Happiness,* ". . . if anything, to judge by soaring rates of depression, the quintupling of the violent crime rate since 1960, the doubling of the divorce rate, and the tripling of the teen suicide rate, we're richer and less happy."

Spending Analysis

Washing your face, brushing your teeth, and exercising regularly are good habits. The financial equivalents of these habits are spending less than you earn and saving enough to meet your future financial objectives.

Despite relatively high incomes compared with the rest of the world, most Americans have a hard time saving a good percentage of their incomes compared with the rest of the world. Why? We spend too much — often far more than is necessary.

The first step to saving more of the income that you work so hard for is to figure out where that income typically gets spent; that's what the spending analysis in the next section helps you determine.

You should do the spending analysis if any of the following apply to you:

- ✔ You aren't saving enough money to meet your financial goals.

- ✔ You feel as if your spending is out of control or you don't really know where all your income goes.

- ✔ You're anticipating a significant life change (for example, marriage, leaving your job to start a business, having children, retiring, and so on).

If you're a good saver already, you may not need to complete the spending analysis. If you're saving enough to accomplish your goals (see Chapter 8), I don't see much value in continually tracking your spending. You've already established the good habit — saving. The good habit is *not* month after month of keeping track of exactly where you spend your money. So long as you're saving enough and simply spending what's leftover, I say, who cares where the money is being spent!

The immediate goal of a spending analysis is to figure out what you typically spend your money on. The long-range goal is to establish a good habit: to maintain a regular, automatic savings routine.

Notice the first four letters in the word *analysis*. (You may never have noticed, but I felt the need to bring it to your attention.) Knowing where your money is going each month is very useful. It's terrific to make changes in your spending behavior and to cut out the fat so that you can save more money and meet your financial goals. But you'll perhaps make yourself and those around you into very unhappy campers if you try to be anal-retentive about documenting precisely where you're spending every single dollar and cent.

Remember: What matters is that you save what you want and need to achieve your goals.

Tracking your spending on paper

Unless you keep meticulous records that detail every dollar you spend, you will not have perfect information. Don't sweat it! You have a number of available sources that should allow you to reconstruct where you have been spending the bulk of your money.

Doing your spending analysis is a little bit like being a detective. Your goal is to reconstruct the crime of *spending*. You probably have some major clues at your fingertips or piled somewhere on your desk or on the table where you plop yourself down to pay bills.

Get out your

- ✔ Recent pay stubs
- ✔ Tax returns
- ✔ Checkbook register or canceled checks
- ✔ Credit and charge card bills

Ideally, you should assemble the documents needed to track one year's (12 months') spending. But, if your spending patterns don't fluctuate greatly from month to month (or if your dog ate some of the old bills), you can reduce your data gathering to one six-month period or to every other or every third month for the past year. If you take a major vacation or spend a large amount on gifts during certain times of the year, make sure to include these months in your analysis.

The hardest transactions to track are cash transactions because they don't leave a paper trail. Over the course of a week or perhaps even a month, you *could* keep track of everything you buy with cash. Tracking cash can be an enlightening exercise — it can also be a hassle. If you're lazy like I sometimes am or lack the time and patience, try *estimating*. Think about a typical week or month — how often do you buy things with cash? For example, if you eat lunch out four days a week at work, paying around $5 a shot, that's about $80 a month.

Try to separate your expenditures into as many useful and detailed categories as possible. Table 4-1 gives you a suggested format — you can tailor it to fit your needs. Remember, if you lump too much of your spending into broad, meaningless categories like *Other,* you'll end up where you started: wondering where all the money went.

Table 4-1	Detail Your Spending	
Category	*Monthly Average ($)*	*Percent of Total Gross Income(%)*
Taxes, taxes, taxes (income)		_____
Social Security	_____	
Federal	_____	
State and local	_____	

(continued)

Table 4-1 (continued)

Category	Monthly Average ($)	Percent of Total Gross Income(%)
The roof over your head		_____
Rent	_____	
Mortgage	_____	
Property taxes	_____	
Gas/electric/oil	_____	
Water/garbage	_____	
Phone	_____	
Cable TV	_____	
Furniture/appliances	_____	
Maintenance/repairs	_____	
Food, glorious food		_____
Supermarket	_____	
Restaurants and takeout	_____	
Getting around		_____
Gasoline	_____	
Maintenance/repairs	_____	
State registration fees	_____	
Tolls and parking	_____	
Bus or subway fares	_____	
Style		_____
Clothing	_____	
Shoes	_____	
Jewelry (watches, earrings)	_____	
Dry cleaning	_____	
Debt repayments		_____
Credit/charge cards	_____	
Auto loans	_____	
Student loans	_____	
Other	_____	

Category	Monthly Average ($)	Percent of Total Gross Income(%)
Fun stuff		_____
Entertainment (movies, concerts)	_____	
Vacation and travel	_____	
Gifts	_____	
Hobbies	_____	
Pets	_____	
Other	_____	
Personal care		_____
Haircuts	_____	
Health club or gym	_____	
Makeup	_____	
Other	_____	
Personal business		_____
Accountant/attorney/financial advisor		_____
Other	_____	
Health care		_____
Physicians and hospitals	_____	
Drugs	_____	
Dental and vision	_____	
Therapy	_____	
Insurance		_____
Homeowners/renters	_____	
Auto	_____	
Health	_____	
Life	_____	
Disability	_____	
Educational expenses		_____
Courses	_____	
Books	_____	
Supplies	_____	

(continued)

Table 4-1 *(continued)*		
Category	**Monthly Average ($)**	**Percent of Total Gross Income(%)**
Children		_____
Day care	_____	
Toys	_____	
Child support	_____	
Charitable donations	_____	_____
Other	_____	_____
_____	_____	
_____	_____	
_____	_____	
_____	_____	
_____	_____	
_____	_____	

Tracking your spending on the computer

More and more software packages are being developed and improved to help you pay bills and track your spending. The main advantage of these software packages is that they continually track your spending as long as you keep entering the information. And, after you learn how to use these packages (not always an easy thing to do), they can speed the process of writing checks.

But you don't need a computer and fancy software packages to figure where you're spending money and to pay your bills. More than a few software purchasers give up entering the data after a few months. If tracking your spending is what you're after, you're likely to have only the information in the software from bills you pay by check. Expenses you pay by credit card and cash need to be entered specially into the software if you want to capture that data, too.

Like home exercise equipment and exotic kitchen appliances, some software ends up in the consumer graveyard.

Paper, pencil, and a calculator work just fine.

If you do want to try computerizing your bill payments and expense tracking, the best software packages currently available are recommended in Chapter 21.

Don't waste your time on financial administration

Tom is the model of financial organization. All his financial documents are neatly organized into color coded folders. Every month, he enters all his spending information into his computer. He even carries a notebook to detail his cash spending so that every penny is accounted for.

Tom also balances his checkbook, "to make sure that everything is in order." He can't remember the last time his bank made a mistake, but he knows a friend who once found a $50 error.

If you spend seven hours per month as Tom does balancing your checkbook and detailing all your spending, you may be wasting nearly two weeks worth of time per year — the equivalent of two-thirds of your vacation time if you take three weeks annually.

Suppose that you're "lucky" enough, every other year, to find a $100 error the bank made in their favor. If you spend just three hours per month tracking your spending and balancing your checkbook to discover this glitch, you'll spend 72 hours over two years to find a $100 mistake. Your hourly pay: $1.39 per hour. You could make more flipping burgers at a burger joint if you wanted to moonlight. (**Note:** If you make significant size deposits into or out of your account, be sure that those were captured on your statement.)

To add insult to injury, after working a full week and doing all your financial and other chores, you may not have the desire and energy left to do the more important stuff. Looking at your big personal financial picture — establishing goals, choosing wise investments, ensuring proper insurance coverage — may continue to be shoved to the back burner. As a result, you may lose thousands of dollars annually. Over the course of your adult life, this could translate into tens or even hundreds of thousands of lost dollars.

Tom, for example, didn't know how much he should be saving to meet his retirement goals. He hadn't reviewed his employer's benefit materials to understand his insurance and retirement plan options. He knows he pays a lot in taxes, but he hasn't educated himself about how to reduce his taxes.

You want to make the most of your money. Unless you truly enjoy dealing with money, you need to prioritize the money activities that you work on. Time is limited and life is short. Working harder on financial administration doesn't earn you bonus points. The more time you spend dealing with your personal finances, the less is available to gab with friends, watch a good movie, read a good novel, and do other things you really enjoy.

Don't get me wrong — nothing is inherently wrong with balancing your checkbook. In fact, if you regularly bounce checks because you don't know how low your balance is, the exercise might save you a lot in returned check fees. However, if you keep enough money in your checking account to rarely reach $0.00, balancing your checkbook is probably a waste of your valuable time, even if your hourly wages aren't lofty. I haven't balanced mine in years (please don't tell my bank as they might start making some "mistakes" and siphon money out).

If you're busy, consider ways to reduce the amount of time spent on financially mundane tasks like bill paying. Increasing numbers of companies, for example, allow you to have your monthly bills paid to them electronically via your bank checking account or charged on your credit card (only do this if you pay your credit card bill in full each month). The fewer bills you have to pay, the fewer separate checks and envelopes you must process each month. That translates into more free time for you and fewer paper cuts!

Spending less: the secret to growing rich on your income

As a financial counselor, I work with people who bring in tiny incomes, incomes of hundreds of thousands of dollars or more, and everything in between. At every income level, people fall into one of the following three categories:

- ✔ People who spend more than they earn (accumulate debt)
- ✔ People who spend all that they earn (save nothing)
- ✔ People who save 2, 5, 10, even 20 percent (or more!)

I've seen $30,000 earners save 20 percent of their income ($6,000), $60,000 earners save just 5 percent ($3,000), and people earning well into six-figures annually who save nothing or who are accumulating debt.

Suppose that you currently earn $30,000 per year and spend all of it. You wonder: "How can I save money?"

Good question!

Rather than knocking yourself out at a second job or hustling for that next promotion, you could try living below your income. In other words, spend less than you earn. (I know spending less than you earn is hard to imagine, but you can do it.) Consider that for every discontented person earning and spending $30,000 per year, someone else is out there making do on $27,000.

A great many people live on less than you make. If you spent as they do, you could save and invest the difference.

As Dr. David Myers, whom you met earlier in this chapter says: "Satisfaction isn't so much getting what you want as wanting what you have. There are two ways to be rich: one is to have great wealth, the other is to have few wants."

Chapter 5

Dealing with Debt and Credit Problems

In This Chapter

▶ Using your savings to reduce your debt

▶ Getting out of debt when you don't have savings

▶ The pros and cons of filing bankruptcy

▶ Dealing with credit problems

*B*orrowing money has a lot in common with eating. You need to eat to live, but some foods are better for you than others. And it's tempting to eat too much of the bad foods.

So it is with debt — some debt is good and some is bad. When debt is used for investing in your future, I call it *good debt*. Borrowing money to afford an education, buy real estate, or invest in a small business is like eating foods rich in calcium for strong bones or eating fruits and vegetables for their vitamins.

But accumulating *bad debt* (consumer debt), is like living on a diet of sugar and caffeine: a quick fix with no long-term nutritional value. Borrowing on your credit card to afford that vacation to Cabo is costly and detrimental to your long-term financial health.

In this chapter, I help you battle the increasing problem of consumer debt. Getting rid of your bad debts may be even more difficult for you than giving up the sugar-laden foods you love. But in the long run, you'll be glad you did; you'll be financially healthier and emotionally happier. And once you get rid of your debts, practice the best way to deal with credit problems: **Don't borrow.**

To decide which debt reduction strategies make sense for you, you first must consider your overall financial situation and calculate your total debts relative to your income.

Using Savings to Reduce Your Debt

Many people have built up a psychological brick wall between their savings and investment accounts and their debt accounts. Failing to view their finances holistically, they have simply gotten into the habit of looking at these accounts individually. The thought of putting a door in that big brick wall has never occurred to them.

Money you may be overlooking

Have you ever reached into the pocket of an old winter parka and found a rolled-up twenty dollar bill you forgot you had? Stumbling across some forgotten funds is always a pleasant experience. But before you root through all your closets in search of stray cash to help you pay down that nagging credit card debt, check out some of these financial jacket pockets that you may have overlooked:

✔ **Borrow against your cash-value life insurance policy.** If you were approached by a life insurance agent, odds are good that this is the type of policy you were sold because it pays high commissions to its agents. Or perhaps your parents bought one for you when you were a little gremlin. Borrow against the cash value to pay down your debts. **(Note:** Continuing with such a policy may not be the best thing to do — see Chapter 17 for more details.)

✔ **Borrow against your employer's retirement account.** Check with your employer's benefits department to see if you can borrow against your retirement account balance. The interest rate is usually reasonable and, best of all, as you repay the loan, the interest payments go back into your account. It's like getting paid to clean out your own garage — you can't beat that!

✔ **Sell investments held outside of retirement accounts.** Maybe you have some shares of stock or a Treasury bond gathering dust in your safety deposit box. Consider cashing in these investments to pay down your loan balances. Just be sure to consider the tax consequences of selling, and if possible, only sell those investments that won't generate a big tax bill.

✔ **Borrow against the equity in your home.** If you're a homeowner, you may be able to tap into your home's *equity*, which is the difference between the property's market value and outstanding loan balance. You can generally borrow against real estate at a lower interest rate and get a tax deduction to boot.

✔ **Borrow from (friends and) family.** They know you, love you, realize your shortcomings, and — heck — probably won't be as cold-hearted as some bankers I know. Money borrowed from family members can have strings attached, of course. Treating the obligation seriously is important. It's also best to write up a simple agreement listing the terms and conditions of your loan to avoid misunderstandings. Unless your family members are like the worst bankers I know, you'll probably get a fair interest rate, and your family will have the satisfaction of helping you out — just don't forget to pay them back.

Using savings to pay down debts may seem like you're losing money. You're *not* losing, you're gaining. Remember that the growth of your money is determined by your *net worth* — the difference between your assets and your liabilities (refer to Chapter 2). Hopefully, your savings and investments are earning a decent return, but if you have consumer debts, odds are that the interest on those debts is high.

If you have loans at, say, 12 percent, paying them off is like finding an investment with a guaranteed return of 12 percent — *tax-free*. You would actually need an investment that yielded even more — around 18 percent — to net 12 percent after paying taxes in order to justify not paying off your 12 percent loans. The higher your tax bracket (see Chapter 7), the higher the return you need on your investments to justify keeping high-interest consumer debt.

If you have the savings to pay off high-interest credit card and auto loans, do it. You diminish your savings, true, but you also reduce your debts. You benefit financially because the interest on your savings is far less than the interest your debt accrues. Make sure to pay off the loans with the highest interest rates first.

Even if you think you're an investment genius and can earn more on your investments, swallow your ego and pay down the debts anyway. In order to chase that higher potential return from investments, you need to take substantial risk. You *may* earn more investing in that hot stock tip or that bargain real estate located on a toxic waste site, but more than likely you won't.

If you use your accessible savings to pay down debts, be careful to leave yourself enough of an emergency cushion. You want to be in a position to withstand an unexpected large expense or temporary loss of income. On the other hand, if you use savings to pay down credit card debt, unless your card gets canceled, you can run your credit card balances back up in a financial pinch (or turn to a family member or wealthy friend for a low-interest loan).

Decreasing Debt When You Lack Savings

"I don't have savings, you nincompoop," you exclaim, "that's why I have all this debt!"

If you read the preceding section, thank you for patiently waiting; I just wanted to make sure that you didn't have any money that you forgot about. (The number of people with consumer debt who can pay it down with savings but haven't done so always surprises me.)

But on to your quandary: You lack savings to pay off your high-interest consumer debt. Well, not surprisingly, you have some work to do. If you're currently spending all your income (and more!), you need to figure out how you can decrease your spending (see Chapter 6 for lots of great ideas) and/or increase your income. In the meantime, you need to slow the growth of your debt. Read the rest of this chapter to learn how.

Investigate lower interest rate credit cards

Different credit cards charge different interest rates. Why in the world should you pay 14, 16, 18 percent, or more when you can pay less? For years, the average credit card interest rate has hovered around 18 percent. The credit card business has become quite competitive. Gone are the days when all banks charged 18 percent or more for VISA and MasterCard.

Here's one of the few times in your life when should want to be below average! Until you get your debt paid off, make it more difficult for your debt to grow. You may be able to accomplish this slowing process by reducing the interest rate you're paying on your debt.

If you are earning a decent income, are not *too* burdened with debt, and have a clean credit record, qualifying for lower-rate cards is relatively painless. Some persistence (and clean-up work) may be required if you have nicks in your credit report or have income and debt problems. Once you are approved for a new, lower-interest rate credit card, you can simply transfer your outstanding balance from your higher-rate card.

Something that you might want to try is simply calling the bank that issued your current high-interest-rate credit card and saying that you want to cancel your card because you found a competitor that offers no annual fee and a lower interest rate. Your bank may choose to match the terms of the "competitor" rather than lose you as a customer.

Table 5-1 lists some of the consistently low-interest-rate credit cards. Please note that these cards charge interest rates that are variable and are offered by banks that are somewhat picky about whom they accept for a low-rate card. But you've got nothing to lose if you apply.

While you're paying down your credit card balance(s), stop making new charges on cards that have outstanding balances. Many people don't realize that interest starts to accumulate *immediately* when they carry a balance. *You have no grace period* — the 20-odd days you normally have to pay your balance in full without incurring interest charges — if you carry a credit card balance month-to-month.

Table 5-1	Lower-Interest-Rate Credit Cards	
Bank	**Interest Rate**	**Annual Fee**
AFBA Industrial Bank 800-776-2265	8.5% first six months, 11.4% thereafter	None
Arkansas Federal 800-477-3348	10.00%	$35
USAA Federal Savings 800-922-9092	12.50%	None
Wachovia Bankcard 800-842-3262	8.25% first year, 12.15% thereafter	$18

For a complete, updated listing of low-interest-rate credit cards, send a check for $4 to the nonprofit Bankcard Holders of America, 524 Branch Drive, Salem, VA 24153.

Cut 'em up, cut 'em all up

If you have a pattern of living beyond your means by buying on credit, get rid of the culprit — the credit card, that is. To kick the habit, a smoker needs to toss the cigarettes, and an alcoholic needs to get rid of the booze. Cut up your credit cards and call the issuers of the cards to cancel your accounts. And when you buy consumer items such as cars and furniture, do not apply for E-Z credit.

The world worked fine back in the years *B.C.* (Before Credit). Think about it: Just a couple of generations ago, credit cards didn't even exist. People paid with cash and checks — imagine that! You *can* function in our increasingly high-tech world without buying anything on a credit card. In certain cases, you may need a card as collateral — like when you rent a car. When you bring back the rental car, however, you can pay with cash or check. Leave the card at home in the back of your sock drawer or freezer and pull (thaw) it out only for the occasional car rental.

If you can trust yourself, keep a separate credit card *only* for new purchases that you absolutely can pay in full each month. Be careful, though — you may be tempted to let that balance roll over for a month or two, and you'll start running up your debt again. Better yet, consider getting a debit card (see the next section) while you pay off your credit card(s).

Debit cards: the best of both worlds

Credit cards are the main reason that today's consumers are consuming more than they can afford. So logic would say that one way you can keep your spending in check is to not use your credit cards. But in a society used to flashing the widely accepted VISA and MasterCard plastic for purchases, changing habits is hard. And you may be legitimately concerned that carrying your checkbook or cash can be a hassle or costly if you're mugged.

Well, *debit cards* truly offer the best of both worlds. The beauty of the debit card is that it offers you the convenience of making purchases with a piece of plastic without the temptation and ability to run up credit card debt. Debit cards keep you from spending money you don't have and help you live within your means.

Debit cards look just like a credit card and have either the VISA or MasterCard logo. The big difference from credit cards is that, as with checks you write, debit card purchase amounts are deducted electronically within days from your checking account. (Your bank ATM card is also a debit card, which most merchants don't accept for purchases.)

If you keep your checking account balance low and don't ordinarily balance your checkbook, you may need to start balancing your checkbook if you switch over to a debit card. Otherwise, you could be facing unnecessary bounced check charges.

Finding a debit card is the challenging part. Banks — the leading issuers of credit cards — have long been cool to promoting debit cards. I remember in the mid-1980s when, as a consultant, I worked with some major credit card issuers that were contemplating these newer debit cards. Although technologically feasible, the card issuers feared debit cards because they thought the cards might cut into their highly profitable credit card business.

Because moving your checking account can be a hassle, first check with the bank where you currently have a checking account to see whether they offer VISA or MasterCard debit cards. If your bank does not offer one, shop among the following banks, which are the larger issuers of debit cards. By opening a checking account at one of them, you can also obtain a debit card.

✔ Bank of America	✔ First Bank	✔ National City
✔ Banc One	✔ First Chicago	✔ NationsBank
✔ Barnett	✔ First Interstate	✔ Norwest Banks
✔ BayBanks	✔ First Union	✔ U.S. Bancorp
✔ Core States	✔ Fleet Financial	✔ Wachovia

A number of investment firms offer VISA or MasterCard debit cards with their investment management accounts. Among the best are Charles Schwab & Co. (800-421-4488), which offers a debit card with its SchwabOne account, and Fidelity Investments (800-343-8721), which offers a VISA debit card with its U.S.A. account. Fidelity requires a higher minimum initial opening balance ($10,000) than does Schwab ($5,000). These investment firm "checking accounts" not only can help you break the credit card overspending habit but may also get you thinking about saving and investing your money.

Resisting the credit temptation

Getting out of debt is not an easy thing to do, but I know you can do it with this book by your side and as your guide. Once you're out of debt, most, but not all, of the battle has been won. Following are some additional tactics you can use to limit the influence credit cards hold over your life in the future:

- **Get rid of your extra credit cards.** You don't need three, five, or ten credit cards! You can live with one (and actually none), given the wide acceptance of most cards. Count 'em up, including retail store and gas cards, and get rid of 'em. Retailers, such as department stores and gas stations, just love to give you one of their cards. Not only do these cards charge outrageously high interest rates, they duplicate VISA and MasterCard. Virtually all retailers that accept credit cards accept VISA and MasterCard. More credit lines mean more temptation to spend what you can't afford.

- **Reduce your credit limit.** Just because your bank keeps raising your credit limit to reward you for being such a profitable customer doesn't mean that you have to accept the increase. Call your credit-card service's 800 number and *lower* your credit limit to a level you're comfortable with.

- **Replace your credit card(s) with a charge card.** A *charge card* (such as the American Express Card) requires you to pay your balance in full each billing period. You have no

credit line or interest charges. Of course, spending more than you can afford to pay when the bill comes due is possible. But, you'll be much less likely to overspend if you know you have to pay in full monthly.

- **Never buy on credit anything that depreciates.** Meals out, cars, clothing, and shoes all depreciate in value. Never buy these things on credit. Borrow money only for investments — education, real estate, or your own business, for example.

- **Think in terms of total cost.** Everything sounds cheaper in terms of monthly payments — that's how salespeople lure you into buying things you don't have the money to afford. Take a calculator along if necessary to tally up the sticker price, interest charges, and upkeep. The total cost will scare you. *It should.*

- **Stop the junk mail avalanche.** Look at your daily mail — I bet half of it is solicitations and mail-order catalogs. Save some trees and your time sorting junk mail by removing yourself from most mailing lists. Write to the Direct Marketing Association, Mail Preference Service, 1101 17th St. NW, Suite 900, Washington, DC 10036-4704.

- **Limit what you can spend.** Go shopping with a small amount of cash and no plastic or checks. That way you can only spend what little cash you have with you!

You should also know about other differences between debit and credit cards.

- ✔ If you pay your credit card bill in full and on time each month, charging on your credit card gives you free use of the money you owe until it's time to pay the bill; debit cards take the money out of your checking account almost immediately. (Some cards are now charging a fee even if you pay off your balance in full. You don't think the banks'll let you use the float for ever, do you?)

- ✔ Also, credit cards more easily allow you to dispute charges for problematic merchandise through the issuing bank. Most banks allow you to dispute charges for up to 60 days after purchase and will credit the disputed amount back to your account pending resolution. Most debit cards offer a much shorter window, typically less than one week, to make disputes.

Filing Bankruptcy

For consumers in over their heads, the realization that their monthly income is increasingly exceeded by their bill payments is usually a painful one. In many cases, years can pass before drastic measures like bankruptcy are considered. Both financial and emotional issues come into play in one of the most difficult, painful, yet potentially beneficial decisions.

When Helen, a mother of two and a sales representative, contacted attorney Harry Orr earlier this year, her total credit card debt of about $20,000 equaled her annual gross income of $20,000. Due to the crushing debt load, she could not meet her minimum monthly credit card payments. Rent and food gobbled up most of her earnings. What little was left over went to the squeakiest wheel.

Creditors were breathing down Helen's back. "I started getting calls from collection departments at home and work — it was embarrassing," relates Helen. Helen's case is typical in that credit card debt was the prime cause of her bankruptcy. "If credit card debt didn't exist, I wouldn't have a job," says bankruptcy attorney Harry Orr.

Helen's case is typical in other regards. Her debt accumulated over a number of years. A former homeowner with a Master's degree from a prestigious university, Helen had good credit until a couple of years before. After divorcing, Helen rented an apartment with her two children while holding down a job. Unfortunately, she was laid off when her employer encountered tough times.

At first, bills to her dentist and doctor went unpaid. Then when Helen went into business for herself, she used her credit cards to purchase office furniture and for other start-up expenses. "I would have done more corner cutting, but the credit cards were easily available cash and allowed me to think in terms of monthly payments," says Helen.

As the debt load grew, partly exacerbated by the double-digit interest rates on the cards, more and more purchases got charged — from the kids' clothing to repairs for the car. Finally, out of cash, she had to take a large cash advance on her credit cards to pay for rent and food.

Despite trying to work out lower monthly payments to keep everyone happy, most of the banks to which Helen owed money were inflexible. "When I asked one bank's VISA department if it preferred that I declare bankruptcy because it was unwilling to lower my monthly payment, the representative said yes," Helen says. Out of options, Helen filed personal bankruptcy.

Bankruptcy benefits

Every year, approximately one million American households (that's about 1 in every 100 households) file personal bankruptcy.

The value or benefit of bankruptcy is that certain types of debts can be completely eliminated or *discharged*. Debts that typically can be discharged include credit card, medical, auto, utilities, and rent. Debts that may not be canceled include child support, alimony, student loans, taxes, and court-ordered damages (for example, drunk driving settlements). Helen was an ideal candidate for bankruptcy because her debts (credit cards) were dischargeable.

Helen also met another important criterion — her level of high-interest consumer debt relative to her annual income was high. When this ratio exceeds more than 25 percent, filing bankruptcy may be your best option.

Eliminating your debt also allows you to start working toward your financial goals. Depending on the amount of debt you have outstanding relative to your income, you may need a decade or more to pay it all off. In Helen's case, at the age of 48, she had no money saved for retirement to supplement Social Security, and she was increasingly unable to spend money on her children.

In addition to the financial benefits are the emotional benefits in filing bankruptcy. "I was horrified at filing, but it is good to be rid of the debts and collection calls — I should have filed six months earlier. I was constantly worried. When I saw homeless families come to the soup kitchen where I sometimes volunteer, I thought that someday that could be me and my kids," she said.

Bankruptcy drawbacks

Filing bankruptcy, needless to say, has a number of drawbacks. First, bankruptcy appears on your credit report for ten years, so you will have difficulty obtaining credit, especially in the years immediately following your filing.

If you already have problems on your credit report, however, because of late payments or failure to pay previous debts, damage has already been done. And, without savings, you're probably not going to be making major purchases, such as a home, in the next several years anyway.

If you do file bankruptcy, getting credit in the future is not impossible. You'll probably be able to obtain a *secured credit card,* which requires you to deposit money in a bank account equal to the credit limit on your credit card. If you can hold down a stable job, most creditors are willing to give you loans within a few years of your filing bankruptcy. Almost all lenders ignore bankruptcy after five to seven years.

Another bankruptcy drawback is that it costs money. I know this seems terribly unfair. You're already in financial trouble — that's why you're filing bankruptcy! Nevertheless, filing bankruptcy will probably set you back from several hundred dollars up to $1,000 in court filing and legal fees.

And, finally, most people find that filing bankruptcy causes emotional stress. Admitting that your personal income can't keep pace with your debt obligations is a painful thing to do. Although filing bankruptcy clears the decks of debt and gives you a fresh financial start, feeling a profound sense of failure is only human. Despite the increasing frequency of bankruptcy, bankruptcy filers are reluctant to talk about it with others, including family and friends.

Another part of the emotional side of filing bankruptcy is that you must open your personal financial affairs to court scrutiny and court control during the several months it takes to administer a bankruptcy. A court-appointed bankruptcy trustee oversees your case and tries to recover as much of your property as possible to satisfy the *creditors* — those to whom you owe money.

Some people also feel that they're shirking responsibility by filing for bankruptcy. One client I worked with who should have filed couldn't bring herself to do it. She said, "I spent that money, and it's my responsibility to pay it back."

What you can keep if you file bankruptcy

In every state, you can retain certain property and assets, even though you're filing for bankruptcy. You may be surprised to learn that in some states (such as Florida, Iowa, Kansas, Minnesota, and Oklahoma), you can keep your home regardless of its value! Most states, though, allow you to protect a certain amount of home equity.

Additionally, you're allowed to retain some other types and amounts of personal property and assets. For example, most states allow you to retain household furnishings, clothing, pensions, and money in retirement accounts. So don't empty your retirement accounts or sell off personal possessions to pay debts unless you're absolutely sure that you won't be filing bankruptcy.

Most banks make gobs and gobs of money from their credit card businesses. As a former consultant who worked in the industry, I can tell you that credit cards are one of the most profitable lines of business for banks. If you don't believe me, consider that, at a banking conference sponsored by the investment bank Salomon Brothers, CEO John Reed referred to the credit card business for banks as a "high-return, low-risk" business. Now you know why your mailbox is always filled with solicitations for more cards even though you're already up to your eyeballs in solicitations.

So if you file for bankruptcy, don't feel bad about not paying back the bank. The nice merchants where you bought the merchandise have already been paid. *Charge-offs* — the banker's term for taking the loss on debt that you discharge through bankruptcy — are part of the business. This is another reason why the interest rate is so high on credit cards and why you shouldn't borrow on credit cards.

Pick a number: 7 or 13

You can file one of two forms of personal bankruptcy:

- **Chapter 7** allows you to discharge or cancel certain debts. Chapter 7 bankruptcy makes the most sense when you have significant debts that you are legally allowed to cancel.

- **Chapter 13** comes up with a repayment schedule that requires you to pay your debts over several years. Besides being an unlucky number, Chapter 13 stays on your credit record just like Chapter 7 *but doesn't eliminate debt,* so its value is limited (usually to dealing with debts like taxes that can't be discharged through bankruptcy). Chapter 13 can keep creditors at bay, though, until a repayment schedule is worked out in the courts.

Bankruptcy advice

Be very careful where you get advice about whether to file for bankruptcy. Many people make the mistake of turning to and solely trusting bankruptcy attorneys or Consumer Credit Counseling Services (CCCS).

BEWARE

Biased advice at CCCS

Every year, hundreds of thousands of debt-burdened consumers seek "counseling" from the more than 1,000 Consumer Credit Counseling Service (CCCS) offices. Unfortunately, people like Leona Davis find that the service may not always work the way it is pitched.

Davis, whose family racked up significant debt largely due to unexpected medical expenses and a reduction in her income, found herself in trouble with too much debt. So she turned to CCCS, which she had heard about through its advertising and marketing materials.

CCCS markets itself as a "nonprofit community service." Davis, like many others I know who have used CCCS, found that the "service" was not objective. After her experience with CCCS, Davis feels that a more appropriate name for this organization would be the Credit Card Collection Agency. I agree.

Unbeknownst to Davis and to most people who use CCCS is the fact that about 85 percent of CCCS's funding comes from fees that creditors pay to CCCS. CCCS collects fees on a commission basis — just as collection agencies do!

CCCS's strategy is to place those who come in for help onto their "debt management program." Under this program, counselees like Davis agree to pay a certain amount per month to CCCS, which in turn parcels out the money to the various creditors. The debt management program usually ignores other non-credit-card debts that the counselees may have: in Davis's case, a mortgage and outstanding medical bills.

Because of Davis's tremendous outstanding consumer debt (it exceeded her annual income) and the fact that she didn't receive budgeting help from CCCS to plan her current expenses, her repayment plan was doomed to failure. Davis managed to make 10 months' worth of payments, largely because she raided a retirement account for $28,000. Unfortunately, Davis did not know and was never told by CCCS that if she filed bankruptcy (which she ultimately needed to do), she could have kept her retirement money.

But Davis's CCCS counselor never discussed the bankruptcy option, "I received no counseling. Real counselors take the time to understand your situation and offer options. I was offered one solution, a forced payment plan," says Davis.

Others who have consulted CCCS, including one of my research assistants who, undercover, visited a CCCS office to seek advice, confirm that CCCS has a cookie-cutter approach to dealing with debt. CCCS typically recommends that debtors go on a repayment plan that has the consumer pay 3 percent of each outstanding loan balance to CCCS, which in turn pays the money to creditors.

Unable to keep up with the enormous monthly payments, Davis finally turned to an attorney and filed for bankruptcy. But not before she had unnecessarily lost thousands of dollars because of CCCS's one-sided approach to debt problems.

Although CCCS's promotional materials and counselors aren't shy about highlighting the drawbacks to bankruptcy, CCCS's counselors are reluctant to discuss the impact of signing up for a CCCS debt payment plan. Davis's CCCS counselor never told her that restructuring her credit card payments would tarnish her credit report. The counselor my researcher met with also neglected to mention this important fact. When asked, the counselor was evasive about the debt "management" program's impact on his credit report.

Attorneys who earn a legal fee from doing bankruptcy filings have a conflict of interest. All things being equal, their bias is to — you guessed it — *recommend bankruptcy,* which generates their fees.

In filing bankruptcy, hiring an attorney makes sense when you have major assets (such as a home) to protect. Attorney fees can easily exceed several hundred dollars to over $1,000 for complicated cases.

CCCS faces the opposite conflict. CCCS says that it is a nonprofit, educational service to help consumers who are in debt. Although it's true that CCCS has some well-intentioned employees, it's also true that CCCS is funded by credit-card issuers. Thus CCCS counselors are loathe to recommend bankruptcy (See the sidebar, "Conflicts of interest at CCCS," for more about how CCCS can skew your options in the wrong direction.)

If you want to learn more about the pros, cons, and details of filing for bankruptcy, pick up a copy of *How to File for Bankruptcy* by attorneys Elias, Renauer, and Leonard (Nolo Press). If you're comfortable with your decision to file and think you can complete the paperwork, you may be able to do it yourself. *How to File for Bankruptcy* comes with all the forms necessary to file. An intermediate approach would be to hire a paralegal typing service to prepare the forms, which can be a cost-effective way to get help with the process if you don't need heavy-duty legal advice. Check your local yellow pages under *Paralegals* or call the National Association of Independent Paralegals (707-935-7951) for members in your area.

Regardless of how you deal with paying off your debt, you're in real danger of falling back into old habits. Backsliding happens not only to people who file bankruptcy but also to those who use savings or home equity to eliminate their debt. If history has shown that you are likely to fall into this trap, the best and only solution is to go cold turkey. Eliminate your access to credit and pay for everything with cash, checks, and debit cards.

Ending the Debt-and-Spend Cycle

As hard as they try to break the habit, some people become addicted to spending and debting. It becomes a chronic problem that starts to interfere with other aspects of their lives. Financial problems can lead to problems at work and with family and even friends.

Officially started in 1976, Debtors Anonymous (DA) is a nonprofit organization that provides support, primarily through group meetings, to people trying to break their debting and spending habits. DA is modeled after the 12-step Alcoholics Anonymous program.

Like AA, Debtors Anonymous works with people from all walks of life and socioeconomic backgrounds. It's typical to find people who are financially on the edge, $100,000-plus income earners, and everybody in between at a DA meeting. Even former millionaires join the program.

DA has a simple questionnaire to help determine whether you are a problem debtor. If you answer *yes* to at least eight of the following 15 questions, you may be developing or already have a compulsive debting habit:

1. **Are your debts making your home life unhappy?**

2. **Does the pressure of your debts distract you from your daily work?**

3. **Are your debts affecting your reputation?**

4. **Do your debts cause you to think less of yourself?**

5. **Have you ever given false information in order to obtain credit?**

6. **Have you ever made unrealistic promises to your creditors?**

7. **Does the pressure of your debts make you careless of the welfare of your family?**

8. **Do you ever fear that your employer, family, or friends will learn the extent of your total indebtedness?**

9. **When faced with a difficult financial situation, does the prospect of borrowing give you an inordinate feeling of relief?**

10. **Does the pressure of your debts cause you to have difficulty sleeping?**

11. **Has the pressure of your debts ever caused you to consider getting drunk?**

12. **Have you ever borrowed money without giving adequate consideration to the rate of interest you are required to pay?**

13. **Do you usually expect a negative response when you are subject to a credit investigation?**

14. **Have you ever developed a strict regimen for paying off your debts, only to break it under pressure?**

15. **Do you justify your debts by telling yourself that you are superior to the "other" people, and when you get your "break," you'll be out of debt?**

To find a Debtors Anonymous support group in your area, check your local phone directory (in the "business" section). Or write to DA's national headquarters for meeting locations in your area and a literature order form at the following address: Debtors Anonymous, P.O. Box 400, Grand Central Station, New York, NY 10163-0400.

Dealing with Credit Mistakes

You may not know (or care), but you probably have a personal credit report. Creditors that are considering loaning you money generally examine your credit report before granting you a loan or credit line.

Many people don't realize that they have a blemish on their credit report until they are turned down for a loan or questioned by the creditor about the glitch. For example, when I applied for my first mortgage, I discovered a minor wart on my own credit report.

Dealing with credit report problems, while taking up some of your time, needn't be difficult if you know what and what not to do.

Obtain a copy of your credit report

If you're turned down for rental housing, employment, or a loan because of derogatory information on your credit report, most states require the prospective lender or the credit reporting bureaus to give you a copy of the report.

If you're applying for a mortgage or other major loan, most lenders will give you a copy of your credit report if you simply ask. And why shouldn't they if you're paying for them to obtain the copy!

Reading a credit report is a challenge given all the abbreviations and jargon, so I recommend that, in addition to getting the report, you ask the lender what specific information on the report led to the denial of credit.

Get others to correct their mistakes

If you obtain your credit report and find a boo-boo on it that you do not recognize as being your mistake or fault, do *not* assume that the information is correct and is simply another indicator of your faulty memory. Credit reporting bureaus and the creditors who report credit information to these bureaus make many mistakes.

You would hope and expect that, if a credit bureau has negative and incorrect information in your credit report and you phone them to bring the error to their attention, they would graciously and expeditiously fix the mistake. If you believe that, then you're the world's greatest optimist; perhaps you also believe that you won't have to wait in line at the department of motor vehicles, post office, or your local bank around noon on paydays.

"Credit Repair" firms

On late night television and in the backs of newspapers and magazines, you may see ads for credit repair companies that claim to fix your credit report problems. In the worst cases I've seen, these firms charge outrageous amounts of money and don't come close to fulfilling their marketing hype.

If you have legitimate glitches on your credit report, credit repair firms *cannot* make the glitches disappear. Hope springs eternal, however — some would like to believe that their credit problems can be fixed.

Remember — if your problems are fixable, you can fix them yourself, and you don't need to pay an outside firm big bucks to do it.

Odds are you're going to have to make more phone calls or write a letter or two to fix the problems. Here's how most errors that aren't your fault are corrected:

- ✔ **It's someone else's credit problem.** A surprising number of personal credit report glitches are the result of someone else's negative information getting on your credit report. If the bad information on your report is completely foreign-looking to you, tell the credit bureau and also explain that you need more information because you don't recognize the creditor.

- ✔ **It's the creditor's mistake.** Creditors make mistakes, too. You need to write or call the creditor to get them to correct the erroneous information that they sent to the credit bureau. Phoning first usually works best (the credit bureau should be able to tell you how to reach the creditor if you don't know how). If necessary, follow-up with a letter.

Whether you're speaking with a credit bureau or an actual lender, make notes of your conversations. If representatives say they can fix the problem, get their name and extension and follow-up with them if they don't deliver as promised. If you're ensnared in bureaucratic red-tape, escalate the situation by speaking with a department manager. By law, bureaus are required to respond to a request to fix a credit error within 30 days — hold the bureau accountable!

Tell your side of the story

With a minor credit infraction, some lenders may simply ask for an explanation. I had a credit report glitch that was the result of being away for several weeks and missing the payment-due date for a couple of small bills. When my proposed mortgage lender saw my late payments, all I had to do was provide a written explanation. You and a creditor may not see eye-to-eye on a problem, and the creditor may refuse to budge. If that's the case, credit bureaus are required by law to allow you to add a 100-word explanation to your credit file.

Chapter 6

Reducing Your Spending

. . . .

In This Chapter

▶ The keys to successful spending

▶ Reducing your spending category by category

. . . .

*T*elling people how and where to spend their money is a risky undertaking because most people like to spend money, and most people hate to be told what to do.

You'll be glad to hear that I'm *not* going to tell you exactly where you must cut spending. I'm simply going to give you strategies that have worked for other people. The final decision for what to cut rests solely with you. Only you can decide what's important to you and what's dispensable — should you cut out your weekly poker games or cut back on your shoe collection?

I assume throughout these recommendations that you value your time. Therefore, I'm not going to tell you to scrimp and save by doing things like cutting open a tube of toothpaste so that you can use every last bit of it. And I won't tell you to have your spouse do your ironing to reduce your dry-cleaning bills (no point in having money in the bank if you lose your Significant Other).

Probably, part of the reason you spend money the way you do is that you're busy. Therefore, the recommendations in this chapter focus on methods that don't involve a lot of time but that produce big savings. In other words, these strategies provide a lot of bang for the buck. I believe in saving wherever possible, but small change is awfully heavy to cart around — better to save the big bucks.

Four Keys to Successful Spending

For most people, spending money is a whole lot easier and more fun than earning it. Far be it from me to tell you to stop having fun and to turn into a penny-pinching, stay-at-home miser. Of course you can spend money. But there's a world of difference between spending money *carelessly* and spending money *wisely*.

Spending too much and not spending wisely or efficiently puts pressure on a limited income. Savings dwindle, debts accumulate, and you can't achieve your financial goals.

Sometimes, when you dive into details too quickly, you miss the big picture. So before I jump into the specific areas where you can trim your budget, here are the four overall keys to successful spending. These four principles run through most of the recommendations coming up in this chapter.

Living within your means

Spending too much is a *relative* problem. Two people can each spend $30,000 per year yet have drastically different financial circumstances. How? Suppose that one of them earns $40,000 annually, and the other makes just $25,000. The $40,000 income earner saves $10,000 each year. The $25,000 earner accumulates $5,000 of new debt (or spends that amount from prior savings). Spend within your means.

Don't let others and their spending habits dictate yours. Certain people — you know who they are — bring out the big spender in you. Do something else with them besides shopping. If you can't find any other activity to share with them, try shopping with limited cash and no credit cards. That way you can't over-spend on impulse.

How much you can safely spend while still working toward your financial goals depends upon what your goals are and where you are financially. Chapter 8 assists you with figuring how much you should be saving and, therefore, what you can afford to spend to accomplish your financial goals.

Finding the best value

You can find high quality and low cost in the same product. Conversely, paying a high price is no guarantee that you're getting high quality. Cars are a good example. Whether you're buying a subcompact, sports car, or luxury four-door sedan, some cars are more fuel efficient and cost less to maintain than rivals that carry the same sticker price.

And when you evaluate the cost of a product or service, you need to think in terms of total, long-term costs. Suppose that you're comparing the purchase of two used cars: the Solid Sedan, which costs $10,000, and the Clunker Convertible, which weighs in at $8,000. On the surface, the Convertible appears cheaper. However, the price that you pay for a car is but a small portion of what a car ultimately costs you. If the Convertible is more costly to operate, maintain, and insure over the years, it could end up costing you much more. Sometimes paying more up front for a higher quality product or service ends up saving you more in the long run.

Those who are selling particular products and services may initially appear to have your best interests at heart if they steer you toward buying something that isn't costly. However, you may be in for a rude awakening once you discover the ongoing service, maintenance, and other fees you'll face in the years ahead. For example, a friend of mine was delighted that a gardener installed a backyard garden so inexpensively. The main reason for the low cost, it turns out, was that many of the plantings required high maintenance and frequent replacement, which — surprise, surprise — the gardener was willing to do for a fee.

Don't waste money on brand names

Be suspicious of companies that spend gobs on image-oriented advertising. Why? Heavy advertising costs many dollars and, as a consumer of that companies' products and services, you're paying for all that advertising.

All successful companies do some advertising — advertising is cost-effective and good business if it brings in enough new business. But consider the products and services and the claims that companies make.

Does a cola beverage really taste better if "It's the real thing" or "The choice of a new generation?" Consider all the silly labels and fluffy marketing of beers. Blind taste testing demonstrates little if any difference between the expensive brand name products and the cheaper, less heavily advertised ones.

Now, if you can't live without your Coca-Cola, Pepsi, or Samuel Adams and think that these products are head and shoulders above the rest, drink them to your heart's content. But question the importance of the name and image in the products you buy. Companies spend a lot of money creating and cultivating an image, which has zero real impact on how their products taste or perform.

"Branding" is used in many fields to sell overpriced, mediocre products and services to consumers. Take the lowly can of paint. Tests show some differences among different brands of paint. However, when you can buy high-quality paints for about $20 a gallon, do you really think that spending $100 or more per gallon on a can of paint blessed with the name of Ralph Lauren or Martha Stewart makes it better?

Newsweek magazine commissioned D/L Laboratories, a testing firm, to compare these $100+ per gallon snooty paints to $20 per gallon high-quality alternatives and found little difference, at least no difference that was worth paying for. In fact, one of the "gourmet" paints splattered more, had a less uniform sheen, didn't cover the surface as well, was more prone to run when applied, and emitted a high level of volatile organic compounds! Some other snooty brands didn't fare much better.

As people in the trade can tell you, thanks to computer-based matching, if you find a particular color of paint you like in a high-brow line, match it and buy it in a high-quality but far less costly line.

Don't compromise on quality, especially where the quality is important to you. But don't be snookered into believing that brand-name products are better or worth a substantially higher price.

Renting-to-own is the most expensive way to buy

$12.95 for a VCR? Talk about cheap!?

Well, there's a big hitch: that's $12.95 *per week*, for many weeks. When all is said and done and paid, buying a $200 VCR through a rent-to-own store ends up costing a typical buyer more than $750!

Welcome to the world of rent-to-own stores, which offer cash-poor consumers the ability to lease consumer items and, at the end of the lease, an option to buy. Many items can be bought on this basis. Although this may be more of a troubling sign of the times, increasing numbers of stores are reported to offer rent-to-own engagement rings! One rent-to-own store manager said, "We do get some people with cold feet."

If you think paying an 18 percent interest rate on a credit card is expensive, imagine what you'll think of renting-to-own when I tell you that the effective interest rate charged on many purchases exceeds 100 percent and in some cases 200 percent or more! Renting-to-own makes buying on a credit card look like a deal.

I'm not sharing this information with you to encourage your buying on credit cards but to point out what a rip-off renting-to-own is. Such stores prey on cash-less consumers who either can't get credit cards or don't understand how expensive renting-to-own really is.

Eliminating fat

If you want to reduce your overall spending by, say, 10 percent, you could just cut all of your current expenditures by 10 percent. Or you can reach your 10 percent goal by cutting some categories a lot and others not at all. You need to set priorities and make choices about what you can and can't live without.

What you spend your money on is sometimes a matter of habit rather than what you really want or value. For example, some people shop at whatever stores are closest because they know where the stores are; they never bother to look elsewhere.

Eliminating fat doesn't necessarily mean cutting back on your purchases. Buying in bulk is a good example. Some stores specialize in selling larger packages or quantities of a product at a lower price because they save money on the packaging and handling. You save money by buying in bulk. And even though that 20-pound bag of rice means more cash up front than the little box of Uncle Ben's, every meal from now on that you make from the 20-pound bag will be a great deal cheaper than the meal out of the box would have been. (If you're single, shop with a friend and split the bulk purchases.)

Avoid buying on credit

As I discuss in Chapters 4 and 5, buying items that depreciate — such as cars, clothing, and vacations — on credit is hazardous to your long-term financial health. Buy today only what you can afford today. If you'll be forced to carry a debt for months or years on end, then you can't really afford what you're buying on credit today.

Consumer credit is expensive and reinforces a bad habit: spending more than you can afford.

Strategies for Reducing Your Spending

Please keep in mind as you read through the following ideas that some of these strategies will make sense for you, and some of them won't. Start your spending reduction plan with the ones that come easily first. Work your way through them. Keep a list of the options that are more challenging for you — ones that require more of a sacrifice but that you can make work if necessary to achieve your spending and savings goals.

The chart in Figure 6-1 assumes that you're in a moderate combined federal and state tax bracket of 35 percent. See Chapter 7 for information on tax brackets.

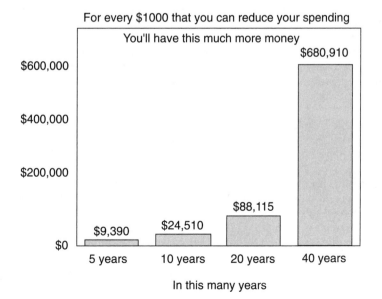

For every $1000 that you can reduce your spending

You'll have this much more money

In this many years

No matter which of the ideas in this chapter you choose for yourself, rest assured that keeping your budget lean and mean pays enormous dividends. After you implement a spending reduction strategy, you'll reap the benefits for years to come. For every $1,000 that you can shave from your annual spending (that's just $83 per month), look how much more money you'll have down the road if you can save that money in a tax-favored retirement account (see Chapter 8) and earn 10% per year on your investments, which I show you how to do in Part III.

Food

One way to reduce your food expenditures is to stop eating. However, this tends to make you weak and dizzy, so it's probably not a viable long-term strategy. The following culinary strategies will keep you on your feet — and perhaps even improve your health — for less money.

Join a wholesale superstore

Superstores such as PriceCostco and Sam's Club enable you to buy groceries in bulk at wholesale prices. And, contrary to popular perception, you *don't* have to buy 1,000 rolls of toilet paper at once — just 24.

I've done price comparisons between these kinds of stores and retail grocery stores and found that wholesalers charge 30 to 40 percent less for the exact same stuff. All without the hassle of clipping coupons or hunting for which store has the best price this month on crackers. Next time you see TV commercials comparing prices at several of your area's retail grocers, you'll know that they missed the real competition!

In addition to saving you lots of money, you'll find that buying in bulk means that you make fewer shopping trips. You'll have more supplies around your humble abode — so there is less need to eat out (which is costly) or make trips to the local grocer, who may be really nice but who charges you out the wazoo.

Perishables run the risk of living up to their name, so don't buy what you can't use. Repackage bulk packs into smaller quantities for the freezer if possible. If you're single, shop with a friend or two and split the order.

Be careful shopping at the warehouse clubs — you might be tempted to buy things you don't really need. These stores carry all sorts of items, including wide-screen TVs, computers, furniture, clothing, complete sets of baseball cards, and giant canisters of M&Ms and biscotti — beware! Try not to make impulse purchases, and be especially careful when you have kids in tow.

Check your local phone directory for superstores. PriceCostco has a toll-free number to help you locate a store nearest you (800-774-2678).

Most of these stores charge a small membership fee and are, frankly, somewhat of a hassle to join. PriceCostco, for example, charges $30 per year and asks for proof that you're a small-business owner or that you work for a nonprofit health-care organization, utility, bank, savings and loan, airline, or the media. You can also join if you hold a professional license or are a member of a credit union.

The reason you need to jump through these hoops is that, if *anyone* could join the warehouse stores, retailers who sell similar merchandise would be upset. Anyone could get the better deals that the warehouse clubs pass on from manufacturers. That's why people with a potential business reason can join.

The reality, though, is that if you really want to join you can. Many community organizations that you may belong to, such as the YMCA/YWCA or Big Brothers/Big Sisters, can get you a membership. A small business owner whom you know well can sponsor you. Or shop with a friend who's a member. Don't give up — the savings you can reap make joining a warehouse club well worth the hassle.

Budgeting to save more money

When most people hear the word budgeting, they usually think unpleasant thoughts — and, like dieting, rightfully so. But budgeting can help you move from knowing how much you spend on various things to successfully reducing your spending to successfully cutting your spending.

The first step in the process of budgeting, or planning your future spending, is to analyze where your current spending is going (refer to Chapter 4). After you've done that, calculate how much more you'd like to be saving per month. Then comes the harder part: Deciding where to make cuts in your spending.

Suppose that you're currently not saving any of your monthly income and that you desire to save 10 percent. If you can save and invest money through a tax-sheltered retirement account such as an employer's 401(k), 403(b) or a self-employed plan such as a SEP-IRA, Keogh, or your own IRA, you don't actually need to cut your spending by 10 percent to reach a savings goal of 10 percent (of your gross income).

When money is contributed into a tax-deductible retirement account, you reduce your federal and state taxes. If you're a moderate income earner and paying say 35 percent in federal and state

taxes on your marginal income, you actually only need to reduce your spending by 6.5 percent to save 10 percent. The "other" 3.5 percent of savings comes from the lowering of your taxes. (The higher your tax bracket, the less you need to cut your spending to reach a particular savings goal.)

So to boost your savings rate to 10 percent, go through your current spending, category by category, until you come up with enough proposed cuts to reduce your spending by 6.5 percent. Make your cuts in those areas that will be least painful and where you're getting the least value from your current level of spending. Even if you don't have access to a tax-deductible retirement account, budgeting still involves the same process.

Rather than examining your current expenses and making cuts from that starting point, another method of budgeting involves starting completely from scratch. Ask yourself how much you'd like to be spending on different categories. The advantage of this approach is that it doesn't allow your current spending levels to constrain your thinking. You'll most likely be amazed at the discrepancies between what you think you should be spending and what you actually are spending in certain categories.

Eat out more frugally

Eating meals out or getting takeout can be a time-saver but can rack up big bills if done too often and lavishly. Eating out is a luxury — think of it as hiring someone to shop, cook, and clean-up for you. Of course, some people hate to cook or don't have the time or space or energy to do much in the kitchen. If this is you, choose restaurants carefully and order from the menu selectively. A couple of tips:

- **Avoid beverages, especially alcohol.** Most restaurants make big profits on beverages. Drink water instead. (Water is healthful and reduces the likelihood of your wanting a nap after a big meal.)

- **Order vegetarian.** Vegetarian dishes, including pasta and rice dishes, generally cost less than meat-based entrees (and are better for you).

I don't want to be a killjoy. I'm not saying that you should live on bread and water. You can have dessert — heck, have some wine, too! But perhaps not every time. Try eating appetizers and dessert at home, where they're a lot less expensive (especially if you follow my advice on shopping for food).

Mom was right about eating those vegetables

Not only is meat expensive, but it is coming under increasing scrutiny as bad for your health. In a landmark report entitled "The Surgeon General's Report on Nutrition and Health" (produced under former U.S. Surgeon General C. Everett Koop, M.D.), reliance on a meat- and dairy-based diet — with its fat and cholesterol — was found to be the cause of the *majority* of premature deaths in the United States. In fact, five out of the top ten causes of death — heart disease, certain types of cancer, stroke, diabetes, and arteriosclerosis — are caused largely by Americans' poor diets.

In developing countries that are poorer economically than the U.S., people eat mainly grains, beans, and vegetables and have significantly lower rates of heart disease and diet-related cancers, such as cancer of the prostate and colon.

Meat is expensive, so the less meat you eat, the more money you save. Even if you choose to merely reduce your meat consumption rather than eliminate it, you can still save significant

dough. If you decide to eliminate meat from your diet, don't try to shift from burgers, pork chops, and meat loaf to tofu and sprouts overnight. Make changes in your diet gradually. For example, I first gave up beef, pork, and lamb, but I still eat some chicken, fish, and low-fat dairy products.

(Besides saving you money and your health, a vegetarian diet is also friendlier to the environment. Compared to other foods, cattle need a great deal more land and water to raise. Livestock also produce a great deal of flatulence, which adds more methane to the atmosphere. Here's a statistical tidbit sure to liven up a dull cocktail party conversation: 100 million tons of the world's annual methane emissions — 20 percent of the total — are from cattle!)

A number of good books can teach you more about the benefits of a vegetarian-based diet and provide recipes, too. Among my favorites are *Diet for a New America* by John Robbins (Stillpoint Publishing) and *Eat for Life* by The Food and Nutrition Board (National Academy Press).

Shelter

Housing and all the costs associated with it (utilities, furniture, appliances, and, if you're a homeowner, maintenance and repairs) can gobble a large chunk of your monthly income. I'm not suggesting that you live in an igloo or teepee (even though they're probably less costly and more energy-efficient), but people often overlook common opportunities to save money in this category.

Don't take rent for granted

Rent can take up a sizable chunk of your monthly take-home pay. Many people consider rent to be a fixed and an inflexible part of their expenses. It's not. Here are some things you can do to cut it down in size:

- ✔ **Move to a lower-cost rental.** Of course, a lower-cost rental may not be as nice — it may be smaller or lack a private parking spot or be in a less popular locale. Make the tradeoff and shave $50 to $100 or more off your monthly rent. Don't forget: The less you spend renting, the more you can save toward buying your own place. Just be sure to factor in all the costs of a new location, including possibly higher commuting costs.

- ✔ **Share a rental.** Living alone has some benefits, but financially speaking, it's a luxury. Rent a larger place with roommates. Your rental costs should go way down, and you'll get more home for your rental dollars. You have to be in a sharing mood, though. Roommates can be a hassle at times but can also be a plus — you meet all sorts of new people and have someone else to blame if the kitchen's a mess.

- ✔ **Negotiate your rental increases.** Every year, like clockwork, your landlord bumps up your rent a certain percentage. If your local rental market is soft or your living quarters are deteriorating, stand up for yourself! You have more leverage and power than you probably realize.

  If you pay your rent on time and are otherwise a good tenant, a smart landlord won't want to lose you. Filling vacancies takes time and money. State your case: You've been a responsible tenant, and your research shows comparable rentals going for less. Crying poor may help, too. At the very least, if you can't stave off the rent increase, maybe you can wrangle some improvements to the place.

- ✔ **Buy rather than rent.** No, I haven't lost my mind. Purchasing your own place can be costly, yes, but in the long run, owning should be cheaper than renting, and you'll have something to show for it in the end. If you purchase real estate with a 30-year fixed-rate mortgage, your mortgage payment (which is your biggest ownership expense) remains constant. Only your property taxes, maintenance, and insurance costs are exposed to the vagaries of inflation.

  As a renter, your entire monthly housing cost can rise with increases in the cost of living (unless you are a beneficiary of a rent-controlled building).

  See Chapter 15 to learn about buying real estate, even if you're short on cash.

Saving on your phone bill

Telephone expenses are a good example of not needing to reduce your usage to save money. Just adjust *when* you place your calls. In most areas, the most expensive time to place local toll or long-distance calls is weekdays between 8 a.m. and 5 p.m. From 5 p.m. to 11 p.m. is cheaper, and the cheapest time to call is late at night (usually 11 p.m. to 8 a.m.), which can save you 50-60 percent (and as a bonus, you may get the thrill of waking up the other party). This bargain rate is also available all weekend, usually beginning after 11 p.m. Friday night and ending Sunday at 5 p.m.

You may be able to save money on your toll calls by switching companies. Despite (or perhaps because of) the millions of dollars that AT&T pours into advertising to persuade you that its quality is better and prices are comparable, consider moving to MCI (800-444-3333) or Sprint (800-877-4000). Quality is virtually the same from company to company, and AT&T is more expensive in most cases. Check with your long distance provider to be sure that you're on the lowest cost calling program given the patterns of your calls.

Sometimes sending a thoughtful letter is cheaper, more appreciated, and longer lasting than placing a phone call. Just block out an hour, grab pen and paper, and rediscover the lost art form of letter writing. Formulating your thoughts on paper can be clarifying and therapeutic to boot. Computer users may find that they save money as well by sending e-mail.

Save on homeowner expenses

As every homeowner knows, houses suck money. You should be especially careful to watch your money in this area of your budget.

✔ **Don't overspend.** If you're on the verge of buying your first home or trading up to a more costly property, crunch some realistic numbers before you jump. The most common mistake people make is overstretching when buying a home. If too little money is left over for other needs — such as taking trips, eating out, enjoying hobbies, or saving for retirement — your new dream house may become a financial prison. Overspending on housing can cause unhappiness by blocking other personal and financial goals.

Calculate how much you can afford to spend monthly on a home by figuring your other needs first. (Doing the exercises in Chapter 4 about where you're spending your money and in Chapter 8 about saving for retirement will help.)

Although real estate can be a good long-term investment, a great deal of your discretionary dollars can end up being poured into your home. In addition to decorating and remodeling, some people feel the need to trade up to a bigger home every few years. Of course, after they're in their new home, the remodeling and renovation cycle simply begins again, which costs even more money. Be happy with what you have. The world will always have people with bigger, nicer houses, and toys than you have.

✔ **Rent out a room.** If you already own your place, selling it and buying a less expensive place can be a big hassle and can cost you some taxes if you sell it for a profit. Have you considered taking in a tenant to reduce your housing expenses? Check out the renter thoroughly: Get references, run a credit report, and talk about ground rules and expectations before sharing your space. Don't forget to check with your insurance company to see whether your homeowner's policy needs adjustments to cover potential liability from renting.

✔ **Refinance your mortgage.** This step may seem like common sense, but surprisingly, many people don't keep up-to-date on mortgage rates. If interest rates are lower than when you obtained your current mortgage, you may be able to save money by refinancing (see Chapter 15 for more information).

✔ **Appeal your property-tax assessment.** In many areas of the country, housing prices have gone down in recent years. If you're still paying property taxes based on a higher valuation, you may be able to save money by appealing your assessment. Check with your local assessor's office for the procedure to follow. You may need to prove that your property is worth less today, and you can prove that by using the sale prices of comparable homes in your area. An appraiser's recent evaluation of your property would do — you may already have one if you refinanced your mortgage recently.

✔ **Reduce utility costs.** Sometimes you have to spend money to save money. Old refrigerators, for example, can waste a lot of electricity. Insulate an attic to save on heating and air-conditioning bills. Install water flow regulators in shower heads and toilet bowls. Even if you don't live in an area susceptible to droughts, why waste water unnecessarily (which isn't free)? If you live in an area where garbage rates depend on the amount of stuff you toss, recycle. Recycling means less garbage, which means lower trash bills. (Even if you don't pay extra, recycle anyway — it benefits the environment by reducing landfill.)

Transportation

America is a car-driven society. In most other countries, cars are a luxury. More than 90 percent of the people in the rest of the world can't afford a new American car. If more people in the United States thought of cars as a luxury, Americans might have far fewer financial problems (and accidents). Cars not only pollute the air and clog the highways but also cost you a bundle. Purchasing the best car you can and using it wisely can save you big dollars. So can using other transportation alternatives.

Contrary to advertising slogans, cars are not built to last — car manufacturers don't want you to stick with the same car year after year. They want you to buy a new one. New models are constantly introduced with new features and styling changes. Getting a new set of wheels every few years is an expensive luxury.

Some professionals like to use their cars to project a successful image. Picking up a prospective client in your spiffy new car is sure to make an impression, all right. I ask my counseling clients what they think when a salesperson arrives in a gleaming new sedan. My clients say that a new car is a sign that the person behind the wheel makes a lot of money — probably at the clients' expense! Many also wonder whether the person is a good financial manager. I don't think either image is one you want to project.

Don't try to keep up with the Joneses as they show off their new cars every year — for all you know, they're running themselves into financial ruin just trying to impress you. Let your neighbors admire you for your thriftiness and wisdom instead.

Research before you buy a car

When you buy a car, not only do you pay the initial sticker price, but you're also on the hook for gas, insurance, registration fees, maintenance, and repairs. Don't compare simple sticker prices; think about total, long-term costs of ownership.

Speaking of total costs, remember that you are also trusting your life to the car. With more than 40,000 Americans killed in auto accidents annually, safety should be an important consideration as well. Air bags, for example, may save your life.

The *Consumer Reports Buying Guide* summarizes all the latest information on cars and includes a list of the most reliable used cars in various price categories. For you data jocks, *The Complete Car Cost Guide* (published by Intellichoice) is packed with information about all categories of ownership costs, warranties, and dealer costs. The guide rates new cars based on total ownership costs. But can you *really* afford a new car?

Buy your car with cash

The main reason people end up spending more than they can really afford on a car is that they finance it. As I discuss in Chapter 2 and elsewhere, you should avoid borrowing money for consumption purchases, especially for items that depreciate in value like cars. A car is most definitely *not* an investment.

In most situations, leasing is even more expensive than borrowing money to buy a car. Leasing is like a long-term car rental. We all know how well rental cars get treated — well, leased cars are treated just as well, which is one of the reasons leasing is so costly.

Sadly, the practice of leasing cars or buying them on credit is increasingly becoming the norm in our society. This is certainly attributable to a lot of misinformation spread by car dealers and, in some cases, the media. Consider the magazine article entitled "Rewards of Car Leasing": compared to buying, the article claims, leasing is a great deal. Placed immediately next to the article were ads for auto dealers advertising auto leasing. The magazine, by the way, is *free* to subscribers — which means that 100 percent of its revenue comes from advertisers such as auto dealers.

Replace high-cost cars

Maybe you've realized by now that your car is too expensive to operate because of insurance, gas, and maintenance costs. Or maybe you bought too much car — people who lease or borrow money to buy a car frequently buy a far more expensive car than they can realistically afford.

Nothing says that you're stuck with it until the bitter end. *Dump* your expensive car and get something more financially manageable. The sooner you switch, the more money you'll save. Getting rid of a car on a lease is more of a challenge but it can be done. I had one client who, when he lost his job and needed to slash expenses, convinced the dealer (by writing a letter to the owner) to take the leased car back.

But I can't buy a new car for cash!

"Come on, Eric" you may be thinking "how can I and most wage earners today afford to buy a new car for cash — who has got that kind of dough sitting around?!"

Some people feel that it's unreasonable of me to expect them to buy a new car using cash. After all, many publications, which not uncoincidentally derive great advertising revenue from auto dealers and lenders, effectively endorse and encourage loaning and leasing to buy a car.

If you knew me, you'd know that I'm a very reasonable kinda guy. Believe me, I'm trying to look out for your best long-term financial interests. Please consider the following:

✔ If you lack sufficient cash to buy a new car, I say "DON'T BUY A NEW CAR!" Ninety percent of the world's population can't even afford a car, let alone a new one! Buy a car that you can afford — namely not a new one.

✔ Don't fall for the new car buying rationalization that says that buying a used car means lots of maintenance, repair expenses, and problems. If you do your homework and buy a good, used car, you can have the best of both worlds. A good used car costs less to buy and should cost you less to operate thanks to lower insurance costs.

✔ A fancy car is not needed to impress people for business purposes. Some people I know say that they absolutely must drive a brand spanking nice new car to set the right impression for business purposes. I'm not going to tell you how to manage your career, but I will ask you to consider that if clients and others see you driving an expensive new car, they may think that you spend money wastefully or that you're getting rich off of them!

Keep cars to a minimum

I've seen households that have one car per person. Four people, four cars! In most cases, this is unnecessary and very costly. In developing countries like China, cars are a luxury. Bikes are used to carry groceries, the kids, and even large pieces of furniture, thereby reducing transportation costs . . . and the need to diet!

Maintaining two or more cars for most middle-income households is an expensive extravagance. Try to find ways to make do with fewer cars.

One of the ways to move beyond the confines of a car is to ride buses or trains or carpool to work. Some employers give incentives for taking public transit to work, and some cities and counties offer assistance in setting up van pools or car pools along popular routes. By leaving the driving to someone else, you can catch up on reading or just relax on the way to and from work. And you're doing your share to cut down on pollution.

When you're considering where to live and the cost of living in different areas, don't forget to consider commuting costs. One advantage of living close to work, or at least close to public transit systems, is that you may be able to make do with fewer cars in your household or with no car at all.

Buy commuter passes

In many areas, you can purchase train, bus, or subway passes to reduce the cost of commuting. Many toll bridges also have booklets of tickets that you can buy at a discount. Some booths don't advertise that they offer these plans — maybe as a strategy to keep revenues up. It took me several years to figure out that even the Golden Gate Bridge — arguably the world's most beautiful bridge — had these booklets.

Buy regular unleaded gas

A number of studies have shown that "superduperultrapremium" gasoline is not worth the extra expense. Fill up your tank when you're on a shopping trip to the warehouse wholesalers (discussed earlier in this chapter). These superstores are usually located in lower-cost areas, so the gas is usually cheaper there, too. Also don't use credit cards to buy your gas if you have to pay a higher price to do so.

Service your car regularly, before problems develop

Sure, servicing your car (for example, changing the oil every 5,000 miles) costs money, but it saves you dough in the long run by extending the operating life of the car. Servicing your car also reduces the chances that your car will crap out in the middle of nowhere, which requires a humongous towing charge to a service station. Even worse is stalling on the freeway during peak rush hour and having thousands of angry commuters stuck behind you.

Clothing and accessories

Given the amount of money that some people spend on clothing and related accessories, I've come to believe that people in nudist colonies must be great savers! But you probably live among the clothed mainstream of American society, so here's a short list of economizing ideas:

- ✔ **Avoid dry cleanables.** When you buy clothing, try to stick with cottons and machine-washable synthetics rather than wools or silks that require dry cleaning. Check labels before you buy stuff.

  Despite his tremendous business success, Jack Bogle, founder of the thrifty Vanguard Group of mutual funds, wore wool ties to work. He proudly declared that his ties were more *efficient,* and he is right. They last longer and require less cleaning than silk ties!

- ✔ **Don't chase the latest fashions.** Fashion designers and retailers are constantly working to tempt you to buy more. Don't do it. Toss the publications that pronounce this season's look.

  In most cases, you simply don't need to buy racks of new clothes or an entire new wardrobe yearly. If your clothes are not lasting you at least ten years, you're probably tossing them before their time or buying clothing that's not durable enough.

  Fashion, as defined by what people wear, changes quite slowly. In fact, the classics don't ever go out of style. If you want the effect of a new wardrobe every year, store last year's purchases away next year and then bring them out the year after! Or rotate your clothing inventory every third year. Set your own fashion standards. Buy basic, buy classic — don't let fashion gurus be your guide or you'll be the best dresser in the poorhouse.

- ✔ **Minimize accessories.** Shoes, jewelry, handbags, and the like can gobble large amounts of money. Again, how many of these accessory items do you really need? The answer is probably very few, and each one should last many years.

Go to your closet or jewelry box and tally up the loot. What else could you have done with all that cash? See the things you regret buying or forgot you even had? Don't make the same mistake again. Have a garage sale if you have a lot of stuff that you don't want.

Debt repayment

In Chapter 5, I discuss strategies to reduce the cost of carrying consumer debt. The *best* way to reduce the costs of debt is to avoid it in the first place when you're making consumption purchases. You can avoid debt by eliminating your access to credit or by limiting your purchase of consumer items that you can pay off each month. Remember, only borrow for long-term investments. (Refer to Chapter 2 for more information.)

If you pay your balance in full each month, you don't need to keep a credit card that charges you an annual fee. Many no fee credit cards exist — some that even offer you a benefit for using them:

- ✔ Discover Card (800-347-2683) rebates 0.25 to 1 percent of purchases in cash
- ✔ GM Card (800-947-1000) gives credits worth 5 percent of charges toward the purchase of a GM-manufactured vehicle (Saturns excluded)
- ✔ Ford Card (800-374-7777) credits 5 percent of charges toward the purchase of a Ford-manufactured vehicle
- ✔ AFBA Industrial Bank (800-776-2265)
- ✔ USAA Federal Savings (800-922-9092)

If you have a credit card that charges an annual fee, try calling the company and saying that you want to cancel the card because you can get a competitor's card without an annual fee. Many banks will agree to waive the fee on the spot. Some require you to call back yearly to cancel the fee — a hassle that can be avoided by getting a true no-fee card.

If you pay in full each month and charge $10,000 or more annually, consider a card that gives you credits toward a purchase, such as a car or airline ticket. *Note:* Be careful, however, because some people are tempted to charge more on a card that rewards them for more purchases. If you spend more than you would otherwise, it defeats the purpose of getting the credits. The following cards may rebate enough to justify a fee:

- ✔ American Advantage (800-359-4444) credits one American Airlines frequent-flier mile per dollar charged. Annual fee: $50.
- ✔ United Mileage Plus (800-537-7783) credits one United Airlines frequent-flier mile per dollar charged. Annual fee: $60.
- ✔ Continental (800-446-5336) credits one Continental frequent-flier mile per dollar charged. Annual fee: $45.

Stuff to make you and others happy

Having fun, taking time out for R & R, and lavishing gifts on those you love can be money well spent. But in these areas, financial overindulgence can wreck an otherwise good budget.

Gifts

Think about how you approach buying gifts throughout the year — and especially during the holidays. I know people who spend so much money on credit cards at this time of year that it takes them until late spring or summer to pay their debts off!

Although I don't want to deny your loved ones gifts from the heart — or you the pleasure of giving them — spend wisely. Homemade gifts are less costly to the giver and may be more dear to recipients. Many children actually love durable, classic, basic toys that aren't necessarily advertised on Saturday morning TV.

Perhaps because we don't like to feel cheap when buying a gift, most people forget their thrifty shopping habits when gift buying. As with other purchases you make, however, careful attention to where and what you buy can save you significant dollars. And don't make the mistake of equating the value of a gift with its dollar cost. How many expensive gifts have you received that were useless or meaningless to you?

In fact, I've got a good suggestion for getting rid of those old, unwanted gifts. One of the most entertaining and memorable holiday parties I've attended involved a "white elephant" gift exchange: everyone brought a wrapped, unwanted gift of the past and exchanged it with someone else. Once the gifts were opened, trading was allowed.

Entertainment

Entertainment doesn't have to cost a great deal of money if you adjust your expectations. Especially in metropolitan areas, many movies, theaters, and museums offer discount prices on certain days and times. Same goes for restaurants.

Cultivate some interests and hobbies that are free or low cost. Seeing friends, reading, hiking, and playing sports can be good for your finances as well as your health.

Vacations

For many people, vacations are a luxury. For others, regular vacations are essential parts of their routine. Regardless of how you recharge your batteries, remember that vacations are not investments, so you shouldn't be borrowing through credit cards to finance your travels. After all, how relaxed will you feel when you have to pay all those bills?

Try vacations that are shorter and closer to home. Have you been to a state or national park recently? Take a vacation at home and see the sights in your local area. Great places probably exist within 50 miles of you that you've always wanted to see but haven't got around to for one reason or another. Or just block out some time and do what my cats do: take a lot of naps and just hang out around your home.

If you do travel far and are heading for a popular destination, travel during the off-season for the best deals on airfares and hotels. Keep an eye out for discounts and "bought-but-unable-to-use" tickets advertised in your local paper. Seniors generally qualify for special fares at most airlines — ask the airline what programs it offers.

Also, be sure to shop around even when working with a travel agent. Travel agents work on commission, so they may not work very hard to find you the absolute best deals. Tour packages, when they meet your interests and needs, can also save you money. If you have flexible travel plans, courier services can cut your travel costs significantly (but make sure that the company is reputable).

Personal care

You have to take care of yourself, but as with anything else, there are ways to do it that are expensive, and there are ways that can save you money.

- ✔ **Hair care.** One way to save money in this category is to go bald. I'm working on this one myself. In the meantime, if you have hair to be trimmed, a number of no-frills, low-cost, hair-cutting joints can do the job — Supercuts is one of the larger chains. I know that some of you will insist that your stylist is the only one who can manage your hair the way you like it. At the prices charged by some of the trendy hair places, you have to really adore what they do to justify the cost. Consider going periodically to a no-frills stylist for maintenance after getting a fabulous cut at a more expensive place. If you're daring, you could try getting your hair cut at a local training school.

- ✔ **Other personal-care services.** As long as we're on the subject of outward beauty, I have to say that in my personal opinion, the billions spent annually on cosmetics are a complete waste of time and money. Women look fine and in most cases better without makeup. Now, deodorant I can understand, but beyond that, you should pay close attention to your spending in this area. And having regular facials, pedicures, and manicures can add up quickly.

- ✔ **Health club expenses.** Expenditure on exercise is almost always money well spent. But you don't have to belong to a trendy club to get benefits. If you belong to a gym or club for the social scene, whether it's for dating or business purposes, you have to judge whether it's worth the cost.

  Low-cost exercise facilities are everywhere — look for them anywhere you see children. Local schools, colleges, and universities almost always have tennis courts, running tracks, swimming pools, basketball courts, and exercise rooms and often provide instruction. Community centers offer fitness programs and classes, too. Metropolitan areas that have lots of health clubs undoubtedly have the widest range of options and prices. *Note:* When figuring the cost of membership, be sure to factor in the cost of travel to and from these clubs (and the realistic likelihood of going there regularly to work out).

  Don't forget that lots of healthy exercise can be done indoors or out, free of charge. Isn't biking in the park at sunset more fun than peddling away on a stationary bike, anyway? If you're dedicated, you may want to buy some basic gym equipment for use at home. Be careful though: lots of rowing machines and free weights languish in a closet after their first week at home.

Look for value in the publications to which you subscribe

Everyone has a favorite and not-so-favorite publication. Some people don't realize how much they are spending on publications partly because they've never tallied up the cost.

Take *The New York Times*. Actually, consider not taking it. At $7.10 per week in the New York Metro area and $9.50 per week elsewhere, that's a whopping $369 and $494 per year! Most areas have decent newspapers that cost a fraction of these amounts. You can also keep up with news and events through weekly news magazines such as *Newsweek* — just $41 per year.

As I discuss elsewhere in this book, "free" publications are often driven by advertisers so I'm not encouraging that you load up on them. But take a close look at how much in total you're spending on publications and how much each one costs. Keep the ones that you're getting sufficient value from and cancel the rest. You can always read them at your local library.

If you took the money that you're spending on *The New York Times*, for example, and invested it in your retirement account and earned a mere 10 percent per year, in 25 years you'd have more than $55,000 (New York metro subscribers) or more than $74,000 (everyone else in the country)! And this assumes that they don't increase the price of their paper, which they always do. Knowing these figures, you'd really have to feel you're getting good value from *The New York Times* to keep subscribing!

Personal business

Accountants, lawyers, and financial advisors can be worth their expense if they're good. But be wary of professionals who create or perpetuate work and have conflicts of interest in their recommendations.

The best way to use professionals for tax, legal, or financial advice is to get organized before you meet with them. Do some background research to evaluate their strengths and biases. Make sure that you set goals and estimate fees in advance so that you know what you're getting yourself into.

Good self-help books and software (see Chapter 21) can be terrific low-cost alternatives to hiring professionals.

Medical care

Health care is a big topic nowadays, and the cost of it is going up fast. Your health insurance — if you have health insurance, that is — probably covers most of your health-care needs (Chapter 17 explains how to shop for health insurance). But many plans require you to pay for certain expenses out of your own pocket.

Medical care and supplies are like any other services and products — price and quality vary. And medicine in the United States, like any other profession, is a business, and a conflict of interest exists whenever the person recommending treatment benefits financially from providing that treatment. Many studies have documented unnecessary surgeries and other medical procedures.

If you don't have health-insurance coverage, you may end up paying a larger amount out of your own pocket. You should really investigate buying minimal coverage. Just remember — as with any other service or product that you buy — shop around. And don't take any one physician's advice as gospel. Always get a second opinion for any major surgery. Most health insurance plans, out of economic self-interest, require one anyway.

Therapy can be useful and even lifesaving. Have a frank talk with your therapist about how much total time and money you can expect to spend and what kind of results you expect. As with any professional service, a competent therapist should be able to give you a straight answer if he or she is looking out for your psychological *and* financial well-being.

Alternative medicine (holistic and chiropractic, for example) is gaining attention because of its focus on preventive care and treatment of the whole body or person. Although alternative medicine can be dangerous to undertake if you are in critical condition, alternative treatment for many forms of chronic pain or disease may be worth your investigation. Alternative medicine may lead to better *and* lower-cost health care.

If you must take certain drugs on an ongoing basis and pay for them out-of-pocket, ordering through a mail-order company can bring down your costs and be more convenient for refilling prescriptions. Your health plan may be able to provide more information about this. The following mail order companies also offer generic drugs, which are medically equivalent to brand-name drugs but cost a lot less:

- ✔ Family Pharmaceuticals of America (800-922-3444)
- ✔ Retired Persons Services, Inc. (AARP) (800-456-2277)

Insurance

Insurance is a vast mine field. Part IV explains the different coverages, suggests what to buy and avoid, and reveals how to save on policies. The following are the most common ways people waste money on insurance.

✔ **Keeping low deductibles.** The *deductible* is the amount of a loss that must come out of your pocket. On an auto insurance policy, for example, if your collision deductible is $100 and you get into an accident, you pay for the first $100 of damage and your insurance company picks up the rest. Low deductibles, however, translate into much higher premiums for you. In the long run, you should save money with a higher deductible, even factoring in the potential for greater out-of-pocket costs to you when you do have a claim. Insurance should protect you from economic disaster. If your savings are quite low, don't get carried away with a really high deductible, which could cause financial hardship if you do have a claim.

If you have a lot of claims, your insurance premiums will escalate, so you still don't come out ahead with lower deductibles. Plus low deductibles mean more claim forms to file for small losses (more hassle). Filing an insurance claim is usually not an enjoyable or quick experience.

✔ **Covering small potential losses or unnecessary needs.** You shouldn't buy insurance for anything that wouldn't be a financial catastrophe if you had to pay for it out of your own pocket. Although the postal service isn't perfect, insuring inexpensive gifts sent in the mail is not worth the price. Buying dental or home warranty plans also doesn't make financial sense for the same reason. And, if no one is dependent on your income, then you don't need to buy life insurance either (who will be around to collect when you're gone?).

✔ **Failing to shop around.** Rates vary *tremendously* from insurer to insurer. In Part IV, I recommend the best companies to call first for quotes and other cost saving strategies.

Taxes

Taxes probably represent one of the largest — if not *the* largest — of your expenditures. (So why is it last here? You will soon see.)

Retirement savings plans are one of the best and simplest ways to reduce your tax burden. I explain more about retirement savings plans in Chapter 12. Unfortunately, most people can't take full advantage of these plans because they spend everything they make. So not only do they have less savings, they also pay higher income taxes — a double whammy.

I've attended many presentations where a fast-talking investment guy in an expensive suit lectures about the importance of saving for retirement and explains how to invest your savings. Yet details and tips about finding the money to save (the hard part for most people) are left to the imagination.

In order to take advantage of the tax savings that come through retirement savings plans, you must first spend less than you earn. Only then can you afford to contribute to these plans. That's why the first part of this chapter is all about strategies to reduce your spending.

Another benefit of spending less and saving more is reduced sales tax. When you buy most consumer products, you pay sales tax. Therefore, the less money you spend and the more you save in retirement accounts, the more you reduce income *and* sales taxes. (See Chapter 7 for other tax-reduction strategies.)

Costly addictions

Human beings are creatures of habit. We all have habits that we wish we didn't have, and breaking those habits can be very difficult. Costly habits are the worst. The following tidbits may nudge you in the right direction toward breaking your own financially draining habits.

✔ **Kick the smoking habit.** Despite the decline over the past few decades in smoking, 25 percent of all Americans still smoke. Using smokeless tobacco, which also causes long-term health problems, is on the increase. Americans spend more than $45 billion annually on tobacco products — that's a staggering $900 per year per tobacco user. The increased medical costs and lost work time costs are even greater, estimated at more than $50 billion every year. Of course, if you continue to smoke, you may be eliminating the need to even save for retirement.

Check with local hospitals for smoking-cessation programs. The American Lung Association (check your local phone directory) also offers Freedom from Smoking clinics around the country. The National Cancer Institute (800-4CANCER) and the Office on Smoking and Health at the Centers for Disease Control (1600 Clifton Road, Atlanta, GA 30333, phone 404-488-5705) offer free information guides containing effective methods to stop smoking.

✔ **Stop abusing alcohol and other drugs.** Nearly three-quarters of a million Americans seek treatment annually for alcoholism or drug abuse. These addictive behaviors, like spending, transcend all educational and socioeconomic lines in our society. Even so, studies have demonstrated that only one in seven alcoholics or drug abusers seeks help. Three of the ten leading causes of death — cirrhosis of the liver, accidents, and suicides — are associated with excessive alcohol consumption.

The National Clearinghouse for Alcohol and Drug Information (800-729-6686) can refer you to local treatment programs such as Alcoholics Anonymous. It also has pamphlets and other literature available on various types of substance abuse. The National Drug Abuse Information and Treatment Hotline (800-662-HELP) can refer you to local drug treatment programs and has literature available as well.

✔ **Don't gamble.** The house *always* comes out ahead in the long run. Why do you think so many governments run lotteries? Because governments make money on people who gamble, that's why.

Casinos, horse and dog racetracks, and other gambling establishments are sure long-term losers for you. Getting hooked on the dream of winning is easy and tempting. And sure, occasionally you win a little bit (just enough to keep you coming back). Every now and then a few folks win a lot. But it's built into the odds that your hard-earned capital mostly winds up in the pockets of the casino owners.

If you go just for the entertainment, take only what you can afford to lose.

Chapter 7

Taking the Trauma Out of Taxes

· ·

In This Chapter

▶ Dealing with the baffling tax system

▶ Figuring your marginal income tax rate

▶ Reducing the taxes on your employment and investment income

▶ Lowering the taxes on your investment income

▶ Increasing your deductions (legally, of course!)

▶ Preparing your return with and without help

▶ What to do if you get an audit notice

· ·

> *"The nation should have a tax system that looks like someone designed it on purpose."*
>
> — Former Treasury Secretary William E. Simon

The Winchester Mystery House is a bizarre tourist attraction near San Jose, California. It is named for its former owner, Sarah Winchester, widow of the rifle-manufacturing magnate. As the story goes, Sarah believed that she would not die as long as she continued to build on her property.

Proving that the prospect of death is a powerful motivator, Ms. Winchester kept builders working on her house around the clock for 38 years! Without a plan in mind, contractors added one room at a time. One hundred and sixty rooms later, you can imagine the result. Some staircases appropriately lead upstairs, but others dead-end at ceilings. Some doors and windows open only to reveal walls.

The Winchester Mystery House provides tour guides to lead you through the property. If you were on your own, of course, you'd need a detailed map and a lot of patience and persistence to get from one end of the house to the other.

And so it is with our tax system, which has quite a bit in common with the Winchester Mystery House. There is no master plan.

It's Not You — It's the System

The U.S. tax code has been changed incrementally over the years but has never been examined globally or given an overhaul. And rather than being a fun and interesting tourist attraction, for weary U.S. taxpayers who must comply with its sometimes frightening and unnecessary complexity, our tax system is like a nightmare that never seems to end.

Nearly every year, elected officials make revisions to the tax code, changing, amending, occasionally deleting, but more often adding to the written rules and regulations that determine what is taxable, which deductions are legal, which aren't, and so forth. The revisions are the results of political bargaining that usually ignores the fact that you, the taxpayer, must understand it all. Very little common sense is ever involved.

Of course, not everyone suffers at the hands of the confusing, cumbersome tax code. Some accountants and tax preparers are guaranteed employment as long as bewildered taxpayers need help. And the category of bewildered taxpayers includes most of us.

You may be interested to know that almost all of the congressional members who sit on the tax-writing committees — the Senate Finance Committee and the House Ways and Means Committee — *hire tax help, too.* An article in *Forbes* magazine found that 11 of the 12 members of the tax-writing committees don't prepare their own tax returns!

So don't feel dumb when the time comes to fill out tax forms, because it's not you — it's the system. Nevertheless, even if you hire a tax advisor to help you navigate the tax morass and prepare your annual return, understanding how the system treats certain financial moves you make is worth some of your time. The more you know about taxes, the smarter the financial strategies you devise and the less you need to spend hiring tax advisors.

The value of understanding the system

You pay a lot of money in taxes — probably more than you realize. Most people remember only whether they got a refund or owed money on their return. But when you file your tax return, all you're doing is settling up with tax authorities over the amount of taxes you paid during the year versus the total tax that you owe based on your income and deductions.

Some people feel lucky when they get a refund, but really, all a refund indicates is that you overpaid in taxes during the year. You should have had this money in your own account all along. If you're consistently getting big refunds, you should be paying less tax throughout the year. (Fill out a simple tax form, the W-4, to determine how much you should be paying in taxes throughout the year. You can obtain a W-4 through your employer's payroll department or Form 1040-ES through the IRS at 800-TAX-FORM if you're self employed.)

Instead of caring about whether you get a refund when you complete your annual tax return, you *should* care about the *total* taxes you pay. The only way to know the *total* taxes you pay is to get out your federal and state tax returns. On each of those returns is a line that shows the *total tax:* This is line 54 on federal 1040 returns. Add up the totals from your federal and state tax returns, and you'll probably see one of the single largest expenses of your financial life (unless you have an expensive home or a huge gambling habit).

The goal of this chapter is to legally and permanently help you reduce the total taxes you pay. The key to reducing your tax burden is to understand the tax system — if you don't, you will surely pay more in taxes than necessary. And your tax ignorance can lead to mistakes, which can be costly if the IRS and your state government catch errors in your favor. With the proliferation of computerized information and data tracking, discovering mistakes has never been easier.

The tax system, like other public policy, is built around incentives to encourage *desirable* behavior and activity. Home ownership, for example, is considered desirable because it encourages people to take more responsibility for maintaining buildings and neighborhoods. Clean, orderly neighborhoods are supposed to be the result of home ownership. Therefore, the government offers all sorts of tax perks, which I discuss later in this chapter, to encourage people to buy and own homes.

To understand the tax system is to understand what your government thinks you should be doing. Naturally, not all people follow the path the government encourages — after all, it's a free country. You've spent years rebelling against your parents. Why should the government get better treatment?

However, the difference between rebelling against your parents and being a rebellious taxpayer, of course, is that as a taxpayer, the cost of defiance comes out of your pocket (I haven't heard of many parents who penalize, in *cash,* their kids' unruliness). The *fewer* desirable activities that you engage in, the *more* you will pay in taxes. If you understand the options, you can choose those that meet your needs as you approach different stages of your financial life.

Many people resent the taxes they pay — they feel that they pay too much and get too little in return. Therefore, another potential benefit to your understanding the tax system is that you can become a more informed voter and citizen in the democratic process.

Your marginal income tax rate: the single most important tax number

"What's marginal about my taxes?" I hear you asking. "They're huge! They're not marginal in my life at all!" *Marginal* is a term often applied to those things that are small or minimally acceptable. Sort of like getting a C- on a school report card (or an A- if you're from an overachieving family).

Marginal tax rates are a powerful concept. Once you understand them, you can understand the implications of many financial strategies that affect the amount of taxes you pay. And because you pay taxes on your income from employment as well as on your investments held outside of retirement accounts, a lot of personal financial decisions are at stake.

First, you must understand that when it comes to taxes, *not all income is treated equally.* This fact is not self-evident. If you work for an employer and have a constant salary during the course of a year, a steady and equal amount in federal and state taxes is deducted from your paycheck. Thus, it appears as though all that earned income is being taxed equally.

In reality, however, you pay less tax on your *first* dollars of earnings and more tax on your *last* dollars of earnings. For example, if you're single and your taxable income (a term I define in the next section) totaled $30,000 during 1996, you paid federal tax at the rate of 15 percent on the first $24,000 of taxable income and 28 percent on income from $24,000 up to $30,000.

Table 7-1 gives federal tax rates for singles and married households filing jointly.

Table 7-1   1996 Federal Income Tax Brackets and Rates

Singles Taxable Income	Married-Filing-Jointly Taxable Income	Federal Tax Rate (Bracket)
Less than $24,000	Less than $40,100	15%
$24,000 to $58,150	$40,100 to $96,900	28%
$58,150 to $121,300	$96,900 to $147,700	31%
$121,300 to $263,750	$147,700 to $263,750	36%
Over $263,750	Over $263,750	39.6%

Your *marginal tax rate* is the rate of tax that you pay on your *last* or so-called *highest* dollars of income. In the example of a single person with taxable income of $30,000, that person's federal marginal tax rate is 28 percent. In other words, she effectively pays 28 percent federal tax on her last dollars of income — those dollars in excess of $24,000.

Alternative minimum tax (say what?)

You may find this hard to believe, but (as if the tax system weren't already complicated enough) there is actually a *second* tax system. This second system may raise your taxes even higher than they would have been normally. Let me explain while you reach for some aspirin.

Over the years, as the government has grown hungrier for revenue, taxpayers who slash their taxes by claiming lots of deductions have come under greater scrutiny. So the government created a second tax system — the *alternative minimum tax* (AMT) — to ensure that those with high deductions pay at least a certain amount of taxes on their incomes.

If you have a lot of deductions from state income taxes, real estate taxes, certain types of mortgage interest, and passive investments (for example, rental real estate), you may fall prey to AMT.

At the federal level lurk two AMT tax brackets: 26 percent for AMT income up to $175,000 and 28 percent for everything over that amount. AMT restricts you from claiming certain deductions and requires that you add back in normally tax-free income (like certain municipal-bond interest). So you have to figure your tax under the AMT system *and* under the other system and pay whichever amount is higher. Hope that aspirin is starting to kick in.

Your marginal tax rate allows you to quickly calculate additional taxes that you would pay on additional income. Conversely, you can delight in quantifying the amount of taxes that you save by reducing your taxable income, either by decreasing your income or by increasing your deductions.

As you are painfully aware, you not only pay federal income taxes but also state income taxes — that is, unless you live in Alaska, Florida, Nevada, South Dakota, Texas, Washington, or Wyoming. Those states have no state income taxes at all.

Your *total marginal rate* includes your federal *and* state tax rates.

You can look up your state tax rate by getting out your most recent year's state income tax-preparation booklet.

Taxable income defined

Taxable income is the amount of income on which you actually pay taxes. You don't pay taxes on your total income for the following two reasons:

  ✔ **Not all income is taxable.** For example, you pay federal tax on the interest you earn on a bank savings account but not on the interest from municipal bonds.

> ✔ **You get to subtract deductions from your income.** Some deductions are available just for being a living, breathing human being. In 1996, single people get an automatic $4,000 standard deduction, and married couples filing jointly get $6,700. (People over age 65 and those who are blind get a slightly higher deduction.) Other expenses, such as mortgage interest and property taxes, are deductible to the extent that your total deductions exceed the standard deductions.

How to Trim Taxes on Employment Income

You are supposed to pay taxes on any income you earn from work. Countless illegal ways are available to reduce your employment income — for example, not reporting it — but you could very well end up with a heap of penalties and extra interest charges on top of the taxes you owe. And you might even get tossed in jail. Because I don't want you to lose even more money by paying unnecessary penalties and serving jail time to boot, this section focuses on the many *legal* ways to reduce your taxes.

Retirement plan contributions

A retirement plan is one of the few painless and completely legal ways to reduce your taxable employment income. Besides reducing your taxes, you build up a nest egg so that you don't have to work for the rest of your life.

From your taxable income you can deduct money that you tuck away into employer-based retirement plans, such as 401(k) or 403(b) accounts, or into self-employed plans like SEP-IRAs or Keoghs. Therefore, if you contribute $1,000 to one of these plans and your combined federal and state marginal tax rate is 35 percent, you reduce your federal and state taxes by $350. Like the sound of that? How about this: Contribute another $1,000, and your taxes drop *another* $350 (so long as you're still in the same marginal tax rate).

If this process sounds easy, that's because it is. In fact, everyone should invest in a retirement plan. You benefit both in the short-term and the long-term. So why don't more people take advantage of this tax break?

Many people miss this opportunity to reduce their taxes because they *spend* all (or too much) of their current employment income and, therefore, have nothing (or little) left to put into a retirement account. If this scenario sounds familiar, you need to reduce your spending first in order to be able to contribute money to a retirement plan. Take an immediate tour through Chapter 6, which explains how to reduce your spending.

If your employer does not offer the option of saving money through a retirement plan, see whether you can drum up support for it. Lobby the benefits and human resource departments. If they resist, you might add this to your list of reasons to consider other employment (but don't leave for this reason alone). Many employers offer this valuable benefit, but others don't. Some company decision-makers themselves don't understand the value of these accounts. Other employers think that these accounts cost an arm and a leg to set up and administer.

If your employer does not offer a retirement savings plan, individual retirement account (IRA) contributions may or may not be tax-deductible, based on your circumstances. You should first exhaust contributions to the previously mentioned accounts that are tax-deductible. Chapter 12 contains all the details you need to determine whether you should contribute to an IRA and if your IRA contribution is tax-deductible.

Income shifting

Income shifting, which has nothing to do with money laundering, is a more esoteric tax-reduction technique and is an option only to those who can control *when* they receive their income.

For example, suppose that your employer tells you in late December that you're eligible for a bonus. You are offered the option to receive your bonus in either December or January. Looking ahead, if you're pretty certain that you will be in a higher tax bracket next year, you should choose to receive your bonus in December.

Or suppose that you run your own business and think that you'll be in a lower tax bracket next year. Perhaps you plan to take time off to be with a newborn or take an extended trip. You can send out some invoices later in the year so that your customers won't pay you until January, which falls in the next tax year.

Investment Income Reducing Techniques

For investments that you hold in *tax-sheltered* retirement accounts (IRAs and 401(k) plans, for example), you don't need to worry about taxes. This money is not taxed until you actually withdraw funds from the retirement account.

For investments that you hold outside of tax-sheltered retirement accounts, the distributions and profits on those investments are exposed to taxation when you receive them. Interest, dividends, and profits (called *capital gains*) from the sale of an investment at a price higher than the purchase price are all taxed.

Taxes on investment income should definitely concern you if you are in a relatively high tax bracket. If you're in the 31 percent or higher federal bracket (which kicks in for singles with taxable income over $58,150 and couples filing jointly over $96,900), you should pay attention to the rest of this section.

If you're in the 28 percent federal tax bracket, these strategies may or may not help. Pay close attention to the issues that increase or decrease the benefits of following each of the strategies.

If you're in the 15 percent federal bracket, you can probably skip this section. Or you may sit quietly at your desk and amuse yourself until the rest of the class is finished.

While this section explains some of the best methods to reduce the taxes on investments exposed to taxation, Chapter 13 discusses in detail how and where to invest money held outside of tax-sheltered retirement accounts.

Fill up those retirement accounts

If you have decent chunks of money invested outside retirement accounts, the distributions and profits on those investments are exposed to taxation. Unless you have that money earmarked for some specific nonretirement account purpose such as buying a home, and so long as hefty taxes aren't involved from selling off those investments at a great profit, the money will probably serve you better in a tax-sheltered retirement account.

Taking advantage of opportunities to direct money into retirement accounts gives you two possible tax bonuses. First, your contributions to the retirement account may be immediately tax-deductible (see Chapter 12 for complete details). Second, the distributions and growth of the investments in the retirement accounts aren't taxed until withdrawal.

Invest in tax-free money market funds and bonds

If you're in a high enough tax bracket, you may find that you come out ahead with tax-free investments. Tax-free investments pay investment income, which is exempt from either federal tax, state tax, or both.

Such investments yield less than comparable investments that produce taxable income. But because of the difference in taxes, the earnings from tax-free investments *can* end up being greater than what you're left with from taxable investments.

Tax-free money market funds can be a better alternative to bank savings accounts, the interest from which is subject to taxation. Likewise, tax-free bonds are longer-term investments that pay tax-free interest and may be a better investment option for you than bank certificates of deposit, Treasury bills and bonds, and other investments that produce taxable income. (See Chapter 13 for more specifics on which tax-free investments may be right for your situation.)

Select other tax-friendly investments

Too often, when selecting investments, people mistakenly focus on past rates of return. We all know that the past is no guarantee of the future. But an even worse mistake is choosing an investment with a reportedly high rate of return without considering tax consequences. What you get to keep — after taxes — is what matters in the long run.

Mutual funds

Mutual funds are a good example. When comparing two similar funds, most people prefer a fund that averages returns of 14 percent per year to a fund earning 12 percent. But what if the 14-percent-per-year fund causes you to pay a lot more in taxes? What if, after factoring in taxes, the 14-percent-per-year fund nets just 9 percent, while the 12-percent-per-year fund nets an effective 10-percent return? In such a case, you'd be unwise to choose a fund solely on the basis of the higher (pre-tax) reported rate of return.

I call investments that appreciate in value and don't distribute much in the way of taxable income *tax friendly*. Examples include growth stocks, which pay low taxable dividends, and mutual funds that invest in such stocks. See Chapter 11 for more information.

Real estate

Real estate is one of the few areas with privileged status in the tax code. In addition to deductions allowed for mortgage interest and property taxes, you can depreciate rental property to reduce your taxable income. Depreciation is a special tax deduction allowed for the gradual wear and tear on rental real estate.

If your rental property shows a loss for the year (when you figure your properties' income and expenses), you may be able to take this loss on your tax return. If your adjusted gross income (AGI) is less than $100,000, and you actively participate in managing the property, you are allowed to deduct your losses on operating rental real estate of up to $25,000 per year. (Your *AGI* is your total wage, interest, dividend, and all other income minus retirement account contributions and losses from investments.)

If you make more than $100,000 per year, you start to lose these write-offs. At an income of $150,000 or above, you cannot deduct rental real estate losses from your other income. People in the real estate business (for example, agents and developers) who work more than 750 hours per year in the industry may not be subject to these rules.

Strategies to Increase Your Deductions

Deductions are just that: You subtract them from your income after totaling your income and before calculating the tax you owe. To make things more complicated, the IRS gives you two methods for determining your total deductions. The good news is that you get to pick the method that leads to greater deductions — and, hence, lower taxes.

Standard deductions

The first method for deductions requires no thinking or calculating. If you have a relatively uncomplicated financial life, taking the so-called standard deduction is generally the better option. Symptoms of a simple tax life are not earning a high income, renting your house or apartment, and lacking unusually large expenses from medical bills, moving expenses, charitable contributions or loss due to theft or catastrophe.

As mentioned earlier in this chapter, single folks qualify for a $4,000 standard deduction, and married couples filing jointly get a $6,700 standard deduction in 1996. If you're 65 or older or blind, you get a slightly higher standard deduction.

Itemized deductions

The other method of determining your allowable deductions is itemizing them on your tax return. This method is definitely more of a hassle, but if you can tally up more than the standard amounts noted in the preceding section, itemizing saves you money. Use Schedule A of IRS Form 1040 for summing up your itemized deductions.

Many of the categories on Schedule A, such as line 10, "Home mortgage interest and points reported to you on Form 1098," are reasonably self-evident. If you own your home and have a mortgage, early in the new year your bank should send you Form 1098, which tells you to the penny how much deductible mortgage interest you paid.

Organizing to deduct

The hard part for most people is locating Form 1098 and all the other scraps of paper you need when you're completing your tax return. Setting up a filing system can be a *very* big time-saver:

- ✔ **One receptacle.** If you have limited patience for setting up neat file folders and you lead an uncomplicated financial life (that is, you haven't saved receipts throughout the year that you need for tax purposes), you can confine your filing to January and February. During those months, you should receive tax summary statements on wages paid by your employer (Form W-2), investment income (Forms 1099), and home mortgage interest (Form 1098) in the mail. Set up a folder that's labeled with something easy to remember ("1996 Taxes" is a brilliant choice) and dump these papers as well as your tax booklet into it. When you're ready to crunch numbers, you should have everything you need to complete the form.

- ✔ **Many receptacles.** A more thorough approach is to organize the bills you pay into individual folders during the entire year. This method is essential if you own your own business and need to tabulate your expenditures for office supplies each year. No one is going to send you a form totaling your office expenditures for the year — you're on your own.

- ✔ **Software as receptacle.** Software programs can help organize your tax information during the year and can save you time and accounting fees come tax-preparation time. See Chapter 21 for more information about tax and financial software.

A number of available resources explain in excruciating detail what you can and cannot deduct on Schedule A. These include IRS instructions, preparation guide books, and software programs, which are reviewed later in the chapter. The following are the most *overlooked* deductions and deduction strategies. Some are listed on Schedule A, and others are on Form 1040 itself.

Purchasing real estate

When you buy a home, two big ongoing expenses of home ownership — the interest on your mortgage and your property taxes — are deductions you can claim on Schedule A. You are allowed to claim mortgage interest deductions for a primary residence (where you actually live) and on a second home for mortgage debt totaling $1,000,000 (and a home equity loan of up to $100,000).

You can also deduct the full amount of your property taxes, even if you live in a multimillion-dollar mansion. Such a deal!

Shifting or bunching deductions

When you total up your itemized deductions on Schedule A and the total is lower than the standard deduction, then you should take the standard deduction. This total is worth checking each year, because you may have more deductions in some years than others, and itemizing may make sense.

Because you can control when you pay particular expenses that are eligible for itemizing, you can *shift* or *bunch* more of them into the select years when you have enough deductions to take advantage of itemizing. Suppose, for example, that you are using the standard deduction this year because you don't have many itemized deductions. Late in the year, though, you become certain that you'll be buying a home next year. With mortgage interest and property taxes to write off, you also know that you can itemize next year. It makes sense, then, to shift and collect as many deductible expenses as possible into next year. For example, if you typically make more charitable contributions in December because of the barrage of solicitations you receive when you're in the giving mood, you may want to write the checks in January rather than in December.

If you're sure that you won't have enough deductions in the current year to itemize, try to shift as many expenses as you can into the next tax year.

Trading consumer debt for mortgage debt

If you own real estate and haven't borrowed the maximum that you can and if you've run up high-interest consumer debt, you may be able to trade one debt for another. If you can refinance your mortgage and pull out extra cash to pay off your credit card, auto loan, or other costly credit lines, you may be able to save yourself money.

You can usually borrow at a lower interest rate for a mortgage and get a tax deduction as a bonus, which lowers the effective borrowing cost further. Consumer debt, such as on auto loans and credit cards, is not tax-deductible.

This strategy involves some danger. Borrowing against the equity in your home can be an addictive habit. I've seen cases in which people run up significant consumer debt three or four times and then refinance their home the same number of times over the years to bail themselves out.

An appreciating home creates the illusion that excess spending isn't really costing you. But debt is debt, and all borrowed money has to be repaid. In the long run, you wind up with greater mortgage debt, and paying it off takes a bigger bite out of your monthly income. Refinancing and establishing home equity lines cost you more in terms of loan application fees and other charges (points, appraisals, credit reports, and so on).

At a minimum, continued expansion of your mortgage debt handicaps your ability to work toward other financial goals. In the worst case, easy access to borrowing encourages bad spending habits that can lead to bankruptcy or foreclosure against your debt-ridden home.

Charitable contributions and expenses

If you itemize, you can deduct contributions made to charities. For example, most people know that when they write a check for $50 to their favorite church or college, they can deduct it. *Note:* Make sure to get a receipt for contributions of $250 or more because a canceled check is no longer sufficient documentation for the IRS.

Many taxpayers overlook the fact that you can also deduct expenses for work you do with charitable organizations. For example, when you go to a soup kitchen to help prepare and serve meals, you can deduct your transportation costs to get there. You just need to keep track of your bus fares or driving mileage. The IRS currently allows a deduction of 12 cents per mile.

You also can deduct the fair market value (which could be determined from thrift stores selling similar merchandise) of donations of clothing, household appliances, furniture, and other goods to charities, many of which will even drive to your home to pick up the stuff. See whether organizations such as the Salvation Army, Goodwill, or others are interested in your donation. Just make sure to keep some documentation — write up an itemized list and get it signed by the charity. Consider taking pictures of more valuable donations.

Auto registration fees and state insurance

If you don't currently itemize, you may be surprised to learn that your state income taxes are itemizable. If you must pay a fee to the state to register and license your car, you can itemize the expenditure as a deduction (line 8, "Other Taxes"). The IRS only allows you to deduct that part of the fee that relates to the value of your car. The state organization that collects the fee should be able to tell you what portion of the fee is deductible. If the organization is user-friendly, it will even show this figure for a fee on your invoice.

Several states — California, New York, New Jersey, and Rhode Island — have state disability insurance funds. If you pay into these funds (check your W-2), you can deduct this fee as state and local income taxes on line 5 of Schedule A.

Bad news — limitations on deductions

If you are a high income earner, the IRS has imposed a limit on how much in itemized deductions you may subtract when calculating your taxable income. You have to reduce your total itemized deductions by 3 percent of your income above $117,950.

Here's how it works. Say that your income is $137,950 and your total itemized deductions come to $30,000. Because your income exceeds $117,950 by $20,000, you have to reduce your itemized deductions by $600 ($20,000 × 3 percent). Although you started with itemized deductions of $30,000, you can deduct only $29,400.

Of course, given a large enough income and low enough total deductions, the 3 percent rule threatens to wipe out any deductions at all. Don't worry. The IRS has benevolently set a limit to the amount that your deductions can be reduced — no more than 80 percent. So if we take the preceding example but boost your income to $1 million, you would still get to deduct $6,000 because your $30,000 in deductions cannot be reduced by more than $24,000 ($30,000 × 80 percent).

If you are in this high income category and your spirits are down, here's a little consolation (and something to make it all a little more complicated). Not all of your deductions are subject to the 3 percent rule: medical and dental expenses, investment interest, casualty and theft losses, and gambling losses (please don't gamble!) are all exempt.

If you are a high income earner, knowing this 3 percent rule and all of its nuances is important because it can affect some of your financial decisions. The 3 percent rule raises your effective tax rate and may encourage you, for example, to spend less on a home or to pay off your mortgage faster because you don't merit a full deduction.

Deducting miscellaneous expenses

A number of so-called *miscellaneous expenses* are deductible on Schedule A. Most of these relate to your job or career and management of your finances.

Educational expenses

You may be able to deduct the cost of tuition, books, and travel to and from classes if your education is related to your career. Specifically, you can deduct these expenses if your course work improves your work skills. Continuing education classes for professionals may be deductible. If the law or your employer requires you to take courses to maintain your position, they are deductible. ***Note:*** Educational expenses that allow you to change or move into a new field or career are not deductible.

Job search and career counseling

After you obtain your first job, you may deduct legitimate costs related to finding another job within your field. For example, suppose that you're a chef in a steak house in Chicago and decide that you want to do stir fry in Los Angeles. You take a crash course in vegetarian cooking and then fly to L.A. a couple of

times for interviews. You can deduct the cost of the course and your trips —
even if you don't change jobs. And if you hire a career counselor to help you
figure everything out, you can deduct that cost as well.

On the other hand, if you're burned out on cooking and decide that you want to
become a professional volleyball player in L.A., that's a new career. You may get
a better tan, but you won't generate deductions from changing jobs.

Unreimbursed expenses related to your job

If you pay for your own subscriptions to trade journals to keep updated in your
field or buy a new desk and chair to ease back pain, you can deduct these costs.
If your job requires you to wear special clothes or a uniform, you can write off
the cost of purchasing and cleaning them, as long as the clothes aren't suitable
for wearing outside of work.

If you buy a computer for use outside the office at your own expense, you may
be able to deduct the cost if it's for the convenience of your employer, is a
condition of your employment, and is used more than half the time for business.

Union dues and membership fees for professional organizations are also
deductible.

Investment and tax-related expenses

Investment and tax-advisor fees are deductible, as are subscription costs for
investment-related publications. Accounting fees for preparing your tax return
or conducting tax planning during the year are deductible, as are legal fees
related to your taxes. If you purchase a home computer to track your investments or prepare your taxes, you can deduct that expense, too.

When you deduct miscellaneous expenses, you get to deduct only the amount
of these costs that exceeds 2 percent of your AGI. AGI (adjusted gross income)
is your total wage, interest, dividend, and all other income minus retirement
account contributions, self-employed health insurance, alimony paid, and
losses from investments.

Self-employment expenses

If you are self-employed, you can deduct a multitude of expenses from your
income before calculating the tax that you owe. If you buy a computer or office
furniture, you can deduct those expenses (sometimes they need to be gradually
deducted or *depreciated* over time). Salaries for your employees, office supplies,
rent or mortgage interest for your office space, and phone expenses are also
generally deductible.

Although some business owners cheat on their taxes, some self-employed folks don't take all the deductions they should. In some cases, people simply aren't aware of the wonderful world of deductions. Others are worried that large deductions will raise the risk of an audit.

If you fall into one of these categories, you should spend some time learning more about tax deductions; you will be convinced that taking full advantage of your eligible deductions makes sense and saves you money.

The following are common mistakes made by people who are their own bosses.

Being an island unto yourself

If you're self-employed, going it alone is usually a mistake when it comes to taxes. You must educate yourself to make the tax laws work for you rather than against you. It's worth the money to hire tax help — either in the form of a tax advisor and/or by using some good tax guide books and computer software. (I recommend some later in this chapter.)

Making administrative tax screwups

When you are self-employed, you are responsible for the correct and timely filing of all taxes owed on your income or on that of your employees. You need to make estimated tax payments on a quarterly basis. And if you have employees, you also need to withhold taxes on their income from each paycheck they receive and make timely payments to the IRS and to the appropriate state authorities. In addition to federal and state income tax, you also need to withhold and send in Social Security and any other state or locally mandated payroll taxes.

For paying taxes on your income, you can obtain Form 1040-ES with instructions from the IRS (call 800-TAX-FORM). This form comes complete with an estimated tax worksheet and the four payment coupons to send in with your quarterly tax payments.

If you want to learn the rules regarding withholding and submitting taxes from employees' paychecks, ask the IRS for Form 941 as well as Form 940, which is for unemployment insurance. And unless you're lucky enough to live in a state with no income taxes, remember to call for your state's estimated income tax package. Another alternative is to hire a payroll firm, such as Paychex (800-428-8170), to do all this drudgery for you.

Overlooking start-up expenses

Many small-business owners use some of their personal assets when starting a business. For example, perhaps you owned a home computer that you put to service for your new business. When you convert the computer to business use, you can deduct some of the original costs of purchase.

Receipts, receipts, and more receipts

When you pay with cash, following the paper trail for all the money you spent is hard for you (and the IRS in the event you're ever audited). At the end of the year, how are you going to remember how much you spent for parking or client meals if you keep no record? For purchases under $75, you don't need a receipt as proof, but you do need a system or written record of your daily petty cash purchases. Most pocket calendars or daily organizers include ledgers that allow you to jot down these small purchases. If you can't be that organized, at least get a receipt for cash transactions and stash them in a file folder in your desk. Or keep receipts in envelopes labeled with the month and year.

Depreciating what is deductible

One of the goodies in the last major tax bill that was passed (in 1993) was a provision that allows you to deduct up to 75 percent more of your equipment purchases annually. Now you can take up to $17,500 as a current year deduction (the previous limit was $10,000).

Choosing the wrong entity or form of organization

When you set up your own business, you can structure its legal and tax organization in a variety of ways. To incorporate or not to incorporate is the first question you want to answer. Those motivated to incorporate do so not out of a love of paperwork (which can be considerable) but out of the desire to shield themselves from liabilities and lawsuits that might be brought against the business.

A *corporation* is a separate legal entity from you, the individual. For example, if a customer slips on a stray banana peel at your office and decides to sue, if you're incorporated, the customer can sue your company but can't go after your personal assets. Incorporating makes more sense if you have employees, customers who visit the office, or if you do business with many vendors.

Incorporating is not always the right answer. For professional services, such as self-employed attorneys, physicians, or tax advisors, incorporating may not necessarily be useful as protection against professional negligence suits related to their work. In such cases, the law treats the business and the professional as one and the same. The answer for these folks is *professional liability insurance*. Check with the professional association(s) in your field for information on insurers who offer such policies.

Not funding a retirement plan

I am always shocked and amazed by the number of accountants who do not encourage their clients to contribute to retirement plans to reduce taxes. You should be saving money toward retirement anyway, and you can't beat the tax break. People who are self-employed are allowed to save up to about 20 percent of their net income on an annual basis. To learn more about SEP-IRAs, Keoghs, and other retirement plans, see Chapter 12.

Not using numbers to help manage business

If you are a small-business owner who doesn't track his income, expenses, staff performance, and customer data on a regular basis, your tax return may be the one and only time during the year when you take a financial snapshot of your business. After you go to all the time, trouble, and expense to file your tax return, make sure that you reap the rewards of all your work: Use those numbers to help analyze and manage your business.

Some bookkeepers and tax preparers can provide you with management information reports on your business from the tax data they compile for you. Just ask! Likewise, software packages can help. See recommendations later in this chapter

Not paying family help

If your children, spouse, or other relatives help with some aspect of your business, consider paying them for the work. Besides showing them that you value their work, this practice may reduce your family's tax liability. For example, a child is usually in a lower tax bracket than you are. So by shifting income to the child, you cut your tax bill.

Tax Preparation and Planning Options

All sorts of ways to prepare your tax return exist. Which approach makes sense for you depends on the complexity of your situation and your level of interest and knowledge in taxes.

Regardless of which approach you take, you should be taking financial moves during the year to reduce your taxes. By the time you actually file your return in the following year, you are usually too late to take advantage of many tax-reduction strategies.

Doing it yourself

Odds are, you do many things for yourself, such as cooking, shopping, and repairing your home. You may do these chores because you enjoy them, because you save money by doing them, or because you want to develop particular skills. For the same reasons, you may also choose to do-it-yourself when it comes time to file your tax return.

By preparing your own tax return, you develop a better understanding of the ins and outs of the tax code and of your own financial situation. Done on your own, a tax return gives you a condensed review of your financial history over the past year; it should also plant some ideas on how to better manage your finances in the year to come.

If your financial situation doesn't change much from year to year, neither does your return. You may need to do a little reading to keep up with the small number of changes in the tax system and laws that might affect your situation.

IRS publications and phone assistance

If you have a simple, straightforward tax return, filing it on your own using only the IRS instructions is fine. This approach is as cheap as you can get. The main costs are time, patience, photocopying expenses (you should always keep a copy for your files), and postage to mail the completed tax return.

This approach has a lot in common with an Easter egg hunt. If you've ever hunted Easter eggs, you know the prizes are well hidden (from a child's perspective, anyway) and require some real searching to ferret out. In my own egg-hunting experience, I don't recall any large, flashing neon signs reading "DON'T MISS THIS ONE!" pointing to hidden eggs. Likewise, IRS publications don't, in general, have Tip or Warning icons like this book has. For example, here's something you won't see in an IRS publication:

STOP! ONE OF THE MOST COMMONLY OVERLOOKED DEDUCTIONS IS A TAX-DEDUCTIBLE RETIREMENT ACCOUNT CONTRIBUTION. YOU STILL HAVE TIME TO START ONE AND SLASH HUNDREDS, MAYBE *THOUSANDS* OF DOLLARS FROM YOUR TAX BILL! HURRY!

Another danger of relying on the IRS is that it has been known to give wrong information on a more-than-infrequent basis. If you call the IRS with a question, be sure to take notes about your conversation to protect yourself in the event of an audit. Date your notes and include the name of the tax employee you talked to, what you asked, and the employee's responses. File your notes in a folder with a copy of your completed return.

In addition to the standard instructions that come with your tax return, the IRS offers some free (actually paid for with your tax dollars) and sometimes useful booklets. Publication 17, *Your Federal Income Tax,* is designed for individual tax-return preparation. Publication 334, *Tax Guide for Small Businesses,* is for (you guessed it) small-business tax-return preparation. These publications are more comprehensive than the basic IRS instructions. Call 800-TAX-FORM to request these booklets.

Other preparation and advice guides

Books about tax preparation and tax planning that are written in clear, simple English and that highlight common problem areas are invaluable. They supplement the official instructions not only by helping you to complete your return correctly but also by showing you how to save as much money as possible. Consider picking up a copy of *Taxes For Dummies* (as co-author, I'm a bit biased).

Software

If you have access to a computer, tax-preparation software can be helpful. Think of it as having a squadron of accountants in your computer. Plus you don't have to go to the library to get all the forms for your particular return only to discover that the library is out of them and then call the IRS and wait for weeks for your forms to arrive in the mail — they're in the software!

Software also has the virtue of automatically recalculating all the appropriate numbers on your return when one number changes — no more whiting out math errors because your dog was sleeping on some of the receipts.

Among the better tax-preparation software packages on the market are

- ✔ TurboTax (for Windows and DOS); MacinTax (for the Macintosh)
- ✔ Kiplinger Taxcut (for DOS, Windows, and the Macintosh)

Hiring help

Some people hire a contractor to help with a home-remodeling project because they lack the time, interest, energy, or skill to do it themselves. For the same reasons, some choose to hire a tax advisor.

Competent tax specialists can save you money — sometimes more than enough to pay their fees — by identifying tax-reduction strategies you may overlook. They can also reduce the likelihood of an audit, which can be triggered by blunders you might make. Mediocre and lousy tax preparers, on the other hand, may make mistakes and not be aware of sound ways to reduce your tax bite.

Tax practitioners come with varying backgrounds, training, and credentials. One credential is not necessarily better than another. The four main types are preparers, enrolled agents (EAs), Certified Public Accountants (CPAs), and tax attorneys. The more training and specialization a tax practitioner has (and the more affluent his clients), the higher his hourly fee usually is. Fees and competence at all levels of the profession vary significantly. If you do hire a tax advisor and you're not sure of the quality of work performed and the soundness of the advice, try getting a second opinion.

Preparers

Among all the tax practitioners, preparers generally have the least amount of training, and a greater proportion of them work part-time. As with financial planners, no national regulations apply to preparers, and no licensing is required.

H&R Block is the largest and most well-known tax-preparation firm in the country with about 9,000 offices nationwide. In addition to Block and other national firms such as Jackson Hewitt and Triple Check, there are also lots of mom-and-pop shops. The appeal of preparers is that they are relatively inexpensive — they can do most basic returns for around $100 or so. The drawback, of course, is that you may be hiring a preparer who doesn't know much more than you do.

Preparers make the most sense for folks who have relatively simple financial lives, who are budget minded, and who hate doing their own taxes. If you're not good about hanging onto receipts or don't want to keep your own files with background details about your taxes, you should definitely shop around for a tax preparer who's going to be around for a few years. You may need all that stuff someday for an audit, and many tax preparers keep and organize their clients' documentation rather than return everything each year. (Can you blame them for keeping it after they went to the trouble of sorting it all out of the shopping bags you brought them?) Also, going with a firm that is open year-round may be safer (some small shops are open only during tax season) in case tax questions or problems arise.

Enrolled agents (EAs)

A person must pass IRS scrutiny in order to be called an *enrolled agent*. This license allows the agent to represent you before the IRS in the event of an audit. Continuing education is also required. Training to become an EA is generally longer and more sophisticated than that for a typical preparer.

Enrolled agents' prices tend to fall between those of a preparer and a CPA. Returns with a few of the more common schedules (such as Schedule A for deductions and Schedule B for interest and dividends) shouldn't cost more than a couple hundred dollars to prepare.

EAs are best for people with moderately complex returns who don't necessarily need complicated tax-planning advice throughout the year (although some EAs provide this service as well as prepare returns). You can get names and telephone numbers of EAs in your area by contacting the National Association of Enrolled Agents (800-424-4339).

Certified public accountants (CPAs)

Certified public accountants go through significant training and examination to receive the CPA credential. In order to maintain this designation, a CPA must also complete a fair number of continuing education classes every year.

CPA fees vary tremendously. Most charge around $100 per hour, but CPAs at large companies and in high cost-of-living areas tend to charge somewhat more.

CPAs are of greatest value to people completing some of the more unusual and less user-friendly schedules, such as K-1 for partnerships, Schedule C for self-employed folks, or Form 8829 for home office deductions.

If your return is uncomplicated and your financial situation is stable, hiring a high-priced CPA year after year to fill in the blanks is a waste of money. A CPA once bragged to me that he was making about $500 per hour from some of his clients' returns that required only 20 minutes of an assistant's time to complete.

Paying for the additional cost of a CPA on an ongoing basis makes sense if you can afford it and if your situation is reasonably complex or dynamic. If you are self-employed and/or file lots of other schedules, it may be worth hiring a CPA. But you needn't do so year after year. If your situation grows complex one year and then stabilizes, consider getting help for the perplexing year and then using preparation guides, software, or a lower-cost preparer or enrolled agent in the future.

Tax attorneys

Tax attorneys deal with more complicated tax problems and issues, which usually have some legal angle. Unless you're a superhigh-income earner with a complex financial life, hiring a tax attorney to prepare your annual return is prohibitively expensive. In fact, many tax attorneys don't prepare returns as a normal practice.

Because of their level of specialization and training, tax attorneys tend to have the highest hourly billing rates — $200 to $300 per hour is not unusual.

Help, I Got an Audit Notice!

On a list of real-life nightmares, most people would rank tax audits right up there with rectal exams and needing to appear in court to contest a speeding ticket.

The primary trauma of an audit is that many people feel like they're on trial and are being accused of a crime. Take a deep breath and don't panic.

First of all, you may be one of the tens of thousands of taxpayers whose returns are audited at random. No, the IRS isn't headed by sadists. Random audits help the IRS identify common areas on tax forms where taxpayers make mistakes or try to cheat.

Second, you might be getting audited simply because a business that reports tax information on you, or someone at the IRS, made an error regarding the data on your return.

About 20 percent of audited returns are left unchanged by the audit — that is, you don't end up owing more money. In fact, if you're the lucky sort, you may be one of the 5 percent of folks who actually gets a refund because the audit finds a mistake in your favor!

Unfortunately, you'll most likely be one of the roughly 75 percent of audit survivors who end up owing more tax money. The amount of additional tax that you owe in interest and penalties hinges on how your audit goes.

Audit preparation

Preparing for an audit is sort of like preparing for a test in school. The IRS informs you of which sections of your tax return the agency wants to examine.

The first decision you face when you get an audit notice is whether to handle it yourself or turn to a tax advisor to represent you. Hiring representation costs money out-of-pocket but may save you time, stress, and money.

If you normally prepare your own return and are comfortable with your understanding of the areas being audited, then do it yourself. If the amount of tax money in question is small in comparison to the fee you'd pay the tax advisor to represent you, self-representation is probably the answer. However, if you're likely to turn into a babbling, intimidated fool and are unsure how to present your situation, hire a tax advisor to represent you (see the "Hiring help" section earlier in this chapter for information about whom to hire).

If you decide to handle the audit yourself, get your act together sooner rather than later. Don't wait until the night before to start gathering receipts and other documentation. You may find, for example, that you can't find certain documents and need to contact others to get copies.

You need to document and be ready to speak with the auditor only about the areas the audit notice said were being investigated. Organize the various documents and receipts into folders. You want to make it as easy as possible for the auditor to review your materials. *Don't* show up, dump shopping bags full of receipts and paperwork on the auditor's desk, and say, "Here it is — *you* figure it out."

Whatever you do, *don't ignore your audit request letter.* The IRS is the ultimate bill-collection agency. And if you end up owing more money (the unhappy result of most audits), the sooner you pay, the less interest and penalties you'll owe.

The day of reckoning

Two people with identical situations can walk into an audit and come out with very different results. The loser can end up owing much more in taxes and have the audit expanded to include other parts of the return. The winner can end up owing less tax money than he or she really should pay under the tax laws.

Here's how to be a winner:

✔ **Treat the auditor as a human being.** Obvious advice, yes, but very often not practiced by taxpayers. You may be resentful or angry about being audited. You may be tempted to gnash your teeth and tell the auditor how unfair it is that an honest taxpayer like you had to spend scores of hours getting ready for this. You might feel like ranting and raving about how the government wastes too much of your tax money or that the party in power is out to get you. Bite your tongue.

Believe it or not, most auditors are decent people just trying to do their job. They are well aware that taxpayers don't like seeing them. Don't suck up, either — just relax and be yourself. Behave as you would around a boss whom you like — with respect and congeniality.

✔ **Stick to the knitting.** Your audit is to discuss *only* the sections of your tax return that are in question. The more you talk about other areas or things that you're doing, the more likely the auditor will probe into other items. Don't bring documentation for parts of your return not being audited. Besides creating more work for yourself, you might be opening a can of worms that needn't be opened.

✔ **Don't argue when you disagree.** State your case. If the auditor wants to disallow a deduction or otherwise increase the taxes you owe and you don't agree, state once why you don't. If the auditor won't budge, don't get into a knock-down, drag-out confrontation. He or she may not want to lose face and is inclined to find additional tax money — that's the auditor's job. *Remember:* If necessary, you can plead your case with several layers of people above your auditor. If that fails and you still feel wronged, you can take your case to tax court.

✔ **Don't be intimidated.** Most auditors are not tax geniuses. The work is stressful — being in a job in which people dislike seeing you is not easy. Turnover is quite high. Thus many auditors are fairly young, just-out-of-school types who majored in something like English, history, or sociology. They may know less about tax and financial matters than you do. The basic IRS tax boot camp that auditors go through doesn't come close to covering all the technical details and nuances in the tax code. So you may not be at such a disadvantage in your tax knowledge after all, especially if you work with a tax advisor (most of whom know more about the tax system than the average IRS auditor).

Chapter 8

Saving for Specific Goals

• •

In This Chapter

▶ Prioritizing your financial goals

▶ Making retirement-account funding a priority

▶ Nonretirement goals and how to fund them

▶ What you need to get through retirement

▶ Ways to make up for lost time

▶ Overcoming objections to saving in retirement accounts

• •

*M*ost people that I know have dreams. Here is a list of some of the most common dreams, in no particular order:

▶ **Become part of the landed gentry.** Renting and dealing with landlords can be a financial and emotional drag, so most folks want to buy into the American dream and own some real estate — the most basic of which is to own your own home.

▶ **Retire.** No, retiring does not imply sitting on a rocking chair watching the world go by while hoping that some long lost friend, your son's or daughter's family, or the neighborhood dog comes by to visit. *Retiring* is a catch-all term for discontinuing full-time work or perhaps not even working for pay at all.

▶ **Educate the kids.** No, all those diaper changes, late-night feedings, and trips to the zoo aren't enough to get junior out of your house and into the real world as a productive, self-sufficient adult. You may want to help your children get a college education, and, unfortunately, that can cost a truckload of dough.

▶ **Own your own business.** Many employees desire to become an employer so that they can face the challenges and rewards that come with being the boss. The primary reason that many people continue to dream without actually plunging into their own small business is that they lack the money to do so. Although many businesses don't require gobs of start-up cash, almost all require that you withstand a substantial reduction in your income in the early years.

Because each of us is unique, each of us can have other goals, unique to our own situation. No matter — accomplishing such goals almost always requires saving money. As one of my favorite Chinese proverbs says, "Do not wait until you are thirsty to dig a well."

The first chapters in this book help you to assess your current financial situation and to begin to develop good savings habits. In this chapter, you move on to more advanced topics, such as determining how much you need to save in order to achieve your important financial goals.

Prioritizing Your Savings Goals

Unless you earn really big bucks or have a large family inheritance to fall back on, your personal and financial desires will probably outstrip your resources. Thus, you must prioritize your goals if you want to accomplish them.

Only you know what's most important to you

One of the biggest mistakes that I see people make is to rush into financial decisions without considering what is really important to them. Because many of us get caught up in the responsibilities of our daily lives, time for reflection often never happens.

From the experience I've had counseling and teaching many people about better personal financial management, I can tell you that the people who accomplish their goals aren't necessarily smarter or higher income earners than those who don't.

People who accomplish their goals identify their goals and work toward them.

The advantages of retirement accounts

Where possible, you should try to save and invest in accounts that offer you a tax advantage. That's precisely what retirement accounts do for you. These accounts — known by such enlightening acronyms and names as 401(k), 403(b), SEP-IRAs, Keoghs, and so on — offer tax breaks to people of all economic means (see Chapter 12):

> ✔ **Contributions are usually tax-deductible.** I think that retirement accounts are misnamed. They should really be called *tax-reduction accounts*. If they were, people might be more excited about contributing to them. For many, avoiding higher taxes is the motivating force that opens the account and starts the contributions.

By putting money in a retirement account, you are not only planning wisely for your future, but you are also getting an immediate financial reward: lower taxes — and lower taxes mean more money available for saving and investing.

Retirement account contributions are generally not taxed at either the federal or state levels. If you're paying say 35 percent between federal and state taxes (refer to Chapter 7 for your tax bracket), a $5,000 contribution into a retirement account would lower your taxes by $1,750.

✔ **Returns on your investment compound over time without taxation.** After money is in a retirement account, any interest, dividends, and appreciation add to your account without being taxed.

Of course, there's no such thing as a free lunch — these accounts don't allow for *permanent* tax avoidance. Yet, you can get a really great lunch at a discount — you get to defer taxes on all of the accumulating gains and profits until you withdraw the money down the road. Thus, more money is working for you over a longer period of time.

Dealing with competing goals

Unless one enjoys paying higher taxes, why would anyone save money outside of retirement accounts? The reason is that accomplishing some financial goals is not possible through saving in these retirement accounts.

If you're accumulating down payment money for a home purchase or to start or buy a business, for example, you'll need to save that money outside of a retirement account. Why? Because if you withdraw funds from retirement accounts before age 59 ½ and you are not retired, you not only have to pay income taxes on the withdrawals, but you also must pay *early withdrawal penalties* — 10 percent in federal charges and varying amounts of state charges.

Because each of us is constrained by our financial resources, we must prioritize our goals. Before funding your retirement accounts and racking up those tax breaks, read the rest of this section to consider the importance of accomplishing other common goals.

Building Emergency Reserves

If your only source of emergency funds right now is a high-interest credit card, it's in your financial interest to save at least three to six months' worth of living expenses in an accessible account before funding a retirement account or saving for other goals.

Avoiding early withdrawal penalties

There are times and ways to avoid the early withdrawal penalties that the tax gods normally apply.

Suppose that you read this book at a young age, develop sound financial habits early, and save enough to retire before age 59½. In that case, you can take money out of your retirement account without triggering penalties. The IRS allows you to withdraw money before 59 ½ if you do so in equal, annual installments based on your remaining life expectancy. The IRS (this is slightly chilling) even has a little table that allows you to look up your life expectancy.

The other conditions under which you can make penalty-free early withdrawals from retirement accounts are not as much fun: If you have catastrophic medical expenses or a disability, you are exempt from the penalties.

If you get in a financial pinch while you're still employed, be aware that some company retirement plans allow you to borrow against your cash balance (it's like loaning money to yourself; the interest payments go back into your account). Another strategy to meet a short-term financial emergency is to withdraw money from your Individual Retirement Account (IRA) and return it within 60 days to avoid paying penalties. I don't generally recommend this because of the penalties invoked if you miss the 60-day deadline, even by just one crummy day.

If you lose your job and simply need money to live on, the penalties do apply. However, if you're earning so little income that you need to raid your retirement account, you are surely in a low tax bracket. The lower income taxes you pay as compared to the taxes you would have paid on that money had you not sheltered it in a retirement account in the first place should make up for most or all of the penalty.

No one can predict the future. There is simply no reliable way to tell what may happen with your job, health, or family. Because you don't know what the future holds in store, preparing for the unexpected is financially wise. Even if you're the lucky sort who sometimes finds $5 bills on street corners or wins radio call-in contests, you can't control the sometimes chaotic world in which you find yourself.

Conventional wisdom says that you should have approximately six months of living expenses put away for an emergency. This particular amount may or may not be right for you because it depends, of course, on how expensive the emergency is. Why six months, anyway? And where should you put it? Unfortunately, no hard and fast rules exist. How much of an emergency stash you need depends on your situation.

I recommend saving the following emergency amounts under differing circumstances (In Chapter 13, I recommend good places to invest this money):

✔ **Three months' living expenses** if you have other accounts such as a 401(k) or family members and close friends that you could tap for a short-term loan. This minimalist approach makes sense when you're trying to maximize investments elsewhere (for example, in retirement accounts) or have very stable sources of income (employment or otherwise).

✔ **Six months' living expenses** if you don't have other places to turn for a loan and/or have some instability in your employment situation or source of income.

✔ **Up to one year's living expenses** if you don't have other places to turn for a loan and if your income fluctuates wildly from year to year. If your profession involves a high risk of job loss, and if it could take you a long time to find another, you also have a greater need for a significant cash reserve.

Establishing an emergency reserve should take priority over saving for other purposes, unless you have access to money through other resources such as family or are willing to borrow from a retirement account.

Saving to Buy a Home or Business

When you're starting out financially, deciding whether to save money to buy a home or to put money into a retirement account presents a real dilemma. In the long run, owning your own home is a wise financial move. On the other hand, starting early to save for retirement makes achieving your goal easier.

The bottom line is: You should be doing both — owning a home and saving for retirement. If you're really eager to own a home, then you can throw all of your savings toward achieving that goal and temporarily put retirement savings on the back burner. If you're not in such a rush, you can save for both purposes simultaneously.

You may be able to have your cake and eat it too if you work for an employer that allows borrowing against retirement account balances. You can save money in the retirement account and then borrow against it for the down payment. Be careful, though. Retirement account loans typically must be paid back within a set number of years (check with your employer) or immediately if you quit or lose your job.

In saving money for starting or buying a business, you face the same dilemma as when deciding to save to buy a house: If you fund your retirement accounts to the exclusion of building money for your small business dreams, your dreams may never become a reality. Generally, I advocate hedging your bets by saving some money in your tax-sheltered retirement accounts as well as some toward your business venture. Although an investment in your own small business can produce great rewards, this type of investment is usually a good deal riskier than investing in real estate in the form of your own home.

Saving for Children's Educational Expenses

Wanting to provide for your children's future is perfectly natural. But doing so before you've saved adequately toward your own goals can be a major financial mistake.

It may sound selfish, but you need to take care of *your* future first. If you're not taking advantage of saving through tax-sheltered retirement accounts, you should do so before you set aside money in custodial savings accounts for your kids. This practice isn't selfish — do you really want to have to leech off your kids when you're old and frail because you didn't save any money for yourself?

Retirement savings accounts are a smart investment for the future of the entire family, and they give you immediate tax breaks. Besides, the college financial-aid system effectively penalizes you for saving money outside of retirement accounts. See Chapter 14 for a complete explanation for how to save for educational expenses.

Don't buy cash-value life insurance plans

Life insurance salespeople who earn commissions selling life insurance are often eager to sell you cash-value life insurance policies, which combine life insurance protection with a type of savings account. Such policies are not anywhere near as good for you as they are for the agents who earn large commissions selling them. Most people are far better off buying term life insurance (see Chapter 17 for more details).

You may very well be suckered into buying a cash-value life insurance policy as a savings vehicle for accomplishing goals such as retiring or paying for a child's educational costs. Don't fall for this sales trap.

Cash-value life insurance policies give you no immediate tax deduction. By contrast, a retirement savings plan like a 401(k), 403(b), SEP-IRA, or Keogh allows you to deduct your contributions from your taxable income. Even if you don't have access to these plans, you're better off saving and investing through an IRA or annuity plan (these are detailed in Chapter 12).

Saving for Big Purchases

If you want to buy a car or a canoe or plane ticket to France, do not, I repeat, *do not* buy such things with credit or a consumer loan. As I explain in Chapter 5, cars, boats, vacations and the like are consumer items, not investments that build wealth, such as real estate or a small business. A car begins to depreciate the moment you drive it off the sales lot. A plane ticket to France is worthless the moment you land in Paris. (I know your memories will be priceless, but they don't pay the bills.)

Don't deny yourself gratification; just learn how to delay it. Get into the habit of saving up for your big consumer purchases and paying for them with cash.

Interest on consumer debt is exorbitantly expensive, up to 18 percent for most credit cards. When contemplating the purchase of a consumer item on credit, add up the total interest you end up paying on your debt and call it the price of instant gratification.

Paying for high-interest consumer debt can cripple your ability not only to save for long-term goals like retirement or a home but also to make major purchases in the future.

If you are saving up for a consumer purchase like a car, a money market account (see Chapter 13) is a good place to store your short-term savings.

Preparing for Retirement

Many people toil away at work, dreaming about the day they can chuck it all and do what they want whenever they want. People often assume that this magical day will arrive when they retire or win the lottery, whichever comes first.

I've never cared much for the term *retire*. It seems to imply idleness or the end of usefulness to society. But if retirement means not having to work at a job (especially one you don't enjoy) and having financial flexibility and independence, then I'm all for it.

Part of the American dream is to be able to retire sooner rather than later. But this idea has some obvious problems. First, you set yourself up for disappointment. If you want to retire by your mid-60s (when Social Security kicks in), you'll need enough money to live for an additional 20 years, maybe longer. Two decades is a long time to be living off your savings. You're going to need a good-sized chunk — more than most people realize. The earlier you hope to retire, the more money you need to set aside and the earlier you have to start saving. Either that or plan to work part-time in retirement to earn more income!

Can you save too much or spend too little?

Anne Scheiber, on a modest income, started saving at a young age and allowed her money to compound in wealth-building investments such as stocks over many years. The result was that she was able to amass $20 million by the time that she passed away at the age of 101.

Scheiber lived in a cramped studio apartment and never used her investments. She didn't even use their interest or dividends — she lived solely on her Social Security benefits and the small pension from her employer. Scheiber was extreme in her frugality and obsessed with her savings. As reported by James Glassman in the *Washington Post*, "She had few friends . . . she was an unhappy person, totally consumed by her securities accounts and her money."

Most people, myself included, would not choose to live and save the way that Scheiber did. She saved for the sake of saving: no goal, no plan, no reward for herself. Saving should be a means to an end, not something that makes you mean to the end.

Even those who are saving for an ultimate goal can often become consumed by their saving habits. I see people pursuing higher-paying jobs and pinching more and more pennies in order to retire early. But sometimes they make too many personal sacrifices today while chasing after some vision of their lives tomorrow.

The problem is that tomorrow might not come. Even if all goes according to plan, will you know how to be happy when you're not working if you spend your entire life making money? More importantly, who will be around to share your leisure time? One of the costs of an intense career is time spent away from friends and family. You may indeed realize your goal of retiring early, but you may be putting off too much living today in expectation of living tomorrow.

As Charles D'Orleans said in 1465, "It's very well to be thrifty, but don't amass a hoard of regrets."

At the other extreme are spendthrifts who live only for today. A friend of mine once said, "I'm not into delayed gratification." *Shop 'til you drop* seems to be the motto of this personality type. "Why bother saving when I might not be here tomorrow?" reasons this type of person.

The danger of this approach is that tomorrow may come after all, and most people don't want to spend all their tomorrows working for a living. The earlier neglect of saving, however, handicaps the possibility of *not* working when you are older. And if for some reason you can't work, and have little money to live on, much less live enjoyably, the situation can be tragic.

Although neither extreme is good, you may be surprised to hear me say that if you must pick an extreme — and I'd rather that you didn't — picking the spendthrift approach is better. At least you're making use of your money and, hopefully, deriving value from it. Just don't live too close to the edge. Remember that the only difference between a person without savings or access to credit and some homeless people is a few months of unemployment. If you're a spendthrift, be sure that you have an emergency reserve and you don't mind continuing to work, assuming your health allows.

Saving money is like eating food. If you don't eat enough, you may suffer. If you eat too much, the overage may go to waste or make you overweight. The right amount, perhaps with some extra to spare, affords you a healthy, balanced, peaceful existence.

Most people I speak with say that they do want to retire, and most say the sooner the better. Yet more than half of Americans between the ages of 18 and 34 and a quarter of those aged 35 to 54 have not begun to save for retirement. When I asked one of my middle-aged counseling clients, who had saved little for retirement, when he would like to retire, he deadpanned, "Sometime before I die." If you're in this group, and even if you're not, you should determine where you stand financially regarding retirement. If you're like most working people, you need to increase your savings rate for retirement.

What you need for retirement

If you hope to someday cease working or reduce the time you spend working for an income, you will need sufficient savings to support yourself. Most people — particularly young people and those who don't work well with numbers — underestimate the amount of money needed to retire.

Many people don't even think about saving for retirement until middle age rolls around. As you may already know or will soon see, this mistake can be costly. To figure out how much you should be saving per month given your retirement goals, you can't avoid crunching a few numbers (but don't worry, this number-crunching is easier than doing your taxes).

Luckily for you, you don't have to start cold. Studies have shown how people typically spend money before and during retirement. Most people need about 70 to 80 percent of their preretirement income throughout retirement to maintain their standard of living.

For example, if your household earns $40,000 per year before retirement, you're likely to need $28,000–$32,000 (70–80 percent of $40,000) per year during retirement to live the way that you're accustomed to living. The 70–80 percent is an average. Some people may need more money simply because they have more time on their hands to spend their money. Others adjust their standard of living and need less.

You, of course, are a shining example of the diversity that makes our country great. You're unique! You're not average in any way! So how do you estimate what *you* will need?

The simplest and easiest method to estimate what you need is for me to tell you what percentage you need. (I know we've only known each other a short time, but let me have a chance to offer some friendly counseling.) The following three profiles provide a rough estimate of the percentage of your preretirement income that you need during retirement. Pick the one that most accurately describes your situation. If you fall between two descriptions, pick a percentage in between.

To maintain your standard of living in retirement:

 ✔ You need **65 percent of your preretirement income** if you

- save a large amount (15 percent or more) of your annual earnings

- are a high-income earner

- will own your home free of debt by retirement, and

- do not anticipate leading a lifestyle in retirement that reflects your current high income.

If you're an especially high-income earner who lives well beneath his or her means, you may be able to do with even less than 65 percent. Try picking an annual dollar amount or percentage of your current income that you believe would allow the kind of retirement lifestyle you need.

 ✔ You need **75 percent of your preretirement income** if you

- save a reasonable amount (5 to 14 percent) of your annual earnings

- will still have some mortgage debt or a small rent to pay by the time you retire, and

- anticipate having a standard of living in retirement that is comparable to what you have today.

 ✔ You need **85 percent of your preretirement income** if you

- save little or none of your annual earnings (less than 5 percent)

- will have a significant mortgage payment or growing rent to pay in retirement, and

- anticipate wanting or needing to maintain your current lifestyle throughout retirement.

Of course, you can use a more precise approach to figure out how much you need per year in retirement. Those who are more data-oriented may feel comfortable tackling this method: You need to figure out where you're spending your money today (worksheets are located in Chapter 4) and then work up some projections for your expected spending needs in retirement (the information in Chapter 20 may help as well.) Be sure to include some of your "dream spending" in your equations. This more personalized method is far more time-consuming, and because you're making projections into an uncertain future, it may not be any more accurate than the first method.

Retirement building blocks

Did you play with Lego blocks or Tinker Toys when you were a child? You start by building a foundation on the ground, and then you build up and out. Before you know it, you're creating bridges, castles, and panda bears. Although preparing financially for retirement isn't exactly like playing with blocks, the concept is the same: You need a basic foundation for your necessary retirement reserves to grow.

If you have been working steadily, you may already have a foundation, even when you haven't been actively saving toward retirement. In the pages ahead, I walk you through the probable components of your future retirement income and how to figure how much you should be saving to reach a particular retirement goal.

Social Security

Social Security is the Rodney Dangerfield of U. S. government programs. According to a *Wall Street Journal*/NBC poll of American adults 18 and older, nearly half of those under the age of 35 and more than a third of those between the ages of 35 and 49 think that there will be *no* Social Security benefits by the time they retire.

Contrary to widespread cynicism, Social Security should be there for you when you retire no matter how old you are today. In fact, it's one of the sacred cow political programs. Although the Republicans' self-described "revolutionary" Contract with America was supposed to relieve the government of things that were better done by the private sector, the Social Security program and its handling were not discussed. And imagine what would happen to the group of politicians that voted not to pay any more benefits.

If you think you can never retire because you have no money saved, I'm happy to inform you that you're probably wrong. You've likely got some Social Security. But Social Security is generally not enough to live on comfortably.

Social Security is intended to provide you with a subsistence level of retirement income for the basic necessities: food, shelter, and clothing. It is *not* intended to be your sole source of income. Few people could maintain their current lifestyles without supplementing Social Security with personal savings and company retirement plans.

How much will I get from Social Security?

Table 8-1 shows the approximate size of your expected monthly allowance from Social Security. The first column gives your average *yearly employment earnings* (in today's dollars) on which you paid Social Security taxes. The second column contains your approximate *monthly benefit amount* (in today's dollars) that you'll receive when eligible for full benefits.

Note: The benefit amounts in Table 8-1 are for an individual income earner. If you're married, and one of you doesn't work for pay, the nonworking spouse collects 50 percent of what the working spouse collects. Working spouses are eligible for either individual benefits or half of their spouses' benefits, which-ever amount is greater.

Don't neglect nonfinancial preparations for retirement

Investing your money is just one, and not even the most important, aspect of preparing for your retirement. In order to enjoy the lifestyle that your retirement savings will provide you, you need to invest energy into other areas of your life as well.

✔ Few things are more important than your health. Without your health, enjoying the good things in life is hard. Unfortunately, many people are not motivated to care about their health until after they discover problems. By then, it may be too late.

Although regular exercise, a balanced and nutritional diet, and avoiding substance abuse cannot guarantee you a healthful future, they go a long way toward preventing many of the most common causes of death and debilitating disease. Regular medical exams also are important in detecting problems early.

✔ In addition to your physical health, invest in your psychic health. It is well documented that people live longer and are happier and healthier when they have a circle of family and friends around them for support.

Unfortunately, as they grow older, many people become more isolated as they lose regular contact with business associates, friends, and family members.

Retirees who are happy seem to be busy and involved in volunteer organizations and in new social circles. They may travel to see old friends or to visit younger relatives who may be too busy to visit them.

Treat retirement life like a bubbly, inviting hot tub at 102 degrees. You want to ease yourself in, nice and slow; taking a hasty plunge can take most of the pleasantness out of the experience. Abruptly leaving your job without some sort of plan for spending all that free time is an invitation to boredom and depression. Everyone needs a sense of purpose, a sense of routine. Establishing hobbies, volunteer work, or a sideline business while gradually cutting back your regular work schedule can be a terrific way to ease the transition into retirement.

Lower yourself into the tub slowly. Take some time to get used to the temperature change. Ahhh . . . nice isn't it?

Table 8-1	Your Expected Social Security Benefits
Annual Earnings	*Approximate Monthly Benefit (Value in Today's Dollars)*
$10,000	$500
$20,000	$750
$30,000	$910
$40,000	$1,030
$50,000	$1,130
$60,000 +	$1,200

When can I collect Social Security?

Prior to changes made in Social Security regulations in 1983, if eligible, you could collect full Social Security payments at age 65. This rule no longer holds true. If you were born before 1938, you're still eligible to collect full Social Security benefits at age 65. If you were born in 1960 or after, you have to wait until age 67 for full benefits. If you were born between 1938 and 1959, full benefits are payable to you at age 66 plus or minus some number of months, depending on the year you were born.

The problem with Social Security is that when the system was created in the 1930s, its designers underestimated how long people would live in retirement (the Roosevelt administration must have included a lot of young people). Thanks to scientific advances and improved medical care, life expectancies have risen substantially since that time. As a result, many of today's retirees get back far more in benefits than they paid into the system.

For this reason, the age at which you can start collecting full benefits has been increased and may be increased again. It may seem unfair, but it's necessary to update the system for the realities of our increased longevity, large federal budget deficits, and aging baby boomers. Without changes, the Social Security system could collapse, because it will be fed by a relatively small number of workers while supporting large numbers of retirees.

In addition to paying for retirement-income checks for retirees, your Social Security taxes also provide for disability insurance for you, survivor income insurance for your financial dependents, and Medicare, the health-insurance program for retirees.

The amount of Social Security benefits that you receive in retirement depends on your average earnings during your working years. Don't worry about the fact that you probably earned a lot less many years ago. The Social Security benefits calculations increase your older earnings to account for the lower cost of living and wages in the good old days.

How much work makes me eligible?

To be eligible to collect Social Security benefits, you need to have worked a minimum number of quarters. If you will reach age 62 after 1990, you need 40 quarters of work credits to qualify for Social Security retirement benefits.

If for some reason you work only the first half of a year or only during summer months, don't despair. You don't need to work part of every quarter to get a quarter's credit. You get credits based on the income you earn during the year. As of this writing, you get the full four quarters credited to your account if you earn approximately $2,500 or more in a year. (In earlier years, folks got one quarter's credit for each actual calendar quarter in which they earned $50.) To get 40 quarters of coverage, you basically need to work ten years.

To get credits, you must report the income and pay taxes on it, including Social Security tax. In other words, you and those you employ encounter problems when you neglect to declare income or if you pay people under the table — you may be cheating yourself or others out of valuable benefits.

In order to get a more precise handle on your Social Security benefits, call the Social Security Administration at 800-772-1213 and ask for Form 7004, which allows you to receive a record of your reported earnings and an estimate of your Social Security benefits. Checking your earnings record is a good thing to do every few years, because occasional errors do arise and — surprise — they are usually not in your favor.

Personal savings/investments

Money that you are saving toward retirement can include money under the mattress as well as money in a retirement account such as an Individual Retirement Account (IRA), 401(k), or similar plan (see Chapter 12). You may have also earmarked investments in nonretirement accounts toward your retirement.

Equity in rental real estate can be counted as well. Deciding whether to include the equity in your primary residence (your home) is trickier. If you don't want to count on using this money in retirement (for example, you don't want to sell the house and move away), then don't include it when you tally your stash.

In reality, many people do sell their homes when they retire to move to a cheaper region of the country, to move closer to family, or to downsize to a more manageable household. And increasing numbers of older retirees are tapping their home's equity through reverse mortgages. So you may want to count a portion of your home equity in your total assets for retirement.

Pensions

Pension plans are a benefit offered by some employers — mostly larger organizations and government agencies. Even if your current employer does not offer a pension, you may have earned pension benefits through a previous job (if you have become fully eligible for retirement benefits, the accumulated amount is still yours when you leave the company).

The plans I'm referring to are known as *defined-benefit plans.* You qualify for a monthly benefit amount to be paid to you in retirement based on your years of service.

Although each company's plan differs, all plans calculate and pay benefits based on a formula. A typical one might credit you with 1.5 percent of your salary for each year of service (full-time employment). For example, if you work ten years, you earn a monthly benefit worth 15 percent of your monthly salary.

This type of benefit is quite valuable. In the better plans, an employer puts away 5–10 percent of your salary to pay your future pension. What the employer is effectively doing is putting money away in an account for your retirement. This money is not quoted as part of your salary — it's in addition to your salary. You never see it in your paycheck and it is not taxed.

To qualify for pension benefits, you don't have to stay with an employer long enough to receive the 20-year gold watch. Under current government regulations, an employee must be fully *vested* (entitled to receive full benefits based on years of service upon attaining retirement age) after five years of full-time service.

Defined-benefit pension plans are becoming rarer for two reasons.

- ✔ First, they are very costly for employers to maintain. Many employees don't understand how these plans work and why they're so valuable, so companies don't get mileage out of their expenditures here — employees don't see the money, so they don't appreciate how generous the company is being.
- ✔ Second, most of the new jobs being generated in the U.S. economy are with small companies that typically don't offer these types of plans.

More and more employers are offering plans like 401(k)s, in which employees elect to save money out of their own paychecks. Known as *defined-contribution plans,* these plans allow you to save toward your retirement at your own expense rather than at your employer's expense. Thus, more of the burden and responsibility for saving for retirement falls on your shoulders in 401(k) and similar plans. You need to be educated about how these plans work.

Employers offering defined-contribution plans should educate employees about how to save by using these plans. Defined-contribution plans transfer the burden of planning for retirement from the employer to the employee. Most people are ill-equipped to know how much to save and how to invest the money. The retirement planning worksheet in the next section should help.

Retirement planning worksheet

Now that you've toured through the components of your future retirement income, I'd like you to take a shot at tallying where you stand in terms of retirement preparations. Don't be afraid to do this exercise — it's not difficult and you may be surprised that you're not in such bad shape. If you find that you are behind in saving for retirement, I provide specific ideas for how to play catch-up.

Note: The following worksheet (Table 8-2 and the Growth Multiplier Minitable) assumes that you will retire at age 66 and that your investments will produce an annual rate of return 4 percent per year higher than the rate of inflation (for example, if inflation is averaging 3 percent, this table assumes you will earn 7 percent per year on your investments).

Table 8-2	Retirement Planning Worksheet
1. Annual retirement income needed in today's dollar (see earlier in this chapter)	$ _____ / year
2. Annual Social Security (see Table 8-1)	– $ _____ / year
3. Annual pension benefits (ask your benefits department). Multiply by 60% if your pension won't increase with inflation during retirement.	– $ _____ / year
4. Annual retirement income needed from personal savings (subtract lines 2 and 3 from line 1)	= $ _____ / year
5. Savings needed to retire at age 66 (multiply line 4 by 15)	$ _____
6. Value of current retirement savings	$ _____
7. Value of current retirement savings at retirement (multiply line 6 by Growth Multiplier in following minitable)	$ _____
8. Amount you still need to save (line 5 minus line 7)	$ _____
9. Amount you need to save per month (multiply line 8 by Savings Factor in following minitable)	$ _____ / month

To get a more precise handle on where you stand in terms of retirement planning, especially if you'd like to retire earlier than your mid-60s, call Fidelity Investments (800-544-8888) or T. Rowe Price (800-638-5660) and ask for their retirement planning booklets. I also recommend retirement planning software in Chapter 21 that can save you a great deal of number crunching.

Growth Multiplier Minitable		
Your Current Age	**Growth Multiplier**	**Savings Factor**
26	4.8	.001
28	4.4	.001
30	4.1	.001
32	3.8	.001
34	3.5	.001
36	3.2	.001
38	3.0	.002
40	2.8	.002
42	2.6	.002
44	2.4	.002
46	2.2	.003
48	2.0	.003
50	1.9	.004
52	1.7	.005
54	1.6	.006
56	1.5	.007
58	1.4	.009
60	1.3	.013
62	1.2	.020
64	1.1	.041

How to make up for lost time

If the amount that you need to save per month to reach your goal seems frightening, don't despair. All is not lost. In fact, there are some tried-and-true ways to make up for lost time. Saving money doesn't have as much sex appeal as spending it does, so don't expect much help or praise from your friends and neighbors. But your mother will think she brought you up well, and you'll have the satisfaction of knowing that you're doing the right thing, unless you want to work for the rest of your life.

✔ **Question your spending.** There are only two ways to boost your savings: Earn more money or cut your spending (or do both). Most people don't spend their money nearly as thoughtfully as they earn it. Refer to Chapter 6 for spending reduction suggestions and strategies.

✔ **Be more realistic about your retirement age.** If you extend the age at which you plan to retire, you get a double financial benefit. You're earning and saving money for more years and spending your nest egg over fewer years. Of course, if your job is making you crazy, this option may not be too appealing.

Try to find work that makes you happy and that provides income now and consider working, at least part-time, during the years typically considered the retirement years.

✔ **Use home equity.** Psychologically, the prospect of tapping the cash in your home can be troubling. After getting together the down payment, you probably worked for many years to pay off that sucker. You're delighted not to have to mail a mortgage payment to the bank anymore. You've been released from that particular prison. But what's the use of owning a house free of mortgage debt when you have no cash? All that money tied up in the house can help to increase your standard of living in retirement.

There are a number of ways to tap your home's equity. You can sell your home and either move to a lower-cost property or rent. If you're over 55, you may be eligible to take a once-in-a-lifetime $125,000 capital-gains tax exclusion. Another option is a *reverse mortgage* — where you get a monthly income check as you build a loan balance against the value of your home. The loan is paid when your home is finally sold (see Chapter 15 for more information about reverse mortgages).

✔ **Get aggressive with your investments.** The faster the rate at which your money grows and compounds, the less you need to save each year to reach your goals. Earning just a few extra percentage points per year on your investments can dramatically slash the amount you need to save. The younger you are, the more powerful the effect.

For example, if you're in your mid-30s and your investments appreciate 6 percent per year faster than the rate of inflation rather than 4 percent, the amount you need to save each month to reach your retirement goals drops by about 40 percent!

✔ **Turn a hobby into supplemental retirement income.** Even if you've earned a living in the same career over many decades, you have skills that are portable and can be put to profitable use. Pick something you enjoy and are good at. Go to the library and do some research on how to market your services and wares. Remember, as people get busier, more special-ized services are being created to support their hectic lives. A demand for quality, homemade goods of all varieties also exists. Be creative! You never know — you may wind up on the cover of some business magazine.

✔ **Invest in a tax-wise way.** A free way to boost the effective rate of return on your investments without taking on additional risk is to insulate more of your money from taxation. Many people who are able to save money do not do so in a way that minimizes their taxes.

I do not want to sound like a broken record, but direct your savings into a tax-favored retirement account like a 401(k) plan. You get an immediate tax deduction for your contribution. For a typical person, a third or more of your contribution represents money you would have had to pay in federal and state taxes. This money gets to work for you, rather than for the government, in the years ahead. Plus the money compounds over the years without taxation.

As for money outside of tax-sheltered retirement accounts, if you're in a relatively high tax bracket, you may earn more by investing in tax-free investments and other vehicles that do not make a great deal of taxable distributions. (Chapter 12 discusses these investments in detail.)

✔ **Take a look at jobs that offer retirement plans.** When you're evaluating employers, cash is usually king. As long as the position includes health insurance, most people are concerned only about the salary. But having access to a retirement savings plan is a valuable benefit. Even more beneficial is a pension plan, which pays you a monthly retirement benefit based on your years of service (a completely pain-free way to plan for retirement). If you're lucky enough to have choices, check out these plans when considering a job offer.

What's a retirement savings plan such as a 401(k) worth in the long run? A lot. Suppose that a person who is 40 years old earns $35,000 per year and pays 35 percent in federal and state taxes on her last dollars of income. If she can contribute 10 percent of her salary, or $3,500, into a retirement savings plan, she reduces her current year's taxes by $1,225. Assume further that the money she contributes this year grows at the rate of 8 percent per year until she withdraws the money at age 65. If she pays taxes at the same rate she is paying today when she withdraws the money at age 65, she'll have about $15,580 left.

If she hadn't saved this money through a retirement plan, she would have only $8,080 at 65. In other words, on *just one year's contribution* of $3,500, she nets $7,500 more in retirement because of the tax-deferred compounding allowed in the retirement account. On top of that, if she's like most people, she probably would have been tempted to spend the money if she had access to it, so she might not have saved even the $8,080 if she hadn't used the retirement account.

✔ **Think about inheritances.** While I don't endorse knocking off rich relatives whom you don't care for, people do die every day, and their estates (large or small) typically go to their children or grandchildren. Although you should never count on an inheritance to support your retirement, in reality, you may inherit money someday. If you want to see what impact an inheritance has on your retirement calculations, simply add the amount (use a conservative estimate) that you expect to inherit to your current total savings in Table 8-2.

Common objections to saving in retirement accounts

Despite all the great tax benefits of saving in retirement accounts, many people aren't jumping at the opportunity to take advantage of them. Everyone has unique priorities. Maybe you're saving for a home purchase or paying off student loans. Some reasons, however, stem from a lack of knowledge and understanding. The following are the objections to contributing to tax-favored accounts that I hear most frequently. Some of these objections can be overcome, whereas others are legitimate excuses.

Retirement's a long way away

When you're in your 20s or 30s, age 65 seems like the distant future. For many people, it's not until middle age that some warning bells start to stimulate thoughts about one's golden years.

Delaying the age at which you start to sock money away is usually a financial mistake. The sooner you start to save, the less painful it is to save each year because your contributions have more years to compound. Each decade you delay approximately doubles the percentage of your earnings you should save to meet your goals. For example, if saving 5 percent per year in your early 20s would get you to your retirement goal, waiting until your 30s may mean socking away 10 percent; 40s, 20 percent; and so on.

When should you start saving towards retirement? Ideally, you should start saving a small portion of your employment earnings with your very first paycheck. Start your kids' saving habits while they're young!

Only losers who don't know how to have fun save for retirement

Some people really believe this statement. But I also know losers who don't save for retirement and still don't know how to have a good time (none of my counseling clients, of course).

This attitude is just a rationalization. The reality is that if you manage your finances efficiently and start working toward your goals sooner, you can spend more and have more fun in the long run. Besides, who says spending all your money is the only way to have fun?

My taxes probably won't decrease in retirement

Some people feel that there's little point in contributing to retirement accounts if their tax rate will be the same in retirement. Others fret that their taxes will increase when they retire. Although your taxes could increase when you retire, the following simple example shows you why your time is better spent worrying about more important issues.

Earlier in this chapter, I create the scenario of a woman earning $35,000 per year who pays 35 percent in federal and state taxes on her last dollars of income. She contributes 10 percent, or $3,500, per year into a retirement savings plan, thereby decreasing her current year's taxes by $1,225. Assume that the money she contributes grows at the rate of 8 percent per year until she withdraws the money at age 65. If she is still in the same tax bracket when she starts withdrawing money at age 65, her $3,500 contribution is worth $15,580. If she had saved this money through a nonretirement plan, she would have had only $8,080 at age 65.

Suppose that her career takes off and she earns more money (and pays more taxes) as she gets closer to retirement. How high would her retirement tax rate have to be before she should regret having saved in the retirement account? Answer: She would have to pay about 67 percent in taxes on the retirement account withdrawals to be worse off, a very unlikely occurrence. Remember, I assume she was paying 35 percent in taxes during her working years.

It's highly unlikely that your tax rate would increase this much. You may actually get an added bonus from deferring taxes on your retirement account assets if you are in a lower tax bracket when you withdraw the money. You may be in a lower tax bracket in retirement, because most people have less income when they're not working.

The only people who may not want to start saving money in retirement accounts are those who are within a few years of retirement. For these people, the small number of years available for funds to compound tax deferred before withdrawal may not be worthwhile, especially if they can expect their tax rate to increase in retirement.

Note: If you are near retirement and already have money in a tax-sheltered type of retirement account — for example, through your employer — by all means continue to keep it in a tax-sheltered account if you leave. You can do this, for example, by rolling the money over into an IRA account. Don't pass up the opportunity to continue the tax-deferred compounding of your money.

There are greener investment pastures elsewhere

Real estate is a good example. Some people find retirement accounts boring and believe that they can get a better return in the real estate market. Rental real estate can appreciate in value and produce increasing rental income over the years. Investing in real estate is a legitimate reason for not maximizing retirement plan contributions.

However, although real estate provides some tax breaks, consider its drawbacks.

- First, while you accumulate the down payment, you may pay higher income taxes if you're sacrificing contributions to retirement accounts that are tax-deductible.

- Second, rental real estate produces income that is taxable and is added to all your other income during the year; it may even push you into a higher tax bracket.

In a retirement account, the earnings continue to compound without taxation, and you decide when you want to start drawing on the money.

There may be a way for you to have your cake and eat it, too. Many types of investments — stocks, bonds, mutual funds, precious metals, and even real estate — can be held in retirement accounts. (See Chapter 12 for more details.)

I have no money left over to save

People who don't save enough and who don't take advantage of the great tax savings that come with retirement accounts most often use this excuse. In a very real sense, the extra taxes that you pay because you can't afford retirement account contributions are an additional cost of overspending today. So if you can reduce your expenditures (refer to Chapter 6), you can more easily meet your retirement goals. You'll have more money to contribute to retirement accounts, and you'll save on your taxes to boot!

In some cases, people have a pile of money not earmarked for specific future needs that's invested outside of tax-sheltered retirement accounts. They may use all of their monthly employment income to meet their ongoing living expenses. As a result, they believe they can't afford to save in a retirement account.

If you think this way, you're compartmentalizing your finances. Look at the big picture. For example, what if you save $300 per month through your tax-deductible retirement plan? Suppose that doing so reduces your taxes by $100 and thus really costs you only $200 a month. You then can take $200 from your savings outside the retirement account and put it toward living expenses.

What you're effectively doing is transferring your savings from outside retirement accounts to inside a retirement account. You're not really saving new money, but you're getting terrific tax savings by playing this perfectly legal investing shell game. Just be careful not to drain your emergency savings reserve down too far.

I love my job and will work forever

Are you one of those people who loves his or her work? You don't plan to retire and therefore don't need to amass a pile of money to live on for 20-plus years? If so, you can get away with saving a lot less than your eager-to-retire friends.

You may not, however, be *able* to work at your current job forever. What if you lose your job? What if something happens to your health? You can't assume that you will always be able to work — plan ahead for these what-ifs.

I've saved enough already

Congratulations! This is the single best excuse for not saving more for retirement. If you have a lot of money outside of tax-sheltered retirement accounts, you may want to contribute to retirement accounts anyway for the tax deductions.

Part III
Investing What You Save

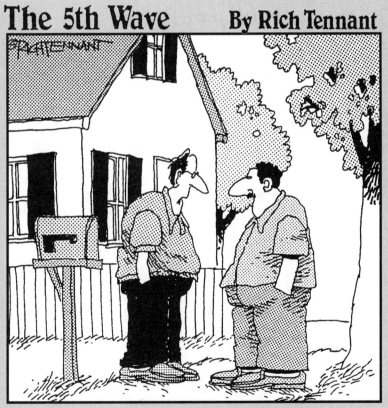

The 5th Wave   By Rich Tennant

"WE TOOK A GAMBLE AND INVESTED ALL OUR MONEY IN A RACE HORSE. THEN IT RAN AWAY."

In this part . . .

You find out what you already know deep down, that earning and saving are hard work and that you should be careful where you invest the fruit of your labor. I lay out the basics of investing and show you how to pick your investments wisely. This part is where you find out the real story on such things as stocks, bonds, mutual funds, the differences between investing in retirement and non-retirement accounts, how to invest for college, and how to buy a home.

Chapter 9

Important Investment Concepts

In This Chapter

▶ Common investment mistakes

▶ Defining your goals

▶ Investment flavors, returns, and risks

▶ Understanding diversification and asset allocation

▶ Where and where *not* to invest

▶ A few words about gurus

*M*aking wise investments need not be complicated. However, many investors get bogged down in trying to analyze and compare the thousands of investments out there. This chapter will help you grasp the important, "bigger picture" issues that will ensure that your investment plan fits with your needs and the realities of the investment marketplace.

Before I jump into the key things you need to know before you begin selecting individual investments, I'd like to give you a quick education in the investing school of hard knocks. Whether you're just starting to save money to invest or have millions to play with, mistakes can cost you dearly. Everyone makes at least one.

I don't define a mistake as an investment that doesn't turn a profit. No one can predict which investments will produce great profits. Aside from doing your homework before making an informed investment decision, there's an occasional element of luck in picking a high-yielding investment.

What I mean by an *investment mistake* is a bad decision that you could or should have avoided — either because better options were available or because the odds were heavily stacked against your making money. A mistake is the result of not doing your homework, surrendering to a sales pitch against your better judgment, or being greedy and believing that you can get something for nothing.

Common Investment Mistakes

This section is one of the most important of the book. As a financial counselor, I always ask new clients to tell me about their mistakes. The following are the most common blunders, costly errors, and painful regrets. If you can avoid major investment errors, you're more than halfway down the road to investment success. So sit back, relax, swallow your pride, and learn from the mistakes of others.

Neglecting to pay off high-interest consumer debt

The first step toward successful investing is to broaden your definition of what it means to invest. While "saving money and watching it grow" may be the most psychologically gratifying approach, you may ultimately be losing money if you are neglecting paying off a credit card bill or an auto loan.

If you're paying 10, 14, or 18 percent interest on an outstanding balance, pay it off first — it's your best investment. To get a comparable return through other investment vehicles (after the government takes its share of your profits), you would have to start a new career as a loan shark. If between federal and state taxes you're in a 33 percent tax bracket, and you're paying 12 percent interest on a consumer loan, you'd need to annually earn a whopping 18 percent on your investments pre-tax to justify not paying off the debt. Good luck!

Even people who have money languishing in savings or money market accounts at 2 or 3 percent interest resist the strategy of using savings to pay down the debt, despite their paying far more in interest charges on their loans than they earn on their savings. Invest your money by paying off high-interest debts as soon as possible.

If your only source of funds to pay off debt is a small emergency reserve equal in size to a few months living expenses, paying off debt may involve some risk. Only tap into your emergency reserves if you have a backup source — for example, the ability to borrow from a willing family member or to borrow against a retirement account balance.

Investing based on sales solicitations

Companies that advertise aggressively or sell investments by telemarketing offer some of the worst financial products with the highest commissions. Companies with great products don't have to reach their potential customers this way.

And never to seek out companies because they have a catchy theme song or because they promise you a piece of some rock. (That firm, by the way, sold billions of dollars of limited partnerships, which led to the loss of billions of investor dollars. If you don't know what a limited partnership is, consider yourself lucky. If you're curious, see Chapter 10.)

Purchasing investments you don't understand

The mistake of not understanding the investments you purchase usually follows from the preceding no-no — buying into a sales pitch. If you don't understand an investment, odds are good that it won't be right for you. Slick-tongued brokers who earn commissions based on what they sell often talk you into these investments. Before you put your money into an investment, you should know its track record, its true costs, and how liquid it is.

Not understanding risks

Many of us have a simplistic understanding of what risk means and how to apply it to our investment decisions. For example, when compared to the yo-yo motions of the stock market, a bank savings account may seem like a less risky place to put your money. Over the long term, however, the stock market usually beats out the rate of inflation; money in a savings account does not. Thus, if you are saving your money for a long-term goal like retirement, a savings account can be a "riskier" place to put your money.

Before you invest, ask yourself three questions:

- First, what am I saving and investing this money for? In other words, what's my goal?

- Second, what is my timeline for this investment?

- And third, what is the historical volatility of this investment and does that suit my comfort level and timeline for this investment?

Armed with answers to these questions, you will have a better understanding of *risk,* and you will be able to match your savings goals to their most appropriate investment vehicles. In Chapter 8, I help you to consider your savings goals and timeline. Investment risk and returns are dealt with later in this chapter.

Paying unnecessary commissions and high management fees

Avoid investments that carry high sales commissions and management expenses (usually disclosed in a *prospectus*). Virtually all investments today can be purchased without a salesperson. Besides paying unnecessary commissions, the danger in investing through a salesperson is that you're far less likely to be directed to a path that's in your best interests.

Management fees create a real drag on investment returns. Not surprisingly, higher-fee investments, on average, perform worse than alternatives with lower fees. High ongoing management fees often go toward lavish offices, glossy brochures, and skyscraper salaries or toward propping up small, inefficient operations. Do you want your hard-earned dollars to support either of these types of businesses?

Putting all your eggs in one basket

Diversification means putting your money in different investments that perform well under differing market conditions. A common mistake is investing too much retirement money in your employer's stock. If your employer falls on hard times, you may lose your job and the value of your investments.

I remember during the earlier 1980s when folks talked about IBM as a super safe investment. IBM may have been a blue chip stock for a while, but employees who were laid off have more than bruised egos — they also have black-and-blue investment portfolios if they invested heavily in IBM stock. After trading as high as $175 $^{7}/_{8}$ per share in 1987, IBM's stock went on a multiyear downward spiral and traded as low as $40 $^{5}/_{8}$ per share in 1994. In case your calculator isn't handy, that is a 77 percent drop! Ouch! It has since rebounded but is still below its level of more than a decade ago.

Another common mistake with diversification is that some conservative-minded investors think that they are diversifying their long-term investment money by buying several bonds, some CDs, Treasuries, and an annuity. The problem, however, is that all these investments pay a relatively fixed-rate of return. There's no real upside or growth potential.

Buying after major price increases

By the time an investment gets front-page coverage and everyone is talking about its stunning rise, it's time to take a reality check. The higher the value of an investment rises, the greater the danger that it's overpriced. Its next move may be downward. Don't follow the herd.

In recent years, some technology stocks have had spectacular rises, thus attracting a lot of attention. Although the U.S. economy is increasingly becoming technologically based, that doesn't mean any price you pay for a technology stock is fine. Some investors who neglected to do basic research and who bought into attention-grabbing, high-flying technology stocks recently have lost 50 percent or more of their investments — and this during a time period when the overall stock market was inching higher. Ouch!

Selling after major price declines

When the New York Mets lost the majority of their games in 1968, their future prospects seemed bleak. But the very next year, the Mets won the World Series. When things look bleak, giving up hope is easy — who wants to be associated with a loser? If you could have invested in the Mets, though, 1968 would have been a great time to do so. Things couldn't have gotten much worse for the team, and the price of stock would have been cheap. But you gotta have faith.

Likewise, the stock market is full of fair-weather fans. Investors who panicked and sold *after* the October 1987 U.S. stock market crash missed out on a tremendous buying opportunity.

People like buying everything from clothing to cars to ketchup on sale — yet whenever the stock market has a clearance sale, most investors stampede for the exits instead of snatching up great buys. Demonstrate your courage; don't follow the herd. After all, lemmings die that way. (By the way, how is it that lemmings haven't gone out of existence?)

Ignoring tax consequences

Even if you never become an investment expert, you're smart enough to know that the less money you pay in taxes, the more you have to invest and play with. Channeling investment money into retirement accounts allows your money to grow without taxation, and therefore faster, over time (see Chapter 12). For investments outside retirement accounts, you need to match the types of investments to your tax situation (see Chapter 13).

Believing self-proclaimed gurus and soothsayers

Ignore the predictions and speculations of self-proclaimed gurus. No one has a crystal ball — and even if someone did, she wouldn't waste her time publishing a mass-market newsletter to tell you what she saw.

Of course, you may want to believe that people can divine the future of the investment world. Believing in gurus makes it easier to accept the risk that you know you're taking to make your money grow. But if you have to believe in something to offset your fears, believe in good information and proven investment managers. And don't forget the value of hope — regardless of What or Whom you believe in!

Setting Your Goals

Jumping right into picking a particular investment is fun and easy. You may have an idea from some reading you've done or from some entertaining-investment-type touting investments on television or online. Or maybe Uncle Louie is whispering in your ear that he's gonna get you in on the ground floor of a great new opportunity — a real sure thing.

Stop! Wait! Hit the brakes!

Before you immerse yourself in a specific investment, you must first determine your investment needs and goals. Why are you saving this pile of money? What are you going to use it for?

You can't and don't need to earmark *every* dollar, but you should set some major objectives. Doing so is important because the expected use of the money determines how much time it's going to be invested. And that, in turn, helps determine which investment you choose to go with.

Suppose the money you plan on using for Uncle Louie's sure-win deal is all the liquid cash you have available. What if Louie's deal is a bust? What are you going to tap in the event of an emergency? Bad things don't just happen to "other" people. You need a safety net in case you lose your job or are hit with unexpected expenses.

If you've been accumulating money toward a down payment on a home that you'd like to buy in a few years, you can't afford much investment risk with that money. You're going to need that money sooner rather than later. Putting that money in the stock market, then, is probably not a wise move. As you see later in this chapter, the stock market can drop a lot in a year or over several consecutive years. So stocks are probably too risky a place to invest down payment money you plan on using soon.

Perhaps you're saving toward a longer-term goal, such as retirement, that is 20 or 30 years away. In this case, you're in a position to take more risk because you have more time to bounce back from temporary losses or setbacks. A retirement account that you leave alone for 20 years may be where you should consider investing in growth investments like stocks. You can tolerate year-to-year volatility in the market — you've got time on your side.

For some people, the thought of putting retirement money in the stock market is horrifying. You want to make sure that your retirement nest egg is intact, and perhaps you know what a roller coaster the stock market can be. These concerns are valid.

The risk level of your investments has to meet your time frame *and your comfort level*. There's no sense investing in high-risk vehicles if you are going to spend all your profits on ulcer-induced medical bills. Learn how to weigh your fears against the potential benefits. What's the investment rate of return that you *need* in order to reach your goals? Let that direct how much risk to take.

The Major Investment Flavors

Remember your childhood friends who always aced their math tests or arranged alphabet soup into ten-letter words before eating it? Well, these little geniuses grew up, went to work on Wall Street, and had fun cooking up hundreds of confusing names and acronyms for different investment products.

Forget all those buzzwords — in many cases, they're only meant to obscure what an investment really is and to hide the hefty fees and commissions it contains. Imagine a world with only chocolate and vanilla ice cream (or low-fat, nondairy frozen dessert for you health-minded folks). Just two choices. Might make the ice cream shop a lot less interesting, but it would sure simplify your decision.

The investment world is really just as simple. If you have money to invest, you have only two choices: you can either be a lender or an owner.

Lending investments

You're a *lender* when you invest your money in a bank certificate of deposit, a Treasury bill, or a bond issued by a company like General Motors, for example. In each case, you are lending your money to an organization — a bank, the federal government, or GM. You are paid an agreed-upon rate of interest for lending your money. You are also promised to have your original investment (the *principal*) returned to you on a specific date.

The best that can happen with a lending investment is that you are paid all of the interest in addition to your original investment — the *principal* — as promised. Given that the investment landscape is littered with carcasses of failed investments, this is not a result to take for granted.

The worst that can happen is that you don't get everything you were promised. Promises can be broken under extenuating circumstances. When a company goes bankrupt, for example, you can lose all or part of your original investment.

Another risk is that you get what you were promised, but because of the ravages of inflation, your money is worth less — it has less purchasing power than you thought it would. Back in the 1960s, for example, high-quality companies were issuing long-term bonds that paid approximately 4 percent interest. At the time, buying a long-term bond seemed like a good deal because the cost of living was increasing only 2 percent per year.

When inflation rocketed to 6, 8, 10 percent and higher, those 4 percent bonds didn't seem so attractive any longer. The interest and principal didn't buy nearly the amount it did years earlier when inflation was lower. After just ten years, look at the reduction in the purchasing power of your money at varying rates of inflation in Table 9-1.

Table 9-1	Reduction in Purchasing Power
Inflation Rate	*Reduction in Purchasing Power After 10 Years*
6 percent	– 44 percent
8 percent	– 54 percent
10 percent	– 61 percent

A final drawback to lending investments is that you do not share in the success of the organization to which you are lending your money. If the organization doubles or triples in size and profits, neither your principal nor your interest rate doubles or triples in size along with it; they stay the same. On the other hand, such success probably ensures that you will get your promised interest and principal back.

Ownership investments

You're an *owner* when you invest your money in an asset, such as a company or real estate, that has the ability to generate earnings or profits. In the first case, suppose that you own 100 shares of Gap stock. With hundreds of millions of shares of stock outstanding, Gap is a mighty big company — your 100 shares represent a tiny piece of it.

What do you get for your small slice of Gap? As a stockholder, you share in the profits of a company in the form of annual dividends as well as an increase (you hope) in the stock price if the company grows and becomes more profitable. That's when things are going well.

The downside is that if Gap's business declines, your stock can become worth less (or even worthless!). The Gap might be taken over by evil aliens who decide to sell all sorts of "socially irresponsible" products. Everyone may boycott the store and your stock plummets in value.

Real estate is another type of ownership investment. Most folks invest in real estate in order to earn a profit. (The two exceptions are homes you live in yourself, in which case you probably hope that it increases in value, and properties you buy for sentimental or conservation reasons.) Real estate can yield profits by being rented out for income (profits come when rental income exceeds the expense of owning the property) or by being sold at a higher price than what you paid to buy it.

As with other ownership investments, the value of real estate depends not only on the particulars of the individual property but also on the health and performance of the local economy. If the local economy grows and more jobs are being produced at higher wages, then real estate should do well. If companies in the community are laying people off left and right and excess housing is sitting vacant because of previous overbuilding, then rents and property values are likely to fall.

A third way many Americans have built substantial wealth is through small business. According to *Forbes* magazine, more of the U.S. and world's wealthiest individuals have built their wealth through their stake in small businesses than through any other vehicle. Small business is the engine that drives much of our economic growth. Although firms with fewer than 20 employees account for about 27 percent of all employees, such small firms in the past two decades were responsible for 47 percent of all new jobs created.

You can participate in small business in a variety of ways. You can start your own business, buy and operate an existing business, or simply invest in promising small businesses.

In the chapters ahead, I explain each of these major investment types in detail.

Investing versus gambling

Although investing if often risky, it's not gambling.

Gambling is putting your money into schemes that are sure long-term losers. That's not to say that everyone loses or that you lose every time you play. However, the deck is stacked against you. The house wins most of the time.

In some cases, as with horse racing, gambling casinos, and lotteries, the system is set up to pay out 50–60 cents on the dollar. The rest goes to administration of the system and — don't forget that these are businesses — profits. Sure, your chosen horse may win a race or two, but in the long run, you're almost guaranteed to lose about 40 to 50 percent of what you bet. Would you put your money in an "investment" where your expected return was negative 40 percent?!

Gambling in the investment world is *speculation* — these opportunities are found in sales and trading of futures, options, and commodities. Futures, options, and commodities are *derivatives*, financial investments with value derived from the performance of another security such as a stock or bond.

You may have heard the radio ad by the firm of Fleecem, Cheatem, and Leavem, advocating that you buy heating oil futures because the cold weather months lead to the use of more heating oil. You call and are impressed by the smooth-talking vice president who spends so much time with little ol' you. His logic makes sense, and he's spent a lot of time with you, so you send him a check for $10,000.

Doing so isn't much different from blowing $10,000 at the craps tables in Las Vegas. Futures prices depend on short-term, highly volatile price movements. As with gambling, you occasionally win when the market moves the right way at the right time. But in the long run, you're gonna lose. In fact, you can lose it all.

Options are the same — you're betting on short-term movements of a specific security. If you have inside information, as Ivan Boesky did, such that you know in advance when a major corporate development is going to occur, you can get rich. But don't forget one minor detail — insider trading is illegal. You may end up in the slammer like Boesky.

That's no way to fund government

More and more states are getting into the gambling business as a way to bring in more revenue. This business is sad and wrong for many reasons. First, it's been well documented that lotteries and casinos obtain most of their business from those least able to afford them — primarily middle- and low-income earners. They end up creating an additional tax on the less economically well off and operate on the basis of false hopes.

Second, government endorsement of gambling promotes the get-rich-quick mentality. Why get an education and work hard over the years when you can solve all your financial concerns with the next ticket you buy or slot you pull? Gambling also contributes to our nationally low personal savings rate.

Finally, gambling, like alcohol and tobacco, can be addictive and destructive. In the worst cases, gambling and gambling debts can split up families and lead to divorce or even suicide.

It's bad enough that legalized gambling exists. It's even worse that, in the pursuit of short-term profits and a quick fix, more local governments are piling into this business. Government is fostering an irresponsible attitude toward money.

Honest brokers who help their clients invest in stocks, bonds, and mutual funds tell you the truth about commodities, futures, and options. A former broker I know who used to work for Merrill Lynch and Shearson Lehman over a period of 12 years told me, "I had one client who made money in options, futures, or commodities, but the only reason he came out ahead was because he was forced to pull money out to close on a home purchase just when he happened to be ahead. The commissions were great for me, but there's no way a customer will make money in them." Remember these words if you're tempted to gamble with futures, options, and the like.

Investment Returns

You know the difference between ownership and lending investments. Hopefully, you can also distinguish gambling and speculation from true investments.

"That's all well and good," you say, "but how do I choose which type of investments to put my money into? How much can I make and what are the risks?"

Good questions. I'll start with the returns you *might* make. I say "might" because I'm looking at history, and history is a record of the past. Using history to predict the future, especially the near future, is dangerous. History may repeat itself, but not always in exactly the same fashion and not necessarily when you expect it to.

This century, ownership investments like stocks and real estate have returned around 10 percent per year, handily beating lending investments such as bonds (around 5 percent) and savings accounts (roughly 4 percent) in the investment performance race. Inflation has averaged 3 percent per year.

If you already know that the stock market can be risky, perhaps you're wondering why it's worth the anxiety and potential loss of money to invest in stocks. Why bother for a few extra percent per year? Well, over many years, a few extra percent per year can really magnify the growth of your money (see Table 9-2). The more years you have to invest, the greater the difference a few percent makes in your returns.

If you invest $10,000 for 25 years or 40 years:

Table 9-2	The Difference a Few Percent Makes	
At This Rate of Investment Return on $10,000	**You'll Have This Much in 25 years**	**You'll Have This Much in 40 years**
4% (savings account)	$26,658	$48,010
5% (bond)	$33,863	$70,399
10% (stocks and real estate)	$108,347	$452,592

Investing is not a spectator sport. You can't earn good returns in stocks and real estate if you keep your money in cash and sit on the sidelines. If you do invest in growth investments such as stocks and real estate, don't chase one new investment after another trying to beat the market average returns. *The biggest value is to be in the market, not to beat it.*

The investing secret of millionaires

Wouldn't it be interesting to see where those who have some discretionary funds to toss around invest their money? They must know some secret. Many millionaires are financially savvy — that's how some of them make their millions. But others are financial dummies — the difference is that they are (or feel) wealthy enough to hire advisors.

Millionaires invest most of their wealth — nearly three-quarters of it — in ownership investments such as corporate stock, real estate, and businesses. They invest the remaining quarter mainly in lending-type investments.

Investment Risks

We should put all of our money in stocks and real estate, right? The returns sure look great. So what's the catch?

Investments with a potential for higher returns carry greater risks. Risk and return go hand-in-hand. If you're not willing to accept more risk, you're not going to be able to achieve higher rates of return.

The risk with ownership investments is the short-term fluctuations in their value. On average, during this century, stocks have declined by more than 10 percent in a year every five years. Drops in stock prices of more than 20 percent occurred, on average, once every ten years. Real estate prices suffer similar periodic setbacks.

Thus, in order to earn those generous long-term returns, you must be willing to tolerate volatility. That's why you absolutely should not put all your money in the stock or real estate market. At a minimum, you should not invest your emergency money or money you expect to use within the next five years in such volatile investments.

The shorter the time period that you have, the lesser the likelihood that growth-oriented investments like stocks will beat out lending-type investments like bonds. Table 9-3 illustrates the historical relationship between stock and bond returns based on number of years held.

Table 9-3	Stocks versus Bonds
Number of Years Investment Held	*Likelihood of Stocks Beating Bonds*
1	60%
5	70%
10	80%
20	91%
30	99%

Some types of bonds have higher yields than others, but the risk-reward relationship remains intact. A bond generally pays you a higher rate of interest as compared to other bonds when it is:

✔ Lower credit — to compensate for the higher risk of default and higher likelihood of losing your investment

✔ Longer-term maturity — to compensate for the risk that you'll be unhappy with the bond's interest rate if interest rates move up

Dollar-cost averaging: Investing lump sums without losing your shirt

Whether through accumulation of funds over the years, an inheritance, or a recent windfall from work that you've done, you've got a problem when you have a large chunk of cash to invest. Many people, of course, would like to have your problem. (You're not complaining, right?) You want to invest your money, but you're a bit skittish, if not outright terrified, at the prospect of investing the lump of money all at once.

If the money is residing in a savings or money market account, you may feel like it's wasting away. You want to put it to work!

My first words of advice: Don't rush. Nothing is wrong with earning only a few percentage points on your money in a money market account (see Chapter 13 for recommendations of the best money funds). Remember that a money market fund beats the heck out of rushing into an investment in which you might lose 20 percent or more. I often get calls from people in a state of near panic. Typically, these folks have CDs coming due and feel that they must decide exactly where they want to invest the money in the 48 hours before the CD matures.

Take a *deeeep* breath. You have absolutely no reason to rush into an important decision. Instruct your friendly banker that when the CD matures, you'd like the proceeds to be put in their highest-yielding savings or money market account. That way, your money still earns interest while you buy yourself some breathing room.

One approach to investing is called *dollar-cost averaging*. Dollar-cost averaging is a process in which you invest your money in equal chunks on a regular basis, such as once a month.

For example, if you have $60,000 to invest, you can invest $2,000 per month until it's all invested, which takes a few years. The money that's awaiting future investment isn't lying fallow. You keep it in a money market-type account earning a bit of interest while it's waiting its turn.

The attraction of dollar-cost averaging is that it allows you to ease into riskier investments instead of jumping in all at once. The benefit may be that if the price of the investment drops after some of your initial purchases, you can buy some later at a lower price. If you had dumped all your money into the "sure win" investment at once and then it dropped like a stone, you'd kick yourself for not waiting.

The flip side of dollar-cost averaging is that if your investment of choice appreciates in value, you may wish that you had invested your money faster. Another possible drawback of dollar-cost averaging is that you may get cold feet continuing to pour money into an investment that's dropping in value. Many people who are attracted to dollar-cost averaging out of fear of buying before a price-drop end up bailing out of what feels like a sinking ship.

Dollar-cost averaging can also cause headaches with your taxes when the time comes to sell investments held outside retirement accounts. If you buy an investment at many different times and prices, accounting is muddied as you sell blocks of the investment.

Dollar-cost averaging is most valuable when the money you want to invest represents a large portion of your total assets and you can stick to a schedule. Making dollar-cost averaging automatic so that you're less likely to chicken out is best. Most investment firms recommended in the next few chapters can provide automatic exchange services.

Focus on the risks that you can control

I always ask students in my personal finance class to write down what they would like to learn. Here's what one student had to say: "I want to learn what to invest my money in now as the stock market is overvalued and interest rates are about to go up, so bonds are dicey and banks give lousy interest — HELP!"

This student recognizes the risk of price fluctuations in her investments, but she also seems to believe, like too many people, that there's a way to expect or predict what's going to happen. How does *she* know that the stock market is overvalued and why hasn't the rest of the world figured it out? How does *she* know that interest rates are about to go up and why hasn't the rest of the world figured that out either?

If you're going to invest in stocks and other growth-oriented investments, you must accept the volatility of these investments. Invest the money that you have earmarked for the longer-term in these vehicles. Minimize the risk of these investments through diversification. Don't buy just one or a two stocks; buy a number of stocks, which you can easily do through a mutual fund.

Low-risk, high-return investments

Despite what professors teach in the nation's leading business and finance graduate school programs, low-risk investments that almost certainly will lead to high returns *are* available.

I can think of at least three such investments:

- ✔ **Your health.** Eat healthy, exercise, relax. Low risk, high return!

- ✔ **Friends and family.** Improve your relationships with loved ones. Invest the time and effort in making them better. Low risk, high return!

- ✔ **Personal and career development.** Learn a new hobby, improve your communication skills, or read widely. Take an adult education course or go back to school for a degree. Your investment will surely pay off in higher paychecks and greater happiness. Low risk, high return!

Diversification

Diversification is one of the most powerful investment concepts. All it really means is that you save and place your eggs (or investments) in different baskets.

Diversification requires you to place your money in different investments with returns that are not completely correlated. This is a fancy way of saying that with your money in different places, when one of your investments is down in value, odds are that others are up.

To decrease the odds of all of your investments getting clobbered at the same time, you must put your money in different types or classes of investments. These include bonds, stocks, real estate, small business, and precious metals. (I cover all these investments and more in Chapter 10). You can further diversify your investments by investing in domestic as well as international markets.

Within a given class of investments such as stocks, to diversify by investing in different types of stocks that perform well under various economic conditions is important. For this reason, mutual funds, which are diversified portfolios of securities such as stocks or bonds, are a highly useful investment vehicle. You buy into the mutual fund, which in turn pools your money with that of many others to invest in a vast array of stocks or bonds.

You can look at the benefits of diversification in two ways:

- Diversification reduces or dampens the volatility in the value of your whole portfolio. In other words, you can achieve the same rate of return that a single investment can provide with reduced fluctuations in value.

- Diversification allows you to obtain a higher rate of return for a given level of risk.

Keep in mind that no one, no matter whom he works for or what credentials he has, can guarantee returns on an investment. You can do good research and you can be lucky, but no one is free from the risk of losing money. Diversification allows you to hedge the risk of your investments. See Figures 9-1, 9-2, and 9-3 to get an idea of how diversifying can reduce your risk (figures in these charts are adjusted for inflation). Notice that different investments did better during various time periods. Because the future can't be predicted, you are safer diversifying your money into different investments.

Asset allocation: spreading it around

How you spread out your investing dollars over different investment options is known as *asset allocation.* When determining how to allocate your assets, study your financial situation, prioritize your goals, and then weigh the pros and cons of various investment options.

Although stocks and real estate offer investors attractive long-term returns, they can and do suffer significant declines in value from time-to-time. Thus, these investments are not suitable for money that you think you may want or need to use within, say, the next five years.

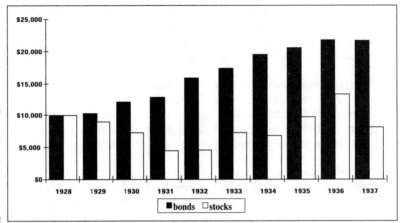

Figure 9-1:
Value of
$10,000
invested
from 1928-
1937.

Figure 9-2:
Value of
$10,000
invested
from 1947-
1956.

Figure 9-3:
Value of
$10,000
invested
from 1972-
1980.

Money market and bond investments are good places to keep money that you expect to use sooner. Everyone should have a reserve of money that they can access in an emergency. Keeping about three to six months' worth of living expenses in a money market fund is a good start. Shorter-term bonds or bond mutual funds can serve as a higher-yielding, secondary emergency cushion (refer to Chapter 8 for more on emergency reserves).

Bonds can also be useful for some longer-term investing for diversification purposes. For example, when investing for retirement, placing a portion of one's money in bonds helps to buffer stock market declines.

Allocating money for the long-term

In almost any type of retirement account, you have investment options. Most people get a big headache when they try to decide how to spread their money across those choices. (If you have to select the investment options yourself, such as in a self-employed SEP-IRA or Keogh plan, you've got other decisions to make as well. More on this in Chapter 12.)

Your current age and the number of years until you retire should be the biggest factors in your allocation decision. The younger you are and the more years you have before retirement, the more comfortable you should be with growth-oriented (and more volatile) investments, such as stocks.

One useful rule of thumb for dividing or allocating your money between longer-term oriented growth investments such as stocks and bonds is to subtract your age from 100 (or 120 if you want to be aggressive) and invest the resulting percentage in stocks. Invest what's left over in bonds.

For example, if you're 30 years old, that would mean that you could invest from 70 (100 minus 70) to 90 (120 minus 30) percent in stocks. What's left over — 10 to 30 percent — would be invested in bonds.

Table 9-4 lists some guidelines for allocating retirement account money. All you need to figure out is how old you are and the level of risk you're comfortable with.

Table 9-4	Allocating Retirement Account Money	
Your Investment Attitude	*Bond Allocation (%)*	*Stock Allocation (%)*
"Play it safe"	= Age	= 100–age
"Middle of the road"	= Age–10	= 110–age
"Aggressive"	= Age–20	= 120–age

For example, if you're the conservative sort who doesn't like a lot of risk but recognizes the value of striving for some growth and making your money work harder, you're a *middle-of-the-road* type. Using Table 9-4, if you're 40 years old, you might consider putting 30 percent (40–10) in bonds and 70 percent (110–40) in stocks.

In most employer retirement plans, mutual funds are the typical investment vehicle. If your employer's retirement plan includes more than one stock mutual fund as an option, you may want to try discerning which options are best by using criteria outlined in Chapter 11. If it's safe to assume that all your retirement plan's stock fund options are good, you can simply divide your stock allocation equally among the choices.

If one or more of the choices is an international stock fund, consider allocating a percentage of your stock fund money to overseas investments: at least 20 percent for *play it safe* investors, 35 percent for *middle-of-the-road* investors, or up to as much as 50 percent for *aggressive* investors.

If the 40-year-old, middle-of-the-roader from the example above is investing 70 percent in stocks, then about 35 percent of the stock fund investments (which works out to be around 25 percent of the total) could be invested in international stock funds.

Historically, most employees haven't had to make their own investing decisions with retirement money. Pension plans, in which the company directs the investments, were more common in previous years. It's interesting to note that in a typical pension plan, companies choose to allocate the majority of money to stocks (about 60 percent), with a bit less in bonds (about 35 percent) and other investments.

Investment Firms Are Not Created Equal

Thousands of firms sell investments and manage money. Banks, mutual fund companies, securities brokerage firms, and even insurance companies all vie for your hard-earned dough.

Just to make matters more complicated, each industry plays in the others' backyards. You can find mutual fund companies that offer securities brokerage, insurance firms that are in the mutual fund business, and mutual fund companies that offer banking-like accounts and services. You benefit somewhat from all this competition and one-stop shopping convenience. On the other hand, some firms are novices at particular businesses and count on the fact that you shop by brand-name recognition.

Where to focus

The firms with whom you should do business are those that do the following:

✔ Offer the best value investments in comparison to their competitors.

Value combines performance and cost. Given the level of risk that you're comfortable with, you want investments that offer the highest possible rates of return, but you don't want to have to pay a small fortune for them. Commissions of all types (front-end, back-end, or ongoing), management fees, maintenance fees, and other charges can turn a high-performance investment into a mediocre or poor one.

✔ Employ representatives that do not have an inherent self-interest in steering you into a particular type of investment.

This criterion has nothing to do with whether an investment firm hires polite, well-educated, or well-dressed people. The most important factor is the way the company compensates its employees. If the investment firm's personnel are paid on commission, I'd pass on that firm. You want to work with firms that do not tempt their employees to push one investment over another in order to generate a better commission. As you see in the rest of this part of the book, plenty of such firms with excellent investment products exist.

No-load (commission-free) mutual fund companies

Mutual funds are an ideal investment vehicle for most investors. *No-load mutual fund companies* are firms in which you can invest in mutual funds without paying sales commissions. In other words, every dollar you invest goes to work in the mutual funds you choose. Not one cent is siphoned off to pay sales commissions. See Chapter 11 for the low-down on investing in mutual funds.

Discount brokers

Prior to May 1, 1975, when investors bought or sold stocks, bonds, and other securities, they were charged fixed commissions. In other words, no matter which brokerage firm an investor did business with, the cost of the firm's services was set. And the level of commissions was high.

In one of the most beneficial changes for investors in this century, the Securities and Exchange Commission (SEC) deregulated the retail brokerage industry. For the first time, brokerage firms could charge people whatever their little hearts desired. You may think that this change opened the door to exorbitantly high rates. In fact, it did the opposite. A fair and open free market is good for consumers. Competition inevitably resulted in more and better choices.

Most firms that were in business before that time, such as Merrill Lynch, Prudential, and E. F. Hutton, continued doing business as usual: That is, they continued to pay their brokers based on the amount of trading their customers did and which investments they sold.

Fortunately, many new brokerage firms opened up that did not do business the old way. They were dubbed *discount brokers* because the fees they charged customers were substantially lower than what brokers charged under the old fixed-fee system.

Even more important than saving the customer money, discount brokers established a vastly improved compensation system that effectively eliminated conflicts of interest. Discount brokers pay their brokers a straight salary. Therefore, they don't have an incentive to encourage the customer to trade, and they also won't steer the customer into one investment over another unless it is truly wiser.

The term *discount broker* is actually not an enlightening one. It is certainly true that this new breed of brokerage firm saves you lots of money when you invest. You can easily save 50–80 percent through the major discount brokers, such as Charles Schwab, Quick & Reilly, and Waterhouse Securities. Fidelity, which is better known for mutual funds, is also a major player in the discount brokerage market. But these firms' investments are not "on sale" or second rate. Discount brokers are simply brokers without major conflicts of interest. Of course, like any other for-profit enterprise, they want your business and they are in business to make money, but they're much less likely to steer you wrong for their own benefit.

Note: Be careful of discount brokers selling load mutual funds.

Places to consider avoiding

The worst places to invest are those that charge you a lot, have mediocre or poorly performing investments, and have major conflicts of interest.

The prime conflict of interest comes with investment firms that pay their brokers commissions on the basis of how much and what they sell. The result: The investment firms sell lots of stuff that pays fat commissions and they churn your account (because each transaction has a fee, the more you buy and sell, the more money they make).

The major firms that historically have compensated their brokers almost exclusively on commissions include Prudential, Smith Barney Shearson, Paine Webber, Dean Witter, Merrill Lynch, and Kidder Peabody.

You probably recognize the names of many of these firms. Think about that. Do you know many people who have made lots of money and beaten the securities market averages by investing with them? Or do you know of them because of all the advertising they do and the negative publicity so many of these firms have received from the press in recent years? Going by a catchy slogan or by brand-name recognition is *not* smart shopping. These firms sold billions of dollars of the dreaded limited partnerships, which I briefly discuss in the next chapter.

Folks who call themselves *financial planners* or *financial consultants* work on commission (discussed in Chapter 3) outside the big brokerage firms. Many of them belong to so-called *broker-dealer networks,* which provide back-office support and investment products to sell. If a person claiming to be a financial planner or advisor is part of a broker-dealer network, odds are quite high you're dealing with an investment salesperson. See Chapter 19 for the questions to ask an advisor you might be considering hiring.

Commissions and their impact on human behavior

Investment products bring in widely varying commissions. The products that bring in the highest commissions tend to be the ones that money-hungry brokers push the hardest.

Table 9-5 lists the commissions that you pay and that come out of your investment dollars when you work with brokers, financial consultants, and financial planners working on commission.

Table 9-5	Investment Sales Commissions	
Investment Type	**Avg. Commission on $20,000 Investment**	**Avg. Commission on $100,000 Investment**
Annuities	$1,400	$7,000
Initial public offerings (new stock issue)	$1,000	$5,000
Limited partnerships	$1,800	$9,000
Load mutual funds	$1,200	$6,000
Options and futures	$2,000+	$10,000+

Besides the fact that you can never be sure that you're getting an unbiased recommendation from a salesperson working on commission, you're wasting unnecessary money. All good investments can be bought on a no-load (commission-free) basis. No-load mutual funds are a good example.

If you're unsure about an investment product that's being pitched to you (and even when you *are* sure), ask for a copy of the prospectus. In the first few pages, check out whether the investment includes a commission (also known as a load). If it does, pitch the prospectus into your circular file and ditch the salesperson who recommended it.

Investment salespeople's conflicts of interest

Financial consultants (also known as stock brokers), financial planners, and others who sell investment products can have enormous conflicts of interest in the strategies and specific investment products that they recommend. Commissions and other financial incentives can't help but skew the advice of even the most earnest and otherwise well-intentioned salespeople.

Numerous conflicts of interest can damage your investment portfolio. The following are the most common conflicts to watch out for:

✔ **Pushing higher-commission products.** As I discuss earlier in this chapter, commissions vary tremendously on investment products. At the worst end of the spectrum for you (and the best for a salesperson) are products like limited partnerships, commodities, options, and futures. At the best end of the spectrum for you (therefore, the worst for a salesperson) are investments such as no-load mutual funds and Treasury bills which are 100 percent commission free.

Surprisingly, commission-based brokers and financial planners need not give you the prospectus (where commissions are detailed) before you buy a financial product that carries commissions (as with a load mutual fund). In contrast, commission-free investment companies, such as no-load mutual fund companies, must send a prospectus in advance of taking a mutual fund order. Commission-based investment salespeople should also have to provide prospectuses in advance of a sale, and they should be required to disclose any commissions up front and in writing. I suppose if that happened, more people would choose to buy investments elsewhere and politicians might start telling the truth!

✔ **Recommending active trading.** Investment salespeople often advise you to trade frequently into and out of different securities. They usually base their advice on current news events or an analyst's comments on the security. Sometimes, these moves are valid; more often they are not. In extreme cases, brokers trade on a monthly basis. By the end of the year, they've churned through your entire portfolio; needless to say, all these transactions cost you big money in trading fees.

Diversified mutual funds (discussed in detail in Chapter 11) make more sense for most people. You can invest in mutuals free of sales commissions. Beside saving money on commissions, you earn better long-term returns by having an expert money manager work for you.

✔ **Failing to recommend investing through employer's retirement plans.** If you're not taking full advantage of retirement savings plans (see Chapter 12), you may be missing out on valuable tax benefits. Your initial contributions to most retirement plans are tax-deductible, and your money compounds without taxation over the years. An investment salesperson is not likely to recommend that you contribute to your employer's retirement plan, a 401(k) for example. Such contributions cut into the total stash of money you have available to invest with your friendly salesperson.

If you're self-employed, salespeople are somewhat more likely to recommend that you fund a retirement plan because they can set up such plans for you. You're better off doing so yourself through a no-load mutual fund company (see Chapters 11 and 12).

✔ **Pushing high-fee products.** Many of the brokerage firms that used to sell investment products only on commission (for example, Prudential, Merrill Lynch, Smith Barney Shearson, Paine Webber, and Dean Witter) are moving into fee-based investment management. This change is an improvement for investors because it reduces some of the conflicts of interest caused by commissions.

On the other hand, these brokers charge extraordinarily high fees (which are usually quoted as a percentage of assets under management) on their managed investment (wrap) accounts.

Wrap or managed accounts

Wrap, or *managed,* accounts are all the rage among commission-based brokerage firms such as those I just mentioned.

These accounts go under a variety of names but are similar in that they charge a fixed percentage of the assets under management to invest your money through money managers.

Two major problems exist with wrap accounts. First, their management expenses are extraordinarily high — often up to 3 percent per year (some even higher) of assets under management. Remember that in the long haul, stocks can return about 10 percent per year before taxes. So, if you're paying 3 percent per year to have the money managed in stocks, 30 percent of your return (before taxes) is siphoned off. But don't forget — because the government sure won't — that you pay a good chunk of money in taxes on your 10 percent return as well. So the 3 percent wrap actually ends up depleting 40–50 percent of your after-tax profits!

Forbes magazine said it best in an article on wrap accounts: "Brokerage firms love wrap accounts because they're so lucrative — for them."

No-load (commission-free) mutual funds offer investors access to the nation's best investment managers for a fraction of the cost of wrap accounts. You can invest in dozens of top-performing funds for an annual expense of 1 percent per year or less. Companies like Vanguard offer many excellent funds for a cost as low as 0.2–0.5 percent.

So how do brokerage firms trick investors into paying 3–15 times as much for access to investment managers? Marketing. Slick, seductive, deceptive, misleading pitches that include some outright lies.

You may be told that you're getting access to investment managers who don't normally take money from small-fry investors like you. Not a single study shows that the performance of money managers has anything to do with the minimum account they handle. Besides, no-load mutual funds hire many of the same managers who work at other money management firms.

You also may be told that you earn a higher rate of return, so the extra cost is worth it. You could have earned 18–25 percent per year, they say, had you invested with the "Star of Yesterday" investment management company. The key word here is "had." History is history. Many of yesterday's winners become tomorrow's losers or mediocre performers.

You also must remember that, unlike mutual funds, whose performance records are audited by the SEC, wrap account performance records may include marketing hype. The most common ploy is showing only the performance of selected accounts — those that performed the best!

The value of brokerage research

One of the arguments frequently advanced by brokerage firms and the brokers who work for them is that their research is better. With their insights and recommendations, they say, you'll do better and "beat the market averages."

Don't believe them. A number of studies clearly demonstrate that their research is barely worth the cost of your morning paper (sometimes not even that)!

If the brokerage firms' research were superior, then their mutual fund returns should be exceptional, right? They're not. Not a single brokerage firm mutual fund family produces above average returns when considering all their funds!

Wall Street analysts are chronically overly optimistic when it comes to predicting corporate profits. (Hey, it's better than being a sad sack all the time!) If analysts were simply inaccurate or bad estimators, you would expect that they would sometimes underestimate and other times overestimate companies' earnings. Doesn't happen. They almost always overestimate. The discrepancy identifies yet another conflict of interest among many of the brokerage firms.

Brokerage firm analysts are loathe to write a negative report about a company because the firms these analysts work for also solicit companies to issue new stock to the public. What better way to show your potential for selling shares at a high price to the public than by showing how much you believe in certain companies and writing up glowing reports about their future prospects?

Brokerage analysts can't be objective. Investment banking (the business of helping companies sell new securities) cannot objectively be done by companies supposedly evaluating and rating the same securities for the investing public.

If you want research on individual securities, check out the *Value Line Investment Survey,* which I mention in Chapter 10.

Experts Who Predict the Future

A common mistake that many investors make is believing that they can increase their investment returns if they follow the prognostications of certain gurus. The sage predictions in an investment newsletter or by an "expert" who is repeatedly quoted in financial publications make you feel protected. It's sort of like Linus and his security blanket.

I have some bad news for you investment newsletter subscribers and guru followers. Go buy yourself a warm blanket. It has a lot more value and costs a whole lot less. No one can predict the future. If they could, they would be so busy investing their own money and getting rich that they wouldn't have the time and desire to share their secrets with you.

Investment newsletters

Many investment newsletters purport to time the markets, telling you exactly the right time to get into and out of certain stocks or mutual funds (or the financial markets in general). Such a time approach is doomed to failure in the long run. By failure, I mean that this approach is not going to beat the tried-and-true strategy of buy and hold.

I see many people paying hundreds of dollars annually to subscribe to all sorts of market-timing and stock-picking newsletters. One client, an attorney, had subscribed to several newsletters. When I asked him why, he said that their marketing materials claimed that if you followed their advice, you would make 20 percent per year return on your money. But in the four years that Ken had followed their advice, he had actually *lost* money, despite appreciating financial markets overall.

Before you ever consider subscribing to any investment newsletter, you should examine its historic track record. The newsletter's marketing materials typically hype the supposed returns that a letter's recommendations have produced. Sadly, newsletters seem to be able to make lots of bogus claims without suffering the timely wrath of securities regulators.

Mark Hulbert tracks the performance of the recommendations made by newsletter writers. Hulbert's organization looks at the cold, hard facts of actual returns and shows how your portfolio would have done if you had followed the recommendations of given newsletters.

If you had been so omniscient as to know in advance which five newsletters would give the best advice during the past 15 years (see Table 9-6), after adjusting for the level of risk that each had taken, you would have done worse in all five cases than the overall rate of return of the Wilshire 5000 index, the broadest measure of the overall performance of small, medium, and large companies' U.S. stocks.

Table 9-6	The "Best" Newsletters
Newsletter	*Risk-Adjusted Performance Ranking*
Value Line Investment Survey	97.5
The Chartist	93.2
Growth Stock Outlook	82.6
No-Load Fund X	73.3
The Prudent Speculator	72.0
Wilshire 5000 Index	100.0

Source: Hulbert's Financial Digest

What to do if you've been fleeced by a broker

You can't sue a broker just because you lose money on that person's investment recommendations. That's life in the big city. However, if you have been the victim of one of the following cardinal financial sins, you may have some legal recourse:

- **Misrepresentation and omission.** If you were told, for example, that a particular investment guaranteed returns of 15 percent per year and the investment ends up plunging in value by 50 percent, you were misled. Misrepresentation can also be charged if you are sold an investment with a hefty commission but were originally told that it was commission-free.

- **Unsuitable investments.** Retirees who need access to their capital are often advised to invest in limited partnerships (discussed in Chapter 10) for safe, high yields. The yields on most LPs end up being anything but safe. LP investors have also discovered how illiquid their investments are — some can't be liquidated for up to ten years or more.

- **Churning.** If your broker or financial planner is constantly trading your investments, odds are that his or her weekly commission check benefits at your expense.

- **Rogue elephant salespeople.** If your planner or broker buys or sells without your approval or ignores your request to make a change, you may be able to collect for losses caused by these actions.

Two major types of practitioners — securities lawyers and arbitration consultants — stand ready to help you recover your lost money. You can find securities lawyers by looking under "Attorneys — Securities" in the Yellow Pages or by calling your local bar association for referrals. Arbitration consultants can be found under "Arbitrators." If you come up dry, try contacting business writers at a major newspaper in your area or at your favorite personal finance magazine. These sources may be able to give you names and numbers of folks they know.

Most lawyers and consultants work on a *contingency-fee basis* — they get a percentage of damages (about 20–40 percent of the amount collected). They also usually ask for an up-front fee ranging from several hundred to several thousand dollars to help them cover their expenses and time. If they take your case and lose, they generally get to keep the up-front money. Securities lawyers are usually a more expensive option.

You generally don't end up in a courtroom *L.A. Law* style. You'll probably go to *arbitration* — an agreement you made (probably not realizing it) when you set up an account to work with the broker or planner.

The good news is that arbitration is usually much quicker, cheaper, and easier for you. You can even choose to represent yourself. Both sides present their case to a panel of three arbitrators who make a decision that both sides can't squabble over or appeal.

If you decide to prepare for arbitration yourself, the nonprofit American Arbitration Association can send you a background package of materials to help with your case. Check your local phone directory or contact their headquarters at American Arbitration Association, 140 West 51st Street, New York, NY 10020, or call 212-484-4000.

Hulbert uses *risk-adjusted returns,* which are corrected for the differences in the amount of risk different newsletters took in their recommendations. For comparative purposes, the risk-adjusted return of the Wilshire 5000 index is set at 100. The best newsletter above, which has a rating of 97.5 has produced a –2.5 percent lower return than expected given the level of risk it takes. The fact that all of the above newsletters have a rating less than 100 implies that their recommendations, given the risk entailed, performed worse than the Wilshire 5000 index.

Because you can actually invest in the Wilshire 5000 index via an index mutual fund (see Chapter 11), don't waste your money subscribing to investment newsletters in the hopes of beating the stock market's overall returns!

If, by bad luck, you had been suckered into following the advice of some of the worst newsletters, your investment results would have been disastrous, especially in comparison to what you could have earned in Treasury bills or the Wilshire 5000 stock index. Check out Table 9-7.

Table 9-7	The Worst Newsletters Compared to the Market
Newsletter Portfolio	**Past Five-Year Return**
Granville Market Letter	- 99 %
Overpriced Stock Price	- 95 %
Futures Hotline	- 88 %
Option Advisor	- 78 %
PQ Wall Street	- 73 %
The Dines Letter	- 52 %
Investment Reporter	- 48 %
Newsletter Portfolio	**Past Five-Year Return**
Wilshire 5000 Index	+ 78 %

Source: Hulbert's Financial Digest

Never use a newsletter for predictive advice. If people were that smart about the future of financial markets, they would be money managers making lots more money.

The only types of investment newsletters and periodicals that you should consider subscribing to are those that offer research and information rather than predictions. I discuss those that fit the bill in the subsequent investment chapters.

Investment gurus

Investment gurus come and go. Some of them get their 15 minutes of fame on the basis of one or two successful predictions that someone in the press remembers (and makes famous). A classic example is a former (she was recently fired) market analyst at Shearson named Elaine Garzarelli.

Now, I don't mean to pick on Ms. Garzarelli. I assume that she's a decent person who has done some good with the money she's been paid since becoming famous for predicting the stock market's plummet in the fall of 1987. Perhaps she happened to be in the right place at the right time (that is, she was out of the market just before the market crashed).

Garzarelli's fund, Smith Barney Shearson Sector Analysis, was established just before the crash. Supposedly, Garzarelli's indicators warned her to stay out of stocks, which she did, and in doing so saved her fund from the plunge.

Shearson, being a money-minded brokerage, quickly motivated its brokers to sell shares in Garzarelli's fund. In addition to her having avoided the crash, it didn't hurt that Shearson brokers were being rewarded a hefty 5 percent sales commission for selling her fund. By the end of 1987, investors had poured nearly $700 million into this fund.

In 1988, Garzarelli's fund was the worst-performing fund among funds investing in growth stocks. From 1988 to 1990, Garzarelli's fund underperformed the S&P 500 average by about 43 percent! In 1987 — the year of the crash — Garzarelli outperformed the S&P 500 by about 26 percent. So what she saved her investors by avoiding the crash she lost back and more in the years that followed. In fact, Garzarelli's performance was so dismal in the years following the crash that Shearson eventually fired her.

Despite her subpar long-term track record, Garzarelli is still widely quoted as a market soothsayer. She now manages money privately and is hawking investment newsletters. From a recent mailed brochure entitled, "The Garzarelli Edge," listen to the marketing hype promoting her newsletter:

> "The proven, scientific system that has produced compounded yearly gains of 20.2% since 1982!"

> "Elaine Garzarelli has called every major turn in the Dow since 1982."

Now, if the above were true, why did Garzarelli's investment fund perform so poorly and why did Shearson fire her?! It's also humorous to note that the 20.2 percent return was reportedly "audited by a Big-6 accounting firm." Down in the fine print, however, it says, "Audit Pending." I bet it's still pending.

Every year, new gurus emerge. All it seems to take to leap to guru status these days is one right call or one good stock pick. Recently, for example, prognosticators who recommended one of the high flying technology stocks were nearly vaulted to instant guru status as the stocks continued climbing.

Pundits who pitched investing in Presstek and Iomega attracted fairly large followings as these stocks seemed to defy gravity and rationale valuations as their stocks rocketed ever skyward. Like Ms. Garzarelli, however, these stocks and their promoters were brought back to reality during 1996 when their stocks plummeted by more than 65 percent.

And like other high-flying stocks and the pundits made famous by them, many investors weren't attracted to invest in Presstek and Iomega until nearly everybody was talking about them. By then, those stocks were peaking and those who bought got clobbered.

Herb Greenberg, a business writer for the *San Francisco Chronicle,* had a stock market contest in which a group of 13-year-olds won. The reason: They put most of their money into Iomega while it was still heading up. Does this make these 13-year-olds investing geniuses to whom we should look to for guidance on the next hot stock? Of course not. Well, then treat other pundits who happened to guess right the same way.

Commentators and experts interviewed in the media can't predict the future. Don't make investing decisions based on any prognostications. The very few people who have a slight leg up on everyone else aren't going to share their investment secrets — they're too busy investing their own money!

Chapter 10

Investment Vehicles

. . . .

In This Chapter

▶ Safe and boring investments: savings accounts and bonds

▶ Growth and exciting investments: stocks, a home, and a business

▶ Oddball investments: metals, annuities, collectibles

. . . .

*I*n the investment world, you can place your money in many different types of investment vehicles. Decent investment vehicles work their way methodically around the racetrack, rarely deterred but also never at a fast rate. The best ones make their way through the course at a faster clip, only occasionally slowed by a bump or detour. The worst ones sputter in fits and starts and sometimes crash and burn in a flaming heap.

Which vehicle you choose for your trip depends on where you're going, how fast you want to get there, and what risks you're willing to take along the way. If you haven't yet read Chapter 9, please do so now. In it, I cover a number of investment concepts, such as the difference between lending and ownership investments, that will enhance your ability to choose among the common investment vehicles I discuss in this chapter.

Lending Vehicles for Slow-Trip Money

Everyone should have some money riding in stable, safe investment vehicles. For example, as I discuss in Chapter 8, money that you have earmarked for your short-term bills, both expected and unexpected, should have a seat belt on in the back seat of a Volvo. Likewise if you're saving money for a home purchase within the next few years, you certainly don't want to risk that money on the roller coaster of the stock market.

The vehicles that follow are appropriate for money that you don't want to put at great risk. In Chapters 12 and 13, you should be happy to know, I recommend the best specific investments to satisfy varying financial needs and goals.

Transaction/checking accounts

These accounts are best used for depositing your monthly income and paying for your expenditures. If you want to have unlimited check-writing privileges and access to your money with an ATM card, checking accounts at local banks are your best bet. Make sure that you shop around for accounts that don't ding you $1 here for use of an ATM machine and $10 there for a low balance.

With interest rates as low as they are now, focus on avoiding monthly service charges rather than chasing after a checking account with a slightly higher interest rate. Some banks, for example, do not require you to maintain a minimum balance to avoid a monthly service charge when you direct deposit your paychecks.

If you don't need access to ATM machines on every other street corner — an option usually available through larger banks — you can generally get a better checking account deal at a credit union or a smaller bank. Because you can easily obtain cash through ATM outlets in supermarkets and other retail stores, you may not need to do business with Big City Bank with branch offices at every intersection.

In any event, you should only keep enough money in the account to service your monthly bill payment needs. If you consistently keep more than a few thousand dollars in a checking account, get the excess out. You can earn more in a savings or money market account, which I describe next.

Some folks I know have no bank checking account at all. How do they do that? They have a discount brokerage account — see Chapter 11 for recommended firms — that allows for unlimited check writing.

Savings and money market accounts

Savings accounts can be found at banks; money market funds are available through mutual fund companies. Savings accounts and money market funds are nearly identical except that money market funds generally pay a better rate of interest. The interest rate paid to you, also know as the *yield,* fluctuates over time, depending on the level of interest rates in the overall economy. (Note that some banks offer money market *accounts* which are basically like savings accounts and should not be confused with money market mutual *funds.*)

Bank savings accounts are backed by the federal government through Federal Deposit Insurance Corporation (FDIC) insurance. Money market funds are not. Should you prefer a bank account because your investment (principal) is insured? No. In fact, you should prefer money market funds because the better ones are higher yielding than the better bank savings accounts. And money market funds offer check writing and other easy ways to access your money.

Money market funds are closely regulated by the U.S. Securities and Exchange Commission. Hundreds of money market funds invest hundreds of billions of dollars in individuals' and institutions' money. Never has the industry caused an individual to lose even a penny of principal.

Money market securities are extremely safe; many are guaranteed or backed by a federal government agency. The risk difference versus a bank account is nil. General-purpose money market funds invest in very safe short-term bank certificates of deposits, U.S. Treasuries and corporate commercial paper (short-term debt), which is issued by the largest and most credit-worthy companies.

Money market fund investments can exist only in the most credit-worthy securities and must have an average maturity of less than 120 days. In the unlikely event that an investment in a money market fund's portfolio goes sour, the mutual fund company that stands behind the money market fund would almost certainly cover the loss.

If the lack of insurance on money market funds still spooks you, here's a way to get the best of both worlds: Select a money market fund that invests exclusively in U.S. government securities, which are virtually risk-free because they are backed by the full strength and credit of the federal government (as is the FDIC insurance system). These types of accounts typically pay less interest, usually $1/4$ percent less (although the interest is free of state income tax).

Bonds

Bonds are the most common lending investments traded on securities markets. When you invest in a bond, you are really lending your money to an organization. When a bond is issued, it includes a specified maturity date at which time the principal will be repaid. Bonds are also issued at a particular interest rate or what's known as a "coupon." That rate is fixed on most bonds. So, for example, if you buy a five-year, 7 percent bond issued by IBM, you're lending your money to IBM for five years at an interest rate of 7 percent per year.

The value of a bond is based on changes in interest rates. For example, if you're holding a bond issued at 8 percent and rates increase to 10 percent on comparable, newly issued bonds, your bond decreases in value. (Why would anyone want to buy your bond at the price you paid if it yields just 8 percent and she can get 10 percent elsewhere?)

More and more bonds issued today are tied to variable interest rates. For example, you can buy bonds that are adjustable-rate mortgages, on which the interest rate can fluctuate. As an investor, you're actually lending your money to a mortgage borrower — indirectly, you are the banker making a loan to someone buying a home.

Bonds differ from each other in the following ways:

✔ The type of institution to which you are lending your money — state government (municipal bonds), federal government (treasuries), mortgage holder (GNMA), or a corporation (corporate bonds).

✔ The credit quality of the borrower to whom you lend your money (in other words, the probability that the borrower will pay you the interest and return your principal as agreed).

✔ The length of maturity of the bond. Bonds generally mature within 30 years. Short-term bonds mature within a few years, intermediate bonds within 7 to 10 years, and long-term bonds within 30 years. Longer-term bonds generally pay higher yields but fluctuate more with changes in interest rates.

Bonds are rated by major credit-rating agencies for their safety, usually on a scale on which AAA is the highest possible rating. For example, high-grade corporate bonds (AAA or AA) are considered the safest (that is, most likely to pay you back). Next in safety are general bonds (A or BBB), which are still safe but just a little less so. Junk bonds (rated BB or lower), made popular by Michael Milken and Drexel Burnham, are actually not all that junky; they're just lower in quality and have a slight (1 or 2 percent) probability of default.

Some bonds are *callable,* which means that the lender can decide to pay you back earlier than the previously agreed-upon date. This event usually occurs when interest rates fall and the lender wants to issue new, lower-interest rate bonds to replace the higher-rate bonds outstanding. To compensate you for early repayment, the lender typically gives you a small premium or bonus over what the bond is really worth.

CDs are overused

Another type of bond is a certificate of deposit (CD), which is issued by a bank. With a CD, as with a real bond, you agree to lend your money to a bank for a predetermined number of months or years. Generally, the longer you agree to lock up your money, the higher the interest rate you receive.

Unlike bonds, CDs are not liquid; that is, you can't get your money back whenever you want it. You pay a penalty for early withdrawal. If you want your money back before the end of the CD's term, you'll get whacked with the loss of a number of months' worth of interest. CDs also don't tend to pay very competitive interest rates. You can usually beat the interest rate on shorter-term CDs (those that mature within a year or so) with the best money market mutual funds, which offer complete liquidity without any penalty.

Ownership Vehicles to Build Wealth

The three best, legal ways to build wealth are to invest in stocks, real estate, and small business.

Stocks

Stocks are the most common ownership investment vehicle and represent shares of ownership in a company. When companies go "public," they issue shares of stock that people like you and me can purchase on the major stock exchanges, such as the New York Stock Exchange, American Stock Exchange, and NASDAQ (National Association of Securities Dealers Automated Quotation system) or the Over-the-Counter market.

As the economy grows and companies grow with it and earn greater profits, stock prices generally follow suit. Stock prices don't move in lockstep with earnings, but over the years, the relationship is pretty close. In fact, the *price-earnings ratio* — which measures the level of stock prices relative to (or divided by) company earnings — of U.S. stocks has averaged approximately 14 during this century. While the ratio has varied and been as high as 27 and as low as 6, it tends to fluctuate around 14. A price-earnings ratio of 14 simply means that stock prices per share on average are selling at about 14 times those company's earnings per share.

Companies that issue stock (called *publicly held* companies) include automobile manufacturers, computer software producers, fast food restaurants, hotels, magazine and newspaper publishers, supermarkets, wineries, zipper manufacturers, and everything in between! By contrast, some companies, known as privately held, elect to have their stock be held generally by senior management and a small number of affluent outside investors. Privately held companies' stocks do not trade on a stock exchange; that means that folks like you and me can't buy stock in such firms.

Companies differ in what industry or line of business they're in and also vary in size. In the financial press, you often hear companies referred to by their *market capitalization,* which is the value of their outstanding stock. When describing the size of companies, Wall Street has done away with such practical adjectives as "big" and "small" and replaced them with babbling expressions like "large cap" and "small cap" (cap standing for capitalization). Such is the language of financial geekiness.

International stocks

Not only can you invest in company stocks that trade on the U.S. stock exchanges, but you can also invest in stocks overseas. Aside from folks with business connections abroad, why would the average citizen want to do so?

Several reasons. First, the majority of investment opportunities are overseas. If you look at the total value of all stocks outstanding worldwide, the value of U.S. stocks is now squarely in the minority (about 35 percent). (*Note:* Because Americans are so good at spending and borrowing, Americans hold a larger share of the debt — bonds — outstanding!)

Another reason for investing in international stocks is that, when you confine your investing to U.S. securities, you're missing a world of opportunities, not only because of business growth available in other countries but also because you get the opportunity to diversify your portfolio further. International securities markets don't move in tandem with U.S. markets. During the 1987 U.S. stock market crash, for example, most international stock markets dropped less. Some actually rose in value.

Some people hesitate to invest in overseas securities for silly reasons. In some cases, people read idiotic columns like one I recently ran across in a fairly big city paper. It was entitled "Plenty of Pitfalls in Foreign Investing: Timing is all in earning a decent return." The piece went on to say, "But as with sex, commuting and baseball, timing is everything in the stock market." Smart stock market investors know better than to try and time their investments. The piece also ominously warned, "Foreign stock markets have been known to evaporate overnight." I wish I could say the same for the jobs of bone-headed financial journalists.

Others are concerned that overseas investing hurts the U.S. economy and contributes to a loss of American jobs. I have some counter-arguments. First, if you don't profit from the growth of economies overseas, someone else will. If there is money to be made, Americans may as well be there to participate. Profits from a foreign company are distributed to all stockholders, no matter where they live. Dividends and stock price appreciation know no national boundaries.

Also, you must recognize that you already live in a global economy — making a distinction between U.S. and non-U.S. companies is no longer appropriate. Many companies that are headquartered in the U.S. also have overseas operations. Some U.S. firms derive a large portion of their revenue from their international divisions. Conversely, many firms based overseas also have operations here. Increasing numbers of companies are worldwide operations.

As with raising children or going mountain climbing, investing in the stock market involves occasional setbacks and difficult moments, but the overall journey should be worth the effort. Over the past two centuries, the U.S. stock market has produced an annual average rate of return of about 10 percent. However, the market, as measured by the Dow Jones Industrial Average, has fallen more than 20 percent during 16 different periods in this century. On average these periods of decline lasted less than two years. So if you can withstand a temporary setback over a few years, the stock market is a terrific place to invest for long-term growth.

You can invest in stocks by making your own selection of individual stocks or by letting a mutual fund manager (discussed in Chapter 11) do it for you.

Isn't the stock market just legalized gambling?

A student in my personal finance class at the University of California at Berkeley brought in a copy of a *The New York Times* article entitled "Gaming on Wall Street." In the piece, the writer said, "Increasingly, the stock market itself has become just another commodity — as its recent volatility has shown."

After having read this, the student put her comment/question to me in writing: "Unless you're a superstar in your field, have stock options in a high tech company, or inherited wealth, it's increasingly difficult for a working person to provide for the future merely with hard work and savings. One is forced to invest in a stock market that is acting more like a commodity and has little to do with economic rules or real value. It is more and more like gambling. I resent turning over my hard-earned money to something that resembles a casino, but there's really no other game in town. Your thoughts?"

First, I suggested to the student that she might choose better reading material. The writer of this piece had not bothered to do his homework.

If he had, he would know that, in the years before this piece was published in early 1996, by historic standards, the U.S. stock market was actually less volatile than normal. He also implied that the increasing stock prices were inflated and unjustified by the economy. In fact, corporate profits have been booming in recent years, and that inevitably drives stock prices higher.

Second, I told my student that, although the stock market can sometimes be temperamental, in the long run the market is driven by the performance of our economy. That's not gambling — that's investing.

Third, as I discuss later in this chapter, the stock market is hardly the only game in town. To build wealth, in addition to the U.S. stock market, you can invest in stocks outside the U.S. as well as in real estate, small business, or your own career.

A capitalistic economy isn't always fair. But it rarely rewards pessimists, spectators, and those unwilling to take some risks.

The danger of individual stocks

Investing in individual stocks generally should be avoided. Success is difficult to attain; the drawbacks and pitfalls are many:

- **Significant research time and cost required.** You should know a lot about the situation of the company you're investing in when you are considering the purchase of an individual security. Relevant questions to understand are: What products does it sell? What are its prospects for future growth and profitability? How much debt does the company have? You need to do your homework not only before you make your initial investment but also on an ongoing basis as long as you hold the investment.

Don't fool yourself or let others fool you into believing that picking and following individual companies and their stocks is simple, requires little time, and is far more profitable than investing in mutual funds.

✔ **High transaction costs.** Even when you use a discount broker (described in Chapter 9), the commissions you pay to buy or sell securities are substantial. It may cost you about $40 to buy 100 shares of a $20 security through a discounter, which amounts to 40 cents per share or 2 percent of the amount invested. A large institution, such as a mutual fund company, that buys securities in blocks of 10,000 shares or more pays a penny or two per share when trading. So you're effectively paying 20–40 times more in commissions than mutual fund companies do.

✔ **Less likely to diversify.** Unless you have tens of thousands of dollars to invest in different stocks, you probably can't cost-effectively afford to develop a diversified portfolio. For example, when you're investing in stocks, you should hold companies in different industries, different companies within an industry, and so on. Not diversifying adds to the risk of losing your shirt.

✔ **Accounting and bookkeeping.** When you invest in individual securities outside retirement accounts, every time you sell a specific security, you must report that transaction on your tax return. Even if you pay someone else to complete your tax return, you still have the hassle of keeping track of statements and receipts.

✔ **Generally forced to do so in taxable accounts.** If you work for an employer, it's highly unlikely that his or her retirement plan allows you to invest in individual stocks. Thus, you may be relegated to investing in individual stocks in a nonretirement account, which thus exposes your stock investments to taxation. You are taxed whenever dividends are paid as well as whenever you sell a stock at a profit.

If you're using your nonretirement savings to play the stock market game and not fully funding your retirement accounts, you are sacrificing substantial tax benefits. That is not wise investing.

Researching individual stocks can be more than a full-time job and if you choose to take this path, remember that you'll be competing against the professionals who do so on a full-time basis.

The relative advantages of mutual funds

Efficiently managed mutual funds offer investors of both modest and substantial means low-cost access to high-quality money managers. Mutual funds span the spectrum of risk and potential returns from nonfluctuating money market funds (which are similar to savings accounts) to bond funds (which generally pay higher yields than money market funds but fluctuate with changes in interest rates) to stock funds (which offer the greatest potential for appreciation but also the greatest short-term volatility).

The danger in buying individual stocks without doing your homework

The ratio of a company's stock price per share to its profits per share — known as the price-earnings, P/E, ratio (discussed earlier in this chapter) is one of the most important stock valuation measures an investor should examine before investing in a stock. Buying a stock without knowing its P/E ratio is like buying an apartment building without knowing its rental income or buying a small business you desire to run without knowing its profitability.

Many people who wouldn't make those foolish mistakes make the mistake of buying individual stocks based solely on tips from friends, newsletter writers, and other self-anointed gurus. In early 1996, investors who bought into some of the high flying technology stocks such as Presstek, which manufactures digital-imaging technology systems; Iomega, which manufacturers removable computer disk drives; and America Online, a commercial online service, saw their stock investments in these companies plunge about 70 to 80 percent in a matter of months.

Presstek, Iomega and America Online were all selling at stratospheric P/Es — all above 200 — well before they crashed. You would know these P/Es were out of line given some important benchmarks. First, the stock market historically has sold at a P/E of about 15. Secondly, the overall stock market was selling at a P/E of about 19 in early 1996.

However, just as real estate is more expensive to buy in desirable areas and relatively cheaper in the boondocks, higher growth companies can command higher P/Es and thus higher stock values. But, as Burton Malkiel, author of the investment classic, *A Random Walk Down Wall Street* (Norton), says, "It is always true that the market values growth, and that higher growth rates and larger price-earnings multiples go hand in hand. But the crucial question: How much more should you pay for higher growth?"

Well, the premium that investors have been willing to pay for growth has fluctuated over the years. During the stock market boom of the 1960s, investors were willing to pay P/Es of 60 to 100 for the growth stocks of those days such as Avon, IBM, Eastman Kodak, and Xerox. During other market periods, growth companies have commanded far less rich premiums, sometimes only a bit above the market average P/E.

Are technology stocks different, somehow subject to different laws and valuation measures? Of course not. The bidding up of some technology stocks to sky high P/Es is not unlike other speculative bubbles ranging from the bloated Japanese stock and real estate markets in 1989 which then collapsed 70 percent, to consumer product stocks in the 1920s in the U.S. stock market which plunged 90 percent or more, to the go-go growth companies of the 1960s which shed 70 percent or more of their value in the late 1960s and early 1970s.

While already beaten down, the still high P/E technology stocks could fall a lot further if the companies don't maintain their breakneck revenue and earnings growth rates. "...beware of the stock with a very high multiple and many years of growth already discounted in the price. If earnings decline rather than grow, you will usually get double trouble — the multiple will drop along with the earnings, and heavy losses will result," says author Malkiel.

If all this talk of P/Es and growth rates gives you a migraine and following the rise and fall of individual stocks unsettles your stomach, rather than heading for the drug store, invest in stocks via stock mutual funds. In addition to properly diversifying, you'll be hiring a professional money manager to do the homework and make the decisions you probably don't have the time, expertise and emotional detachment to make.

Dividend reinvestment plans for individual stock purchases

Increasing numbers of corporations allow existing shareholders to reinvest their dividends in more shares of stock without paying brokerage commissions. In some cases, companies allow you to make additional cash purchases of more shares of stock, also commission-free.

In order to qualify, you must first buy some shares of stock in a company that seems strong and attractive. Ideally, you should purchase these initial shares through a discount broker to keep your commission burden as low as possible. Some investment associations also have a plan that allows you to buy one or just a few shares to get started.

I don't think that these plans are worth the bother.

✔ First, investing this way is only available and cost-effective for investments held outside retirement accounts. Doing so increases your tax bill, especially with stocks that pay dividends.

✔ Second, you need to complete a lot of paperwork to invest in a number of different companies' stock. Life is too short to bother with these plans for this reason alone.

✔ Third, some companies that offer these plans are hungry — for whatever reason, they need to drum up support for their stock. These investments may not be the best ones for the future.

✔ Finally, you're probably better off in the long run using professional money managers such as those available through no-load mutual funds (see Chapter 11).

Mutual funds make better sense than individual securities for investors with small or large amounts of money to invest. To illustrate, imagine the following scenario. You just bought your first home. It's an older, lived-in property with barf-brown carpets that have accumulated 20-plus years of food spills and pet accidents. You want to tear out the yucky old carpet and install hardwood floors.

Imagine that you can either redo your flooring work yourself or pay a contractor just $200 to do it for you. You would hire the contractor if you could hire him this cheaply. The only type of person who would choose to go it alone is someone who really enjoys this type of work. You're not going to be able to do a faster, better job than a full-time contractor if you do a decent job searching for a good one.

The same thinking process should go into investing in stocks and bonds. Investing in individual securities should be done only by those who really enjoy doing it. Mutual funds, if properly selected, are a low-cost way to hire professional money managers.

In the long haul, you're not going to beat full-time professional managers who are investing in the securities of the same type and risk level that you are. As with hiring a contractor, you need to do your homework to find a good money manager. Even if you think that you can do as well as the best, remember that most "superstar" money managers have only beaten the market averages by a few percent per year.

My experience is that more than a few otherwise smart, fun-loving people choose to invest in individual securities because they think that they're smarter or luckier than the rest. I don't know you personally, but it's safe to say that in the long run, your investment choices are not going to outperform those of a full-time investment professional.

I've noticed a distinct difference between the sexes on this issue. Perhaps because of differences in how people are raised, testosterone levels, or whatever, men tend to have more of a problem swallowing their egos and admitting that they're better off not going with individual securities. Maybe men's' desires to be stock pickers are genetically linked to not wanting to ask for directions.

If you derive sheer ecstasy from picking and following your own stocks or want an independent opinion of some stocks you happen to own now, probably the best research reports available are from the *Value Line Investment Survey.* This superb publication provides concise, user-friendly, single-page summaries of about 1,700 stocks. Libraries with good business sections usually carry this publication. You can subscribe for $525 per year or on a 10-week trial basis for $55 by calling Value Line at 800-833-0046.

Real estate

Investing in real estate is another time-tested method for building wealth. Over the generations, real estate owners and investors have enjoyed rates of return comparable to the stock market.

Real estate is not a gravy train or a simple way to get wealthy. Like stocks, real estate goes through good and bad performance periods. Most people who make money investing in real estate do so because they invest over many years.

The best place to start investing in real estate is to buy your own home. The *equity* (difference between the market value of the home and loan owed on it) in your home that builds over the years can become a significant part of your net worth. Among other things, this equity can be tapped to help finance other important financial goals such as retirement, college, and starting or buying a business.

Over your adult life, owning a home should be less expensive than renting a comparable home. The reason: as a renter, your housing costs are fully exposed to inflation (unless you're the beneficiary of a rent-controlled apartment). As a homeowner, the bulk of your housing costs — your monthly mortgage — is not exposed to inflation if you financed your home purchase with a fixed-rate mortgage. And your mortgage interest and property tax costs are generally deductible expenses for tax purposes.

See Chapter 15 to learn the best ways to buy and finance your home purchase.

Real estate: not your ordinary investment

Besides providing solid rates of return, real estate is quite different from most other investments. Here's what makes real estate unique as an investment.

- ✔ **Usability.** You can't live in a stock, bond, or mutual fund (although I suppose you could build yourself a pretty substantial fortress with all the paper these companies fill your mailbox with each year). Real estate is the only investment that you can use (live in or rent out) to produce income.

- ✔ **Land is in limited supply.** Last time I checked, the percentage of the Earth occupied by land wasn't increasing. And because humans like to reproduce, the demand for land and housing continues to grow. Consider the areas that have the most expensive real estate prices in the world — Hong Kong, Tokyo, Hawaii, San Francisco, and Manhattan. In these densely populated areas, there is virtually no new land upon which to build.

- ✔ **Zoning shapes potential value.** Local government regulates the zoning of property, and zoning determines what a property can be used for. In most communities these days, local zoning boards are against big growth. This bodes well for future real estate values. Also know that in some cases a particular property may not have been developed to its full potential. If you can see how to develop the property, you can reap large profits.

- ✔ **Leverage.** Real estate is also different from other investments because, to buy it, you can borrow a lot of money — up to 80–90 percent or more of the value of the property. This is known as exercising *leverage*: with only a small investment of 10–20 percent down, you are able to purchase, own, and control a much larger investment. If the value of your real estate goes up, you make money on your investment and on all the money that you borrowed.

  For example, suppose that you plunk down $20,000 to purchase a property for $100,000. If the property appreciates to $120,000, on paper you've made a profit of $20,000 on an investment of just $20,000. In other words, you've made a 100 percent return on your investment. But leverage cuts both ways. If your $100,000 property decreases in value to $80,000, even though it's only dropped 20 percent in value, you've actually lost (on paper) 100 percent of your original $20,000 investment.

> ✔ **Hidden values.** In an *efficient market*, the price of an investment accurately reflects its true worth. Some investment markets are more efficient than others because of the large number of transactions and easily accessible information. Real estate markets can be *in*efficient at times. Information is not always easy to come by, and you may find an ultramotivated or uninformed seller. If you are willing to do some homework, you may be able to purchase a property below, perhaps by as much as 10–20 percent, its fair market value.

Good real estate investment options

If you wish to invest directly in real estate, residential housing — such as single family homes or small multi-unit buildings — is a straight-forward and attractive investment for most people. Before you venture into real estate investing, be sure that you have sufficient time to devote to it. Also be careful not to sacrifice contributions to tax-deductible retirement accounts in order to own investment real estate. In the early years of rental property ownership, many investors find that their property's expenses exceed its income. This "negative cash flow" can siphon off money that you could otherwise direct into your retirement accounts to earn tax benefits.

Although it is in some ways unique, real estate is like other types of investments in that prices are driven by supply and demand. You can invest in homes or small apartment buildings and rent them out. In the long run, investment-property buyers hope that their rents and the value of their properties will increase faster than their expenses.

When selecting real estate for investment purposes, remember that local economic growth is the fuel for housing demand. In addition to a vibrant and diverse job base, a limited supply of both existing housing and land on which to build is a thing to look for. When you identify potential properties in which you might invest, run the numbers to understand the cash demands of owning the property and the likely profitability. See Chapter 15 for background on how to think about the costs of real estate ownership.

If you don't want to be a landlord — one of the biggest drawbacks of investment real estate — consider investing in real estate through real estate investment trusts (REITs). *REITs* are diversified real estate investment companies that purchase and manage rental real estate for investors. A typical REIT invests in different types of property, such as shopping centers, apartments, and other rental buildings.

You can invest in REITs either through purchasing them directly on the major stock exchanges or through a real estate mutual fund that invests in numerous REITs. Both Fidelity and Cohen & Steers offer no-load (commission-free) funds that invest mostly in REITs. Fidelity's is called the Fidelity Real Estate Investment fund. Cohen & Steers' is called Cohen & Steers Realty and must be bought through discount brokers (see Chapter 11 for more information on buying mutual funds).

Real estate versus stocks

Real estate and stocks have historically produced comparable returns. Deciding between the two depends less on the performance of the markets than it does on you and your situation. Consider the following major issues in deciding which investment may be better for you.

The first and most important question to ask yourself is whether you're cut out to handle the responsibilities that come with being a landlord. Real estate is a time-intensive investment. Investing in stocks can be time-intensive as well, but it doesn't have to be if you use professionally managed mutual funds.

An often-overlooked drawback to investing in real estate is that you earn no tax benefits while you're accumulating your down payment. Retirement accounts such as 401(k)s, SEP-IRAs, Keoghs, and so on (discussed in Chapter 12) give you an immediate tax deduction as you contribute money to them. If you haven't exhausted your contributions to these accounts, consider doing so before chasing after investment real estate.

Also ask yourself which investments you know more about. Some folks feel uncomfortable with stocks and mutual funds because they don't understand them. If you have a better handle on what makes real estate tick, you have a good reason to consider investing in it.

Finally, what will make you happy? Some people enjoy the challenge that comes with managing and improving rental property. It's a bit like running a small business. If you're good at it and have some good luck, you can make money and derive endless hours of enjoyment.

Although few will admit it, some real estate investors get an ego rush from a tangible display of their wealth. Sufferers of this "edifice complex" can't obtain similar pleasure from a stock portfolio that is detailed on a piece of paper (although others have been known to boast of their stock market prowess and wealth).

Not so good real estate investments

Not all real estate investments are good; some are not even real investments. The bad ones are characterized by burdensome costs and problematic economic fundamentals:

✔ **Limited partnerships.** Limited partnerships (LPs) sold through brokers and financial consultants should be avoided at all costs. LPs are inferior investment vehicles. They are so burdened with high sales commissions and ongoing management fees that deplete your investment that you can do better elsewhere. The investment salesperson who sells you such an investment stands to earn a commission of up to 10 percent or more — so only 90 cents of your dollar gets invested. Each year, LPs typically siphon off another several percent for management and other expenses. Most partnerships have little or no incentive to control costs. In fact, they have a conflict of interest to charge more to enrich the managing partners.

Unlike a mutual fund, you can't vote with your dollars. If the partnership is poorly run and expensive, you're stuck. LPs are *illiquid*. You can't get out your money until the partnership is liquidated, typically seven to ten years after you buy in.

Brokers who sell LPs often tell you that, while your investment is growing at 20 percent or more per year, you get handsome dividends of 8 percent or so per year. Many of the yields on LPs have turned out to be bogus. In some cases, partnerships propped up their yields by paying back investors' principal (without telling them, of course). As for returns — well — most LP investors of a decade ago are lucky to have half their original investment left.

The only thing limited about a limited partnership is its ability to make you money.

✔ **Time shares.** Time shares are another nearly certain money loser. With a time share, what you buy is a week or two per year of ownership, or usage, of a particular unit, usually a condominium in a resort location. If you pay $8,000 for a week (in addition to ongoing maintenance fees), you're paying the equivalent of more than $400,000 for the whole unit, but a comparable unit nearby may sell for only $150,000. All the extra mark-up pays the salespeople's commissions, administrative expenses, and profits for the time share development company.

People usually get lured into buying a time share when they're enjoying a vacation someplace. They're easy prey for salespeople who want to sell them a souvenir of the trip. The cheese in the mousetrap is an offer of something free (for example, a free night's stay in a unit) for going through the sales presentation.

If you can't live without a time share, consider buying a used one. Many previous buyers, who almost always have lost a good hunk of money, are trying to dump their shares (which should tell you something). You may be able to buy a time share at a fair price. But why commit yourself to taking a vacation in the same location and building at the same time each year? Many time shares let you trade your weeks for other times and other places; however, doing so is a hassle, you will be charged an extra fee, and your choices are usually limited to time slots that other people don't want — that's why they're trading them!

✔ **Second homes.** A sometimes romantic notion and extended part of the so-called American dream is the weekend getaway — a place you can escape to a couple of times a month. When it's not in use, you may be able to rent it out and earn some income to help defray the expense of keeping it up.

If you can realistically afford the additional costs of a second, or vacation, home, I'm not going to tell you how to spend your extra cash. But please don't make the all-too-common mistake of viewing a second home as an investment. The way most people use them, they're not. Most second home owners rent out their property very little — 10 percent or less of the time. As a result, second homes are usually money drains.

Part of the allure of a second home is the supposed tax benefits. Even when you qualify for some or all of them, tax benefits only partially reduce the cost of owning a property. I've seen more than a few cases in which the second home is such a cash drain that it prevents its owners from contributing to and taking advantage of tax-deductible retirement savings plans.

If you don't rent out a second home property most of the time, ask yourself whether you can afford such a luxury. Can you accomplish your other financial goals — saving for retirement, paying for the home in which you live, and so on — with this added expense? Keeping a second home is more of a consumption than an investment decision. Few people can afford more than one home.

Investing in small business

With what type of investment have more people built great wealth? If you said the stock market or real estate, you're wrong. The answer is small business. You can invest in small business by starting one yourself (and thus finding yourself the best boss you've ever had), buying an existing business, or investing in someone else's small business.

Launching your own enterprise

If you have self-discipline and a product or service you can sell, starting your own business can be both profitable and fulfilling. Consider first what skills and expertise you possess that you can use in your business. You don't need a "eureka"-type idea or an Eli Whitney-type invention to justify going into small business. Millions of people operate successful businesses such as dry cleaners, restaurants, tax preparation firms, and so on that are hardly unique.

Start exploring your idea first by developing a written business plan. Such a plan should detail what your product or service will be, how you will market it, who your customers and competitors are, and what the economics of the business are, including the start-up costs.

Of all your small business options, starting your own business involves the greatest amount of work. Although you can do this work on a part-time basis in the beginning, most people end up in their business full-time — it's your new job, career, or whatever you want to call it.

I've run my own business for most of my working years, and, wouldn't give it up. That's not to say that running my own business doesn't have its drawbacks and down moments. But in my experience counseling small business owners, I've seen many people of varied backgrounds, interests, and skills succeed and be happy with running their own business.

In the eyes of most people, starting their own business is the riskiest of all small business investment options. But if you're going into a business that utilizes your skills and expertise, the risk is not nearly as great as you may think.

Many businesses can be started with little cash by leveraging your existing skills and expertise. You can build a valuable company and job if you have the time to devote to building "sweat equity." As long as you check out the competition and offer a valued service at a reasonable cost, the principal risk with your business is that you won't do a good job marketing what you have to offer. If you can market your skills, you're home free.

As long as you're thinking about the risks of starting a business, consider the risks of staying in a job you don't enjoy or that isn't challenging or fulfilling you. If you never take the plunge, you may regret that you didn't pursue your dreams.

Buying someone else's business

If you don't have a specific product or service you desire to sell but are skilled at managing and improving the operations of a company, buying a small business might be for you. Finding and buying a good small business takes much time and patience so be willing to devote at least several months to the search. You will probably also need to enlist the help of financial and legal advisors to help inspect the company, look over its financial statements, and put a deal together.

Although you don't have to go through the riskier start-up period if you take this route, you will likely need more capital to buy a going enterprise. You also need to be able to deal with stickier personnel and management issues. The history of the organization and the way things work will predate your ownership of the business. If you don't like making hard decisions, firing people who don't fit with your plans, and coercing people into changing the way they did things before you arrived on the scene, buying an existing business likely isn't for you.

Some people perceive buying an existing business as safer than starting one. Buying someone else's business can actually be riskier. You're likely to shell out far more money, in the form of a down payment, up front to buy a business. If you don't have the ability to run the business and it does poorly, you have a lot more to lose financially. Another risk is that the business is for sale for a reason — it's not very profitable, it's in decline, or it's generally a pain in the neck to operate.

Good businesses for sale don't come cheaply. If the business is a success, the current owner has removed the start-up risk from the business, so the price of the business should be at a premium to reflect this lack of risk. If you have the capital to buy an established business and you have the skills to run it, consider going this route.

Sticking your money in someone else's business

If you like the idea of profiting from successful small businesses but don't want the day-to-day headaches of being responsible for managing the enterprise, investing in someone else's small business may be for you. Although this route may seem easier, fewer people are actually cut out to be investors in other people's businesses. The reason: finding and analyzing opportunities isn't easy.

Are you astute at evaluating corporate financial statements and business strategies? Investing in a small, privately held company has much in common with investing in a publicly traded firm. One difference is that private firms aren't required to produce comprehensive, audited financial statements that adhere to certain accounting principles the way that public companies are. Thus, you have a greater risk of not having sufficient or accurate information when evaluating a small private firm.

Another difference is that it's harder to unearth private small business investing opportunities. The best private companies seeking investors don't generally advertise but instead find prospective investors through networking with people such as business advisors. Increase your chances of finding private companies to invest in by speaking with tax, legal, and financial advisors who work with small businesses. You can also find interesting investing opportunities through your own contacts or experience within a given industry.

You should consider investing in someone else's business only if you can afford to lose what you're investing. Unlike investing in a diversified stock mutual fund (see Chapter 11), you can lose all your investment when investing in a small, privately held company. Also, you should have sufficient assets so that what you are investing in small, privately held companies is only a small portion (20 percent or less) of your total financial assets.

Investment Odds and Ends

In Chapter 9, I tell you that the investment world offers you only two flavors: lending investments and ownership investments. Well, I sort of oversimplified.

The investments that I discuss in this section sometimes belong on their own planet. Here's the basics on these other common, but odd, investments.

Precious metals

Gold and silver have been used by many civilizations as currency or as a medium of exchange. One advantage of precious metals as a currency is that they can't be debased by the government. With a paper-based currency, such as U.S. dollars, the government can print more to pay off debts. This process can lead to the devaluation of a currency and inflation. It takes a whole lot more work to make more gold. Just ask Rumplestiltskin.

Holdings of gold and silver can provide a so-called *hedge* against inflation. In the U.S. in the late 1970s and early 1980s, inflation rose dramatically. This largely unexpected rise in inflation depressed stocks and bonds. Gold and silver, however, rose tremendously in value — in fact, more than 500 percent (even after adjusting for inflation) from 1972 to 1980 (refer to Figure 9-3 in Chapter 9).

Periods like 1972 to 1980 are unusual. Over many decades, precious metals tend to be lousy investments. Their rate of return will keep up with the rate of inflation, but it won't come out ahead.

If you want to invest in precious metals as an inflation hedge, your best option is to do so through mutual funds. For more information about determining how mutual funds fit with the rest of your investments and how to buy them, be sure to read Chapter 11.

Don't purchase precious metals futures. They are not investments; they are short-term gambles on which way gold or silver prices might head over a short period of time. You should also stay away from firms and shops that sell coins and *bullion* (not the soup but bars of gold or silver). Even if you can find a legitimate firm (not an easy task), the cost of storing and insuring gold and silver is quite costly. You don't get good value for your money. I hate to tell you, but the Gold Rush is over.

Annuities

Annuities are a peculiar type of insurance and investment product. They are a sort of savings-type account with slightly higher yields that are backed by insurance companies.

As in other types of retirement accounts, money placed in an annuity compounds without taxation until withdrawal. However, unlike most other types of retirement accounts 401(k)s, SEP-IRAs, and Keoghs, your contributions into an annuity give no tax benefits (deductions). Thus considering an annuity only after you fully fund tax-deductible retirement accounts makes sense.

The best annuities available today are distributed by no-load (commission-free) mutual fund companies. For more information on deciding whether to invest in an annuity, be sure to read Chapter 12.

Collectibles

Collectibles are a catchall category for antiques, art, autographs, baseball cards, clocks, coins, comic books, diamonds, dolls, gems, photographs, rare books, rugs, stamps, vintage wine, and writing utensils — in other words, any material object that through some kind of human manipulation has become more valuable to certain humans.

However, as an investment vehicle, collectibles are far from valuable; in fact, they're lousy. Dealer markups are enormous, maintenance and protection costs are draining, research is time-consuming, and people's tastes are quite fickle. All this for returns that, after you factor in the huge markups, rarely keep up with inflation.

If you buy collectibles, do it for your love of the object, not for financial gain; treat it as a hobby, not as an investment.

When buying a collectible, try to avoid the big markups by cutting out the middlemen. Buy directly from the artist or producer if you can.

Life insurance with a cash value

Life insurance should not be used as an investment, especially if you haven't exhausted your contributions to retirement accounts. Agents love to sell it for the high commissions. Life insurance that combines life insurance protection with an account that has a cash value is usually known as *universal, whole,* or *variable life.*

The only reason to consider buying cash value life insurance is that the proceeds paid to your beneficiaries can be free of estate taxes. You need to have a fairly substantial estate at your death to benefit from this feature. (See Chapter 17 for more on life insurance and why term is best for the vast majority of people.)

Chapter 11

Mutual Funds: Investments for All of Us

In This Chapter

▶ Why funds?

▶ The different types of funds

▶ Choosing the best mutual funds

▶ Good and bad information sources

▶ Making sense of fund performance numbers

Mutual funds are managed by investment companies that pool your money with that of thousands of other like-minded individuals and invest it in stocks, bonds, and other securities. It's kind of like a big investment club without the meetings. When you invest through a typical mutual fund, several hundred million to a billion dollars or more is invested along with your money.

Mutual Fund Benefits

Mutual funds rank right up there with microwave ovens, videocassette recorders, sticky notes, and plastic wrap as the best inventions of modern times. To understand their success is to grasp how and why funds can work for you. Read on to discover their benefits:

✔ **Professional management.** Mutual funds are managed by a portfolio manager and research team whose full-time jobs are to screen the universe of investments for those that best meet the stated objectives of the fund. The portfolio management team calls and visits companies, analyzes companies' financial statements, and speaks with companies' suppliers and customers. In short, the team does more due diligence and research than you can ever hope to do in all of your free time.

Fund managers are typically graduates of the top business and finance schools in the country, where they learn the principles of portfolio management and securities valuation and selection. (Despite their time in the groves of academe, most of them do a good job of investing money.) The best fund managers typically have five or more years of experience in analyzing and selecting investments.

✔ **Low cost.** The most efficiently managed stock mutual funds cost less than 1 percent per year in fees (bonds and money market funds cost much less). Because mutual funds typically buy or sell tens of thousands of shares of a security at a time, their transaction fees are generally 80 to 90 percent less per share than what you pay to buy or sell a few hundred shares on your own. Recent innovations in the technology of information management further reduce the cost of monitoring and managing billions of dollars of investor money.

In addition, when you buy a *no-load fund,* you avoid paying brokerage commissions on your transactions. I write more about these types of funds later in this chapter.

✔ **Diversification.** Mutual fund investing enables you to achieve a level of diversification that is difficult without several hundred thousand dollars and a lot of time to invest. To go it alone, you need to invest money in at least 8 to 12 different securities in different industries to ensure that your portfolio can withstand a downturn in one or more of the investments. Proper diversification allows a mutual fund to receive the highest possible return at the lowest possible risk given its objectives.

I'm not suggesting that mutual funds are able to escape share price declines during major market downturns. For example, mutual funds that invested in U.S. stocks certainly declined during the October 1987 U.S. stock market crash. However, the most unlucky investors that month were individuals who had all of their money riding on only a few stocks. Some shares plunged in price by as much as 80 to 90 percent that month. (Of course, if you held on to your stocks during the plunge, you would have enjoyed the past decade's generous returns.)

✔ **You don't need big bucks.** Most mutual funds have low minimum-investment requirements, especially for retirement account investors. And when you invest in a mutual fund, you get the same attention given to the rich and famous: full-time, professional money management.

Even if you have a lot of money to invest, you should also consider mutual funds. Join the increasing numbers of companies and institutions, (who have the biggest bucks of all) who are turning to the low-cost, high-quality money-management services that you can get in a mutual fund.

✔ **Audited performance records and expenses.** In the prospectuses, all mutual funds are required to disclose historical data on returns, operating expenses, and other fees. The Securities and Exchange Commission (SEC) and accounting firms oversee these disclosures for accuracy.

The rise of the mutual fund industry

Just as computers have replaced typewriters because they allow for more efficient word processing, mutual funds are replacing less-efficient institutions that manage money. That's not to say that banks and commission-based brokerage firms are going to disappear — but you'll probably see fewer of them in the coming years.

As for safety, mutual funds have a virtually zero risk of bankruptcy. Unlike banks and insurance companies, which have failed and will continue to fail, mutual funds have never failed and probably won't in the future. The situation in which the demand for money back (*liabilities*) exceeds the value of a fund's investments (*assets*) cannot occur with a mutual fund.

Of course, the value of a fund fluctuates with the value of the securities in which it is invested. But this variation doesn't lead to the failure or bankruptcy of a mutual fund company. In fact, because the Investment Company Act of 1940 was passed to regulate the mutual fund industry, no fund has ever gone under.

In contrast, hundreds of banks and dozens of insurance companies have failed in the past decade alone. Banks and insurers can fail because their liabilities can exceed their assets. When a bank makes too many loans that go sour at the same time depositors want their money back, the bank fails. Likewise, if an insurance company makes several poor investments or underestimates the number of claims that will be made by insurance policy holders, it too can fail.

And you don't have to worry about fund companies stealing your money. The specific securities in which a mutual fund is invested are held at a *custodian* — a separate organization independent of the mutual fund company. The employment of a custodian ensures that the fund management company can't embezzle your funds and use assets from a better-performing fund to subsidize a poor performer.

✔ **Flexibility in risk level.** Among the enormous variety of different mutual funds, you can choose a level of risk that you're comfortable with and that meets your personal and financial goals. If you want your money to grow over a long period of time, you may want to select funds that invest more heavily in stocks. If you need current income and don't want investments that fluctuate in value as widely as stocks, you may choose more conservative bond funds. If you want to be sure that your invested principal does not drop in value because you may need your money in the short term, you can select a money market fund.

✔ **Freedom from salespeople.** Stock brokers (a.k.a. financial consultants) and commission-based financial planners make more money by encouraging trading activity and by selling you investments that provide them with high commissions — limited partnerships and mutual funds with high load fees, for example. No-load (commission-free) mutual fund companies do not push products. Their toll-free telephone lines are staffed with knowledgeable people who earn a salary, not a commission. Their recommendations don't carry inherent conflicts of interest.

Fund Types

One of the major misconceptions about mutual funds is that they are all invested in stocks. They're not. Figure 11-1 shows how the money currently invested in mutual funds breaks down:

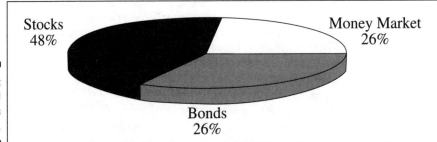

Figure 11-1:
How mutual
fund assets
are invested.

So as you can see, the majority of mutual fund money is *not* invested in stocks.

When you hear folks talk about the "riskiness" of mutual funds, even in the media, you'll know that they're overlooking this fact: All mutual funds are not created equal. Some funds, such as money market funds, carry virtually *no* risk that your investment will decline in value.

Throughout this discussion, remember that when mutual fund companies package and market their funds, the names they give their funds aren't always completely accurate or comprehensive. For example, a stock fund may not be *totally* invested in stocks. Twenty percent of it may be invested in bonds. Don't assume that a fund invests exclusively in U.S. companies, either — it may invest in international firms as well.

Note: If you haven't yet read Chapters 9 and 10, which provide an overview of investment concepts and options, doing so will enhance your understanding of the rest of this chapter.

Money market funds

Money market funds are the safest type of mutual funds if you are worried about losing your principal. Money market funds are like bank savings accounts in that the value of your original investment does not fluctuate.

Money market funds have several advantages over bank savings accounts.

✔ The best money market funds have higher yields.

✔ If you're in a higher tax bracket, you have the option of using tax-free money market funds. No savings account pays tax-free interest.

✔ Most money market funds come with free check-writing privileges. (The only stipulation is that each check must be written for a minimum amount — $250 is common.)

As with money you'd put into bank savings accounts, money market funds are suitable for money that you can't afford to let fluctuate in value.

Bond funds

Bonds are IOUs. When you buy a bond, you are lending your money, typically to a corporation or government agency. A bond mutual fund is nothing more than a large group (pack, herd, gaggle, whatever) of bonds.

Bond funds typically invest in bonds of similar *maturity* (the number of years to elapse before the borrower must pay back the money you lend). The names of most bond funds include a word or two to provide clues about the average length of maturity of their bonds. For example, a short-term bond fund concentrates its investments in bonds maturing in the next 2 to 3 years. An intermediate-term fund generally holds bonds that come due within 7 to 10 years. The bonds in a long-term fund usually mature in 20 years or so.

In contrast to an individual bond that you buy and hold until it matures, a bond fund is always replacing bonds in its portfolio to maintain its average maturity objective.

Like money market funds, bond funds can invest in tax-free bonds, which may be appropriate for investing money you hold outside retirement accounts if you're in a reasonably high tax bracket.

Bond funds are useful when you want to live off dividend income or when you don't want to put all your money in riskier investments such as stocks and real estate (perhaps because you plan to use the money soon).

Hybrid funds

Hybrid funds invest in a mixture of different types of securities. Most commonly, they invest in bonds and stocks. These funds are usually less risky and volatile than funds investing exclusively in stocks. In an economic downturn, bonds usually hold up in value better than stocks do. However, during good economic times when the stock market is booming, the bond portions of these funds tend to drag down their performance a bit.

Hybrid mutual funds are typically known as balanced or asset allocation funds. *Balanced funds* generally try to maintain a fairly constant percentage of investment in stocks and bonds. *Asset allocation funds* tend to adjust the mix of different investments according to the portfolio manager's expectations of the market. Of course there are exceptions — some balanced funds make major shifts in their allocations whereas some asset allocation funds maintain a relatively fixed mix. You should note that most funds that shift money around instead of staying put in good investments have done a dismal job in beating the market averages.

Hybrid funds are a way to make fund investing simple. They give you instant diversification across a variety of investing options. They also make it easier for stock-skittish investors to invest in stocks while avoiding the high volatility of pure stock funds.

Stock funds

Stock mutual funds, as their name implies, invest in stocks. These funds are often referred to as *equity* funds. (Equity [not to be confused with equity in real estate] is another word for stocks.) Stock mutual funds are usually categorized by the type of stocks they invest in.

Stock types are first defined by size of company (small, medium, and large). The total market value (capitalization) of a company's outstanding stock determines its size. Small-company stocks, for example, are usually defined as companies with total market capitalization of less than $1 billion.

Stocks are further categorized as growth or value. *Growth stocks* are companies that are experiencing rapidly expanding revenues and profits.

These companies tend to reinvest most of their earnings back into their infrastructure to fuel future expansion. Thus, growth stocks pay low dividends.

At the other end of the spectrum are *value stocks.* Value stock investors look for good buys. They want to invest in stocks that are cheaply priced in relation to the assets and profits of the company.

These categories are combined in various ways to describe how a mutual fund invests its money. One fund may focus on large-company growth stocks; another fund limits itself to small-company value stocks. Funds are further qualified by the geographical locations of their investments: U.S., international, worldwide, and so on.

For more background on stocks, please see Chapter 10.

Funds of funds

Increasing numbers of fund providers are responding to overwhelmed investors and offering a simplified way to construct a portfolio: a mutual fund that diversifies across numerous other mutual funds. When a fund of funds is done right, it helps focus fund investors on the important big picture issue of asset allocation — how much of your investment money will you put into bonds versus stocks.

Although the best of such funds of funds appear to deliver a high quality, diversified portfolio of funds in one fell swoop, funds of funds are not all created equal and are not all worthy of your investment dollars.

The funds of funds concept is not new. In fact, it's been around many years. High fees gave the earlier funds of funds, run in the 1950s by the late Bernie Cornfeld, a bad name. He established a fund of funds outside the U.S. and tacked on many layers of fees. While profitable for his enterprise, duped investors suffered a continual drain of high fees. The Cornfeld episode is an important reason why the Securities and Exchange Commission has been slow in approving new funds of funds.

The newer funds of funds being developed by the larger fund companies are investor-friendly. Both Vanguard's LifeStrategy and T. Rowe Price's Spectrum funds of funds add no extra fees for packaging together the individual funds. Annual operating fees on the underlying funds at Vanguard are a razor thin one-third of one percent.

Other funds of funds, which layer on high fees, merit a much more skeptical look. For example, the Fund Manager Merriman and API family funds of funds charge annual operating expenses of 1.7 to 2.8 percent on top of the fees of the underlying mutual funds that they invest in. When you add it all up, investing in mutual funds through these funds can siphon off a whopping 3 to 4 percent annually of your investment balances.

Remember that stocks' historic annual returns average just 10 percent. So paying 3 to 4 percent in fees gives away about 30 to 40 percent of your expected returns. Not surprisingly, in terms of performance, the high fee funds of funds have badly lagged the stock market indexes.

U.S., international, and global funds

Most funds focus their investments in the U.S. unless they have words like *international, global, worldwide,* or *world* in their names. But even funds without one of these terms attached often invest money internationally.

The only way to know for sure where a fund is currently invested (or where the fund may invest in the future) is to ask. You can start by calling the 800 number of the mutual fund company that you're interested in.

The term *international* typically means that a fund can invest anywhere in the world except the U.S. The term *worldwide* or *global* generally implies that a fund can invest anywhere in the world, including the U.S. I generally recommend avoiding worldwide or global funds for two reasons. First, thoroughly following the financial markets and companies in so many parts of the world is difficult for a fund manager. Following financial markets and companies is hard enough to do so solely in U.S. or in a specific international market. Second, most of these funds charge high operating expenses — often well in excess of 1 percent per year — which puts a drag on returns.

Exceptions to this rule are the funds of funds — T. Rowe Price's Spectrum funds and Vanguard's Star and Life Strategy funds — I discuss earlier in this chapter. With these funds, you have multiple managers at work.

Index funds

Index funds are funds that can be (and are, for the most part) managed by a computer. An index fund's assets are invested to replicate an existing market index such as Standard & Poor's 500, an index of 500 large U.S. company stocks.

Over long periods (ten years or more), index funds outperform about three-quarters of their peers! How is that possible? How can a computer making mindless, predictable decisions beat out an intelligent, creative, MBA-endowed portfolio manager with a crack team of research analysts scouring the market for the best securities? The answer is cost. The computer does not demand a high salary nor does the computer need a big corner office. And index funds don't need a team of research analysts.

Most active fund managers cannot overcome the handicap of high operating expenses that pull down their funds' rates of return. As I discuss later in this chapter, operating expenses include all the fees and profit that a mutual fund extracts from a fund's returns before the returns are paid out to you. For example, the average U.S. stock fund has an operating expense ratio of 1.2 percent per year. So a U.S. stock index fund with an expense ratio of just 0.2 percent per year has an advantage of 1 percent per year.

Another not so inconsequential advantage of index funds is that you can't underperform the market. Some funds do just that due to the burden of high fees and poor management. If you were unfortunate enough to have been involved in the following loser mutual funds in the past ten years, you fared about 15 to 30 percent worse per year in your rate of return than if you had invested in a boring old index fund (Vanguard S&P's 500 Index over the same time period provided an average annual rate of return of 13.5 percent). See Table 11-1.

Table 11-1 Mutual Funds That Will Fetch a Stick (Bow Wow!)	
Fund	*Average Annual Rate of Return (10 years)*
Steadman Tech. Growth	–16.4%
Steadman American Industry	–13.8%
Steadman Investment	–6.1%
Centurion T.A.A.	–3.2%
Steadman Associated	–2.3%
American Heritage	–1.9%

For money invested outside retirement accounts, index funds have an added advantage: Fewer taxable distributions (discussed later in this chapter) are made to shareholders because less trading of securities is conducted and a more stable portfolio is maintained.

Yes, index funds may seem downright boring. When you invest in them, you give up the opportunity to brag to others about your shrewd investments that beat the market averages. On the other hand, you have no chance of doing much worse than the market, which more than a few mutual fund managers do.

Index funds make sense for a portion of your investments because it's very difficult for portfolio managers to beat the market. The Vanguard Group (800-662-7447), headquartered in Valley Forge, Pennsylvania, is the largest mutual-fund provider of index funds.

Specialty (sector) funds

Specialty funds don't fit neatly into the previously discussed categories. These funds are often known as *sector* funds because they tend to invest in securities in specific industries.

In most cases, you should avoid investing in specialty or sector funds. Investing in stocks of a single industry defeats a major purpose of investing in mutual funds — diversification. Another good reason to avoid sector funds is that they tend to carry much higher expenses than other mutual funds.

Specialty funds that may make sense for a small portion (10 percent or less) of your investment portfolio are funds that invest in real estate or precious metals (refer to Chapter 10). These types of funds can help diversify your portfolio because they can do better during times of higher inflation.

Selecting the Best Mutual Funds

When you go camping in the wilderness, you can do a number of things to maximize your odds of happiness and success. You take maps to keep you on course, food to keep you from getting hungry, proper clothing to stay dry and warm, and some first-aid gear to treat minor injuries. But regardless of how much advance preparation you do, you may have a less-than-perfect experience. You may take the wrong trail, trip on a rock and break your ankle, or lose your food to a tenacious bear that comes romping through camp one night.

And so it is with mutual funds. Although most mutual fund investors are rewarded for their efforts, there are no guarantees. You can, however, follow some simple, common sense guidelines that will keep you on the trail and increase your chances of investment success and happiness. The following issues in this section are the main ones you should consider.

Cost

The charges you pay to buy or sell a fund, as well as the ongoing fund operating expenses, can have a big impact on the rate of return you earn on your investments. Many novice investors pay too much attention to a mutual fund's prior performance (in the case of stock funds) or to the fund's current yield (in the case of bond funds). Doing so is dangerous because a fund can inflate its return or yield in many (risky) ways. And what worked yesterday may flop tomorrow.

Socially responsible funds

Increasing numbers of mutual funds that are popping up are labeling themselves *socially responsible.* This term means different things to different people. In most cases, though, it implies that the fund avoids investing in companies, such as tobacco manufacturers, that are harming people or the world at large. Because cigarettes and other tobacco products kill hundreds of thousands of people and add billions of dollars to health-care costs, most socially responsible funds shun tobacco companies.

Socially responsible investing presents a couple of problems. For example, your definition of social responsibility may not match the definition of the investment manager who's running a fund. Another problem is that even if you can agree on what's socially irresponsible (such as selling tobacco products), funds aren't always as clean as you would think or hope. Although a fund may avoid tobacco manufacturers, it may well invest in retailers that sell tobacco products.

If you want to consider a socially responsible fund, call the investment company and ask them to send you a recent report that lists the specific investments that the fund owns.

A recent study conducted by the Investment Company Institute confirmed what I've long observed among fund buyers. Only 43 percent of recent fund buyers who were surveyed bothered to examine the fees and expenses of the fund they ended up buying. The majority of fund buyers — 57 percent to be exact — don't know what funds are charging them to manage their money!

Fund costs are an important factor in the return that you earn from a mutual fund. Fees are deducted from your investment. All other things being equal, high fees and other charges depress your returns.

Loads

Loads are up-front commissions paid to brokers who sell mutual funds. Loads typically range from 4 percent to as high as 8.5 percent of your investment. Sales loads have two problems:

✔ First, sales loads are a needless cost that drags down the returns of your investment money.

Because commissions are paid to the salesperson and not to the fund manager, the manager of a load fund does not work any harder and is not any more qualified than a manager of a no-load fund. Common sense suggests and studies confirm that load funds perform *worse,* on average, than no-loads when the load is factored in.

And don't think that spotting a load fund is easy. Just as some jewelers flog fake diamonds on late-night TV commercials, increasing numbers of brokers and financial planners sell bogus funds that they *call* no-loads, but these funds are *not* no-loads — they just hide the sales commission.

"Stay in this fund for five to seven years," the broker will tell you, "and you don't have to pay the back-end sales charge that would normally apply upon sale of the investment." Although this claim may be true, it is also true that the fund is probably charging you very high ongoing operating expenses (usually 1 percent more per year than true no-load funds) that the fund uses to pay the salesperson a hefty commission. So one way or another, the broker gets his pound of flesh (that is, his commission) from your investment dollars.

✔ The second problem with sales loads is the power of self-interest.

Although this issue is rarely discussed, it is even more problematic than the issue of extra sales costs. Brokers who work for a commission are interested in selling you commission-based investment products; there-fore, their best interests often conflict with your best interests.

Although you may be mired in high-interest debt or underfunding your retirement plan, salespeople almost never advise you to pay off your credit cards or put more money into your 401(k). To get you to buy, they tend to exaggerate the potential benefits and obscure the risks and drawbacks of what they sell. They don't take the time to educate investors. I've seen too many people purchase investment products through brokers without understanding what they're buying, how much risk they are taking, and how these investments will affect their overall financial lives.

Invest in no-loads and avoid load funds and investment salespeople. The only way to be sure that a fund is truly no-load is to look at the prospectus for the fund. Only there, in black and white and without marketing hype, must the truth be told about sales charges and other fund fees. (An astonishing 73 percent of fund buyers surveyed by the Investment Company Institute didn't review whether the fund they bought charged a sales load!) If you need advice about investing, hire a financial advisor on a fee-for-service basis (see Chapter 19). Doing so ends up costing you less and eliminates potential conflicts of interest in product sales and recommendations.

Operating expenses

All mutual funds charge ongoing fees. The fees pay for the operational costs of running a fund — employees' salaries, marketing, servicing the toll-free phone lines, printing and mailing published materials, computers for tracking investments and account balances, accounting fees, and so on.

A fund's operating expenses are quoted as an annual percentage of your investment. A mutual fund's operating expenses are essentially invisible to you. That's because they're deducted before you're paid any return. The expenses are charged on a daily basis, so you have no need to worry about trying to get out of a fund before these fees are deducted.

You can find a fund's operating expenses in the fund's prospectus. Look in the expenses section and find a line that says something like "Total Fund Operating Expenses." You can also call the fund's 800 number and ask a representative.

Within a given sector of mutual funds (for example, money market, short-term bonds, or international stock), funds with low annual operating fees can more easily produce higher total returns for you.

Although expenses matter on all funds, some types of funds are more sensitive to high expenses than others. Expenses are critical on money market mutual funds and very important on bond funds. Fund managers already have a hard time beating the averages in these markets; with higher expenses added on, it's nearly impossible.

With stock funds, expenses are a less important (but still important) factor in picking a fund. Don't forget that over time, stocks have averaged returns of about 10 percent per year. So if one stock fund charges 1 percent in operating expenses more than another, you're already giving up an extra 10 percent of your expected returns.

Some people argue that stock funds that charge high expenses may be justified in doing so if they generate higher rates of return. Evidence doesn't show that they do generate higher returns. In fact, funds with higher operating expenses tend to produce *lower* rates of return. This trend makes sense because operating expenses are deducted from the returns that a fund generates.

Stick with funds that maintain low total operating expenses and that don't charge sales loads (commissions). Both types of fees come out of your pocket and reduce your rate of return.

You have no reason to pay a lot for the best funds, as Table 11-2 shows.

Table 11-2	Mutual Fund Operating Expense Ratios	
Fund Type	*Expense Ratio Range*	*Who's Got Good Ones*
Money market funds	0.2% to 0.4%	Vanguard, Fidelity (Spartan), USAA
Bonds funds	0.2% to 0.5%	Vanguard, Fidelity (Spartan), PIMCO, Benham, USAA
Hybrid	0.2% to 1%	Vanguard, Dodge & Cox, Fidelity
U.S. stock	0.2% to 1%	Fidelity, Vanguard, T. Rowe Price, others
International stock	0.4% to 1.3%	Vanguard, T. Rowe Price, others
Index	0.2% to 0.5%	Vanguard, Schwab
Specialty	0.4% to 1.0%	Fidelity, Vanguard

Historic performance

A fund's *performance*, or historic rate of return, is another important factor to weigh when selecting a mutual fund. As all mutual funds are required to tell you, past performance is no guarantee of future results. Analysis of historic mutual fund performance proves that some of yesterday's stars turn into tomorrow's skid-row bums.

Many former high-return funds achieved their results by taking on high risk. Funds that assume higher risk should produce higher rates of return. But high-risk funds usually decline in price faster during major market declines. Thus, in order for a fund to be considered a *best* fund, it must consistently deliver a favorable rate of return given the degree of risk it has taken.

When assessing an individual fund, compare its performance and volatility over an extended period of time (five or ten years will do) to a *relevant* market index. For example, compare funds which focus on investing in large U.S. companies to the Standard & Poor's' 500 Index. Funds that invest in U.S. stocks of all sizes can be compared to the Wilshire 5000 Index. Indexes also exist for bonds, foreign stock markets, and most any other type of security you can imagine.

Fund manager and fund family reputation

Much is made of who manages a specific mutual fund. As Peter Lynch, retired and famous former manager of the Fidelity Magellan fund, said, "The financial press made us Wall Street types into celebrities, a notoriety that was largely undeserved. Stock stars were treated as rock stars. . . ."

Although the individual fund manager is important, no fund manager is an island. The resources and capabilities of the parent company are equally important. Different companies have different capabilities and levels of expertise in relation to different types of funds. For example, Fidelity has a pool of talented U.S. stock fund managers upon which to draw when a manager leaves the firm or moves to another fund while Vanguard is terrific at money market, bond, and conservative stock funds, thanks to its low operating expenses.

When you're considering a particular fund — for example, the Barnum & Barney High-Flying Foreign Stock fund — examine the performance history and fees not only of that fund but also of similar foreign stock funds at the Barnum & Barney company. If Barnum's other foreign stock funds have done poorly or Barnum & Barney offers no other such funds because it's focused on its circus business, those are strikes against their High-Flying fund.

Tax-friendliness

Investors often overlook tax implications when selecting mutual funds for nonretirement accounts. Numerous mutual funds effectively reduce their shareholders' returns because of their tendency to produce more taxable distributions — that is capital gains and dividends — which I discuss later in this chapter).

"Ranking Mutual Funds on an After-Tax Basis," a pioneering study conducted by John B. Shoven and Joel M. Dickson at Stanford University, demonstrated that mutual fund capital gains distributions have a significant impact on an investor's after-tax rate of return. The Shoven and Dickson study found large differences between the before-tax and after-tax rates of return generated by stock mutual funds.

The following example highlights the dangers of picking a stock mutual fund for a nonretirement account simply on the basis of its reported rate of return.

Over a recent five-year period, the Founders Special fund averaged a 20.6 percent annual rate of return, outpacing the 20th Century Heritage fund, which averaged 17.6 percent per year. On the surface, it would seem that Founders, beating its rival by 3 percent per year, is the better of the two funds.

But that's only part of the story. All mutual fund managers buy and sell stocks during the course of a year. Whenever a mutual fund manager sells securities, any gain or loss from those securities must be distributed to fund shareholders. Securities sold at a loss can offset those sold at a profit.

If a fund manager has a tendency to cash in more winners than losers, investors in the fund receive a high amount of taxable gains. Over the past five years, the Founders Special fund has made capital gains distributions averaging a whopping 9.5 percent of shareholder principal per year. The 20th Century Heritage fund, on the other hand, has averaged just 3.3 percent in annual capital gains distributions. So, even though the Founder's fund says it produces higher total returns, *after* factoring in taxes, it doesn't.

Choosing mutual funds that minimize capital gains distributions helps you as the investor to defer taxes on your profits. By allowing your capital to continue compounding as it would in an IRA or other retirement account, you as a fund shareholder receive a higher total return.

In addition to capital gains distributions, mutual funds also produce dividends that may be subject to higher income tax rates for some investors, both for high-income earners and Social Security recipients (refer to Chapter 7 for details).

If you're a long-term investor, you benefit most from choosing mutual funds that minimize capital gains distributions. The more years that appreciation can compound without being taxed, the greater the value to you as the investor.

Investors who purchase mutual funds outside tax-sheltered retirement accounts should also consider the time of year they purchase shares in funds. December is the most common month in which mutual funds make capital gains distributions. When making purchases late in the year, ask if and when the fund may make a significant capital gains distribution. Consider delaying purchases in such funds until January.

Your needs and goals

Selecting the best funds for you requires an understanding of your investment goals and risk tolerance. A good fund for your next-door neighbor is not necessarily a good fund for you. You have a unique financial profile.

Reading prospectuses and annual reports

Mutual fund companies produce information that can help you make decisions about mutual fund investments. Every fund is required to issue a *prospectus.* This legal document is reviewed and audited by the U.S. Securities and Exchange Commission. Most of what's written isn't worth the time it takes to slog through it.

The most valuable information — the fund's in-vestment objectives, costs, and performance history — is summarized in the first few pages of the prospectus. This part you should read. Skip the rest, comprised mostly of tedious legal details.

Funds also produce annual reports that discuss how the fund has been doing and provide details on the specific investments that a fund holds. If, for example, you want to know which countries an international fund invests in, you can find this information in the fund's annual report.

If you've determined your needs and goals already, terrific! If you haven't, refer to Chapter 8. Understanding yourself is a good part of the battle. But don't shortchange yourself by not being educated about the investment you're considering. If you do not understand what you are investing in and how much risk you are taking, then you should stay out of the game.

Best Places for Fund Investing

The mutual fund field has attracted a lot of new competitors tempted by the riches that early winners have accumulated. Banks, insurance companies, and even airlines have jumped on the bandwagon. Unfortunately, most of these companies sell funds with high fees, subpar performance, or both.

Here's a short list of the leading firms to consider when investing in funds. Please note that fund companies not on this short list have some excellent funds and not all funds offered by each of the top companies are worthy of your fund dollars.

Vanguard Group

The Vanguard Group (800-662-7447), headquartered in Valley Forge, Pennsylva-nia, is the nation's largest exclusively commission-free mutual fund provider with over $200 billion under management. Vanguard is a solid base for safety-minded investors who want to invest in money market, bond, and conservative stock funds.

To understand and appreciate Vanguard, you need to know a bit about John Bogle, founder of the Vanguard Group of mutual funds. Bogle came up with a unique ownership structure for Vanguard. He insisted that the management of individual funds be contracted out to the private money-management firms with whom Vanguard negotiates the best deal.

Vanguard mutual fund investors (now numbering around 5 million) own the company. Thus Vanguard, the company, makes no profit. You can buy its funds at cost — that is, with no markup.

Mutual fund operating expenses, which are deducted from a fund's returns before shareholders are paid, are by far lower at Vanguard than at any other company in the industry. In comparison to 1.11 percent for the average mutual fund, Vanguard's fund operating expenses average just 0.31 percent.

Thus, Vanguard investors begin the investment performance race with a head start of about 0.7 percent per year in return. Vanguard is also the mutual fund innovator of index funds (discussed earlier in this chapter), which are unmanaged portfolios of the representative securities that comprise an index, such as the S&P 500. Vanguard offers the broadest selection and lowest cost index funds in the business.

Vanguard also offers discount brokerage services (800-992-8327) through which, if you're so inclined, you can trade individual securities or buy mutual funds from a handful of other good fund companies (a service similar to that offered by other discount brokers, which I discuss in this chapter). Vanguard charges a flat fee of $35 per transaction for non-Vanguard fund purchases or sales.

Such mutual fund shopping services allow you to consolidate all of your no-load funds into one account. It simplifies your paperwork, reducing your desk's build-up of fund applications and account statements.

Cost is the main drawback to using such mutual fund supermarkets rather than buying funds from fund companies on your own. If you buy funds directly from their companies, you avoid any unnecessary transaction fees.

Fidelity Investments

Fidelity Investments (800-544-6666), headquartered in Boston, Massachusetts, is the nation's largest mutual fund company with more than $400 billion under management. Fidelity has about 100 local branch offices around the U.S. and offers 24-hour customer service.

Fidelity's roots trace back to the 1940s, when Edward C. Johnson II took over the then-fledgling Fidelity Fund from its president, who felt that he couldn't make enough money as the head of an investment fund! Johnson's son, Ned (Edward C. Johnson III), took over management of Fidelity in 1972.

Fidelity offers a number of excellent mutual funds, particularly those that invest in U.S. stocks. If you're the kind of person who likes to pick among 30 different brands of potato chips at the store, you'll love Fidelity. They offer more than 200 different funds, more than any other mutual fund company.

Consider using Fidelity particularly for investments in retirement accounts. Nonretirement accounts in many of their best stock funds typically cost you 2 to 3 percent in sales fees (which you should avoid whenever possible).

Beware of Fidelity Advisor funds, which are sold through commission-based investment salespeople and carry high sales and ongoing management fees.

Like Vanguard, Fidelity offers discount brokerage services (800-544-8666) through which you can invest in individual securities as well as mutual funds from companies other than Fidelity.

Fidelity offers several hundred non-Fidelity funds without transaction fees (that is, at the same cost as buying from the mutual fund company directly). These are called *no transaction fee* funds. Approach these funds with caution. Many of them, particularly the bond funds, carry higher operating expenses.

Most of the better funds that you'll buy through Fidelity or other discount brokers will charge transaction fees. Fidelity charges a flat fee of $35 per purchase or sale.

Charles Schwab & Company

Charles Schwab & Co. (800-526-8600), headquartered in San Francisco, California, is the nation's largest discount brokerage firm with assets of more than $200 billion. It offers 24-hour customer service and has more than 200 local branch offices. Schwab was founded in 1974 by Charles R. Schwab, an innovator in the industry.

To speak of Schwab as a discount broker, a term applied to firms that trade individual securities, is not really appropriate anymore. The majority of customer assets at Schwab now are in mutual funds.

Schwab's mutual fund supermarket is among the biggest. In addition to offering hundreds of funds, Schwab also offers a small family of its own funds. As with the fees it charges for individual security trades, Schwab's Mutual Fund Transaction Fees are among the costlier in the business, especially for larger investment amounts. For trades up to $5,000, you'll pay the minimum of $39. On a $10,000 trade, it costs $70 and for a $30,000 trade, $135. If you place your mutual fund trade through Schwab's computer software packages (see Chapter 21) or by touch-tone phone, you get a 10 percent discount on these fees.

Jack White & Company

Founded in 1975, Jack White & Company (800-323-3263) is a discount brokerage firm based in San Diego, California, with approximately $7 billion in customer account assets. Like Schwab and a handful of other discount brokers, it offers a mutual fund service, too.

White's fee schedule is a bit more complicated than some of the previously discussed discount brokers. White charges $27 for investments of up to $5,000, $35 for amounts up to $25,000, and $50 for amounts in excess of that.

White is a no-frills broker. You won't find a local branch office in your area (unless you live in the San Diego area). However, White's representatives are available by phone 24 hours a day, seven days a week.

White also offers a useful service, called Connect, that allows holders of load (commission-based) mutual funds to sell their shares to another buyer. The buyer pays a flat $200 fee instead of the normal 4 to 8.5 percent commission that he must normally pay to an investment salesperson. For purchases of $5,000 or more of a mutual fund, this service can save a buyer hundreds or thousands of dollars. The seller benefits, too — getting paid $100 to sell a load fund through White's service.

Tracking Fund Rankings and Performance

Whether you're a novice or an experienced mutual fund investor, trying to get a handle on which funds are the best in various categories (such as international stocks or mortgage bonds) through mutual fund information and rating services can be overwhelming. Value Line and Morningstar, for example, track thousands of funds. These services are big, heavy, and awfully unwieldy for beginners to use.

Many publications track and recommend load mutual funds, which are sold through investment brokers. As discussed earlier in the chapter, sales commissions on load funds typically amount to 4 to 8.5 percent of your investment dollars. Perhaps more dangerous is the possibility that you'll end up in the hands of a salesperson who will recommend investments and other financial products that are not in your best interests.

Finding and investing in good funds isn't rocket science. Chapters 12 and 13 recommend the best mutual funds using criteria discussed earlier in the chapter. If you're still not satiated, pick up a copy of *Mutual Funds For Dummies*, another book I've written in this infamous series.

Beware the worst sources

With the popularity of mutual funds, more and more business, personal finance, and news magazines publish mutual fund articles and rankings. For a variety of reasons, much of this information isn't useful to folks trying to make informed decisions. In fact, making decisions based on some of these so-called mutual fund studies is downright dangerous.

One of the nation's largest business magazines committed a number of major errors in its recent "Top Funds" analysis. First of all, the article awarded high returns without paying any attention to risk or volatility. Funds that took more risk and were able to generate higher rates of return were awarded higher rankings.

The most egregious error was the ranking of funds solely on the basis of rate of return over a three-year period. Three years is a very short time to look at fund performance. This particular three-year period witnessed a nearly uninterrupted upward march in stock and bond prices. Imagine betting on an athlete to win the Olympic decathlon after the shot-put competition. Sure, a stocky, muscular type can shot-put farther than his competitors, but he may be huffing and puffing his way around the track in the mile run.

Another example of the "garbage in, garbage out" phenomenon is the ranking done by Lipper Analytic Services, which are often published in newspapers and magazines. This organization assigns letter grades to funds just like your junior high school teacher did, except your teacher's system was probably more sound. Lipper grades funds within broad categories based solely on total return, completely ignoring risk. The performance rankings that wind up in some newspapers can be for periods as short as *one year.*

Another mistake that some publications commit in published mutual fund rankings is dumping a truckload of data on you. They then order the mutual funds alphabetically so that you sift through page after page of rows and columns of numbers. You have better things to do with your time.

Sadly, one of the reasons some publications confuse more than they convey is *advertising.* I once got a call from a financial reporter. Mr. Reporter had an outline for an article he wanted to write about mutual fund investing in which he would profile mutual fund investors that had specific fund companies' investments. The list included a number of load funds, all of which were heavy advertisers in the magazine.

As best I could tell, the reporter, who came from a political background, had little — if any — experience with the financial services industry. A few minutes into our conversation, he asked me to explain a couple of terms I had used. He didn't know the difference between a stock fund and a bond fund! To this day, I marvel about this experience. I hope you enjoy the fact that, having read this chapter, you know a lot more about mutual funds than this reporter did.

Consider fund directories

Both Value Line and Morningstar put out behemoth mutual fund directories that track thousands of mutual funds. They're reference publications, not newsletters or magazines. If you already have a large portfolio of funds that you've invested in and want to check out a large number of other funds, these publications may be of use to you.

The services are more similar than they are different. Value Line is the newer kid on the block, having launched its service in late 1993. Both use a similar format, devoting a single page packed with all sorts of details, numbers, and a bit of commentary to each fund. Funds are ranked on a scale of one to five (Morningstar uses stars; Value Line uses numbers).

The most common mistake investors make in using these publications is focusing too much on the ranking of specific funds. Both publications' lengthy guidebooks (which most people don't read) warn against doing so, although they don't say it strongly enough for my taste.

Their ratings are somewhat useful in that they look at *risk-adjusted performance* — the performance of a fund in relation to the risk (or volatility) that it took to achieve it. The rankings have a number of limitations, however. One fatal flaw with both services is that they lump funds into broad categories, when in fact, many funds within the category invest in different types of securities.

For example, in the various stock fund categories, you find funds that invest exclusively in stocks and others that invest some of their money in bonds or other high-dividend-paying securities, such as preferred stocks. These types of securities tend to reduce the volatility of a portfolio and do well in times of declining interest rates (such as we've had since the early 1980s).

Funds that invest in U.S. securities as well as those overseas are another example. Mutual funds that call or classify themselves as worldwide are put in a *global* or *worldwide* category. The others end up scattered throughout the U.S. stock and balanced fund categories. These misclassified funds, which invest worldwide but don't self-classify themselves as global, have a leg up on their U.S.-focused competitors in the ratings because international securities tend to reduce the volatility of a fund.

The rankings also ignore fund operating expenses. Because the past is at best a weak predictor of things to come, you're more likely to succeed with funds that keep expenses down. As I explain earlier in this chapter, high expenses are a handicap to generating good future returns.

Brokers and financial planners love the rating system because they can sell you funds with commissions (load funds) easier. They push those with high ratings, saying, "Here's an independent rating service's assessment of the fund we talked about."

Lipper (which I discuss in the previous section) is now peddling fund reports for brokers to use. As *The Wall Street Journal* reported, these slick reports are, ". . . designed as a tool to help brokers sell mutual-fund shares."

Few publications in this world should be called *independent.* Morningstar, Value Line, and Lipper are not among them. Many of those who subscribe to these publications are investment salespeople who sell load (commissionable) mutual funds. A contributing editor at Morningstar, who has since left, once told me, "We could never say to avoid load funds — otherwise we'd lose a large number of subscribers."

Both services are packed with too much information and too many funds for the nonexpert investor. These publications are not for you unless you're willing to spend a lot of time learning how to digest all the information they contain.

The services are also not cheap. Check your local library, where you can use the Value Line and Morningstar directories, or obtain the three-month trial subscription that they each offer.

Understanding your fund's performance

When you look at a statement for your mutual fund holdings, odds are that you're not going to understand it. It's not you — it's the statement.

The hardest part is getting a handle on how you're doing. Most people want to know, and have a hard time figuring out, how much they've made or lost on their investment.

You cannot deduce your return by comparing the share price of the fund today versus the share price that you originally paid for the fund. Why not? Because mutual funds make distributions, both of dividends and capital gains, which lead to your getting more shares of the fund (see the section on taxes and funds earlier in this chapter).

Distributions create an accounting problem because they reduce the share price of a fund. (Otherwise, you could buy into a fund just before it made a distribution and make a profit from the distribution). Therefore, over time, following just the share price of your fund doesn't tell you how much money you've made or lost.

Imagine that the share price of your mutual fund is like a balloon with a small rock tied to the end of a string attached to it. The balloon (representing fund share price) struggles to rise, but the rock (representing fund distributions) keeps pulling down on the balloon.

The only way to figure out exactly how much you've made or lost on your investment is to compare the total value of your holdings in a fund today versus the total dollar amount you originally invested. If you've invested chunks of money at various points in time, this exercise becomes much more complicated, if you want to factor in the timing of your various investments. (Check out recommended investment software in Chapter 21 if you want your computer to help you crunch your own numbers.)

The *total return* of a fund is the percentage change of your investment over a specified period. For example, a fund may tell you that in 1996 its total return was 15 percent. Therefore, if you had invested $10,000 in the fund on the last day of 1995, your investment would be worth $11,500 at the end of 1996. To get a fund's total return, you can call the fund company's 800 number or you can read the fund's annual report.

The following three components make up your total return on a fund:

- ✔ Dividends
- ✔ Capital gains
- ✔ Share price changes

Dividends

Dividends are income paid by investments. Both bonds and stocks can pay dividends. Bond fund dividends tend to be higher (as a percentage of the amount you have invested in a fund). When a dividend distribution is made, you can receive it as cash (which is good if you need money to live on) or as more shares in the fund. In either case, the share price of the fund drops by an amount to offset the payout. So if you are hoping to strike it rich by buying into a bunch of funds just before their dividends are paid, don't bother. You'll just end paying more in income taxes.

If you hold your mutual fund outside a retirement account, the dividend distributions are taxable income (unless they come from a tax-free municipal bond fund). Dividends are taxable whether or not you reinvest them as additional shares in the fund.

Capital gains

When a mutual fund manager sells a security in the fund, net gains realized from that sale (the difference from the purchase price) must be distributed to you as a *capital gain.* Typically, funds make one annual capital gains distribution in December.

As with a dividend distribution, you can receive your capital gains distribution as cash or as more shares in the fund. In either case, the share price of the fund drops by an amount to offset the distribution.

For funds held outside retirement accounts, your capital gains distribution is taxable. As with dividends, capital gains are taxable whether or not you re-invest them in additional shares in the fund.

As I discuss in more detail in the next chapter, you may want to check with a fund to determine when capital gains are distributed if you want to avoid making an investment in a fund that is about to make a capital gains distribution. This increases your current-year tax liability for investments made outside of retirement accounts.

Share price changes

You also make money with a mutual fund when the share price increases. This occurrence is just like investing in a stock or piece of real estate. If it's worth more today than when you bought it, you have made a profit (on paper, at least). In order to realize or lock in this profit, you need to sell your shares in the fund.

There you have it — the components of a mutual fund's total return are the following:

Dividends + Capital Gains + Share Price Changes = Total Return

Following and selling your funds

How closely you follow your funds is up to you, depending on what makes you happy and comfortable. I do not recommend tracking the share prices of your funds (or other investments for that matter) on a daily basis. It's time-consuming, nerve-racking, and will make you lose sight of the long term. You are more likely to panic when times get tough. And for investments held outside of retirement accounts, every time you sell an investment at a profit, you get hit with taxes.

Weekly, monthly, or quarterly check-in is more than frequent enough to follow your funds. Many newspapers now carry total return numbers over varying periods, so you can determine the exact rate of return that you've been earning.

Trying to time and trade the markets to buy at lows and sell at highs rarely works. Yet an entire industry of investment newsletters, hotlines, online services, and the like have sprung up purporting to be able to tell you when to buy and sell. Don't waste your time and money on such nonsense (refer to Chapter 9 to read about gurus and newsletters).

You should consider selling a fund when it no longer meets the criteria mentioned in the section "Selecting the Best Mutual Funds" located earlier in this chapter. If a fund has underperformed its peers for at least a two-year period or if a fund jacks up its management fees, it may be a good time to sell. But if you do your homework and buy good funds from good fund companies, you should need to do little trading.

Chapter 12

Investing Money Inside Retirement Accounts

In This Chapter

▶ Types of retirement accounts

▶ Investments to avoid in retirement accounts

▶ How to allocate money in employer-sponsored plans

▶ How to allocate in plans that you design

▶ How to transfer retirement accounts

*T*his chapter explains how to make decisions about investing money you currently hold inside retirement accounts or money you plan to contribute to a retirement account.

Compared to the often overwhelming world of investing outside retirement accounts, investing inside tax-sheltered retirement accounts — IRAs, 401(k)s, SEP-IRAs, and Keoghs — is far less complicated. Two reasons for this:

✔ **The range of possible retirement account investments is more limited.** Direct investments, such as real estate and investments in small, privately owned companies, are not generally available or accessible in most retirement accounts.

✔ **When investing in a retirement account, your returns aren't taxed as you earn them.** Money inside retirement accounts compounds and grows without taxation. You only pay taxes on these funds when you withdraw money from the account (direct transfers to another investment firm are not withdrawals, so they are not taxed). So when you are choosing an investment for your retirement account, don't rack your brain over dividends and capital gains; save all that worry for your money in nonretirement accounts.

Types of Retirement Accounts

Retirement accounts offer numerous benefits. In most cases, your contributions are tax-deductible. And once inside the retirement account, your money compounds without taxation until you withdraw it. The rest of this section describes the major types of accounts and explains how to determine whether you are eligible for them.

Employer-sponsored plans

Your employer sets up these retirement plans. No muss, no fuss — the employer does all the work, including the selection of investment options. All you have to do is contribute away!

401(k) plans

For-profit companies offer 401(k) plans. The silly name comes from the section of the tax code that establishes and regulates these plans. A 401(k) generally allows you to save up to approximately $9,500 per year (for 1996). Your employer's plan may have lower limits, though, because not enough employees save enough. Your contributions to a 401(k) are excluded from your reported income and thus are free from federal and state income taxes.

Some employers don't allow you to contribute to a 401(k) plan until you've worked for them for a full year. Others allow you to start contributing right away. Some employers also match a portion of your contributions. They may, for example, match half of your first 6 percent of contributions, so in addition to saving a lot of taxes, you get a bonus from the company.

If your company does offer a matching money program and if you earn a high enough income such that you hit the plan maximum before the end of year, you may lose out on some of that matching money if you don't spread your contributions over the full calendar year. Check with your company's benefits department for your plan's specifics.

Thanks to technological innovations and the growth of the mutual fund industry, smaller companies (those with fewer than 100 employees) can consider offering 401(k) plans, too. In the past, it was prohibitively expensive for smaller companies to administer 401(k)s. If your company is interested in this option, contact a mutual fund organization, such as T. Rowe Price, Vanguard, or Fidelity, or a discount brokerage house, such as Charles Schwab or Jack White.

Can your employer steal your retirement plan money?

The short answer, unfortunately, is yes. However, the vast majority of employees, particularly those who work for larger and more established companies, need not worry.

Some companies that administer 401(k) plans have been cited by the U.S. Labor Department for being too slow in putting money that employees had deferred from their paychecks into employee 401(k) investment accounts. In the worst cases, companies diverted employees' 401(k) money to pay for corporate bills. Many business owners who engaged in such practices, rather than intent on fraud, used 401(k) money as a short-term emergency fund.

In cases where companies failed and funds were diverted from employee 401(k) accounts, the funds were lost. In cases where the money was delayed in being put into the employees' 401(k) accounts, employees simply lost out on earning return on their investments during the period. Once your contributions are in your 401(k) account, they are financially and legally separate from your employer. Thus, your funds will still be protected even if your employer goes bankrupt.

After conducting hundreds of investigations, the Labor Department issued rulings requiring employers to contribute employee retirement contributions into their proper accounts within 90 days. In addition to keeping tabs on your employer that money withheld from your paycheck is contributed into your account within this time frame, you should also periodically check your 401(k) statement for accuracy.

403(b) plans

Nonprofit organizations offer 403(b) plans to their employees. As with 401(k)s, your contributions to these plans are federal and state tax-deductible. The 403(b) plans are more often known as *tax-sheltered annuities,* the name for insurance company investments that satisfy the requirements for 403(b) plans. For the benefit of 403(b) retirement-plan participants, *no-load* (commission-free) mutual funds can be used in 403(b) plans.

Nonprofit employees are allowed to annually contribute up to 20 percent or $9,500 of their salary, whichever is less. Employees who have 15 or more years of service may be allowed to contribute a few thousand dollars beyond the $9,500 limit. Ask your employee benefits department or the investment provider for the 403(b) plan about eligibility requirements and details about your personal contribution limit.

If you work for a nonprofit or public-sector organization that doesn't offer this benefit, make a fuss and insist on it. Nonprofit organizations have no excuse not to offer a 403(b) plan to their employees. Unlike a 401(k), this type of plan includes virtually no out-of-pocket expenses to the employer. The only requirement is that the organization must deduct the appropriate contribution from employees' paychecks and send the money to the investment company handling the 403(b) plan.

What's a 457 retirement plan?

Some nonprofit organizations offer what are called 457 plans. Like 403(b) or 401(k) plans, 457 plans offer participants the ability to contribute money out of their paycheck on a pre-tax basis and thus save on federal and state taxes.

457 plans, however, differ in the following important ways. First, money that you contribute into a 457 plan is not separate from the organization's finances. Thus, if the non-profit goes belly up — a rare but not impossible occurrence in the non-profit world — your retirement funds could be in jeopardy. Second, 457 plan contributions are limited to $7,500 per year.

Don't consider contributing to a 457 plan until you've exhausted contributions to your 403(b).

Self-employment plans

If you work for yourself, then you obviously don't have an employer to do the legwork to set up a retirement plan. You need to take the initiative. Although there's more work for you, the good news is that you can select and design a plan that meets your needs. Self-employment retirement savings plans allow you to put *more* money away on a tax-deductible basis than most employers' plans do.

If you have employees, you are required to provide coverage for them under these plans with contributions comparable to the company owners' (as a percentage of salary). Some part-time (fewer than 1,000 hours per year) and newer employees (less than a few years of service) may be excluded. Many small-business owners don't know about this requirement or choose to ignore it; they set up plans for themselves but fail to cover their employees. The danger is that the IRS and state tax authorities may discover small-business owners' negligence, sock them with big penalties, and disqualify their prior contributions. Because self-employed people and small businesses get their taxes audited at a relatively high rate, don't muck up this area.

Don't avoid setting up a retirement savings plan for your business just because you have employees and you don't want to make contributions on their behalf. If you look at contributions for your employees as an additional cost of doing business, you need to take a fresh look at the world. In the long run, you build the contributions you make for your employees into their total compensation package — which includes salary and other benefits like health insurance. Making retirement contributions need not increase your personnel costs.

To get the most from contributions as an employer, consider the following:

- ✔ Educate your employees about the value of retirement savings plans. You want them to understand, but more importantly, you want them to appreciate your investment.

- ✔ Select a Keogh plan that requires employees to stay a certain number of years to vest fully in their contributions. Reward long-term contributors to your company's success.

- ✔ Consider offering a 401(k) plan if you have more than 20 employees.

SEP-IRAs

Simplified employee pension individual retirement account (SEP-IRA) plans require little paperwork to set up. SEP-IRAs allow you to sock away 13 percent (13.04 percent, to be exact) of your self-employment income (business revenue minus deductions), up to a maximum of $22,500 per year. Each year, you decide the amount you want to contribute — there are no minimums. Your contributions to a SEP-IRA are deducted from your taxable income, saving you big-time on federal and state taxes. As with other retirement plans, your money compounds without taxation until you withdraw it.

If you're wondering what's with the oddball percentage — 13.04 percent — a somewhat reasonable explanation exists. SEPs actually allow you to contribute 15 percent of your *net* self-employment income. However, you need to subtract your SEP contribution and half of your self-employment (Social Security) taxes to arrive at your net self-employment income. Multiplying by 13.04 percent is simpler; it factors in the necessary subtractions for you.

Don't be hoodwinked into a "private pension plan"

Employers who don't want to make retirement plan contributions on behalf of their employees are bait for insurance salespeople selling so-called private pension plans. Basically, these plans are cash-value life insurance policies — which combine life insurance protection with a savings type account (see Chapter 17 for more details).

The selling hook of these plans is that you can save money for yourself but need not contribute money on your employees' behalf. And your contributions compound without taxation over the years.

Sound good? Well, life insurance salespeople who earn hefty commissions from selling cash value life policies won't tell you about the big negatives of these plans. Unlike contributions to true retirement savings plans such as SEP-IRAs and Keoghs, you derive *no* up-front tax deduction.

Also, if you don't need life insurance protection, the cost of such coverage is wasted if you save through these plans.

Keoghs

Keogh plans require a bit more paperwork to set up and administer than SEP-IRAs. The appeal of certain types of Keoghs is that they allow you to put away a greater percentage (20 percent) of your self-employment income (revenue less your deductions), up to a maximum of $30,000 per year.

All types of Keogh plans allow *vesting schedules*, which require employees to remain with the company a number of years before they earn the right to their full retirement account balances.

Keogh plans also allow for *Social Security integration*. Without going into all the gory tax details, *integration* effectively allows those in the company who are high-income earners (usually the owners) to receive larger percentage contributions for their accounts than the less highly compensated employees. The logic behind this idea is that Social Security benefits top out once you earn more than $62,700 (for 1996). Social Security integration allows you to make up for this ceiling.

Just to make life complicated, Keoghs come in four main flavors:

- ✔ **Profit-sharing plans.** These plans have the same contribution limits as SEP-IRAs. So why would you want the headaches of a more complicated plan when you can't contribute more to it? These plans appeal to owners of small companies who want to minimize the contributions to which employees are entitled, which is done through use of vesting schedules and Social Security integration.

- ✔ **Money-purchase pension plans.** You can contribute more to these plans than you can to a profit-sharing plan or SEP-IRA: 20 percent of your self-employment income up to a maximum of $30,000 per year. While allowing for a larger contribution, there is *no* flexibility allowed on the percentage contribution you make each year — it's fixed. Thus, these plans make the most sense for employers who are comfortable enough financially to continue making contributions that are a high percentage of their salary.

If the simplicity of the money-purchase pension plan appeals to you, don't be overly concerned about the consequences of some unforeseen circumstance that might make you unable to make the required contribution. You can amend your plan and change the contribution percentage starting the next year.

As long as you have a reason, the IRS generally allows you to discontinue the plan altogether. Prior contributions can remain in the Keogh account — you can even transfer them to other investment providers if you like. Discontinuing the plan simply means that you won't be making further contributions. You don't lose the money.

Usually, people reduce contributions because their business income drops off. The silver lining to your shrinking income is that Keogh plan contributions are set as a percentage of your earnings. So less income means proportionately smaller contributions.

✔ **Paired plans.** These plans combine the preceding profit-sharing and money-purchase plans. Although they require a little more paperwork to set up and administer, paired plans take the best of both individual plans.

You can attain the maximum contribution possible (20 percent) that you get with the money-purchase pension plan but have some of the flexibility that comes with a profit-sharing plan. You can fix your money-purchase pension plan contribution at 8 percent and contribute anywhere from 0 to 12 percent of your net income to your profit-sharing plan.

✔ **Defined-benefit plans.** These plans are for people who are able and willing to put away more than $30,000 per year. As you can imagine, only a very small percentage of people can afford these plans. Consistently high-income earners older than 45 or 50 who want to save more than $30,000 per year in a retirement account should consider these plans. If you are interested in defined-benefit plans, hire an actuary to crunch the numbers to calculate how much you can contribute to such a plan.

Individual Retirement Accounts (IRAs)

Anyone with employment income can contribute to IRA accounts. You may contribute up to $2,000 each year. If you don't earn $2,000 a year, you can contribute as much as you'd like (and can afford) up to that amount. If you are a nonworking spouse, you're eligible to put $250 per year into a so-called *spousal IRA.*

An exception to earning employment income makes you eligible to contribute to an IRA: Receiving alimony also qualifies you for an IRA contribution.

Your contributions to an IRA may or may not be tax-deductible. If you're single and your adjusted gross income is $25,000 or less for the year, you can deduct your full IRA contribution. If you're married and file your taxes jointly, you're entitled to a full IRA deduction if your AGI (adjusted gross income) is $40,000 per year or less.

If you make more than these amounts, you can take a full IRA deduction if and only if you (or your spouse) are *not* an active participant in any retirement plan. The only way to know for certain whether you're an active participant is to look at your W-2 Form: that smallish (4 by 8 ¹/₂-inch) document your employer sends you early in the year to file with your tax returns. Little boxes in box number 15 on that form indicate whether or not you are an active participant in a pension or deferred-compensation plan. If either of these boxes is checked, you're an active participant.

If you are a single income earner with an adjusted gross income above $25,000 but below $35,000, or part of a couple with an AGI above $40,000 but below $50,000, you're eligible for a partial IRA deduction, even if you're an active participant in another plan. The size of the IRA deduction that you may claim depends on where you fall in the income range.

- ✔ For example, a single income earner at $30,000 is entitled to half ($1,000) of the full IRA deduction because his or her income falls halfway between $25,000 and $35,000.

- ✔ A couple earning $42,500 loses just a quarter of the full IRA amount because their incomes are a quarter of the way from $40,000 to $50,000. Thus they can take a $1,500 IRA deduction.

The IRS 1040 instruction booklet comes with a worksheet that allows you to do the calculations for your situation.

Even if you can't deduct a portion or all of a $2,000 IRA contribution, you can still contribute to an IRA. This misunderstanding is common among people who used to contribute to IRAs before tax laws changed in 1986 (before then, anyone could deduct their IRA contributions, but lots of restrictions on deductions were added in 1986).

An IRA contribution that is not tax-deductible is called, not surprisingly, a *nondeductible* IRA contribution. The benefit of this type of contribution is that the money can still compound and grow without taxation. For a person who plans to leave contributions in the IRA for a long time (a decade or more), this tax-deferred compounding makes even nondeductible contributions worthwhile. However, you should consider such an IRA only after you have exhausted the possibilities of contributing to retirement accounts that do provide an immediate tax deduction, such as 401(k)s, SEPs, Keoghs, and so on.

Annuities: an odd investment

Annuities, like IRAs, allow your capital to grow and compound without taxation. You defer taxes until withdrawal. Annuities carry the same penalties for withdrawal prior to age 59 1/2 as do other retirement accounts.

Unlike an IRA that has a $2,000 annual contribution limit, you can deposit as much as you want in any year into an annuity — even a million dollars plus if you've got it! As with a so-called nondeductible IRA, you get no up-front tax deduction for your contributions.

Annuities are peculiar investment products. They are contracts that are backed by an insurance company. If you, the annuity holder (investor), die during the so-called *accumulation phase* (that is, prior to receiving payments from the annuity), your designated beneficiary is guaranteed to receive the amount of your original investment. In this sense, annuities look a bit like life insurance.

Retirement account inequities

To put everyone on more equal footing, those who don't work for employers with retirement savings plans should be allowed to contribute more to their IRAs. It's not fair that people who work for companies that have no retirement savings plans can deduct only $2,000 per year from their taxable income for an IRA.

Take an example of two households that each have annual employment income of $50,000. One household has access to a 401(k) plan, while the other household has no access to retirement plans other than an IRA. The household with the 401(k) can put away and deduct from their taxable income thousands of dollars more per year than the household with just the IRA.

This inequity has persisted because of the federal government's budget deficit. Allowing more people to make larger tax-deductible contributions to retirement accounts would reduce government revenue in the short-term. Tax deductions for retirement savings are included in the tax system to encourage people to provide for their own retirement. But telling people the importance of saving for retirement and not giving them more equal access to do so is hypocritical.

Because the initial contribution to an annuity is not tax-deductible, contributing to an annuity only makes sense if

- You have exhausted contributions to employer-sponsored and self-employed plans. Your contributions to these plans are tax-deductible; annuity contributions are not.

- You have also made the maximum contribution that you can to an IRA account, even if it's not tax-deductible. Annuities carry higher fees (which reduce your investment returns) because of the insurance that comes with them; IRA investments offer you better returns.

- You expect to leave the money compounding in the annuity for at least 15 years. It typically takes this long for the benefits of tax-deferred compounding to outweigh the higher annuity fees. If you're close to or actually in retirement, tax-friendly investments made outside of retirement accounts (discussed in Chapter 13) are preferable.

For more details about other investment options and the best places to purchase annuities, see Chapter 13 about investing money outside of retirement accounts.

Inappropriate Retirement Account Investments

Some investments for retirement accounts are simply inappropriate. The basic problem stems from otherwise intelligent folks forgetting, ignoring, or simply not knowing that retirement accounts are sheltered from taxation so you want to maximize that benefit by selecting investment vehicles that would otherwise be taxed. This section discusses investments that you should *not* make in retirement accounts.

Tax-free bonds

Investments that produce income that is tax-free either at the federal or state level don't make much sense inside retirement accounts. Tax-free securities always yield less than their taxable counterparts, so you are essentially giving away free yield when you invest in such securities inside retirement accounts. Remember, your retirement account investments are sheltered from taxation.

A big no-no is investing in municipal bonds inside a retirement account. Municipals are free from federal and/or state taxation. As such, they yield significantly less than an equivalent bond that pays fully taxable dividends. Municipal bonds definitely don't belong in a retirement account. The better investment firms don't let you make this mistake.

"Okay," you may be saying, "I'm smart enough to know not to invest in municipal bonds inside a retirement account." Terrific, I say. But lots of people make the mistake, albeit a smaller one, of investing in Treasuries — that is, U. S. Treasury bills, notes, or bonds — inside of retirement accounts.

When you buy Treasuries, although you get the safety net of a government guarantee, you also get a bond that produces interest free of state tax. (By the way, I've never understood why investors think that lending their money to the U.S. government, an organization with more than $5 trillion in debt outstanding, is 100-percent safe.) Fully taxable bonds yield more than state-tax-free Treasuries. And, the safety of Treasuries can easily be replicated in other bonds.

Some diversified mutual funds invest a portion of their funds in Treasuries. Holding such a fund is not a mistake as long as the portion in these tax-free holdings is less than about 20 to 30 percent of the portfolio. Avoid funds that have the majority or all of their assets in Treasuries. A surprising number of company retirement plans offer treasury mutual funds (which are nearly all Treasuries) as an investment option. If you see such an offer, send a copy of this book to your company's benefits department!

Annuities

Annuities, although retirement vehicles as noted earlier in this chapter, have no place inside retirement accounts. Annuities allow your investment dollars to compound without taxation. In comparison to other investments that don't allow such tax deferral, annuities carry much higher annual operating expenses, which depress your returns.

Purchasing an annuity inside an IRA, 401(k), or other type of retirement account is like wearing a belt and suspenders together. Either you have a peculiar sense of style, or you are spending too much time worrying about your pants falling down. In my experience, many people who mistakenly invest in annuities inside retirement accounts have been misled into it by investment salespeople.

Annuities pay hefty commissions, sometimes as high as 10 percent or more of the amount invested. In some cases, I think, the salespeople aren't being conniving and unethical — they just don't know any better. The insurance companies behind these products, in their enthusiasm to pump up salespeople to peddle them, conveniently skip over the details about when it's inappropriate and when it's not to invest in annuities.

If you work for a nonprofit organization, your employer may allow you to contribute some of your paycheck into *tax-sheltered annuities* (TSAs). If you have other options, don't. TSAs are also inferior investment choices. Since 1986, the tax laws allow nonprofit employees to invest their retirement money in mutual funds. Well-managed no-load (commission-free) funds have lower operating expenses and other advantages over TSAs. I discuss nonprofit retirement plans, known as 403(b) plans, later in the chapter.

Limited partnerships

Limited partnerships, which are sold through investment salespeople, are treacherous, high-commission, high-cost, and hence low-return investments. Part of their supposed allure, however, is the tax benefits that they generate. But when you buy and hold a limited partnership in a retirement account, you lose the ability to take advantage of many of the tax deductions. The illiquidity of LPs may also mean that you can't make required retirement account withdrawals when needed. These are just some of the many reasons to avoid investing in limited partnerships. For more reasons see Chapter 10.

Allocating Your Money in Retirement Plans

With good reason, people are concerned about placing their retirement account money in investments that can decline in value. You may feel that you're gambling with dollars intended for the security of your golden years.

But in order to attain that security, most working folks need to make their money work hard in order for it to grow fast enough. That involves taking some risk; you have no way around it. Luckily, if you have 15 to 20 years or more before you need to draw on the bulk of your retirement account assets, time is on your side. If some of your investments drop a bit over a year or two, what's the big deal as long as the value of your investments has time to recover? The more years until you are going to retire, the greater your ability to take risk.

If you haven't yet done so, read the section in Chapter 9 on asset allocation. That section helps you decide how to divide your money among different investment options based upon your time frame and risk tolerance.

Prioritizing retirement contributions

If you have access to more than one type of retirement account, prioritize which accounts to use first by what they give you in return. Your first contributions should be to employer-based plans that match your contributions. After that, contribute to any other employer or self-employed plans that allow tax-deductible contributions. If you've contributed as much as possible to tax-deductible plans or do not have access to such plans, contribute to an IRA. If you've maxed out on contributions to an IRA or don't have this choice because you lack employment income, consider an annuity (discussed earlier in this chapter).

Setting up a retirement account

No-load, or commission-free, mutual fund and discount brokerage firms are your best bet for setting up a retirement account. (You find specific recommendations about investments to use inside of your retirement account later in this chapter.)

Investments and account types are different issues. People sometimes get confused when discussing the investments they make in retirement accounts, especially people who have a retirement account, such as an IRA, at a bank. They don't realize that you can have your IRA at a variety of financial institutions (for example, a mutual fund company or brokerage firm). At each financial institution, you can choose among the firm's investment options for putting your IRA money to work.

Allocating money when your employer selects the investment options

In some company-sponsored plans, such as 401(k)s, you are limited to the predetermined investment options your employer offers. Plans differ in the specific options they offer, but they usually offer similar basic choices. In what follows, I discuss a 401(k) plan's typical investment options, in order of increasing risk and hence, likely return.

Money market/savings accounts

For regular contributions coming out your paycheck, the money market or savings account option makes little sense. Some people who are skittish about the stock and bond markets are attracted to money market and savings accounts because those accounts cannot drop in value. However, the returns are low . . . so low that you run the risk — I would venture to say high probability — that your investment will not stay ahead of, or even keep up with, inflation and taxes (which are due upon withdrawal of your money from the retirement account).

For those of you who may be tempted to use a money market fund as a parking place until the time that you think stocks and bonds are cheap, don't. In the long run, you won't be doing yourself any favors if you do so. As I discuss in Chapter 9, timing your investments to attempt to catch the lows and avoid investing at the peaks is impossible. If you can figure out how to do that, you're wasting your time in whatever occupation you're now employed. You could make a fortune as a money manager.

You may need to keep money in the money market investment option if you utilize the borrowing feature that some retirement plans allow. Check with your employee benefits department for more details.

Bond mutual funds

Bond mutual funds (which I describe in Chapter 11) invest in a mixture of typically high-quality bonds. Bonds pay a higher rate of interest or dividends than money funds. Depending on whether your plan's option is a short-term, intermediate-term, or long-term fund, the bond fund's current yield is probably a couple percent or so higher than the money market fund's yield.

Bond funds carry higher yields than money market funds, but they also carry greater risk because their value can fall if interest rates increase. However, bonds tend to be more stable in value than stocks.

Aggressive, younger investors should keep a minimum amount of money in bond funds. Older folks who want to invest more conservatively may want to invest more money this way.

Guaranteed-investment contracts (GICs)

GICs are backed by an insurance company and typically quote you a rate of return projected one or a few years forward. The return is always positive and certain — thus you don't have the uncertainty that you would normally face with bond or stock investments (unless, of course, the insurance company fails).

The attraction of these investments is that your account value does not fluctuate (at least, not that you can see). The insurance company normally invests your money mostly in bonds and maybe a bit in stocks. The difference between what these investments generate for the insurer and what they pay in interest is profit to the insurer. The yield is usually comparable to that of a bond fund.

For people who would hit the eject button the moment that a bond fund slides a bit in value, GICs are soothing to the nerves. And they're certainly higher yielding than a money market or savings account.

Like bonds, however, GICs don't give you the opportunity for long-term growth of your money. Over the long haul, you should earn a better return in a mixture of bond and stock investments. In GICs, you pay for the peace of mind of a guaranteed return in the form of lower long-term returns.

GICs also have another minor drawback: Insurance companies, unlike mutual funds, can and do fail, putting GIC investment dollars at risk. Some employers' retirement plans have been burned by insurance company failures.

Balanced mutual funds

Balanced mutual funds invest in a mixture primarily of stocks and bonds. This one-stop shopping concept makes investing easier and smoothes out fluctuations in the value of your investments — funds investing exclusively in stocks or in bonds make for a rougher ride. These funds are solid options and, in fact, can be used for a significant portion of your retirement plan contributions. Refer to Chapter 11 to learn more about balanced funds.

Stock mutual funds

Stock mutual funds invest in stocks, which usually provide greater long-term growth potential but also wider fluctuations in value from year to year. Some companies offer a number of different stock funds, including funds that invest overseas. Unless you plan to borrow against your funds for a home purchase (if your plan allows), you should have a healthy helping of stock funds.

Stock in the company you work for

Some companies offer employees the option of investing in the company's stock. I generally advocate avoiding this option for the simple reason that your future income and other employee benefits are already riding on the success of the company. If the company hits the skids, you may lose your job and your benefits. You certainly don't want the value of your retirement account to be dependent on the same factors.

If your employer does not offer you other retirement account investing options, complain. Start with your benefits department. If they don't already know, they should know that 401(k) plans are supposed to offer several diversified investment options. If your employer's stock is the one and only option, that doesn't pass muster.

If you think that your company has its act together and the stock is a good buy, investing a portion of your retirement account is fine — but no more than 25 percent. Now, if your company is on the verge of hitting it big and the stock is soon to soar, you'll of course be kicking yourself for not putting more of your money into the company's stock. But if you place a big bet on your company's stock, be prepared to suffer the consequences if the stock tanks. Don't forget that lots of smart investors track companies' prospects, so odds are that the current value of your company's stock is fair.

Some employers offer employees the ability to buy company stock at a discount, sometimes as much as 15 percent, compared to its current market value. If you can do this, so much the better. If you sell the stock when your employer's plan allows, usually after a certain length holding period, you should be able to lock in a decent profit.

Some examples

Using the methodology that I outline in Chapter 9 for allocating money, Table 12-1 shows a couple of examples of how people in different employer plans might choose to allocate their 401(k) investments among the plan's investment options.

Table 12-1	Allocating 401(k) Investments		
	25 Year-Old, Aggressive Risk	45 Year-Old, Moderate Risk	60 Year-Old, Moderate Risk
Bond Fund	0%	35%	50%
Balanced Fund (50% stock/50% bond)	10%	0%	0%
Blue Chip/Larger Company Stock Fund(s)	20%	20%	25%
Aggressive/Smaller Company Stock fund(s)	25%	20%	10%
International Stock Fund(s)	45%	25%	15%

Please note that making allocation decisions is not a science. Use the formulas in Chapter 9 as a guideline.

Allocating money in plans that you design

With self-employed plans (SEP-IRAs and Keoghs), certain 403(b) plans for nonprofit employees, and IRAs, you get to select the investment options as well as the allocation of money among them.

In the sections that follow, I give some specific recipes that you may find useful for investing at the premier investment companies that I profile in Chapter 11. To establish your retirement account at one of these firms, simply pick up your telephone and dial the company's 800 number and ask it to mail you an account application for the type of account (for example, SEP-IRA, 403(b), and so on) you desire. At the time you call, you can also have it mail you background on specific mutual funds that you may be interested in.

Note: For each firm, I recommend a conservative and an aggressive portfolio. These terms are used in a relative sense. Because some of the recommended funds do not maintain fixed percentages of their different types of investments, the actual percentage of stocks and bonds that you end up with may vary slightly from the targeted percentages. Don't sweat it.

Where you have more than one fund choice, you can pick one or split the suggested percentage between them. If you don't have enough money today to divide it up as I suggest, you can achieve the desired split over time as you add more money to your retirement accounts.

Vanguard

The following two Vanguard (800-662-7447) recommendations are for a conservative mix and an aggressive mix.

A conservative portfolio with 50 percent stocks, 50 percent bonds

Vanguard Index Total Bond Market — 25 percent

Vanguard Star (fund of funds) — 55 percent

Vanguard International Growth — 20 percent

An aggressive portfolio with 80 percent stocks, 20 percent bonds

Vanguard Star (fund of funds) — 50 percent

Vanguard Total Stock Market Index — 10 percent

Vanguard International Growth — 40 percent

or

Vanguard LifeStrategy Growth (fund of funds) — 100 percent (note that this portfolio places less money overseas than the previous one).

Should I use one investment firm or more than one?

The recommended firms listed in this chapter offer a large enough variety of investment options, managed by different fund managers, that you can feel comfortable concentrating your money at one firm. The advantages of a focused approach are needing to learn the nuances and choices of just one form rather than several, and having fewer administrative hassles.

If you like the idea of spreading your money around, you may want to invest through a number of the different firms. If you open a discount brokerage account (refer to Chapter 11), you can have your cake and eat it, too. You can diversify across different mutual fund companies through one brokerage firm. However, you will pay small transaction fees on some of your purchases and sales of funds (refer to Chapter 11 for more details).

Fidelity

The following two Fidelity (800-544-8666) recommendations are for a conservative mix and an aggressive mix.

A conservative portfolio with 50 percent stocks, 50 percent bonds

Fidelity Balanced — 1/3

Fidelity Puritan — 1/3

Dodge & Cox Balanced — 1/3

An aggressive portfolio with 80 percent stocks, 20 percent bonds

Fidelity Puritan — 35 percent

Fidelity Contrafund — 20 percent

Fidelity Stock Selector — 25 percent

Warburg Pincus International Equity
and/or Vanguard International Growth — 20 percent

Charles Schwab or Jack White

The following recommendations are for a conservative mix and an aggressive mix from the discount brokerage firms of either Charles Schwab (800-526-8600) or Jack White (800-323-3263).

A conservative portfolio with 50 percent stocks, 50 percent bonds

Vanguard Fixed-Income Short-term Corporate — 20 percent

PIMCO Low Duration — 20 percent

Dodge & Cox Balanced — 20 percent

Mutual Beacon *and/or* Dodge & Cox Stock — 25 percent

T. Rowe Price International Stock
and/or Warburg Pincus International Equity
and/or Vanguard International Growth — 15 percent

An aggressive portfolio with 80 percent stocks, 20 percent bonds

PIMCO Total Return — 20 percent

Brandywine *and/or* Dodge & Cox Stock
and Neuberger & Berman Focus *and/or* Mutual Discovery — 40 percent

T. Rowe Price International Stock
and/or Warburg Pincus International Equity
and/or Vanguard International Growth
and/or Schwab International Index — 40 percent

Transferring Retirement Accounts

With the exception of plans maintained by your employer that limit your investment options, such as most 401(k)s, you can move your money held in SEP-IRAs, Keoghs, IRAs, and many 403(b) plans (also known as *tax-sheltered annuities*) to most any major investment firm you please. Moving the money is pretty simple. If you can dial an 800 number, fill out a couple of short forms, and send them back in a postage-paid envelope, you can transfer an account. The investment firm to which you are transferring your account does the rest.

Here's a step-by-step list of what you need to do to transfer a retirement account to another investment firm. Even if you're working with a financial advisor, you should be aware of this process to ensure that no hanky-panky takes place on the advisor's part:

1. **Decide where you want to move the account.**

   I profile the best investment companies in Chapter 11, and I recommend specific investment options within those firms in the previous section of this chapter.

2. **Obtain an account application and asset transfer form.** Call the 800 number of the firm you are transferring the money to and ask for an *account application and asset transfer form* for the type of account you are transferring — for example, SEP-IRA, Keogh, IRA, or 403(b).

Note: Asking for the form for the *same* type of account you currently have at the company from which you are transferring the money is important. You can determine the account type by looking at a recent account statement — the account type should be near the top of the form or in the section with your name and address. If you can't figure it out on a cryptic statement, call the firm where the account is currently held and ask a representative to tell you what kind of account you have.

Never, ever sign over assets such as checks and security certificates to a financial advisor, no matter how trustworthy and honest he or she may seem. The advisor could abscond with them quicker than you can say Bonnie and Clyde. Transfers should not be completed this way. Besides, you'll find it easier to handle the transfer the way I describe in this section.

3. **Complete and mail the account application and asset transfer form.** Completing these for your new investment firm opens your new account and authorizes the transfer.

You shouldn't take possession of the money in your retirement account yourself to get it over to the new firm. The tax authorities impose huge penalties if you do a transfer incorrectly. Let the company to which you're transferring the money do the transfer for you.

If you have questions or problems, the firm(s) to which you are transferring your account have armies of capable employees waiting to help you. Remember, these firms know that you are transferring your money to them, so they should roll out the red carpet.

4. **Figure out which securities you want to transfer and which need to be liquidated.** Transferring existing investments in your account to a new investment firm can sometimes be a little sticky. If you're transferring cash (money market funds) or securities that trade on any of the major stock exchanges, transferring such assets is not a problem.

If you own publicly traded securities, transferring them *as is* to your new investment firm is better, especially if the firm offers discount brokerage services. You can then sell your securities through that firm more cheaply.

If you own mutual funds unique to the institution you're leaving, check with your new firm to see if it can accept them. If not, you need to contact the firm that currently holds them to sell them.

CDs are tricky to transfer. Ideally, you should send in the transfer forms several weeks or so before the CDs mature — few people do this. If the CD matures soon, call the bank and instruct them that when the CD matures, you would like the funds to be invested in a savings or money market account that you can access without penalty when your transfer request lands in their mailbox.

5. **(Optional) Let the firm from which you're transferring the money know that you are doing so.** If the place you're transferring from doesn't assign a specific person to your account, definitely skip this step. If you're moving your investments from a brokerage firm where you've dealt with a particular broker, the decision is more difficult.

   Most people feel obligated to let their representative know that they are moving their money. In my experience, calling the person with the bad news is usually a mistake. Brokers or others who have a direct financial stake in your decision to move your money will try to sell you on staying. Some may try to make you feel guilty for leaving, and some may even try to bully you.

   Writing a letter may seem the coward's way out, but writing usually makes leaving your broker easier for both of you. You can polish what you have to say, and you don't put the broker on the defensive. Or (although I don't mean to encourage lying) not telling the *whole* truth may be better. Excuses, such as you have a family member in the investment business who will manage your money for free, may help you to avoid an uncomfortable confrontation.

   Then again, telling an investment firm that its charges are too high or that it misrepresented and sold you a bunch of lousy investments may help the firm to improve in the future. Don't fret too much — do what's best for you and what you're comfortable with. Brokers are not your friends. Even though the broker may know your kids' names, your favorite hobbies, and your birthday, you have a *business* relationship.

Transferring your existing assets typically takes a month to complete. If the transfer is not completed within a month, get in touch with your new investment firm to determine what the problem is. If your old company is not cooperating, call a manager to help get the ball rolling.

The unfortunate reality is that an investment firm will cheerfully set up a new account to *accept* your money on a moment's notice, but it will drag its feet, sometimes for months, when the time comes to relinquish your money. To light a fire under the behinds of the folks at the investment firm, tell a manager at the old firm that you're sending letters to the National Association of Securities Dealers (NASD) and the Securities and Exchange Commission (SEC) if it doesn't complete your transfer within the next week.

Moving Money from Your Employer's Retirement Account

If you leave a job, you are confronted with a slightly different transfer challenge: moving money from an employer plan into one of your own retirement accounts. Typically, employer retirement plan money can be rolled over into your own IRA. Check with your employer's benefits department or a tax advisor for details.

A relatively new tax law requires employers to withhold as a tax 20 percent of any retirement account disbursements to plan participants. So if you are personally taking possession of your retirement account money in order to transfer it to an IRA, you must wait to be reimbursed by the government for this 20 percent withholding until you file your annual tax return.

My advice is: Never take personal possession of money from your employer's retirement plan. To avoid the 20 percent tax withholding and a lot of other hassles, simply inform your employer where you want your money to be sent. Prior to doing so, you should establish an appropriate account (an IRA, for example) at the investment firm you intend to use. Then tell your employer's benefits department what investment firm you would like your retirement money transferred to. Ideally, you can send your employer a copy of your account statement, which contains the investment firm's mailing address and your account number.

When you leave a job, particularly if you are retiring or being laid off after many years of service, money-hungry brokers and financial planners probably will be on you like a pack of bears on a tree leaking sweet honey. Tread carefully and slowly if you seek financial help — be sure to read Chapters 3 and 19 to avoid the pitfalls in hiring such assistance.

Issues Unique to 403 (b) Plans

403(b) plans are retirement savings plans available through nonprofit organizations. Some nonprofits don't offer 403(b)s, or in addition to 403(b)s offer insurance company tax-sheltered annuities. No-load (no sales charges) mutual funds are superior investment vehicles compared to insurance company annuities on several fronts:

> ✔ Mutual fund companies have a longer and more successful investment track record than do insurance companies, many of which have only recently entered the mutual fund arena.

> ✔ Insurance annuities charge higher annual operating expenses, often two to three times that of efficiently managed no-load mutual funds. These high expenses reduce your returns.
>
> ✔ Insurance company insolvency can risk the safety of your investment in an annuity, whereas the value of a mutual fund depends only on the value of the securities in the fund.
>
> ✔ Insurance annuities come with severe charges and fees for early surrender; 403(b) plans with mutual funds do not.

With some 403(b) plans, you may borrow against your fund balance without penalty. If this capability is important to you, check with your employer to see whether the company plan allows you to borrow without penalty. Although many insurance annuities advertise borrowing as an advantage, it is also a drawback because it may encourage you to raid your retirement savings.

Vanguard, Fidelity, and T. Rowe Price are good firms for 403(b) accounts (specific fund recommendations are given earlier in the chapter for investing at Fidelity and Vanguard). Jack White and Charles Schwab don't offer 403(b)s. However, if you have a 403(b) or tax-sheltered annuity to which you are no longer contributing, you can roll over this money into an IRA account through one of these firms or another mutual fund company.

Chapter 13

Investing Money Outside Retirement Accounts

. . . .

In This Chapter

▶ Taking advantage of frequently overlooked investment options

▶ Factoring taxes into your investment decisions

▶ Where to invest your emergency reserve

▶ Recommended short-, intermediate-, and long-term investments

. . . .

*I*n this chapter, I discuss investment options for money held *outside* retirement accounts and I include specific mutual fund recommendations. Chapter 12 reviews investments for money *inside* retirement accounts. This distinction may seem somewhat odd — this distinction is not one that is made in most financial books and articles — but I have my reasons.

Thinking of the two pots of money differently is useful.

✔ Investments held outside retirement accounts are subject to taxation. You have a whole range of different investment options to consider when taxes come into play.

✔ Money held outside retirement accounts is also more likely to be used sooner than funds held inside retirement accounts. Why? Because you'll generally have to pay far more in income taxes to access money inside rather than outside retirement accounts.

✔ Funds inside retirement accounts have their own nuances. For example, when you invest through your employer's retirement plan, your investment options are usually limited to a handful of choices. And special rules govern transfer of your retirement account balances.

Getting Started

Suppose you've got some money sitting around in a bank savings account or money market mutual fund. Your money is earning several percent in interest, but you want to invest it more profitably. Never forget two things about investing this type of money:

- ✔ **Earning a few percent is better than losing 20 to 50 percent or more.** Just talk to anyone who was sold a limited partnership in the past decade (refer to Chapter 10). So be patient. Educate yourself first *before* you invest.

- ✔ **To earn a higher rate of return, you must be willing to take more risk.** (This is true unless you jump into a higher-yielding money market fund, discussed later in this chapter). Earning a better rate of return means considering investments that can fluctuate in value — and, of course, the value can drop as much as it can rise.

You approach the vast sea of investment options and start stringing up your rod to go fishing. You hear stories of people catching big ones — cashing in big on stocks or real estate that they bought years ago. Even if you don't have delusions of grandeur, you'd at least like your money to grow faster than the cost of living.

But before you cast your investment line, consider the following frequently overlooked ways to put your money to work and earn higher returns without as much risk. These options may not be as exciting as hunting the big fish out there, but they're financially astute and should improve your financial health.

Pay off high-interest debt

Many folks have credit card or other consumer debt that costs more than 10 percent per year in interest. Paying off this debt with savings is like putting your money in an investment with a guaranteed return equal to the rate you are paying on the debt.

For example, if you have credit card debt outstanding at 14-percent interest, paying off that loan is the same as putting your money to work in an investment with a sure 14-percent annual return. Remember that the interest on consumer debt is not tax-deductible, so you actually need to earn *more* than 14 percent investing your money elsewhere in order to net 14 percent after paying taxes. Refer to Chapter 5 for more details if you're still not convinced.

Paying off some or all of your mortgage may make sense, too. This financial move isn't as clear because the interest rate is lower than on consumer debt and is usually tax-deductible. (See Chapter 15 for more details on this decision.)

Contribute to retirement accounts

If you have a chunk of money, make sure that you take advantage of the *terrific* tax benefits offered by a retirement account. If you work for a company that offers a retirement savings plan such as a 401(k), you should try to fund it at the highest level you can manage. If you earn self-employment income, look into SEP-IRAs and Keoghs. (All retirement-plan options are discussed in Chapter 12.)

If you need to save money outside retirement accounts for short-term purposes (for example, to buy a car or a home), then by all means, save money outside retirement accounts. But remember that investing money outside retirement accounts does not afford you tax deductions and requires greater thought and consideration because your investments can produce taxable distributions.

Taxes and Your Investments

When you invest money outside of a retirement account, *investment distributions* — such as interest, dividends, and capital gains — are all exposed to taxation. Too many folks (and too many of their financial advisors) ignore the tax impact of their investment strategies. You need to pay attention to the tax implications of your investment decisions *before* you invest your money.

Consider a person in the combined 40 percent tax bracket (federal plus state taxes) who keeps extra cash in a taxable savings account paying 3 percent interest. If she pays 40 percent of her interest earnings in taxes, she ends up keeping just 1.8 percent. With a tax-free money market fund from the major mutual fund providers (stay tuned to this chapter for more on these), she could easily earn more than this amount, completely free of federal and/or state taxes. See Chapter 7 to understand your tax bracket.

Another mistake some people make is investing in securities that produce tax-free income when the those people are not in a high enough tax bracket to benefit. Consider a person in a combined 20 percent tax bracket who is investing in securities that produce tax-free income. Suppose that he invests in a tax-free investment that yields 4.5 percent. A comparable taxable investment is yielding 7 percent. If he had instead invested in the taxable investment at a 7 percent yield, the after-tax yield would be 5.6 percent. Thus, he is losing out on yield being in the tax-free investment, even though he may feel happy in it because all the yield isn't taxed.

To decide between comparable taxable and tax-free investments, you need to know your tax bracket and the rates of interest or yield on each investment. Here are some general guidelines based upon your federal income tax bracket:

- ✔ **31 percent or higher federal tax bracket.** If you're in this bracket, you should definitely avoid investments that produce taxable income. For tax year 1996, the 31 percent federal bracket starts at $58,150 for singles and $96,900 for married couples filing jointly.

- ✔ **28 percent federal bracket.** In most cases, you should be as well or better off in investments that do not produce taxable income when investing outside retirement accounts. This may not be the case, however, if you're in tax-free money market and bond funds whose yields are depressed due to high operating expenses (you won't find them recommended in this chapter!).

- ✔ **15 percent federal bracket.** Investments that produce taxable income are just fine for you. You may end up with *less* if you purchase investments that produce tax-free income.

In the sections that follow, I give specific advice about investing your money while keeping an eye on taxes.

Investing Your Savings/Emergency Reserve

In Chapter 8, I explain the importance of keeping sufficient money in an emergency reserve account. From such an account, you need two things:

- ✔ **Accessibility.** When you need to get your hands on the money for an emergency, you want to be able to do so quickly and without penalty.

- ✔ **Highest possible return.** You want to get the highest rate of return possible without risking your principal. This doesn't mean that you should simply pick the money market or savings option with the highest yield, because taxes are a consideration. What good is earning a slightly higher yield if you pay a lot more in taxes?

Bank and credit union accounts

If you have a few thousand dollars or less, your best and easiest path is to keep this excess savings in a local bank or credit union. Look first to the institution where you keep your checking account.

Keeping this stash of money in your checking account, rather than in a separate savings account, makes financial sense if the extra money helps you avoid monthly service charges because your balance occasionally dips below the minimum. Compare the service charges on your checking account with the interest earnings from a savings account.

For example, suppose that you have $2,000 that you're keeping in a savings account to earn 4 percent interest versus earning no interest on your checking account money. So over the course of a year, you're earning $80 interest on that savings account. If you're incurring a $9 per month service charge on your checking account, that's $108 per year. So, keeping your extra $2,000 in a checking account may be better if that keeps you above a minimum balance and erases that monthly service charge. (However, if you're more likely to spend the extra money if it's in your checking account, keeping it in a separate savings account where you won't be tempted to spend it might be better.)

Money market mutual funds

Money market funds, a type of mutual fund, are just like bank savings accounts — but better, in most cases (refer to Chapter 11). The best money market funds pay higher yields than bank savings accounts and offer you check-writing privileges. And if you're in a higher tax bracket, you can select a tax-free money market fund, which pays interest that is free from federal and/or state tax. You cannot get this feature with a bank savings account.

The yield on a money market is an important consideration. The operating expenses deducted before payment of dividends is the single biggest determinant of yield. All other things being equal (which they usually are with different money market funds), lower operating expenses translate into higher yields for you.

Another factor that may be important in your choice of a money market fund is what other types of fund investing you can do at the fund company where you establish a money market fund. Doing most or all of your fund shopping, money-market and otherwise, at one good fund company can reduce the clutter in your investing life; chasing after a slightly higher yield offered by another company is sometimes not worth the extra paperwork and administrative hassle. On the other hand, there's no reason why you can't invest in funds at multiple firms (as long as you don't mind the extra paperwork), using each for its relative strengths.

Most mutual fund companies don't have many local branch offices (Fidelity and Schwab are notable exceptions), so you'll probably open and maintain your money market mutual fund through the fund's toll-free 800 phone line and the mail. Distance has its advantages. Because you can conduct business by mail and phone, you don't need to go schlepping into a local branch office to make deposits and withdrawals. I'm *happy* to report that I haven't visited a bank office in years.

Despite the distance, your money is still accessible via check writing, and you can also have money wired to your local bank on any business day. If you're worried about a deposit being lost in the mail, don't. It rarely happens, and no one can legally cash a check made payable to you anyway. Just be sure to endorse the check with the notation "for deposit only" under your signature.

(For that matter, driving or walking to your local bank isn't 100 percent safe, either. Imagine all the things that could happen to you or your money en route to the bank. You could slip on a banana peel, drop your deposit down a sewer grate, get mugged, kidnapped, or run over by a bakery truck. Who knows — you could walk into a bank holdup and end up being taken hostage.)

Watch out for "sales"

Beware of money market mutual funds running specials. Some mutual funds aren't above resorting to some of the same marketing gimmicks that make retailers so endearing. The most common ploy is for funds to have a "sale." They do so by temporarily waiving (sometimes called *absorbing*) operating expenses, which results in a fund being able to boost its yield. But these sales never last long; the operating expenses come back and deflate that too-good-to-be-true yield like a nail in a bike tire.

Unlike the purchase of an item from a retailer, the decision to invest in a money market fund is usually a long-term proposition. Some fund companies run sales because they know that a good percentage of the fund buyers lured in won't bother leaving when they jack up the prices (operating expenses).

You're better off sticking with funds that maintain "everyday low prices" (for operating expenses) to get the highest long-term yield. I recommend such funds later in this chapter. If you want to move your money to companies having specials and then move it back out when the special's over, be my guest. If you have lots of money and don't mind paperwork, it may be worth the bother.

Recommended money market mutual funds

In the sections that follow, I recommend good money market mutual funds. Remember that, as you peruse these lists, the money market fund that works best for you depends upon your tax situation. Throughout the list, I try and guide you to funds that generally make sense for people in particular tax brackets.

Money market funds that pay taxable dividends are appropriate when you're not in a high tax bracket (less than or equal to 28 percent federal). See Table 13-1 for my recommendations.

Fidelity: 800-544-8888. Vanguard: 800-662-7447. Schwab: 800-526-8600.

Table 13-1	Recommended Taxable Money Market Funds	
Fund	**Operating Expense**	**Minimum to Open**
Vanguard Money Market Reserves Prime Portfolio	0.3%	$3,000
Fidelity Spartan Money Market	0.4%	$20,000
Schwab Value Advantage	0.4%	$25,000

U.S. Treasury money market funds are appropriate if you prefer a money fund that invests in U.S. Treasuries, which have the safety of government backing, or if you're not in a high federal tax bracket (less than or equal to 28 percent) but *are* in a high state tax bracket (5 percent or higher). Table 13-2 lists a few that I recommend.

Table 13-2	Recommended U.S. Treasury Money Market Funds	
Fund	**Operating Expense**	**Minimum to Open**
Vanguard Money Market Reserves U.S. Treasury	0.3%	$3,000
Vanguard Admiral U.S. Treasury Money Market	0.15%	$50,000
Fidelity Spartan U.S. Treasury Money Market	0.4%	$20,000

The tax-free money market funds such as those in Table 13-3 are appropriate when you're in a high federal (31 percent and up) *and* state tax bracket (5 percent or higher).

Fidelity: 800-544-8888. Vanguard: 800-662-7447. USAA: 800-531-8100.

Table 13-3	Recommended State-and-Federal-Tax-Free Money Market Funds	
Fund	**Operating Expense**	**Minimum to Open**
Vanguard CA Tax-Free Money Market	0.2%	$3,000
Fidelity Spartan CA Muni Money Market	0.3%	$25,000
Fidelity Spartan CT Muni Money Market	0.3%	$25,000
Fidelity Spartan FL Muni Money Market	0.4%	$25,000

(continued)

Table 13-3 *(continued)*

Fund	Operating Expense	Minimum to Open
USAA Tax-Exempt FL Money Market	0.5%	$3,000
Fidelity Spartan MA Muni Money Market	0.3%	$25,000
Vanguard NJ Tax-Free Money Market	0.2%	$3,000
Fidelity Spartan NY Muni Money Market	0.5%	$25,000
USAA Tax-Exempt NY Money Market	0.5%	$3,000
Vanguard OH Tax-Free Money Market	0.3%	$3,000
Vanguard PA Tax-Free Money Market	0.2%	$3,000
USAA Tax-Exempt VA Money Market	0.5%	$3,000

A number of states do not have money market fund options listed in Table 13-3 (and some that do may have minimums that are too high for you). In some cases, none exists. In other cases, the funds available (and not on the recommended list) for that state have such high annual operating expenses, and therefore such low yields, that you are better off in a more competitively run federal-tax-free-only fund listed in Table 13-4.

Federally tax-free only money market funds (the dividends on these are state taxable) are appropriate when you're in a high federal (31 percent and up) but *not* state (less than 5 percent) bracket or if you live in a state that doesn't have competitive state and federally tax-free funds available (refer to Table 13-3 to make sure).

Table 13-4   Federally Tax-Free Only Money Market Funds

Fund	Operating Expense	Minimum to Open
Vanguard Municipal Money Market	0.2%	$3,000
Fidelity Spartan Municipal Money Market	0.4%	$25,000
USAA Tax-Exempt Money Market	0.5%	$3,000

Investing Money for the Longer-Term

Important Note: This section (together with its recommended investments) assumes that you have a sufficient emergency reserve stashed away and are taking advantage of tax-deductible retirement account contributions already. Refer to Chapter 8 for more on these goals.

Which investments you should consider depends on your comfort level with risk. But your choice of investments should also be suited to how much *time* you have until you plan to use the money. I'm not talking about investments that you won't be able to sell on short notice if need be (most of them you can). Investing money in a more volatile investment is riskier if you need to liquidate it in the short term.

For example, suppose that you're saving money for a down payment on a house and are about one year away from having enough to make your foray into the real estate market. If you had put this "home" money into the U.S. stock market in the beginning of 1987 (or 1972 or 1968 for that matter), a year later, you'd have been a mighty unhappy camper. You could have seen 30 to 40 percent of your money *vanish* in short order and your home dreams put on hold.

Most of the following recommended investments are different types of *no-load* (commission-free) mutual funds. Mutual funds are very *liquid* — they can be sold on any business day with a simple phone call. Funds come with all different levels of risk, so you can choose funds that match your time frame and desire to take risk. (Chapter 11 discusses all the basics of mutual funds.)

The different investment options in the remainder of this chapter are organized by time frame. All the recommended investment funds that follow assume that you have *at least* a several-year time frame. The recommended investments are also organized by your tax situation. (If you don't know your current tax bracket, be sure to pay a visit to Chapter 7.) The following are summaries of the different time frames:

✔ **Short-term investments.** These investments are suitable for a period of a few years — perhaps you're saving money toward a home or some other major purchase in the near future.

When investing for the short-term, look for liquidity and stability — features that rule out real estate on one hand and stocks on the other. Recommended investments include shorter-term bond funds, which are higher-yielding alternatives to money market funds. If interest rates increase, these funds drop slightly in value — a couple of percent or so (unless rates rise tremendously). I also discuss Treasuries and certificates of deposit later in this chapter.

Intermediate-term investments. These investments are appropriate for more than a few but less than ten years. Investments that fit the bill are intermediate-term bonds and very low-risk, well-diversified hybrid funds that include some stocks.

Long-term investments. If you have a decade or more, then you can consider potentially higher-return (and therefore riskier) investments. Stocks, real estate, and other growth-oriented investments can earn the most money if you're comfortable with the risk involved.

Asset allocation

Asset allocation is the process of figuring out how much of your vast wealth you should invest in different types of investments. You frequently (and most appropriately) practice asset allocation with retirement accounts. Ideally, more of your saving and investing should be conducted through tax-sheltered retirement accounts. That's generally the best way to lower your long-term tax burden (refer to Chapter 12 for more details).

If you have sufficient assets that you plan to invest outside retirement accounts, specific recommendations follow this section. For that portion of your investments that you intend to hold for the long term (ten or more years), you can allocate according to the "Suggested asset allocations" section in Chapter 9.

Bond funds

Bond funds that pay taxable dividends are appropriate when you're not in a high tax bracket (less than or equal to 28 percent federal). Table 13-5 lists some bond funds that I recommend. *Note:* The asterisks and other symbols are explained after each table.

Table 13-5	Recommended Taxable Bond Funds		
Fund	**Investments**	**Operating Expense**	**Minimum to Open**
Short-term			
Benham Adjustable Rate Government Securities */**	Adjustable-rate mortgages	0.5%	$1,000
1 PIMCO Low Duration **	Mostly corporate and mortgage bonds	0.4%	$1,000
Vanguard F/I Short-Term Corporate	Mostly corporate, some treasuries	0.3%	$3,000
Intermediate-term			
Benham GNMA */**	Mortgages	0.5%	$1,000
Dodge & Cox Income	Mostly corporate	0.5%	$1,000
1 PIMCO Total Return **	Corporate and mortgage bonds; small % overseas	0.4%	$1,000

Fund	Investments	Operating Expense	Minimum to Open
1S PIMCO Total Return III **	Corporate and mortgage bonds; small % overseas	0.5%	$1,000
Vanguard GNMA	Mortgages	0.3%	$3,000
Vanguard Index Total Bond Market	Corporate and mortgages; some treasuries	0.2%	$3,000
Long-term			
Vanguard Long-Term Corporate	Corporate bonds; some treasuries	0.3%	$3,000
Vanguard High Yield Corporate	Lower-quality corporate bonds	0.3%	$3,000

* = Available through Schwab without transaction fees (refer to Chapter 11).

**= Available through Jack White without transaction fees (refer to Chapter 11).

1 = Purchase through Schwab or Jack White because of high minimum or unavailable elsewhere (refer to Chapter 11 for details on buying funds through such discount brokers).

S = Socially responsible (refer to Chapter 11 for information on such funds).

U.S. Treasury bond funds

U.S. Treasury bond funds are appropriate if you prefer a bond fund that invests in U.S. Treasuries (which have the safety of government backing) or when you're not in a high federal tax bracket (less than or equal to 28 percent) but *are* in a high state tax bracket (5 percent or higher). See Table 13-6 for a list of good Treasury Bond funds.

Table 13-6	Recommended U.S. Treasury Bond Funds		
Fund	Investments	Operating Expense	Minimum to Open
Short-term			
Vanguard Short-Term U.S. Treasury	Treasuries	0.3%	$3,000
Vanguard Admiral Short-Term U.S. Treasury	Treasuries	0.15%	$50,000
Intermediate-term			
Vanguard Intermediate-Term U.S. Treasury	Treasuries	0.3%	$3,000

(continued)

Table 13-6 *(continued)*

Fund	Investments	Operating Expense	Minimum to Open
Vanguard Admiral Inter-mediate-Term U.S. Treasury	Treasuries	0.15%	$50,000
Long-term			
Vanguard Long-Term U.S. Treasury	Treasuries	0.3%	$3,000
Vanguard Admiral Long-Term U.S. Treasury	Treasuries	0.15%	$3,000

Inflation-indexed Treasury bonds

In 1996, the U. S. Treasury announced the future availability of new *inflation-indexed* Treasury bonds. Because a portion of their return is pegged to the rate of inflation, these bonds offer investors a safer type of Treasury bond investment option.

To understand the relative advantages of an inflation-indexed bond, take a brief look at the relationship between inflation and a normal bond.

When an investor purchases a normal bond, he is committing himself to a fixed yield over a set period of time — for example, a bond that matures in 10 years and pays 7 percent interest. However, changes in the cost of living (inflation) are not fixed and are difficult to predict.

TIP

Buying Treasuries direct

There's an even cheaper method of investing in Treasury Bonds than through the thrifty Vanguard Treasury funds: You can purchase Treasuries directly from the Federal Reserve Bank. To open an account through the Treasury Direct program, look in your local phone book under the Federal Government for the nearest Federal Reserve Bank.

The Federal Reserve Bank charges $25 annually for accounts with more than $100,000 in Treasury bonds. Smaller accounts are free of any maintenance or management fees or charge. The operating expenses of even the leanest mutual funds cannot compete with these rates!

You do sacrifice a bit of liquidity, however, when purchasing Treasury bonds directly from the government. If you need immediate access to your money, buying the recommended Vanguard funds and paying their low management fees may be worth it.

Suppose an investor had put $10,000 into a regular bond in the 1970s. During the life of his bond, he would have unhappily watched escalating inflation. During the time he held the bond and by the time his bond matured, he would have witnessed the erosion of the purchasing power of his $700 of annual interest and $10,000 of returned principal.

Enter the inflation-indexed Treasury bond. Although various versions are under consideration in the U.S., here's how one, based on Canada's version, works.

Say you have $10,000 to invest and you buy a 10-year, inflation-indexed bond that pays you a *real rate of return* (this is the return above and beyond the rate of inflation) of say 3.5 percent. This portion of your return would be paid out in interest. The other portion of your return would be from the inflation adjustment to the principal you invested. The inflation portion of the return in the Canadian model gets put back into principal. So if inflation were running at about 3 percent, as it has in recent years, your $10,000 of principal would be indexed upwards after one year to $10,300. In the second year of holding this bond, the 3.5 percent real return of interest would be paid on the increased ($10,300) principal base.

If inflation skyrocketed and was running at say 10 percent rather than 3 percent per year, your principal balance would grow 10 percent per year and you'd still get your 3 percent real rate of return on top of that. Thus, an inflation-indexed Treasury bond investor would not see the purchasing power of his invested principal or annual interest earnings eroded by unexpected inflation.

In issuing inflation-indexed bonds, the U.S. is following the leads of Argentina, Brazil, New Zealand, Canada, Sweden, Australia, Israel, and Britain. Based on supply and demand, the real return of inflation-indexed bonds in these countries has been running around 4 percent.

As long as inflation doesn't unexpectedly take off, we in the U.S. can expect inflation-indexed bonds to yield slightly lower returns — perhaps 0.5 to 0.75 percent less — than normal Treasury bonds: Such is the cost of insurance against inflation.

If well designed, the inflation-indexed Treasuries could be a good investment for conservative, inflation-worried bond investors, as well as taxpayers who want to hold the government accountable for increases in inflation.

State-and-federal-tax-free bond funds

The state-and-federal-tax-free bond funds listed in Table 13-7 are appropriate when you're in high federal (31 percent and up) *and* state (5 percent or higher) tax brackets.

Table 13-7 Recommended State-and-Federal-Tax-Free Bond Funds

Fund	Investments	Operating Expense	Minimum to Open
Intermediate-term			
Benham CA Tax-Free Intermediate-Term */**	CA Municipals	0.5%	$1,000
Schwab CA Short-Intermediate Tax-Free *	CA Municipals	0.5%	$1,000
Vanguard CA Tax-Free Insured Intermediate Term	CA Municipals	0.2%	$3,000
Fidelity Spartan NY Intermed.	NY Municipals	0.2%	$10,000
Long-term			
Benham CA Tax-Free	CA Municipals Long-Term */**	0.5%	$1,000
Fidelity Spartan CA Muni Income	Lower-quality CA Municipals	0.5%	$10,000
Vanguard CA Tax-Free Insured Long-Term	Insured CA Municipals	0.2%	$3,000
Fidelity Spartan CT Muni Income	Lower-quality CT Municipals	0.5%	$10,000
Fidelity MA Tax-Free Muni Income	Lower-quality MA Municipals	0.5%	$2,500
Fidelity MI Tax-Free Muni Income	Lower-quality MI Municipals	0.6%	$2,500
Fidelity MN Tax-Free Muni Income	MN Municipals	0.6%	$2,500
Vanguard NJ Tax-Free Insured Long-Term	Insured NJ Municipals	0.2%	$3,000
Vanguard NY Insured Tax-Free	Insured NY Municipals	0.2%	$3,000
Vanguard OH Tax-Free Insured Long-Term	Insured OH Municipals	0.2%	$3,000
Vanguard PA Tax-Free Insured Long-Term	Insured PA Municipals	0.2%	$3,000

* = Available through Schwab without transaction fees (refer to Chapter 11).

** = Available through Jack White without transaction fees (refer to Chapter 11).

A number of states do not have bond fund options listed in Table 13-7 (some that do may have minimums that are too high for you). In some cases, none exists. In other cases, the funds that are available for that state (and not on the recommended list) have such high annual operating expenses, and therefore such low yields, that you would be better off in the more competitively run federal-tax-free-only funds listed in Table 13-8. If a bond fund is not listed for your state, or if you're only in a high federal tax bracket, check out Table 13-8 — federal-tax-free bond funds.

Table 13-8	Federal-Tax-Free-Only Bond Funds		
Fund	*Investments*	*Operating Expenses*	*Minimum to Open*
Short-term			
Vanguard Muni Short-Term	Municipals	0.2%	$3,000
Vanguard Muni Limited-Term	Municipals	0.2%	$3,000
Intermediate-term			
Vanguard Muni Intermediate-Term	Municipals	0.2%	$3,000
Long-term			
Vanguard Muni Insured Long-Term	Insured Municipals	0.2%	$3,000
Vanguard Muni Long-Term	Municipals	0.2%	$3,000

Federal-tax-free-only bond funds

Federal-tax-free-only bond funds (the dividends on them are state taxable) are appropriate when you're in a high federal bracket (31 percent and up) but lower state bracket (less than 5 percent) or when you live in a state that doesn't have state and federal-tax-free funds available (refer to Table 13-7 to make sure).

Certificates of deposit (CDs)

For many decades, bank CDs have been the investment of choice for folks with some extra cash that is not needed in the near-term. The attraction is that you get a higher rate of return on a CD than on a bank savings account. And unlike bond funds, your principal does not fluctuate in value.

Compared to bonds, however, CDs have a number of drawbacks.

TIP

Don't buy CDs for the FDIC insurance

Much is made, particularly by bankers, of the FDIC insurance that comes with bank CDs. The lack of this insurance on high-quality bonds shouldn't be a big concern. High-quality bonds rarely default; even if a fund held a bond that defaulted, it would probably be a tiny fraction (less than 1 percent) of the value of the fund, so it would have little overall impact.

Besides, the FDIC itself is no Rock of Gibraltar. Banks have failed and will continue to fail. Yes, you are insured if you have less than $100,000 in a bank, but in reality, if the bank crashes, you may have to wait a long time and settle for less interest than you thought you were getting. You are not immune from harm, FDIC or no FDIC.

If the U.S. government backing through FDIC insurance allows you to sleep better, you can invest in Treasuries (see the earlier discussion in this chapter), which are government-backed bonds.

> ✔ First, in a CD, your money is not accessible unless you cough up a fairly big penalty — typically six months' interest. With a no-load (commission-free) bond fund, if you need some or all of your money next week, month, or year, you can access it without penalty.

> ✔ Second, and less-often noted drawback, CDs come in only one tax flavor — taxable. Bonds, on the other hand, come in tax-free (federal and/or state) and taxable flavors. So if you're a higher tax bracket investor, bonds offer you a tax-friendly option that CDs can't.

TIP

In the long run, you should earn more — perhaps one to two percent more per year — and have better access to your money in bond funds than in CDs. Bond funds make particular sense when you're in a higher tax bracket and would benefit from tax-free income on your investments. If you're not in a high tax bracket (15 percent federal), and you have a bad day whenever your bond fund takes a dip in value, then consider CDs. Just make sure that you shop around to get the best interest rate.

Stock funds

Listed in Table 13-9 are stock funds, which are appropriate if you don't want current income or are in a high federal tax bracket (28 percent and up). Note that *all* the funds in Table 13-9 are intended as long-term investments. That's because funds that avoid bonds and dividend-producing stocks focus on growth stocks.

If you're not in a high tax bracket (less than 28 percent federal), you can also consider some of the stock funds recommended in Chapter 12 in the section "Great Investment Recipes."

Table 13-9	Relatively Tax-Friendly Stock Funds	
Parent	*Fund*	*Operating Expense*
U.S. funds		
Dodge & Cox	Stock	0.6%
Schwab*	Schwab 1000	0.5%
Vanguard	Tax-Managed Capital Appreciation	0.2%
Vanguard	Index Total Stock Market	0.2%
International funds		
Schwab	International Index	0.6%
USAA	Investment International	1.2%
Vanguard	International Growth	0.5%
Vanguard	Total International	0.4%
Warburg Pincus */**	International Equity	1.3%

* = Available through Schwab without transaction fees.

**= Available through Jack White without transaction fees.

Annuities

As I discuss in Chapter 12, *annuities* are accounts that are partly insurance but mostly investment. You should only consider contributing to an annuity after you've exhausted contributions to all your available retirement accounts. Because annuities carry higher annual operating expenses than comparable mutual funds, you should only consider them if you plan to leave your money invested for at least 10 years and preferably 15 or more years. Even if you have that long, the tax-friendly funds discussed in the previous sections of this chapter can allow your money to grow without excessive annual taxation.

The best annuities can be purchased from no-load (commission-free) mutual fund companies — specifically Vanguard (800-662-7447) and T. Rowe Price (800-638-5660).

Real estate

Real estate can be a financially and psychologically rewarding investment. It can also be a money pit and a real headache if you buy the wrong property or get a tenant from hell. (I discuss real estate as an investment in Chapter 10 and the basics of real estate in Chapter 15.)

Small-business investments

Investing in your own business or someone else's established small business can be a high-risk but potentially high-return investment. The best options are those you understand well. Refer to Chapter 10 for more information about small-business investments.

Chapter 14

Investing for Educational Expenses

● ●

In This Chapter

▶ The right and wrong ways to save for college

▶ How the financial aid system works

▶ How to pay for college when the time comes

▶ Calculating how much to save

▶ Good and bad investments for educational costs

● ●

*I*f you're like most parents or potential future parents, just turning to this chapter makes you break out in a cold sweat. Your anxiety is understandable. Much of what you read about educational expenses, particularly college expenses, says that if costs keep rising at the current rate, you have to spend several hundred thousand dollars to give your youngster a quality education.

Quality education for your child need not, and probably won't, cost you as much as those gargantuan projections suggest.

Whether you've already started saving or are about to begin a regular college investment plan, odds are quite high that your emotions are leading you astray. The hype about educational costs may scare you into taking a path that is less financially beneficial than others that are available.

The Big Mistake Nonwealthy Parents Make when Saving for Their Kids' Education

If you're a parent, it's a given that you want what's best for your children. Not only do you want to be able to provide good learning opportunities for them when they are young, but you also want to give them choices. When little Homer and Gwendolyn are filling out their college applications, you don't want to have to say that you can't afford to send them to their dream school.

Being considerate and thoughtful parents, you may start investing money in a separate account for them, perhaps in their name or through some other financial product, such as a life insurance policy. Doing so is usually a major financial mistake in both the short- and long-term.

I know that you're going to think that my advice sounds selfish. But you have to provide for your own financial security *before* saving for your child. Let me explain.

If you're a frequent flier, think back to your most recent trip by airplane. Remember what the flight attendants instructed you to do in an emergency? In the event of a loss of air pressure that necessitates the use of oxygen masks, you are instructed to put your oxygen mask on *first.* Only then should you help your children with their oxygen masks.

Consider for a moment why airlines recommend this approach. Although your instinct may be to ensure that your children are safe before taking care of yourself, by taking care of yourself first, you are stronger and better able to help your children.

Similarly, in regard to your personal finances, you need to take care of yourself first. You should be saving and investing through retirement accounts, such as a 401(k), SEP-IRA, Keogh, or other retirement account (described in Chapter 12), that give you significant tax benefits.

The mistake many, particularly middle-class, parents make is saving for future educational expenses by putting money in accounts in their child's name (called *custodial accounts*) or saving outside retirement accounts in general. Although a small amount of the interest earned on these accounts is taxed at the child's income tax rate rather than yours, you receive no tax deduction on your contributions to these accounts. And, as I discuss later in this chapter, the more money you accumulate outside tax-sheltered retirement accounts, the less assistance you're likely to qualify for from federal and state sources.

How the Financial Aid System Works

Just as your child shouldn't choose a college based solely on whether she thinks she can get in, she shouldn't choose a college on the basis of whether you think you can afford it. Everyone should apply for financial aid. More than a few parents who don't think that they qualify for financial aid are pleasantly surprised to find that they have access to loans as well as grants (grants are free money that you don't pay back).

Mary paid for the full cost of her daughter's first year at an expensive private college. In her 50s, Mary had little put away for retirement. "I didn't bother applying for financial aid," she says, adding, "with the value of my home and savings, I thought I was too rich to qualify."

Mary was wrong. In fact, for her daughter's junior year, Mary was delighted and shocked to learn that her daughter would receive nearly $9,000 in grants as well as access to moderate-interest loans. Two things did the trick. First, Mary applied for aid, and second, before she did, she invested a hefty chunk of savings into an annuity, which is a type of retirement account. In a moment you'll see why this worked.

The first step in the financial aid process is to complete the Free Application for Federal Student Aid (FAFSA), which is available from any high school or college. As its name makes clear, you pay nothing for submitting this application other than the time you take to complete the paperwork (completing the application takes more time than watching a TV sitcom but probably less time than getting a driver's license). Some private colleges also require that you complete the Financial Aid Form (FAF), which asks for more information than the FAFSA.

States have their own financial aid programs, so check with your local high school or college financial aid office to get the forms to apply to these as well if you're planning on attending an in-state college. Some colleges also require submission of supplementary forms directly to them.

The data you supply through student aid forms is run through a *financial needs analysis,* a standard methodology approved by the U. S. Congress. The needs analysis considers a number of factors, such as parents' income and assets, age and need for retirement income, number of dependents, number of family members in college, and unusual financial circumstances, which you explain on the application.

The needs analysis calculates how much money you as the parent(s) and your child as the student can be expected to contribute toward educational expenses. Even if the needs analysis determines that you don't qualify for *needs-based* financial aid, you will still have access to loans that are *not* based on need if you go through the financial aid application process. So make sure that you apply for financial aid!

One of the more damaging things that you can do for preparing financially for college costs is to neglect saving in your retirement accounts and instead save in custodial accounts in your child's name, which gives you no tax deduction and reduces your chances to qualify for financial assistance, whether federal or state.

Treatment of retirement accounts

Under the current needs analysis, the value of your retirement plans is *not* considered an asset. Money that you save *outside* retirement accounts, including money in the child's name, is counted as an asset and reduces your eligibility for financial aid.

Therefore, forgoing contributions to your retirement savings plans in order to save money in a taxable account for Junior's college fund doesn't make sense. When you do, you pay higher taxes both on your current income and on the interest and growth of this money. In addition to paying higher taxes, you are expected to contribute more to your child's educational expenses.

So while your children are years away from applying to college, make sure that you fully fund your retirement accounts such as 401(k)s, SEP-IRAs, and Keoghs. In addition to getting an immediate tax deduction in the year you contribute money, future growth on your earnings will grow without taxation while you're maximizing your child's chances of qualifying for aid.

Let me stress the need to get an early start on saving. If you read about Mary earlier in the chapter, you remember that she waited until the last minute (with her daughter already in college, you could say she waited even beyond the last minute), and she had to resort to an annuity (explained in Chapter 12) because it was the only avenue open to her to put tens of thousands of dollars away at once into a retirement account. Her procrastination cost her thousands of dollars in tax-deductions she could have had over the years.

In recent years, some schools have begun to use "Profile" forms to supplement the FAFSA described earlier in the chapter. This is a four-page form mainly used by costly private schools to differentiate need among financial aid applicants. Individual schools may attach their own questions, which require you to list information about money held in retirement accounts. The information on this form is used to help determine how much money you will receive from the school's privately endowed funds. Does this mean you should ignore retirement accounts? Not at all. The vast majority of schools don't consider retirement account funds at all when making financial aid determinations. And even if your child ends up going to one of the schools that does examine such accounts, it's not at all clear that the reduction in your financial aid offer will outweigh the tax benefits gained from the accounts.

Treatment of money in the kids' names

If you plan to apply for financial aid, saving money in your name rather than in your children's names (custodial accounts) is a good idea. Colleges expect a much greater percentage of money in your child's name (35 percent) to be used for college costs than money in your name (6 percent).

Comparing the plans of the Selfish family and the Good Intentions family

Imagine two families, the Selfish family and the Good Intentions family, who both live in identical neighborhoods. They own identical homes that they purchased at exactly the same cost. They have identical mortgages and identical jobs that pay the same salaries.

Both families give birth to twin children on the same day. The only financial difference between these two families is that the Good Intentions family wants to start saving $100 per month in a nonretirement account when their twins are born to help pay for the children's future college expenses. (Because they have to pay income tax on this money, however, the Good Intentions family is actually putting only about $63 per month per child to work.)

The Selfish family saves the same amount, $100 per child per month, in their retirement savings plans. Because they pay no federal and state income tax on this money, all of their contributions go to work in the retirement savings plan.

Assuming that both families' investments average an 8-percent-per-year rate of return before taxes, the Good Intentions family ends up with about $22,100 per child when the kids turn 18. The Selfish family, on the other hand, has more than $48,500 per child when their twins celebrate their 18th birthdays. (Later in the chapter, I discuss how you can help pay for Junior's college expenses if you're socking money away into retirement accounts.)

Apart from deciding where to invest money for college, these two families continue to live parallel financial lives in every other way. When the children of the two families apply for financial aid, however, the Selfish family kids qualify for a good deal more aid. The Selfish family actually holds higher assets, but given the current financial aid criteria and regulations, the Good Intentions family looks wealthier on paper because they hold more money outside their retirement accounts.

If you're affluent enough that you expect to pay for your kid's entire educational costs, investing through custodial accounts can save you on taxes. Prior to your child reaching age 14, the first $1,300 of interest and dividend income is taxed at your child's income tax rate rather than yours. After age 14, *all* income generated by investments in your child's name is taxed at your child's rate.

Treatment of home equity and other assets

Your family's assets also include equity in real estate and businesses that you own. Although the federal financial aid analysis no longer counts equity in your primary residence as an asset, many private (independent) schools continue to ask parents for this information when making their own financial aid determinations. Thus paying down your home mortgage more quickly instead of funding retirement accounts can harm you financially. You may end up with less financial aid and pay more in taxes.

The need to reform the financial aid system

To some, structuring your finances to maximize financial aid seems, well, a bit underhanded. Let me discourage you from this type of thinking. The government has set up a both a financial aid and a tax system that encourage you to save for retirement. Therefore, retirement saving is not selfish — it's financially responsible for you and your children (and the government that doesn't want to get stuck caring for you if you don't save for retirement). Because so many parents — probably including you before you read this chapter — do not understand this, they are not receiving the financial aid that they deserve.

Perhaps we can criticize the government for not publicizing its intentions more effectively. But compare financial aid to the tax system. The tax system also rewards certain types of behavior, but if you ask the IRS for help, they will not tell you *how* to reduce your taxes. The same is true of financial aid: It is *your* responsibility to understand the system in order to receive the financial aid that your child deserves.

Of course, the system is far from perfect, but it is also our responsibility to work for changes. One suggestion that I have is a revision to the tax code that allows parents to take money out of tax-sheltered retirement accounts without penalty when used for paying educational expenses.

Another inequity in the current financial aid determination process is that it makes no allowance for differences in the cost of living across the country. If you live in a high-cost urban area, such as New York, Los Angeles, or San Francisco, the financial aid system makes the erroneous assumption that you are able to contribute the same amount for college costs as someone with equivalent income who lives in a low-cost rural area. Some adjustment for differences in cost of living should be considered in the system.

How Will I Pay for Educational Expenses?

Now you may be wondering how you'll come up with the money to pay for educational expenses if you keep stashing money into retirement accounts. I don't have just one correct solution because how you'll help pay for your child's college costs depends on your own unique situation. However, in most cases, even if you have some liquid cash that can be directed to pay the college bills as they come in, you will, in all likelihood, have to borrow *some* money.

Some tips: Loans, grants, and scholarships

If you're a homeowner, you can borrow against the equity (market value less the outstanding mortgage loan) in your property. This is a great option because you can borrow against your home at a relatively low interest rate, and the interest is generally tax-deductible. Some company retirement plans — for example, 401(k)s — allow borrowing as well.

A host of financial aid programs, including a number of loan programs, allow you to borrow at reasonable interest rates. As with some mortgage loans on real estate, federal government educational loans have variable interest rates — which means that the interest rate you're charged floats, or varies, with the overall level of interest rates. Most programs add 3.1 percent to the current interest rates on three-month to one-year Treasury bills. Thus, current rates on educational loans are in the vicinity of 9 percent. The rates are also capped so that the interest rate on your loan can never exceed a few percent more than the initial rate on the loan.

A number of loan programs, such as *Unsubsidized Stafford Loans* and *Parent Loans for Undergraduate Students (PLUS),* are available even when your family is not deemed financially needy. Only *Subsidized Stafford Loans,* on which the federal government pays the interest that accumulates while the student is still in school, are limited to students deemed financially needy.

Most loan programs limit the amount that you can borrow per year as well the overall total you can borrow for a student's educational career. If you need more money than your limits allow, PLUS loans can fill the gap: Parents can borrow the full amount needed after other financial aid is factored in. The only obstacle is that you must go through a credit qualification process. Unlike privately funded college loans, federal loans' main qualification stipulation is that you don't have negative credit (recent bankruptcy, more than three debts over three months past due, and so on). For more information from the federal government about these student loan programs, call the Federal Student Financial Aid Information Center at 800-433-3243.

In addition to loans, a number of grant programs are available through schools and the government as well as through independent sources. You can apply for federal government grants via the FAFSA. Grants available through state government programs may require a separate application. Specific colleges and other private organizations (including employers, banks, credit unions, and community groups) also offer grants and scholarships.

Many scholarships and grants don't require any extra work on your part — simply apply for financial aid through colleges. Other programs need seeking out — check directories and databases at your local library, your child's school counseling department, and college financial aid offices. Also try local organizations, churches, employers, and so on. You have a better chance of getting scholarship money through these avenues.

College scholarship search services are generally a waste of money; in some cases, they are actually scams. Some of these services charge up to $100 just to tell you about scholarships that either you're already being considered for or that you're not even eligible for. The legitimate services may tell you about scholarships for, say, $500 that require you to obtain and complete an application and essays. Most people who lack the initiative to use the free references that I described earlier in this chapter probably won't go to the time and trouble to apply for these small potato scholarships.

Your child can work and save money during high school and college. In fact, if your child qualifies for financial aid, he or she is expected to contribute a certain amount to education costs from savings and from employment during the school year or summer breaks. Besides giving Junior a stake in his or her own future, this training encourages sound personal financial management down the road.

The borrowing versus saving debate

More than a few investment firms and financial planners argue that, in the long run, saving for your children's college expenses is far cheaper than borrowing for them.

This claim is not true. If you are able to save in retirement accounts and choose decent investments and then separately borrow the money needed for college costs later, you can come out ahead, thanks to the tax benefits that retirement accounts provide and the increased financial aid you may receive.

The conflict of interest of these organizations and planners is that they can't sell you investments if you channel your savings into your employer's retirement plan. They have every reason to scare you into action (and into their hands).

What's college going to cost?

College can cost a lot. The total costs vary substantially from school to school. The average annual cost (including tuition, fees, books, supplies, room, board, and transportation) at private colleges is running around $20,000 per year and around $9,500 at public colleges and universities. The more expensive schools can cost up to 35 percent more.

Is all this expense worth it? Although many critics of higher education claim that the cost of a college education should not be rising faster than inflation and that costs can, and should, be contained, denying the value of going to college is hard. Whether it is a local community college, your friendly state university, or a selective Ivy League school, investing in education is usually worth the effort and the cost.

The definition of an *investment* is an outlay of money for an expected profit. Unlike a car that depreciates in value each year that you drive it, an investment in education yields monetary, social, and intellectual profit. A car is more tangible in the short term, but an investment in education (even if it means borrowing money) gives you more bang for the buck in the long run.

Colleges are now finding themselves subject to the same types of competition that for-profit companies confront on a daily basis. As a result, schools are having to clamp down on rising costs. As with any other product or service purchase, it pays to shop around. You can find good values — schools that don't cost an arm and a leg and provide a quality education.

Setting realistic savings goals

If you have money left over *after* taking advantage of retirement accounts, by all means try to save for your children. As discussed earlier, you should ideally save in your name unless you know that you won't need or want to apply for financial aid, including those loans that are available regardless of your economic situation.

Be realistic about what you can afford for college expenses given your other financial goals, especially saving for retirement (refer to Chapter 8). Being able to pay the full cost of a college education or anything approaching the full cost, especially at a four-year private college, is a luxury of the affluent. If you're not a high income earner, consider trying to save enough to pay a third or at most half of the cost. You can easily make up the balance through loans, your child's employment before and during college, and the like.

Fill out Table 14-1 to help get a handle on how much you should be saving.

Table 14-1	How Much to Save for College
Figure Out This	**Write It Here**
1. Cost of school you think your child will attend.	$ _____
2. Percent of costs you'd like to pay (for example, 20% or 40%).	x _____ %
3. Line 1 times line 2 is amount you'll pay (in today's dollars).	= $ _____
4. Number of months until your child reaches college age.	_____ months
5.*Amount to save per month (today's dollars). Line 3 answer divided by line 4 answer.	= $ _____ / month

*The amount you need to save (calculated in line 5) needs to be increased once per year by the increase in college inflation — 5 or 6 percent should do.

Note: Don't worry about correcting for inflation. This worksheet takes care of that through the assumptions made on the returns of your investments as well as the amount that you save over time. This way of doing the calculations works because you assume that the money you're saving will grow at the rate of college inflation.

If your child has expensive taste in schools, you may want to tack on 20 to 30 percent to the following average figures.

- ✔ Average cost of a four-year private college education today: $80,000.
- ✔ Average cost of a four-year public college education today: $38,000.

Good and Bad Investments for Educational Funds

Many financial companies pour millions of dollars into advertising for investment and insurance products that they claim are the best ways to make your money grow for your little gremlins — I mean, children.

What makes for good and bad investments in general applies to investments for educational expenses, too. Stick with basic, proven, lower cost investments. Chapter 10 gives a thorough overview of what to look for and what to beware of. This section focuses on considerations specific to college funding.

Good investments: no-load mutual funds

As discuss in Chapter 11, the professional management and efficiency of no-load mutual funds makes them a tough investment to beat. Chapters 12 and 13 provide recommendations for investing money in funds both inside as well as outside tax-sheltered retirement accounts. The important issue is to gear the investments to the time frame involved until your children need to use the money. The closer your child gets to attending college and using the money saved, the more conservatively the money should be invested.

Bad investments

Life insurance policies that have cash values are some of the most oversold investments to fund college costs. The usual pitch is: Because you need life insurance to protect your family, why not buy a policy that you can borrow against to pay for college? Makes sense, doesn't it?

The reason you shouldn't is that you're better off contributing to retirement accounts. These investments give you an immediate tax deduction that saving through life insurance does not. Because life insurance that comes with a cash value is more expensive, parents are more likely to make a second mistake — not buying enough coverage. If you need and want life insurance, you're better off buying lower-cost term life insurance (see Chapter 17).

Another poor investment for college expenses is one that fails to keep you ahead of inflation, such as savings or money market accounts. You need your money to grow to afford educational costs down the road.

Prepaid tuition plans should generally be avoided. A few states have developed plans to allow you to pay college costs at a specific school (calculated for the age of your child). The allure of these plans is that by paying today, you eliminate the worry of not being able to afford rising costs in the future.

This logic doesn't work for several reasons. First, odds are quite high that you don't have the money today to pay in advance. If you have that kind of extra dough around, you're better off using it for other purposes (and you're unlikely to worry about rising costs anyway). You can invest your own money — that's what the school's going to do with it anyway.

Besides, how do you know which college your child will want to attend and how long it might take Junior to get through? Coercing your child into the school you've already paid for is a sure ticket to long-term problems in your relationship with your teenager.

Overlooked investments: Time and attention

Too often, I see parents knocking themselves out to make more money so that they can afford to send their kids to more expensive (and therefore supposedly better) private high schools and colleges. Sometimes families want to send younger children to costly elementary schools, too. Families stretch themselves with outrageous mortgages or complicated living arrangements to get into neighborhoods with top-rated public schools or to send their kids to expensive private elementary schools that they can barely afford.

The best school in the world for your child is you and your home. The reason many people I know, including me and my siblings, were able to attend some of the top educational institutions in this country is that concerned parents worked hard, not just at their jobs, but at spending time with the kids while they were growing up. Rather than working to make more money (with the best of intentions to buy educational games or trips or to send the kids to better schools), in my humble opinion, some parents could do more for their kids by focusing more time on the child.

I see parents scratching their heads about their child's lack of interest and achievement academically — they blame the school or TV or society at large. These factors may contribute, but education begins in the home. Schools can't do it alone.

This is another reason not to live up to your income (that is, to continually raise your spending and living standards to use your income fully). Living within your means not only allows you to save more of your income, but it also can free more of your time to raise and educate your children.

Chapter 15

Real Estate 101

. . . .

In This Chapter

▶ To buy or not to buy

▶ Determining how much to spend and what to buy

▶ Understanding mortgages

▶ Finding a great property

▶ How to work with real estate agents

▶ Putting a deal together

▶ Issues after you buy

. . . .

*B*uying a home or investing in real estate can be a financially and psychologically rewarding experience. On the other hand, owning real estate can
be a real pain in the butt. Purchasing and maintaining property can be one of
the most time-consuming, emotionally draining, and financially painful experi-
ences in managing your personal finances.

Perhaps you are looking to escape your rented apartment and buy your first
home. Or maybe you're interested in cornering the local real estate market and
making millions in investment property. In either case, you can learn many
lessons from real estate buyers who have traveled before you.

Note: Although this chapter focuses primarily on real estate in which you would
live — otherwise known by those in the trade as owner occupied property —
much of what is in the chapter is relevant to real estate investors. For additional
information on buying investment real estate — property that you rent out to
others — see Chapter 10.

To Buy or Continue Renting?

You may be tired of moving from rental to rental. Perhaps your landlord doesn't
keep up the place as well as you'd like, or you have to ask permission to hang a
picture on the wall. You may desire the financial security and rewards that seem
to come with home ownership. Or maybe you just want a place to call your own.

Any one of these reasons is a good enough reason to *want* to buy a home. But you still need to take stock of your life and your financial health *before* you know if you can or should buy a home and how much you can really afford to spend. Time to ask yourself some bigger questions.

What's my timeline?

From a financial standpoint, you really shouldn't buy a place unless you can anticipate being there for at least three years and preferably five or more. Buying and selling a property entails a lot of expenses, including the cost of getting a mortgage (points, application, and appraisal fees), inspection expenses, moving costs, real estate agents' commissions, and title insurance. To cover these transaction costs plus the additional costs of ownership, a property needs to appreciate about 15 percent.

If you may need or want to move in a couple of years, counting on that kind of appreciation is risky. If you're lucky and happen to buy before a sharp upturn in housing prices, you may get it. If you're not, you will probably lose money on the deal.

Some people are willing to invest in real estate even when they don't expect to live in it for long and would consider turning their home into a rental. Doing so can work well financially in the long haul, but don't underestimate the responsibilities that come with being a landlord. Also, most people need to sell their first home in order to tap all the cash that they have in it to buy the next one.

The advantages of renting

Renting has its advantages. Some financially successful renters that I've seen include people who pay low rent, either because they've made housing sacrifices or live in a rent-controlled building. If you're consistently able to save a good percentage of your earnings (10 percent or more), you're probably well on your way to achieving your future financial goals.

As a renter, you can also enjoy your free time away from work not worrying about or being responsible for fixing up the property — that's your landlord's responsibility. You also have more financial and emotional flexibility as a renter. If you want to move, you can generally do so a lot easier as a renter than as a home owner.

Another problem that you won't have in renting over the long haul is having a lot of your money tied up in your home. Many people enter their retirement years with a substantial portion of their wealth in their homes. As a renter, you have all your money in financial assets that you can probably tap into more easily.

Can I afford it?

Although buying and owning your own home can be a wise financial move in the long run, it is a major purchase which can and probably will send shock waves through the rest of your personal finances. You will probably take out a 15- to 30-year mortgage to finance your purchase. The home you buy will need all sorts of maintenance over the years. Owning a home is a bit like running a marathon: Just as you have to be in good physical shape to run a marathon, you have to be in good financial health when you buy a house. For as long as you own the home, you will be paying for something or other all the time. *Before* you make a commitment to buy, you must take stock of your overall financial health.

Lenders look primarily at annual income when determining how much a potential home buyer can borrow; they pay no attention to a borrower's global financial picture. Whether you have no money already tucked away into retirement savings or have several children to clothe, feed, and help pay for college, you qualify for the same size loan as other people with the same income (assuming equal outstanding debts).

So don't trust the lender when she tells you what you can afford according to some formulas that the bank uses to determine what kind of a credit risk you are. Only you can figure out how much you can afford, because only you know what your other financial goals are and how important they are to you.

Here are some important financial questions no lender will ask you or care about but that you should ask yourself before buying a home:

- ✔ Are you saving enough monthly to reach your retirement goals?
- ✔ How much do you spend (and want to continue spending) on fun things such as travel and entertainment?
- ✔ How willing are you to budget your expenses in order to meet your monthly mortgage payments and other housing expenses?
- ✔ How much of your children's expected college educational expenses do you want to be able to pay for?

The other chapters in this book can help you answer these important questions. Chapter 8 in particular will help you with thinking through saving for important financial goals.

Many new home owners run into financial trouble because they don't know their spending needs and priorities and don't know how to budget for them. Some of these owners have trouble curtailing their spending despite the large amount of debt they just incurred; in fact, some spend even more because all sorts of furniture and remodeling expenditures can be made for their home.

Many people prop up their spending habits with credit. For this reason, a surprisingly large percentage — some studies say about half — who borrow additional money against their home equity use the funds to pay consumer debts.

Don't let your home control your financial future. I have seen too many people fall in love with a home and make a rash decision without taking a hard look at the financial ramifications. Take stock of your overall financial health, especially where you stand in terms of retirement planning *before* you buy property or agree to a particular mortgage.

How much will lenders allow you to borrow?

All mortgage lenders want to know your ability and the likelihood of your repaying the money you borrow. So you have to pass a few tests that calculate the maximum amount the lender is willing to lend you. For a home in which you will reside, lenders total up your monthly housing expense. They define your housing costs as:

> Mortgage Payment + Property Taxes + Insurance

Lenders typically loan you up to about 33 percent of your monthly gross (before taxes) income for the housing expense. If you're self-employed, this figure is the net income from the bottom line of your federal tax form Schedule C.

Lenders also consider your other debts when deciding how much to lend you. A lot of other debt diminishes the funds available to pay your housing expenses. To your monthly housing expense, lenders will add the amount you need to pay down your other consumer debt (auto loans, credit cards). The monthly total costs of these debt payments plus your housing costs typically cannot exceed 38 percent.

An old rule of thumb says that you can borrow up to three times (or two and one-half times) your annual income when buying a home. But this is a really rough estimate. The maximum that a mortgage lender loans you depends on interest rates. If rates fall (as they have during much of the past decade), the monthly payment on a mortgage of a given size also drops.

Table 15-1 gives you a ballpark idea of the maximum that you're probably eligible to borrow. Multiply your gross annual income by the number in the second column to determine the maximum size mortgage you can get. For example, if you're getting a mortgage with a rate around 7 percent and your annual income is $50,000, multiply 3.5 x $50,000 to get $175,000, the approximate maximum mortgage allowed. Lower interest rates make buying real estate much more affordable.

Table 15-1 What's the Approximate Maximum You Can Borrow?	
When Mortgage Rates Are	*Multiply Your Gross Annual Income* by This Figure to Determine the Maximum You May Be Able to Borrow*
4%	4.6
5%	4.2
6%	3.8
7%	3.5
8%	3.2
9%	2.9
10%	2.7
11%	2.5

*If you're self-employed, this is your net income (after expenses but before taxes).

What's more expensive: owning or renting?

An important financial consideration for many renters is the cost of owning a home. Some people assume that owning costs more. In fact, owning a place doesn't have to cost a truckload of money. It may even cost less than renting.

On the surface, buying a place seems a lot more expensive than renting. You're probably comparing your monthly rent (a couple hundred dollars to more than $1,000, depending on where you live) to the purchase price of a property, which is usually a number with a whole lot more digits — $100,000, $200,000, or more. When you consider a home purchase, you're forced to think about your housing expenses in one huge chunk rather than in small monthly installments like a rent check.

Tallying up the costs of owning a place can be a useful and not-too-complicated exercise. To make fair the comparison between ownership and rental costs, you need to figure what it would cost on a *monthly basis* to buy a place you desire versus what it would cost to rent a *comparable* place. The worksheet in Table 15-2 enables you to do such a comparison. *Note:* In the interest of reducing the number of variables, all this "figuring" assumes a fixed-rate mortgage, *not* an adjustable (I discuss mortgages later in this chapter).

Table 15-2 Monthly Expenses: Renting Versus Owning

Figure Out This	Write It Here ($ per month)
1. Monthly mortgage payment (see "Mortgage" below)	$ _____
2. Plus monthly property taxes (see "Property tax" below)	+ $ _____
3. Equals total monthly mortgage plus property taxes	= $ _____
4. Your income tax rate (see Table 7-1)	% _____
5. Minus tax benefits (line 3 multiplied by line 4)	− $ _____
6. Equals after-tax cost of mortgage and property taxes (subtract line 5 from line 3)	= $ _____
7. Plus insurance ($30 to $150/mo., depending on property value)	+ $ _____
8. Plus maintenance (1% of property cost divided by 12 months)	+ $ _____
9. Equals total costs of owning (add lines 6, 7, and 8)	= $ _____

Now, compare Line 9 in Table 15-2 with the monthly rent on a comparable place to see which comes out (roughly) ahead, owning or renting.

Mortgage

To determine the monthly payment on your mortgage, simply multiply the relevant number ("Multiplier") from Table 15-3 by the size of your mortgage expressed in (divided by) thousands of dollars. For example, if you are taking out a $100,000, 30-year mortgage at 8 percent, then multiply 100 by 7.34 for a $734 monthly payment.

Table 15-3 Your Monthly Mortgage Payment "Multiplier"

Interest Rate	15-Year Mortgage	30-Year Mortgage
4.0%	7.40	4.77
4.5%	7.65	5.07
5.0%	7.91	5.37
5.5%	8.17	5.68
6.0%	8.44	6.00
6.5%	8.71	6.32
7.0%	8.99	6.65

Interest Rate	15-Year Mortgage	30-Year Mortgage
7.5%	9.27	6.99
8.0%	9.56	7.34
8.5%	9.85	7.69
9.0%	10.14	8.05
9.5%	10.44	8.41
10.0%	10.75	8.78

Property taxes

Ask a real estate person, mortgage lender, or your local assessor's office what your annual property tax bill would be for a house of similar value to the one you are considering buying (the average is 1.5 percent of your property's value). Divide this amount by 12 to arrive at your monthly property tax bill.

Tax savings in home ownership

The following shortcut works quite well in determining your tax savings in home ownership: Multiply your federal tax rate (refer to Chapter 7) by the total amount of your property taxes and mortgage. Technically speaking, not all of your mortgage payment is tax-deductible — only the portion of the mortgage payment that goes to interest is tax-deductible. In the early years of your mortgage, the portion that goes toward interest is nearly all of it. On the other hand, your property taxes will probably rise over time.

You may earn state tax benefits as well from your deductible mortgage interest and property taxes. On the other hand, you probably won't capture its full value due to the intricacies of claiming itemized deductions in the income tax system.

If you want to know more precisely how home ownership may affect your tax situation, get out your tax return and try plugging in some reasonable numbers to "guesstimate" how your taxes will change. You can also speak with a tax advisor or utilize the tax software I discuss in Chapter 7.

Consider the long-term cost of renting

When you crunch the numbers to see what owning rather than renting a comparable place may cost you on a monthly basis, you may discover that owning isn't quite as expensive as you thought. Or you may find that owning costs somewhat more than renting. This discovery may tempt you to think that, financially speaking, renting is cheaper than owning.

Be careful not to jump to conclusions. Remember that you're looking at the cost of owning versus renting *today*. What about 5, 10, or 30 years from now? As an owner, your biggest monthly expense — the mortgage payment — does not increase (assuming that you buy your home with a fixed-rate mortgage). Your property taxes, homeowner's insurance, and maintenance expenses — which are generally far less than your mortgage payment — are the items that increase with the cost of living.

As a renter, however, your entire monthly rent is subject to the vagaries of inflation. The exception to this rule is when you live in a rent-controlled unit, where the annual increase allowed in your rent is capped. Rent control does not eliminate price hikes; it just limits them.

Suppose that you are comparing the costs of owning a home that costs $160,000 to renting that home for $800 a month. Table 15-4 compares the cost of owning the home per month (after factoring in tax benefits) to your rental costs over 30 years. This assumes that you take out a mortgage loan equal to 80 percent of the cost of the property at a fixed rate of 7 percent and that the rate of inflation of your homeowner's insurance, property taxes, maintenance, and rent is 4 percent per year.

Table 15-4	Cost of Owning versus Renting Over 30 Years	
Year	*Ownership Cost per Month*	*Rental Cost per Month*
1	$ 920	$800
5	$ 980	$940
10	$1,080	$1,140
20	$1,360	$1,690
30	$1,800	$2,500

As you can see in Table 15-4, it costs a little bit more in the first few years to own the home than to rent it. In the long run, however, owning becomes less expensive. This is because more of your rental expenses increase with inflation. And don't forget that you're building equity in your property as a home owner, and that equity will be quite substantial by the time that you have your mortgage paid off.

If you've been paying attention, you may be thinking that if inflation doesn't rise 4 percent per year, renting could end up being cheaper. This is not necessarily so. Suppose that no inflation exists at all. Your rent shouldn't escalate, but home ownership expenses (property taxes, maintenance, and insurance) shouldn't, either. And with no inflation, you can probably refinance your mortgage at a rate lower than 7 percent. If you do the math, you find that owning should still cost less in the long run with lower inflation, but the advantage compared to renting is less than during periods of higher inflation.

Mortgages: Side Effect of the American Dream

Once you've looked at your financial health, figured out your timeline, and compared renting to owning costs, you can give yourself the green light to pursue the American dream of owning your own home. Well, now you need to face the reality that part of the American dream is acquiring a large amount of debt — in this case, it's called a mortgage. The *mortgage* is the loan from a bank or other source that makes up the difference between the cash you have already and the agreed-upon selling price of a piece of real estate. Without a mortgage, most people can't buy the homes their hearts desire.

The monthly mortgage payments, which consist of interest and principal to repay your loan balance, are huge expenses. Did you know that you may end up paying more for the *interest* on your mortgage than you will for your humble abode itself?

Assume that your new pad costs $150,000. To buy it, you borrow $120,000 and contribute $30,000 from your savings for the down payment. If you borrow that $120,000 with a 30-year fixed-rate mortgage at 7 percent, you end up paying more than $167,000 *in interest* over the life of your loan. (Although you'll pay back some of these interest dollars many years from now when the dollar will likely, thanks to inflation, be worth less than it is today, you're still going to spend a truckload of dollars in interest.)

So taking the time to educate yourself about how to get the best possible deal on a mortgage and ancillary fees is a very wise financial move. More importantly, you won't be able to buy your dream home unless you can finance its purchase.

For many households, mortgage payments are the single largest monthly expenditure (besides taxes). Like many other financial products, zillions of different mortgages are available to choose from. The differences can be important or trivial, expensive or cost-free.

First, the big differences. Two major types of mortgages exist — those with a *fixed interest rate* and those with a *variable* or *adjustable rate*.

Fixed-rate mortgages

Usually issued for a 15- or 30-year period, fixed-rate mortgages have interest rates that never, ever change. The interest rate you pay the first month is the same one that you pay the last month and every month in between.

Because the interest rate stays the same, your monthly mortgage payment amount does not change. You have no uncertainty or interest rate worries. If you like getting your daily newspaper delivered at the same time everyday, you're gonna like fixed-rate mortgages.

Fixed-rate loans are not without risks, however. If interest rates fall significantly after you obtain your mortgage, you face the danger of being stuck with your higher-cost mortgage if you're unable, because of a deterioration in your financial situation or a decline in the value of your property, to *refinance* your mortgage (refinancing is discussed later in this chapter). And, even if you are eligible to refinance, you'll probably have to spend a good amount of time and money to complete it.

Be wary of balloon loans, which look like fixed-rate loans but really aren't. With a *balloon loan,* the large remaining loan balance becomes fully due at a prede-termined time — typically within three to ten years. Balloon loans are danger-ous because you may not be able to refinance into a new loan to pay off the balloon loan when it comes due. What if you lose your job or your income drops? What if the value of your property drops, and the appraisal comes in too low to qualify you for a new loan? What if interest rates rise and you can't qualify for the higher rate on a new loan? Taking a balloon loan is a high-risk maneuver that can backfire.

You should take such a loan *only* if the following three conditions are true: You *really, really* want a certain property; the balloon loan is your *only* financing option; you're *positive* that you'll be able to refinance when the balloon comes due. If you take a balloon loan, get one with as much time as possible before it comes due.

Adjustable-rate mortgages (ARMs)

In contrast to a fixed-rate mortgage, an *adjustable-rate mortgage* (ARM) carries an interest rate that varies over time. Like a fidgeting child, it rises, falls, and otherwise can't sit still.

Some adjustables are more hyperactive and tend to get you into more trouble than others — again, like kids. You can start with one interest rate this year and have different ones for every year, possibly every month, during a 30-year mortgage. Thus the size of your monthly payment fluctuates. Because a mortgage payment makes an unusually large dent in most homeowners' checkbooks anyway, signing up for an adjustable without understanding its risks is dangerous.

The attraction of adjustables is the potential interest savings. For the first few years of an adjustable loan, the interest rate is typically lower than on a compa-rable fixed-rate loan. After that, it depends on the overall trends in interest rates. When interest rates drop, stay level, or rise just a little, you continue to pay less for your adjustable. On the other hand, when rates rise more than a percent or two and stay elevated, the adjustable is going to cost you more than a fixed-rate loan.

Choosing between fixed- and adjustable-rate mortgages

Ideally, you should weigh the pros and cons of each mortgage type and decide what's best for your situation *before* you go out to purchase a piece of real estate or refinance a loan. In the real world, most people ignore this advice. The excitement of purchasing a home tends to cloud one's judgment. My experience has been that few people look at their entire financial picture before making major real estate decisions.

Consider the issues that I discuss in this section before you decide which kind of mortgage — fixed or adjustable — is right for you.

How willing and able are you to take on financial risk?

Take stock of how much of a gamble you can take with the size of your monthly mortgage payment. If you start making offers on properties before you resolve this issue, you're putting the cart before the horse. You may end up with a mortgage that could someday seriously overshadow your delight in your little English herb garden out back.

For example, if your job and income are unstable and you need to borrow a lot, you can't afford much risk. I define *a lot* as close to the maximum that a bank is willing to lend you. *A lot* can also mean that you have no slack in your monthly budget — that is, you're not saving any money on a regular basis. If you're in this situation, stick with a fixed-rate loan.

Don't take an adjustable simply because the initially lower interest rates allow you to afford the property you want to buy (unless you're absolutely certain that your income will rise to meet future payment increases). Try setting your sights on a property that you can afford — with a fixed-rate mortgage.

If interest rates rise, a mushrooming adjustable mortgage payment may test the lower limits of your checking account balance. If you don't have emergency savings that you can tap to make the higher payments, how can you afford the monthly payments — much less all the other expenses of home ownership?

And don't forget to factor in reasonably predictable future expenses that may affect your ability to make payments. For example, are you planning to start a family soon? If so, your income may fall while your expenses will surely rise.

If you can't afford the highest allowed payment on an adjustable-rate mortgage, you have no business taking one. You shouldn't take the chance that the interest rate might not rise that high — it could, and you could lose your home! Ask your lender to calculate the highest possible *maximum monthly payment* on your loan. That's the payment you would face if the interest rate on your loan went to the highest level allowed, or the *lifetime cap*.

Consider also your stress level. If you have to start reading the daily business pages to check interest rates, it's probably not worth gambling on rates. Life is too short!

On the other hand, maybe you're in a position to take the financial risks that come with an adjustable-rate mortgage. An adjustable places more (but not all as most adjustables limit, or *cap,* the rise in the interest rate allowed on your loan) of the risk of fluctuating rates on you. In return, lenders cut you a deal — an adjustable's interest rate starts lower and stays lower if the overall level of interest rates don't rise substantially. Even if rates go up, they will probably come back down over the life of your loan. So if you can stick with your adjustable for better and for worse, you may still come out ahead in the long term. Typical caps are 2 percent per year and 6 percent over the life of the loan.

You might feel financially secure in choosing an adjustable loan if you have a hefty financial cushion that is accessible in the event that rates go up, if you take out a smaller loan than you're qualified for, or if you're saving more than 10 percent of your income.

How long do you plan to keep the mortgage?

A mortgage lender takes extra risk in committing to a constant interest rate for 15 to 30 years. Lenders generally don't know any better than you or me what may happen in the intervening years, so they charge you a premium for their risk.

Savings on most adjustables is usually guaranteed in the first two or three years as an adjustable-rate mortgage starts at a lower interest rate than a fixed one. If rates rise, you can end up giving back or losing the savings you achieve in the early years of the mortgage. In most cases, if you aren't going to keep your mortgage more than five to seven years, you're probably paying unnecessary interest costs to carry a fixed-rate mortgage.

Another mortgage option is a *hybrid loan,* which combines features of fixed- and adjustable-rate mortgages. For example, the initial rate may hold constant for a number of years — three to five years is common — and then adjust once a year or every six months thereafter. These hybrid loans may make sense for you if you foresee a high probability of keeping your loan seven to ten years or less but want some stability in your monthly payments. The longer the initial rate stays locked in, the higher the rate is.

How to buy with less money down

When you buy a home, ideally you should make a down payment of at least 20 percent of the purchase price of the property. Why? Because you'll generally be able to qualify for the most favorable terms on a mortgage with such a down payment and you'll also be able to avoid the added cost of private mortgage insurance (PMI). Lenders usually require PMI, which on a typical mortgage costs several hundred dollars per year, to protect against their losing money in the event you default on your loan.

Many people don't have the equivalent of 20 percent or more of the purchase price in savings to buy a home without private mortgage insurance. Here are a number of solutions coming up with that 20 percent faster or buying with less money down and solving the down payment blues:

- **Go on a spending diet.** One sure way to come up with a down payment is to raise your savings rate by slashing your spending. Take a tour through Chapter 6 to learn strategies for doing so.

- **Consider lower-priced properties.** Some buyers want their first home to be a palace. Smaller properties and ones that need some work can help to keep down the purchase price and, therefore, the required down payment.

- **Find partners.** You can usually get more home for your money when you buy a building in partnership with one, two, or a few people. Make sure to write up a legal contract to specify what will happen if a partner wants out.

- **Seek reduced down payment financing.** Some property owners or developers may be willing to finance your purchase with as little as 5 to 10 percent down. You can't be as picky about properties because not as many are available under these terms — many need work or haven't yet sold for other reasons.

- **Get assistance from family.** If your parents, grandparents, or other relatives have money dozing away in a savings or CD account, they may be willing to lend (or even give) you the down payment. You can pay them a higher rate of interest than they have been earning (but still lower than what you would pay to borrow from a bank) and thus be able to buy a home — a win/win situation.

- **Obtain private mortgage insurance (PMI).** Some lenders may offer you a mortgage even though you may be able to put down only 5 to 10 percent of the purchase price. Once the property rises enough in value or you pay down the mortgage enough to have 20 percent equity in the property, you can drop the PMI.

15-year versus 30-year mortgages

Many people don't have a choice between 15- and 30-year mortgages. To afford the monthly payments on their desired home, they need to spread the loan payments over a longer period of time, and a 30-year mortgage is the only answer. A 15-year mortgage has higher monthly payments because you pay it off more quickly. With fixed-rate mortgages hovering around 8 percent, a 15-year mortgage comes with payments that are about 30 percent higher than those for a 30-year mortgage.

If you can afford these higher payments, taking the 15-year option is not necessarily better. The money for making extra payments doesn't come out of thin air. You might have better uses, which I discuss later in this section, for your excess funds.

And, if you opt for a 30-year mortgage, you maintain the flexibility to pay it off faster (except in those rare cases where there is a prepayment penalty). By making additional payments, you can create your own 15-year mortgage. But you can fall back to making only the payments required on your 30-year schedule when the need arises.

There's risk in locking yourself into higher monthly payments with a 15-year mortgage. If money gets too tight in the future, you can fall behind in your mortgage payments. You *may* be able to refinance your way out of the predicament, but you can't count on it. If your finances worsen or your property declines in value, odds are that you'll have trouble qualifying for a refinance.

Should you consider faster mortgage payoff?

Suppose that you can qualify for a 15-year mortgage and you're financially comfortable with the higher payments. The appeal of paying off your mortgage 15 years sooner is enticing. Besides, the interest rate is lower on a 15-year mortgage. So if you can afford the higher payments on the 15-year mortgage, you'd be silly not to take it, right? Not so fast. You're really asking whether you should pay off your mortgage slowly or more quickly. And the answer isn't as simple as you think. It depends.

You need to think through this decision despite the fact that entire books have been written extolling the virtues of owning your home without mortgage debt as soon as possible. Those books come complete with endless rows and columns of numbers so that you can look up how much you save through a quicker payback.

The decision about whether to pay off a mortgage faster is not that simple.

If you have the time and inclination (and a good financial calculator), you can calculate how much interest you can save or avoid through a quicker payback. I have a friendly word of advice about spending hours crunching numbers: *don't.* You can make this decision by considering some qualitative issues.

Consider alternative uses for savings

First, think about *alternative uses* for the extra money you'd be throwing into the mortgage paydown. What's best for you depends on your overall financial situation and what else you can do with the money. If you would end up blowing the extra money at the racetrack or on an expensive car, pay down the mortgage. That's a no-brainer.

But suppose that you take the extra $100 or $200 per month that you were planning to add to your mortgage payment and contribute it to a retirement account instead. That step may make financial sense. Why? Because additions to 401(k)s, SEP-IRAs, Keoghs, and other types of retirement accounts (discussed in Chapter 12) are tax-deductible.

When you add an extra $200 to your mortgage payment to pay off your mortgage faster, you get no tax benefits. Zero, *nada,* zippo! When you dump that $200 into a retirement account, you get to subtract that $200 from the income on which you pay taxes. If you're paying 35 percent in federal and state income taxes, you shave $70 (that's $200 multiplied by 35 percent) off your tax bill.

In most cases, you get to deduct your mortgage interest on your tax return. So if you're paying 8 percent interest, your mortgage may really only cost you around 5 percent after you factor in the tax benefits. If you think you can do better by investing elsewhere, go for it. Investments such as stocks and real estate have generated better returns over the long haul. These investments carry risk, though, and are not guaranteed to produce any return.

If you're uncomfortable investing and would otherwise leave the extra money sitting in a money market fund or savings account, you're better off paying down the mortgage. Paying down the mortgage is investing your money in a sure thing with a modest return.

If you have pre-college age kids, you have an even greater reason to fund your retirement accounts before you consider paying down your mortgage quickly. Under current rules for determining financial aid for college expenses, money in your retirement accounts is not counted as an asset. Equity in your home (the difference between its market value and your loan balance), by contrast, is still counted by many schools as an asset.

When you pay down your mortgage balance faster, you're building more equity in your home. On paper, you appear wealthier to financial aid officers than when you save the money in a retirement account. Your reward for paying down your mortgage balance may be less financial aid!

Paying down your mortgage faster, especially when you have children, is rarely a good financial decision when you haven't exhausted contributions to retirement accounts. Save first in retirement accounts and get the tax benefits.

Selecting the best fixed-rate mortgage

If you've decided that you want a fixed-rate mortgage, the good news is that shopping for a fixed-rate loan is easier than shopping for an adjustable. Fixed-rate loans don't come with all the bells and whistles that adjustables do.

Still, the many different lenders in a given market try to differentiate themselves. And lenders have just enough bells and whistles on fixed-rate loans to give you a minor migraine. Here's how to sift among the fixed-rate mortgages out there.

Interest rate

The *interest rate* is the rate of interest that a lender charges you for borrowing their money. Unlike credit-card interest rates, which are usually in the double-digits, fixed-rate loans are much lower. As of this writing, fixed-rate loans can be found around 8 percent.

Points

Just as a seesaw doesn't work with one rider missing, an interest rate quote on its own is completely meaningless. The interest rate on a fixed-rate loan must always be quoted with the points on the loan. If one lender offers 30-year mortgages at 7.75 percent and another lender offers them at 8 percent, the 8-percent loan is not necessarily worse. You need to know how many points each lender charges, too.

Points are up-front fees paid to your lender when you close on your loan. Points are actually percentages: One point is equal to 1 percent of the loan amount. So when a lender tells you that 1.5 points are on a quoted loan, you pay 1.5 percent of the amount you borrow as points. On a $100,000 loan, for example, 1.5 points cost you $1,500.

The seesaw analogy explains how the interest rate and points on a fixed-rate loan go together and move in opposite directions. On a given loan, if you are willing to pay more points (one end of the seesaw goes up), the lender is usually willing to reduce the interest rate (the other end of the seesaw goes down). Paying more in up-front points can save you a lot of money in interest because the interest rate on your loan determines your payments over a long, long time — 15 to 30 years.

If you want to pay fewer points, your interest rate increases. Paying less in points might appeal to you if you don't have much cash to close on your loan. Be wary of lenders advertising no-point loans as though they're offering something for nothing. Remember, if a loan has no points, it's *guaranteed* to have a higher interest rate. That's not to say that it's better or worse than comparable loans from other lenders. But don't get sucked in by a no-points sales pitch. Most lenders who spend big bucks on advertising these types of loans rarely have the best deals anyway.

Suppose Lender X quotes you 7.75 percent on a 30-year fixed-rate loan and charges one point (1 percent). Lender Y, who quotes 8 percent, doesn't charge any points. Which is better? The answer depends mostly on how long you plan to keep the loan.

The 7.75-percent loan is 0.25 percent less than the 8-percent loan. Year in and year out, the 7.75-percent loan saves you 0.25 percent. But because you have to pay 1 percent (one point) up front on the 7.75-percent loan, you take about four years to earn back the savings to cover the cost of that point. So if you expect to keep the loan less than 4 years, go with the 8 percent option.

To perform an apples-to-apples comparison of mortgages from different lenders, get interest rate quotes at the same point level for each mortgage. For example, ask each lender for the interest rate on a loan for which you pay one point.

Other lender fees

In addition to charging you points and the ongoing interest rate, lenders tack on all sorts of other up-front fees in processing your loan. You need to know the total of all lender fees so that you can determine how much completing your home purchase will cost you and can compare different lender's mortgage options.

Lenders can nickel and dime you with a number of fees other than points. Actually, you pay more than nickels and dimes — $300 here and $50 there adds up in a hurry! Here are the main culprits:

- ✔ **Application and processing fees.** Most lenders charge a couple hundred dollars to complete your paperwork and process it through their underwriting (loan evaluation) department. The justification for this fee is that if your loan is rejected or you decide not to take it, the lender needs to cover the costs. Some lenders return this fee to you upon closing when you go with their loan (after you're approved).

- ✔ **Credit report.** Many lenders charge a fee to pay for the cost of obtaining a copy of your credit report. This report tells the lender whether you've been naughty or nice to other lenders in the past. If you have problems on your credit report, clean them up before you apply (see my discussion of this issue later in this chapter).

- ✔ **Appraisal.** The property for which you are borrowing money needs to be valued. If you default on your mortgage, a lender doesn't want to get stuck with a property worth less than you owe. The appraisal cost is typically several hundred dollars for most residential properties.

Get a written itemization of charges from all lenders you are seriously considering so that you have no surprises when you close on your loan and so that you can more readily compare different lenders' mortgages. And to minimize your chances of throwing money away on a loan for which you might not qualify, ask the lender whether you might not be approved for some reason. Be sure to disclose any problems on your credit report or problems with the property that you are aware of.

Some lenders offer loans without points or other lender charges. Remember: Lenders aren't charities. If they don't charge points or other fees, they have to make up the difference by charging a higher interest rate on your loan. Only consider such loans when you lack cash for closing or when you're planning to use the loan for just a few years.

Selecting an adjustable-rate mortgage

If sorting through fixed-rate mortgage options is enough to give you a headache, then comparing the bells and whistles of adjustable-rate mortgages will give you a full-blown migraine. *Caps, indexes, margins,* and *adjustment periods* — you can spend weeks figuring it all out. If you're clueless about personal finances — or just think that you are — shopping for adjustables scores a 9.9 degree of difficulty on the financial frustration scale.

Unfortunately, you have to wade through a number of details to understand and compare one adjustable to another. Bear with me. And remember throughout this discussion that calculating exactly which adjustable mortgage should cost you the least is impossible, because the cost depends on so many variables. Selecting an adjustable-rate mortgage has a lot in common with selecting a home to buy. You have to make trade-offs and compromises based upon what's important to you.

Start (initial) rate

Just as the name implies, the start rate is the interest rate that your adjustable mortgage begins with. Don't judge a loan by this rate alone. You won't be paying this attractively low rate for long. The interest rate will rise as soon as the terms of the mortgage allow.

Beware prepayment penalties

Avoid loans with prepayment penalties. You pay this charge, usually 2 to 3 percent of the loan amount, when you pay off your loan before you're supposed to.

Typically, prepayment penalties don't apply when you pay off a loan because you sell the property.

But if you refinance such a loan in order to take advantage of lower interest rates, you'll almost always get hit by the prepayment penalties.

The only way to know whether a loan has a prepayment penalty is to ask. If the answer is yes, find yourself another mortgage.

Start rates are probably one of the least important items to focus on when comparing adjustables. You'd never know this from the way some lenders advertise adjustables — you see ads with the start rate in 3-inch bold type and everything else in microscopic footnotes!

The formula (which includes index and margin) and rate caps are far more important in determining what a mortgage is going to cost you in the long run.

Some people have labeled the start rate a *teaser rate* because the initial rate on your loan is set artificially low to entice you. In other words, even if the market level of interest rates doesn't change, your adjustable is destined to increase — 1 to 2 percent is not uncommon.

The formula

You'd never (I hope) agree to a loan if your lender's whim and fancy determined your future interest rate. You need to know exactly how a lender figures how much your interest rate increases. All adjustables are based on the following formula, which specifies how the future interest rate on your loan is set:

Index + Margin = Interest Rate

The *index* measures the overall level of interest rates from which the lender chooses to calculate the specific interest rate on your loan. Indexes are generally (but not always) widely quoted in the financial press. For example, the six-month Treasury bill rate is an index used on some mortgages.

The *margin* is the amount added to the index to determine the interest rate you pay on your mortgage. Most loans have margins of around 2.5 percent.

So for example, the interest rate of a mortgage, driven by the following formula

Six-month Treasury bill rate + 2.5 percent

is set at the going rate for six-month Treasuries plus 2.5 percent. So when six-month Treasuries are yielding 5.5 percent, the interest rate on your loan should be 8 percent. This figure is known as the *fully indexed rate*. If this loan starts at 5 percent and if the rate on six-month Treasuries stays the same, your loan should eventually increase to 8 percent.

The margin is very important. When you are comparing two loans that are tied to the same index and are otherwise the same, the loan with the lower margin is better. The margin determines the interest rate for every year you hold the mortgage.

Representatives at one large mortgage lender told me that their market research shows that most borrowers care more about the start rate than the margin on their mortgage. So they happily jacked up their loans' margins and lowered the start rates. Rather than educating their borrowers about the longer-term importance of the margin, they chose to pursue short-term profits.

Indexes differ mainly in how rapidly they respond to changes in interest rates. The following are the more common indexes:

- **Treasury bills (T-bills).** These indexes are issued by the U.S. government. Because they are government IOUs, a whole lot of them are out there. Most adjustables are tied to the interest rate on 6-month or 12-month T-bills.

- **Certificates of deposit (CDs).** Certificates of deposit are interest-bearing bank investments that lock you in for a specific period of time. Adjustable-rate mortgages are usually tied to the average interest rate banks are paying on six-month CDs. Like T-bills, CDs tend to respond quickly to changes in the market level of interest rates. Unlike T-bills, CD rates tend to move up a bit more slowly when rates rise and come down faster when rates decline.

- **11th district cost of funds.** This index tends to be among the slower moving. Adjustable-rate mortgages tied to 11th district cost of funds tend to start out at a higher interest rate. A slower moving index has the advantage of moving up less quickly when rates are on the rise. On the other hand, you must be patient to realize the benefit of falling interest rates.

Adjustment period or frequency

Every so many months, the mortgage-rate formula is applied to recalculate the interest rate on an adjustable-rate loan. Some loans adjust monthly. More typical is an adjustment every 6 or 12 months.

In advance of each adjustment, the lender should send you a notice telling you what your new rate is. All things being equal, the less frequently your loan adjusts, the less financial uncertainty you have in your life. Less-frequent adjustments usually indicate that your loan starts at a higher interest rate, though.

Rate caps

Once the initial interest rate expires, the interest rate fluctuates based on the formula of the loan. Almost all adjustables come with rate *caps*. The *adjustment cap* limits the maximum rate change (up or down) allowed at each adjustment. On most loans that adjust every six months, the adjustment cap is 1 percent.

Loans that adjust more than once per year usually limit the maximum rate change allowed over the entire year as well. On most such loans, 2 percent is the annual rate cap.

Avoid loans with negative amortization

As you make mortgage payments over time, the loan balance you still owe is gradually reduced — this process is known as *amortizing* the loan. The reverse of this process — increasing your loan balance — is called *negative amortization.*

Negative amortization is allowed by some adjustable-rate mortgages. Your outstanding loan balance can grow even though you're continuing to make mortgage payments when your mortgage payment is less than it really should be.

Some loans cap the increase of your monthly payment but not that of the interest rate. The size of your mortgage payment may not reflect all the interest that you owe on your loan. So rather than paying the interest that is owed and paying off some of your loan balance (or *principal*) every month, you're paying off some but not all of the

interest you owe. Thus the extra unpaid interest you still owe is added to your outstanding debt.

Taking on negative amortization is like paying only the minimum payment required on a credit card bill. You keep racking up greater interest charges on the balance as long as you make only the artificially low payment. Doing so defeats the whole purpose of borrowing an amount that fits your overall financial goals. And you may never get the mortgage paid off!

Avoid adjustables with negative amortization. The only way to know whether a loan includes it is to ask. Some lenders aren't forthcoming about telling you. You'll find it more frequently on loans that lenders consider risky. If you're having trouble finding lenders willing to deal with your financial situation, be especially careful.

Finally, almost all adjustables come with *lifetime caps,* which limit the highest rate allowed over the entire life of the loan. Adjustable loans commonly have lifetime caps of 5 to 6 percent higher than the initial start rate. Before taking an adjustable, figure out the maximum possible payment at the lifetime cap to be sure that you can handle it.

Finding the best lender

As with other financial purchases, you can save a lot of money by shopping around. It doesn't matter whether you do so on your own or hire someone to help you. Just do it!

On a 30-year, $120,000 mortgage, for example, getting a mortgage that costs 0.5 percent less per year saves you about $13,000 in interest over the life of the loan (given current interest rate levels). That's enough to buy a nice car! On second thought, save it.

Doing it yourself

You can find many mortgage lenders in most areas. Although having a large number to choose from is good for competition, it also makes shopping a chore.

Large banks whose names you recognize from their advertising usually don't offer the best rates. Make sure that you check out some of the smaller lending institutions in your area as well. Also, check out mortgage bankers, which unlike banks, only do mortgages. The better ones offer some of the most competitive rates.

Real estate agents can also refer you to lenders with whom they've done business. Those lenders don't necessarily offer the most competitive rates — the agent simply may have done business with them in the past.

Look also in the real estate section of one of the larger Sunday newspapers in your area for charts of selected lender interest rates. These tables are by no means comprehensive or reflective of the best rates available. In fact, many of them are sent to newspapers for free by firms that distribute mortgage information to mortgage brokers. Use them as a starting point by calling the lenders who list the best rates.

HSH Associates (800-873-2837) publishes mortgage information for most metropolitan areas. For $20, they'll send you a list of dozens of lenders' rate quotes. You need to be a real data junkie to wade through these multipage reports full of numbers and abbreviations, though.

Hiring a mortgage broker

Insurance agents peddle insurance, real estate agents sell real estate, and mortgage brokers deal in mortgages. They buy mortgages at wholesale from lenders and then mark them up to retail to you. The difference, or *spread,* is their income. The terms of the loan obtained through a broker are generally the same as you would obtain from the lender directly.

A mortgage broker gets paid a percentage of the loan amount — typically 0.5 to 1 percent. This commission is negotiable, especially on larger loans that are more lucrative. You have no reason not to ask a mortgage broker what his cut is. Many people don't, so some brokers may act taken aback when you inquire. Remember, it's your money!

The chief advantage of using a mortgage broker is that the broker can shop among various lenders to get you a good deal. If you're too busy or disinterested to shop around for a good deal on a mortgage, a competent mortgage broker can probably save you money. A broker can also help you through the tedious and draining process of filling out all those horrible documents lenders demand before giving you a loan. And if you've got credit problems or an unusual property, a broker may be able to match you with a hard to find lender willing to offer you a mortgage.

In evaluating a mortgage broker, be on guard for those who are lazy and don't continually shop the market looking for the best mortgage lenders. Some brokers place their business with the same lenders all the time, who don't necessarily offer the best rates. Also watch out for those who are salespeople who earn big commissions pushing certain loan programs that are not in your best interests. They aren't interested in taking the time to understand your needs and discuss your options. Check a broker's references.

Even if you plan to shop on your own, talking to a mortgage broker may be worthwhile. At the very least, you can compare what you find with what brokers say they can get for you. Just be careful. Some brokers tell you what you want to hear — that is, that they can be your best find — and then aren't able to deliver when the time comes.

If a loan broker quotes you a really good deal, make sure to ask who the lender is. (Most brokers refuse to reveal this information until you pay the few hundred dollars to cover the appraisal and credit report.) You can check with the actual lender to verify the interest rate and points the broker quotes you and make sure that you're eligible for the loan.

Increasing your approval chances

A lender can take several weeks to complete your property appraisal and evaluation of your loan package. When you're under contract to buy a property, having your loan denied after waiting several weeks could mean that you lose the property as well as the money you spent applying for the loan and having the property inspected. Some property sellers may be willing to give you an extension, but others won't. Spending all that time and emotional energy getting so close to owning a special property and then losing it can be disappointing.

You can do a number of smart things to increase your chances of having your mortgage approved:

- **Get your finances in shape before you shop.** You're not going to have a good handle on what you can afford to spend on a home until you whip your personal finances in shape. Do so before you begin to make offers on properties. This chapter and book can help you.

  If you have consumer debt, get rid of it, pronto! The more credit card, auto loan, and other consumer debt you rack up, the less mortgage you qualify for. In addition to the high interest rate on consumer debt and the fact that it encourages you to live beyond your means, you now have a third reason to get rid of it. Hang onto the dream of a home and plug away at paying off your debts before you buy a home.

- **Clear up credit report problems.** Late payments, missed payments, or debts that you never bothered to pay can come back to haunt you. If you think there are problems on your credit report, get a copy (the major agencies are listed in the Yellow Pages and TRW [800-392-1122] offers one free copy per year) before you apply for your mortgage.

For mistakes to crop up on credit reports is not unusual. The only way to fix them, unfortunately, is to get on the phone to the credit bureaus and start squawking. If specific creditors have reported erroneous information, call them, too. If the customer service representatives you talk with are no help, dash off a nice letter to the president of each company. Let the head honcho know that his or her organization is tarnishing your credit report and that you're going to report them to the Better Business Bureau and other consumer agencies.

If bona fide problems are documented on your credit report, start by trying to explain them to your lender. If the lender is unsympathetic, try calling other lenders. Tell them your credit problems up front and see whether you can find one willing to give you a loan. Mortgage brokers (discussed earlier) can also help you shop for lenders in these cases.

✔ **Get preapproved or prequalified.** *Prequalified* means that a you've spoken with a lender about your financial situation and they've calculated the maximum they will lend you based upon what you've told them. *Preapproval* is more in-depth and includes a lender's actual review of your financial statements. Although neither is binding upon a lender to actually make you a mortgage loan, preapproval means more, especially in qualifying you financially in the eyes of a seller. Just be sure not to waste your time and money getting preapproved if you're not really ready to get serious about buying.

✔ **Be up-front about problems.** The best defense against loan rejection is to avoid it in the first place. You can sometimes head off potential rejection by disclosing to your lender anything that may cause a problem before you apply for the loan. That way, you have more time to correct problems and find alternate solutions.

✔ **Work around low/unstable income.** If you're self-employed or have been changing jobs, your recent economic history may be as unstable as a communist country trying out capitalism. One way around this problem is to make a larger down payment. If you put down 30 percent or more, you may be able to get a no-income verification loan.

If you are a lending risk because you don't have the income to qualify for the loan you want, you may need to get a cosigner. You can try parents, other relatives, or even rich friends as potential cosigners. As long as they aren't borrowed up to their eyeballs, they can help you qualify for a larger loan than you can get on your own. Be sure that all parties understand the terms of the agreement, including who is responsible for monthly payments!

✔ **Consider a back-up loan.** You certainly should shop among different lenders and you may even want to apply to more than one for a mortgage. Although applying for a second loan means additional fees and work, it can increase your chances of getting a mortgage if you're attempting to buy a difficult-to-finance property or your financial situation makes some lenders leery. Also be sure to disclose what you're doing to each lender — the second lender to pull your credit report will see that another lender has been there already.

Should you lie to get a mortgage?

I know more than a few folks who have lied to get a mortgage. It's not that I associate with unethical people. Working in the financial services industry, I just tend to hear a lot of juicy tales. Mortgage brokers, who end up working with more of the borrowers who have less-than-perfect situations, can tell you lots of war stories of trickery and deception to close a deal. Some brokers even coach people into lying so they can qualify for a loan.

In most cases, not qualifying for the loan that you want is for your own good. Lenders have criteria to ensure that you will be able to repay and don't get in over your head.

On the other hand, I am sympathetic to some of the complaints I hear about bankers and other mortgage lenders who can sometimes be as compassionate and flexible as a totalitarian government agency. They have their rules and regulations and qualifying ratios. You either meet them or you don't. It's black or white. They have their reasons, but sometimes their rules don't fit your situation.

Don't lie. Besides the obvious legal ramifications, you could end up with more mortgage debt than you can really afford and possibly worse. You have alternatives if you're cash-constrained. For example, loans that don't require documentation of income are available when you make a large down payment, generally 30 percent or more. These loans cost a little more than conventional loans, but they also allow you to avoid lying. You could also get a cosigner.

Finding the Right Property and Location

Shopping for a home can be fun. You get to peek inside other people's refrigerators and drawers. But for most people, finding the right house at the right price can take a lot of time. It can also entail a lot of compromise when you're buying with partners or a spouse (or children, if you choose to share the decision making with them).

A good agent (or several in different areas) can help with the legwork. Here are the main things to consider:

Condos, townhouses, co-ops or detached home?

Some people's image of a house is a single-family dwelling — a stand-alone house with a lawn and white picket fence. In some areas, however, particularly in higher-cost neighborhoods, nonsingle-family housing is more common. *Condominiums* (you own the unit and a share of everything else), *townhomes* (attached or row houses), and *cooperatives* (you own a share of the entire building) are higher-density housing units.

The allure of nonsingle family housing is that it is generally less expensive. In some cases, as an owner, you don't have to worry about some of the general maintenance because the owner's association (which you pay for, directly or indirectly) takes care of it.

If you don't have the time, energy, or desire to keep up a property, these types of shared housing can make sense. They may also provide you with better security than a stand-alone home and you generally get more living space for your dollar.

As investments, however, single-family homes generally do better in the long run. Shared housing is easier to build and hence easier to overbuild; on the other hand, single-family houses are harder to put up because more land is required. But most people, when they can afford it, still prefer a stand-alone home.

That said, you should remember that a rising tide raises all boats. In a good real estate market, all types of housing appreciate, although single-family homes tend to do better. Shared housing values tend to increase best in densely populated urban areas with little available land for new building.

If you can afford a smaller single-family home instead of a larger shared-housing unit, buy the single-family home. Be especially wary of buying shared housing in suburban areas with lots of developable land.

Cast a broad net

Before you start your search, you may have an idea about the type of property and location that you are interested in or think you can afford. You may think, for example, that you can afford only a condominium in the neighborhood you want. But if you take the time to check out other communities, you may be surprised to find one that meets most of your needs and has affordable single-family homes. You'd never know that, though, if you narrowed your search too quickly.

Even if you've lived in an area for a while and think that you know it well, look at different types of properties in a number of different areas before you start to narrow your search. Be open minded and be sure to know which of your many criteria for a home you *really* care about. You may have to be flexible on some of your preferences.

If you're working with an agent, make sure you don't overlook homes that are *for sale by owner* (that is, not listed with real estate agents). Otherwise, you may miss out on some good properties.

Find out actual sale prices

Don't look at just a few homes listed at a particular price and get depressed because they're all dogs or you can't afford what you really want. Before you decide to renew your lease on your apartment, remember that properties often sell for less than the price at which they are listed.

Find out how much some of the places you look at end up selling for. Doing so gives you a better sense of what you can really afford as well as what some places seem to be really worth. If you're working with a real estate agent, he or she can easily obtain such sales price information.

Research the neighborhood and area

Even (and especially) if you fall in love with a house at first sight, go back to the neighborhood at different times of day and on different days of the week. Knock on a few doors and meet your potential neighbors. You may discover, for example, a flock of chickens in the backyard next door or that the street and basement flood every other winter.

What are the schools like? Go visit them. Don't rely on statistics about test scores. Talk to parents and teachers — what's really going on at the school? Even if you don't have kids, the quality of the local school has direct bearing on the value of your property. Is crime a problem? Call the local police department. Will future development be allowed? If so, what type? Talk to the planning department. What will your property taxes be? Is the property located in an area susceptible to major risks, such as floods, mud slides, fires, or earthquakes? Consider these issues even if they are not important to you, because they can affect the resale value of your property.

Once you buy a home, you're stuck with it. Make sure that you know what you're getting yourself into *before* you buy.

Working with Real Estate Agents

Odds are that when you buy (or sell) a home, you'll work with a real estate agent. Real estate agents, like many people who call themselves "financial consultants," earn their living on commission. As such, their incentives are different from yours and can sometimes be at odds with what's best for you.

Unlike commission-based financial consultants, who are really salespeople with a loftier sounding title, real estate agents do not hide the fact that they get a cut of the deal. Property buyers and sellers usually understand the real estate commission system. I credit the real estate profession for calling its practitioners "agents" and not coming up with some silly title such as "housing consultants."

A top-notch real estate agent can be of significant help in your purchase or sale of property. On the other hand, a mediocre, incompetent, or greedy agent can be a real liability. Real estate agents don't have as bad a reputation as used car salespeople, but it's not great, either. The following quotations capture some fundamental problems among real estate agents:

> ". . . Commissions are overpriced, quality of service bears no relation to commission levels, agents face serious conflicts of interest, most buyers are inadequately represented by agents, and agents dominate most state regulatory bodies. The residential real estate industry functions as a cartel that overcharges home buyers and sellers over $10 billion a year."
>
> — Consumer Federation of America (a nonprofit consumer advocacy group)
>
> "For the most part agents look out for themselves. The problem . . . is the commission. The only way you're going to get someone to really look out for your interests is to pay him an hourly fee. If he gets a commission, his overwhelming motivation is to see that the deal closes with a minimum of effort on his part."
>
> — John T. Reed, *Residential Property Acquisition Handbook*

Real estate agents' top conflicts of interest

Real estate agents, because they work on commission, face numerous conflicts of interest. Some agents may not even recognize the conflicts in what they're doing. This section discusses what to watch out for in recognizing agent's most common conflicts of interest.

Buy now, sell now

"You must buy now! Prices and interest rates are low, but they could rise any day."

"The market could worsen before it gets better — you better sell now."

Because agents work on commission, it costs them when they spend time with you and you don't buy or sell. They want you to complete a deal, and they want that deal as soon as possible — otherwise, they don't get paid.

Don't expect an agent to give you objective advice about what you should do given your overall financial situation. Examine your overall financial situation *before* you decide to begin working with an agent.

Spend more (and take an adjustable mortgage)

Because real estate agents get a percentage of the sales price of a property, they have a built-in incentive to encourage you to spend more. Adjustable-rate mortgages (discussed earlier in this chapter) allow you to spend more because the interest rate starts at a lower level than that of a fixed-rate mortgage. Thus real estate agents are far more likely to encourage you to take an adjustable. But adjustables are a lot riskier — you must understand these drawbacks before signing up for one.

Buy my company's listings

Agents also have a built-in incentive (higher commission) to sell the listings of their office mates. Agents often receive a higher commission selling listings belonging to other agents in their office. Beware.

Especially problematic are cases in which the same agent represents both the property seller and the property buyer in the transaction. Agents holding open houses for sales sometimes try to sell to an unrepresented buyer whom they meet at the open house. There's no way one person can represent the best interests of both sides.

I don't waste my time working with small fries like you

Because agents work on commission and get paid a percentage of the sales price of the property, many are not interested in working with you if you can't or simply don't want to spend a lot. Some agents may reluctantly take you on as a customer but then give you little attention and time. Before you hire an agent, check references to make sure that they've worked well with buyers like you.

Buy in my area

Real estate agents typically work a specific territory. As a result, they usually can't objectively tell you the pros and cons of the surrounding region. Most won't admit that you may better meet your needs by looking in another town (or some other part of town) where they don't normally work. Before you settle on an agent (or an area), spend time on your own learning the pros and cons of different territories. If you do want to look seriously in more than one area, find an agent in each who specializes in that area.

Get your loan from my favorite lender

If you don't get approved for a mortgage loan, your entire real estate deal will unravel. So it's a good thing that real estate agents want you to get approval for a loan. But it may cause them to refer you to a more expensive lender who has the virtue of high approval rates. Be sure to shop around — you can probably get a loan and get it more cheaply.

Buyer's brokers

Increasing numbers of agents are marketing themselves as *buyer's brokers.* Supposedly, they represent your interests as a property buyer exclusively.

Legally speaking, buyer's brokers may sign a contract saying that they represent your — and only your — interests. Before this enlightened era, all agents contractually worked for the property seller.

The title, buyer's broker, is one of those things that sounds better than it really is. Agents representing you as buyer's brokers still get paid only when you buy. And they still get paid on commission as a percentage of the purchase price. So they still have an incentive to sell you a piece of real estate, and the more expensive it is, the more commission they make.

Also, beware of agents who may refer you to mortgage lenders and mortgage brokers who pay agents referral fees. Such payments clearly bias a real estate agent's "advice."

Use this inspector — he's easy

Home inspectors are supposed to be objective third parties who are hired by prospective buyers to evaluate the condition of a property. The inspector's job is to uncover problems that your novice eye can't see. I've heard of tougher (nit-picky) inspectors referred to as "deal killers" by disgruntled real estate agents. Some inspectors get more referrals from agents because they aren't tough. But you'll be the one who's sorry if your newly acquired home has undiscovered problems due to an inadequate inspection.

I'm helping the seller cover up problems

Some agents, under pressure to sign a seller, agree to be criminal accomplices and not disclose known defects or problems with the property. In most cases, it seems, the seller may not explicitly ask an agent to help cover up a problem, but the agent may look the other way or not tell the whole truth. Never buy a home without having a home inspector look it over from top to bottom.

I'd rather credit back than reduce the purchase price

After an initial agreement on a sales price, negotiations in real estate deals can begin again if circumstances change or new information surfaces. For example, your inspections may uncover problems you weren't previously aware of. Agents involved in your deal are far more likely to suggest and favor a *credit back,* wherein the seller credits money to you at closing instead of reducing the original sales price.

Agents prefer the credit back because it does not reduce their commission, which is based on the sales price. But a price reduction may benefit both the buyer, whose property taxes usually are based on the sales price, and the seller, who pays a sales commission as a percentage of the sales price. Some agents are willing to go along with an overall price reduction if their commission is based on the previously agreed upon (higher) price.

They scratch my back and I scratch theirs

Some agents (as do many in other occupations) refer you to lenders, inspectors, and title insurance companies that have referred them business. A referral, of course, should first and foremost be based on the competence of the person to whom you're being referred. Too often in referrals, this criterion is minor or, in some cases, nonexistent. Some agents also solicit and receive referral fees (or bribes) from mortgage lenders, inspectors, and contractors to whom they refer business.

Qualities to look for in real estate agents

Whether you're hiring an agent to work with you as a buyer or seller, you want someone who is competent and with whom you can get along. Working with an agent costs you a lot of money — make sure that you get your money's worth.

Interview several agents. Check references. Ask agents for the names and phone numbers of at least three clients with whom they've worked in the past six months in the geographical area in which you are looking.

You should look for these traits in any agent you work with:

- ✔ **Full-time employment.** Some agents work in real estate as a second or even third job. Information in this field changes constantly — keeping track of it is hard enough on a full-time basis. To be a really good agent, an agent must work full-time to stay on top of the market.

- ✔ **Experience.** With a real estate deal, you've got a lot at stake financially and emotionally. You want to do the best that you can. Hiring someone with experience doesn't necessarily mean looking for an agent who's been kicking around for decades. Many of the best agents come into the field from other occupations, such as business or teaching. Some sales, marketing, negotiation, and communication skills can certainly be learned in other fields, but experience in this field does count.

- ✔ **Honesty and integrity.** You're trusting your agent with a lot. If the agent doesn't level with you about what a neighborhood or particular property is really like, you suffer the consequences.

✔ **Interpersonal skills.** An agent has to be able to get along not only with you but also with a whole host of other people involved in a typical real estate deal: other agents, property sellers, inspectors, mortgage lenders, and so on. An agent doesn't have to be Mr. or Ms. Congeniality, but he or she should be able to put your interests first without upsetting others.

✔ **Negotiation skills.** Putting a real estate deal together involves negotiation. Is your agent going to exhaust all avenues to get you the best deal possible? Be sure to ask the agent's references how well the agent negotiated for them.

✔ **High quality standards.** Sloppy work can lead to big legal or logistical problems down the road. If an agent neglects to recommend an inspection, for example, you may be stuck with undiscovered problems after the deal is done.

Buying and selling real estate require somewhat different skills. Few agents can do both equally well. No law or rule says that you must use the same agent when you sell a property as when you buy. Don't feel obliged to sell through the agent who worked with you as a buyer just because he sends you holiday cards every year asking how the garden is growing. Remember, he works on commission.

Agents sometimes market themselves as *top producers,* which means that they sell a relatively larger volume of real estate. This title doesn't count for much for you, the buyer. It may be a red flag for an agent that focuses on completing as many deals as possible. When you're buying a home (as opposed to selling), you need an agent who has the following additional traits:

✔ **Patience (not a hard-sell).** When you're buying a home, the last thing you need or want is an agent who tries to push you into making a deal. You need an agent who is patient and willing to allow you the necessary time to get educated and make the best decision for yourself.

✔ **Local market and community knowledge.** If you're looking to buy a home in an area in which you're not currently living, an informed agent can have a big impact on your decision.

✔ **Financing knowledge.** As a buyer, especially a first-time buyer or someone with credit problems, you should look for an agent who can refer you to lenders who can handle your type of situation, which can save you a lot of legwork.

Buying without a real estate agent

A competent and ethical real estate agent can add enough value to your purchase to warrant the commission you pay. However, the claim that it doesn't cost you anything as a buyer to buy through an agent is false. If you're not working with an agent, a seller may be willing to accept a lower offer because he or she needs to pay just one agent's commission.

You can purchase on your own if you're willing to do some additional legwork. You need to do the things that a good real estate agent does, such as searching for properties, scheduling appointments to see them, and negotiating and coordinating inspections. If you're experienced or savvy about real estate and have found a

property on your own, there's no reason you can't put a deal together yourself.

If you don't work with an agent, you should consider having an attorney review the contracts, unless you're a legal expert yourself. Besides, in most cases, real estate agents are not legal experts anyway. In some states, you need to hire an attorney in addition to the real estate agent.

One possible drawback to working without an agent is that you have to do the negotiations yourself. If you're a good negotiator, doing so can work to your advantage. But if you get too caught up emotionally in the situation, negotiating for yourself can backfire.

Putting Your Deal Together

Once you've done your homework on your personal finances, understood how to choose a mortgage, and researched neighborhoods and home prices, you'll hopefully soon close in on your goal. Eventually you'll find a home you'd like to buy. Before you make that first offer, though, you need to understand the importance of negotiations, inspections, and other elements of a real estate deal.

Negotiating 101

When you work with an agent, the agent usually carries the burden of the negotiation process. But you need to have a plan and strategy in mind — otherwise, you might overpay for your home. Here are some recommendations for getting a good deal:

- **Never fall in love with a property.** If you've got money to burn and you can't imagine life without the home you've just discovered, then pay what you will. Otherwise, always remind yourself that other good properties are out there. Having an actual back-up property in mind never hurts.

- **Learn about the property and owner before you make your offer.** How long has the property been on the market? What are its flaws? Why is the owner selling it? For example, if the seller is moving because she got a job in another town where she's about to close on a home purchase, she may be eager to get her money out and may be willing to reduce the price. The more you understand about the property that you want to buy and the seller's motivations, the better you will be able to draft an offer that meets both parties' needs.

✔ **Get comparable sales data to support your price.** Too often, home buyers and their agents pick a number out of the air when making an offer. But if the offer has no substance behind it, the seller will hardly be persuaded to lower his asking price. Pointing to recent and comparable home sales to justify your offer price strengthens your case.

✔ **Remember that price is only one of several negotiable items.** Sometimes sellers get fixated on selling their homes for a certain amount. Perhaps they want to get at least what they paid for it themselves several years ago. You may be able to get a seller to pay for certain repairs or improvements or to offer you an attractive loan without all the extra loan fees that a bank would charge. Likewise, the real estate agent's commission is negotiable, too.

Games real estate agents play to get a deal done

The thirst for a commission brings out the worst in agents. They'll tell you numerous fibs to motivate you to buy on the seller's terms. One common one is to say that other offers are coming in on the property you're interested in. Or they'll say that the seller already turned down an offer for x dollars because he is holding out for a higher offer.

Another tactic is the car dealer trick — blaming the office manager for not allowing them to reduce their commission. The bottom line is that if it's not in writing, be skeptical. Be sure to spend the time needed to find a good agent and to understand agent's potential conflicts of interest (see the section on agents earlier in the chapter).

Negotiating a real estate agent's commission as a buyer

Conventional wisdom says that the seller pays the agent's commission, so it doesn't concern or cost you as a buyer. Wrong! If the agents involved in your real estate deal are amenable to reducing their commissions, the seller may be willing to accept less money for the property.

If the buyer and the property seller aren't that far apart on price, suggest that the agents lower their commissions. To get a deal done, you may be surprised at what agents are willing to do. Read the section later in this chapter about negotiating real estate agents' commissions.

Inspect, inspect, inspect

When you buy a home, you're probably making one of the biggest (if not *the* biggest) financial purchases and commitments of your life. Unless you've built homes and done contracting work yourself, you probably have no idea what you're getting yourself into when it comes to furnaces and termites.

Spend the money and time to hire inspectors and other experts to evaluate the major systems and potential problem areas of the home. Areas that you want to check include

- Overall condition of the property
- Electrical, heating, and plumbing systems
- Foundation
- Roof
- Pest control and dry rot
- Seismic/slide risk

Inspection fees often pay for themselves. If you uncover problems that you weren't aware of, the inspection reports give you the information you need to go back and ask the property seller to fix the problems or reduce the purchase price of the property to compensate you for correcting the deficiencies yourself.

As with other professionals whose services you retain, interview a few inspection companies. Ask which systems they inspect and how detailed a report they will prepare for you (ask for a sample copy). Ask them for names and phone numbers of three people who used their service within the past six months.

Never accept a seller's inspection report as your only source of information. When a seller hires an inspector, they may hire someone who won't be as diligent and critical of the property. What if the inspector is buddies with the seller or agent selling the property? By all means, review the seller's inspection reports if available, but get your own as well.

And here's one more inspection for you to do. The day before you close on the purchase of your home, do a brief walk-through of the property to make sure that everything is still in the condition it was before and that all the fixtures, appliances, curtains, and other items that were to be left as per the contract are still there. Sometimes, sellers (and their movers) "forget" what's to be left or try to test your powers of observation.

Title insurance and escrow fees

Mortgage lenders require *title insurance* to protect against someone else claiming legal title to your property. This can happen, for example, when a husband and wife split up and the one who remains in the home decides to sell and take off with the money. If both spouses were listed as owners on the title, the spouse who sold the property (possibly by forging the other's signature) had no legal right to do so.

If you bought the home that this divided couple was selling, both you and the lender could get stuck holding the bag. But title insurance will be the salvation for you and your lender. Title insurance protects you against the very real possibility in a case like this that the other spouse (whose name was forged to sell the home) could come back and reclaim rights to the home even after it had been sold.

If you're in the enviable position of paying cash for a property, you should still buy title insurance even though a mortgage lender won't prod you to do so. You need to protect your investment.

Escrow charges pay for neutral third-party services to ensure that the instructions of the purchase contract or refinance are fulfilled and that everyone gets paid.

Many people don't seem to know that title insurance and escrow fees vary from company to company. As a result, they don't bother to shop around and simply use the company that their real estate agent or mortgage lender suggests.

When you call around for title insurance and escrow fee quotes, make sure that you understand all the fees. Many companies tack on all sorts of charges for things such as courier fees and express mail. If you find a company with lower prices and want to use it, it doesn't hurt to ask for an itemization in writing so that you don't have any surprises.

Real estate agents and mortgage lenders can be a good starting point for referrals as they usually have a broader perspective on cost and service quality of different companies. Call other companies as well — agents and lenders may be biased toward certain companies simply because they are in the habit of using them or have referred clients to them before.

After You Buy

After you buy a home, over the months and years ahead, you'll make a number of important decisions regarding your castle (or shoe box). This section discusses key issues and what you need to know to make the best decision for each.

Refinancing your mortgage

Three reasons motivate people to *refinance* — obtaining a new mortgage to replace your old one. One is obvious — to save money because interest rates have dropped. Refinancing also can be a way of raising capital for some other purpose. A final reason is to get out of one type of loan and into another. The following discussion should help you to decide upon the best option in each case.

Spending money to save money

If your current loan has a higher rate of interest than comparable new loans now available, you may save money by refinancing. Because refinancing almost always costs money, whether you can save enough to justify the cost is a bit of a gamble. Your odds of saving money by refinancing go up a lot when the new loan is available at at least one percent less than your current loan and you're planning to keep the property for at least five years. If you can recover the costs of the refinance within a few years, go for it. If it takes longer, refinancing may still make sense if you anticipate keeping the property and mortgage that long.

Be wary of mortgage lenders or brokers who brag about how soon your refinance will pay for itself; they usually oversimplify their calculations. For example, if the refinance costs you $2,000 to complete (accounting for appraisals, loan fees and points, title insurance, and so on) and reduces your monthly payment by $100, the lender or broker typically says that it takes 20 months for you to save back the refinance costs. This isn't accurate, however, because you lose some tax write-offs if your mortgage interest rate and payment are reduced. You can't simply look at the reduced amount of your monthly payment (mortgage lenders like to look at it, however, because it makes refinancing more attractive). And your new mortgage will be reset to a different term than the number of years remaining on your old one.

If you want a better estimate of your likely cost savings but don't want to spend hours crunching numbers, take your tax rate — for example, 28 percent — and reduce your monthly payment savings on the refinance by this amount (see Chapter 7). Continuing with the example in the preceding paragraph, if your monthly payment drops by $100, you're *really* only saving around $72 a month after factoring in the lost tax benefits. So it takes 28 months ($2,000 divided by $72) — not 20 — to recoup the refinance costs.

Note that not all refinances cost tons of money. So-called *no-cost* refinances or *no-point* loans minimize your out-of-pocket expenses but, as discussed earlier in this chapter, may not be your best long-term options. Such loans usually come with higher interest rates.

Using money for another purpose

Refinancing to pull out cash from your home for some other purpose can make good financial sense because, under most circumstances, mortgage interest is tax-deductible.

A common reason for borrowing against a home is to pay off other higher-interest consumer debt — such as on credit cards or on an auto loan. The interest on consumer debt is not tax-deductible. Plus you can usually borrow at a much lower interest rate than what consumer loans charge you.

If you're starting a business, consider borrowing against your home to finance the launch of your business. You can usually do so at a lower cost than on a business loan.

The most critical question is whether a lender is willing to lend you more money against the equity in your home (which is the difference between the market value of your house and the loan balance). You can "guesstimate" whether you can afford larger payments by using Table 15-1 to find the maximum loan for which you may qualify.

Changing loans

You might want to refinance even though you're not forced to raise cash or can save money. Perhaps you're not comfortable with your current loan — holders of adjustable-rate mortgages often face this problem. You may find out that a fluctuating mortgage payment makes you a nervous wreck in addition to wreaking havoc on your budget. The certainty of a fixed-rate mortgage may be your salvation.

Paying money to go from an adjustable into a fixed is a lot like buying insurance. The cost of the refinance is "insuring" you a level mortgage payment. Consider this option only if you want peace of mind and you plan to stay with the property for a number of years.

Sometimes jumping from one adjustable to another makes sense. Suppose you can lower the maximum lifetime interest rate cap and the refinance won't cost too much. Your new loan should have a lower initial interest rate than the one you're paying on your current loan. Even if you won't save megabucks, the peace of mind of a lower ceiling can make it worth your while.

Mortgage life insurance

Shortly after you buy a home or close on a mortgage, you'll start getting mail from all kinds of organizations who keep track of publicly available information about mortgages. Most of these organizations want to sell you something, and they don't tend to beat around the bush.

"What will your dependents do if you meet with an untimely demise and they are left with a gargantuan mortgage?" they ask.

Fair enough. In fact, this is a good financial-planning question. If your family is dependent upon your income, can they survive financially if you and your income disappear from life as we know it?

Don't waste your money on mortgage life insurance. You may need life insurance to provide for your family and help meet large obligations such as mortgage payments or educational expenses for children. But mortgage life insurance is grossly overpriced. (Read the life insurance section in Chapter 17 for advice about term life insurance.) You should consider mortgage life insurance only if you have a health problem and the mortgage life insurer does not require a physical examination. Be sure to compare it with term life options.

Is getting a reverse mortgage a good idea?

Increasing numbers of homeowners are finding, particularly in their later years of retirement, that they lack cash. Their largest asset is usually the home in which they live. Unlike other investments, such as bank accounts, bonds, or stocks, a home does not provide any income to the owner unless he or she decides to rent out a room or two.

A *reverse mortgage* allows a homeowner who's low on cash to tap into home equity. For an elderly homeowner, this can be a difficult thing to do psychologically. Most people work hard to feed a mortgage month after month, year after year, until finally it is all paid off. What a feat and what a relief after all those years!

Taking out a reverse mortgage reverses this process. Each month, a bank or other financial institution sends you a check that you can spend on food, clothing, travel, or whatever suits your fancy.

The money you receive each month is really a loan from the bank against the value of your home, which makes the monthly check free from taxation. Other advantages of a reverse mortgage are that it allows you to stay in your home and use its equity to supplement your monthly income.

The main drawback is that a reverse mortgage can deplete the estate that you may want to pass onto your heirs or use for some other purpose. Also, some loans require repayment within a certain number of years. The fees and the effective interest rate you are charged to borrow the money can also be quite high.

Because some loans require the lender to make monthly payments to you as long as you live in the home, lenders assume that you will live a very long time so that they don't lose money in making these loans. If you end up keeping the loan for only a few years because you move, for example, the cost of the loan is extremely high.

An excellent book that explores all the mechanics of reverse mortgages and how to shop for them is *Your New Retirement Nest Egg* by Ken Scholen. Call 800-247-6533 or write to him at 7373 147th St., Apple Valley, MN 55124. The American Association of Retired Persons (AARP) also publishes a free information booklet entitled *Home Made Money,* which can be requested by writing AARP at 1909 K St. NW, Washington, D.C. 20049 or by calling 202-434-2277.

You may be able to create a reverse mortgage within your own family network. This technique can work if you have family members who are financially able to provide you with monthly income in exchange for ownership of the home when you pass away.

There are also other alternatives to tapping home equity. One is to simply sell your home and buy a less expensive property or rent a place. Current tax laws allow homeowners 55 and older to take a once-in-a-lifetime $125,000 capital gains exclusion when they sell a home and buy a less expensive one.

Selling your house

The day will someday come when you will want to sell your house. If you're going to sell, make sure that you can afford to buy the next home you desire. Be especially careful if you're a trade-up buyer — that is you're going to buy an even more expensive home. All of the affordability issues discussed at the beginning of this chapter apply. Also consider the following issues.

Selling through an agent

Selling and buying a home demand agents with different strengths. When you're selling a property, you want an agent who can get the job done efficiently and for as high a price as possible. As a seller, you should seek agents who have marketing and sales expertise and are willing to put in the time and money necessary to get your home sold. Don't necessarily be impressed by an agent who works for a large company. What matters more is what the agent is going to do to market your property.

When you list your home for sale, the contract that you sign with the listing agent includes specification of the commission to be paid if the agent is successful in selling your home. In most areas of the country, agents usually ask for a 6 percent commission. In an area that has lower-cost housing, they may ask for 7 percent.

Regardless of the commission an agent says is "typical," "standard," or "what my manager requires," *always* remember that commissions are negotiable.

Because the commission is a percentage, you have a much greater ability to get a lower commission on a higher-priced home. If an agent makes 6 percent selling both a $200,000 home and a $100,000 home, the agent makes twice as much on the $200,000 home. Yet selling the higher-priced home does not take twice as much work. (Selling a $400,000 home certainly doesn't take four times the effort of a $100,000 home sale.)

If you live in an area with higher-priced homes (above $200,000), you have no reason to pay more than a 5 percent commission. For expensive properties ($400,000 and up), a 4 percent commission is reasonable. You may find, however, that your ability to negotiate a lower commission is greatest when an offer is on the table.

In terms of the length of the listing sales agreement you make with an agent, three months is reasonable. If you give an agent too long a listing (6 to 12 months), the agent may simply toss your listing into the multiple listing book and not expend much effort to get your property sold. Practically speaking, you can fire your agent whenever you want, regardless of the length of the listing agreement. But a shorter listing may be more motivating for your agent.

Selling without a real estate agent

The temptation to sell without an agent is usually to save the commission that an agent deducts from your home's sale price. If you have the time, energy, and marketing experience, you can sell your home and possibly save some money.

The major problem with attempting to sell your home on your own is that you can't list it in the *multiple listing service* (MLS), which only real estate agents can access. Some people have said, and I concur, that the MLS functions as an effective near monopoly over the selling of homes. And if you're not listed in the MLS, many potential buyers will never know that your home is for sale. Agents working with buyers don't generally look for or show their clients homes that are for sale by owner.

Besides saving you time, a good agent can help ensure that you're not sued for failing to disclose known defects of your property. If you decide to sell your home yourself, make sure that you have access to a legal advisor who can review the contracts.

Discount brokers charge less than traditional real estate agents to help you sell your home. They may help you develop advertisements, prepare contracts, and negotiate with potential buyers. You may be responsible for showing the home to prospective buyers.

Discounters usually charge a fixed fee or a percentage of the sales price. The cost should be much less than a traditional agent would charge. Try contacting Help-U-Sell (800-366-1177), a discounter that has 350 offices nationwide. Alternatively, try negotiating a better commission from a regular agent.

Should you keep your home until prices go up?

Many homeowners are tempted to hold onto their properties when they need to move if the property is worth less than when they bought it or if the real estate market is soft. It's probably not worth the hassle of renting out your property or the financial gamble of holding onto it. If you need to move, you're better off in most cases selling your home.

You may reason that in a few years, the real estate storm clouds will clear and you can sell your property at a much higher price. Here are three risks associated with this way of thinking:

- ✔ First, you can't know what's going to happen to property prices in the next few years. They might rebound, but they could stay the same or drop even further. A property generally needs to appreciate at least a few percent per year just to make up for all the costs of holding and maintaining it.

- ✔ If you haven't been a landlord, don't underestimate the hassle and headaches associated with this job.

- ✔ Once you convert your home into a rental property, you need to pay capital gains tax on your profit when you sell it if it does appreciate (talk to your friendly neighborhood tax advisor for more details). This tax wipes out much of the advantage of having held onto the property until prices recovered. (If you want to be a long-term rental property owner, you can do a *tax-free exchange* into another rental property once you sell.)

The only good reason I can think of to hold onto a home that has plunged in value is that you would realize little cash from selling *and* lack other money to come up with the down payment to purchase your next property.

Should you keep your home as investment property if you move?

It's worth considering converting your home into rental property if you need to or want to move. Don't consider doing so unless it really is a long-term proposition (ten or more years). As discussed in the preceding section, selling rental property has tax consequences.

One advantage to keeping your current home as an investment property after you move is that you already own it. Locating and buying investment property takes time and money. You also know what you have with your current home. If you go out and purchase a property to rent, you're starting from scratch.

If your property is in good condition, consider what damage renters might do — few renters will take care of your home the way that you will. Also consider if you're cut out to be a landlord.

For more information, read the section in Chapter 10 that discusses real estate as an investment.

Part IV
Protecting What You've Got

The 5th Wave   **By Rich Tennant**

"You may want to talk to Phil—he's one of our more aggressive financial planners."

In this part . . .

You discover that just because insurance is boring doesn't mean you can ignore it. Therefore, I show you how to obtain the right kind of insurance to shield you from the brunt of unexpected major expenses and protect your future earnings and your assets. I reveal which types of insurance you do and do not need, what you should avoid, what to include and what not to include in your policies, and how much of which things you should insure. Plus, you finally face other creepy but important stuff such as wills, probate, and inheritance taxes.

Chapter 16

Insurance Basics

· ·

In This Chapter

▶ How the insurance industry works

▶ Eric's three laws of buying insurance

▶ How to save thousands of dollars and get the insurance coverage you need

▶ What to do if you are denied coverage

▶ How to get 'em to cough up your claim money

· ·

*U*nless you work in the industry (by choice), insurance is, for most people, a dreadfully boring topic. Most people associate insurance with disease, death, and disaster and would rather do just about anything other than review or spend money on insurance. But because you don't want to deal with money hassles when you are coping with catastrophes — illness, disability, death, fires, floods, earthquakes — you must take care of insurance well before you need it.

Insurance is probably the least understood and least monitored area of personal finance. Studies by the nonprofit National Insurance Consumer Organization show that more than nine in ten Americans purchase and carry the wrong types and amounts of insurance coverage. My own experience as a financial counselor confirms this statistic. Most people are overwhelmed by all the jargon in sales and policy statements. As a result, people get insurance from the wrong companies, pay more than is necessary for their policies, or get insured through companies with poor reputations for servicing customers with claims on their policies.

Insurance: A Big, Inefficient Business

Consider these tantalizing tidbits about the insurance industry: More than 35,000 insurance companies employ more than 1.5 million people, half of whom are the agents and brokers who sell the stuff. Nearly 1 in every 12 dollars spent in our economy goes to pay for insurance.

In *The Invisible Bankers,* an insightful book on the insurance industry, author Andrew Tobias makes the observation that the insurance industry, like the IRS and postal service, interacts with all Americans; however, to accomplish their goals, the insurance companies need 20 times more employees than the IRS and 3 times more employees than the U. S. Postal Service!

Unlike mutual funds or mortgages, which are often available directly from the companies that issue them, virtually all insurance is sold through insurance agents who work on commission. Because of the commission structure, shopping around for the best deal and figuring out — and buying — policies and features that are in your best interests are difficult tasks.

One of the primary reasons that the insurance industry is so inefficient is that it enjoys a unique (and unfair) exemption from federal antitrust regulations. The McCarran-Ferguson Act of 1945, a little-known piece of legislation, allows insurance companies to dictate a fixed price for a specific policy and effectively eliminate competition among their commission-based agents. That makes shopping for a specific insurance policy very different from shopping for a Sony 19-inch color television set or a Ford Taurus GL. Although some auto dealers or stereo stores will cut you a better deal than others, an insurance policy "model" will have the same price from every agent who sells it. (Please note that although price competition does not exist among different agents of a specific policy, it does exist among different insurance companies.)

Equally problematic is the fact that insurers exert tremendous control and influence, through lobbying and representation on state insurance regulatory boards, over the entities that are supposed to oversee them — the state governments.

Why all these details about the insurance industry? Because understanding the industry will help you comprehend the weird stuff on policies, the high costs of many policies, and the inefficiency of most insurers. And, hopefully, you will also become informed enough to make your voice heard when you speak to insurers and government regulators about ways to improve insurance for consumers.

Eric's Three Laws of Buying Insurance

I know your patience and interest in learning about insurance may be limited, so I've boiled it down to three fairly simple but powerful concepts that can easily save you thousands of dollars over the rest of your insurance-buying years. And while you're saving money, you can still get the coverage you need to avoid a financial catastrophe.

Law 1: Insure for the big stuff, don't sweat the small stuff

Imagine, for a moment, that you're offered a chance to buy insurance that reimburses you for the cost of a magazine subscription in the event the magazine folds and you don't get all the issues you paid for. Because a magazine subscription doesn't cost much, I don't think you would buy that insurance.

What if you could buy insurance that pays for the cost of a restaurant meal if you get food poisoning? Even if you're splurging at a fancy restaurant, you don't have a lot of money at stake, so you'd probably decline that coverage as well.

The point of insurance is to protect against losses that would be financially catastrophic to you, not to smooth out the bumps of everyday life. The examples above are silly, but some people buy equally silly policies without knowing it, as I illustrate in this section.

Avoid small potato policies

A good insurance policy can seem expensive. A policy that doesn't cost much, on the other hand, can fool you into thinking that you're getting something for next to nothing. Policies that cost little also cover little — they are priced low because they aren't covering large potential losses.

As you read through this list, you may very well find examples of policies that you yourself have bought and that you feel more than paid for themselves. I can hear you saying, "But I collected on that policy you're telling me not to buy!" Sure, getting the satisfaction (the revenge?) of being "reimbursed" for the hassle of something being lost or going wrong is always nice. But consider all such policies that you have bought or could buy over the course of your life. You're not going to come out ahead in the aggregate — if you did, insurance companies would lose money! These policies aren't worth the cost relative to the small potential benefit. On the average, insurance companies pay out just 60 cents in benefits on every dollar collected. Many of the following policies pay you back even less — around 20 cents in benefits (claims) for every dollar you spend in insurance premiums.

The following are examples of common, "small potato" insurance policies that are generally a waste of your hard-earned dollars.

Extended warranty and repair plans

Isn't it ironic that right after the salesperson persuades you to buy a television, computer, or car — in part by saying how reliable the goods are — he or she tries try to convince you to spend more money to insure against the failure of the item? If the stuff is so good, why do you need insurance?

Product manufacturers' warranties typically cover any problems that occur in the first three months to a year. And should you need to pay for a repair out of your own pocket, it won't be a financial catastrophe. Extended warranty and repair plans are expensive and unnecessary insurance policies.

Home warranty plans

If your real estate agent or the seller of the home wants to pay the cost of a home warranty plan for you, turning down the offer would be ungracious (as grandma would say, you shouldn't look a gift horse in the mouth). But don't buy this type of plan for yourself. In addition to requiring some sort of fee (around $30 to $50) if you need a contractor to come out and look at a problem, home warranty plans limit how much they'll pay for major problems.

Your money is much better spent on hiring a competent inspector to uncover problems and fix them *before* you buy the home. Everyone buying a house should expect to spend money on repairs and maintenance — that's just being realistic! To buy insurance for the smaller repairs and maintenance is a waste of money.

Dental insurance

If your employer pays for dental insurance, take advantage of it. But you shouldn't pay for this coverage on your own. Dental insurance generally covers a couple of teeth cleanings each year and limits payments for more expensive work.

Credit life and credit disability policies

Many direct mail firms try to sell policies that pay a small benefit in case you die with an outstanding loan (a credit life policy) or that pay a small monthly income in the event of a disability (a credit disability policy). These policies are usually sold by credit card companies such as VISA, MasterCard, Discover, and American Express. Some companies even sell you insurance to pay off your credit card bill in the event of your death or disability.

The cost of this insurance seems low, but that's because the potential benefits are small. In fact, given how little insurance you're buying, these policies are extraordinarily expensive. If you need life or disability insurance, purchase it. But get enough coverage and buy it in a separate, cost-effective policy (see Chapter 17 for more details).

One exception to the above rule is if you are in poor health and you can buy these insurance policies without a medical evaluation. In that case, these policies may be the only ones you have access to. This is another reason that these policies are expensive. If you're in good health, you are paying for the people with poor health who can enroll without a medical examination and who undoubtedly make more claims.

Daily hospitalization insurance

Hospitalization insurance policies that pay a certain amount per day, usually $75 to $100, are often sold to older people. These policies prey on people's fears of running up whopping hospital bills. Health care is expensive — there's no doubt about that.

But what you really need is a comprehensive (major medical) health insurance policy. One day in the hospital can lead to several thousand dollars in charges, so that $100 per day policy might pay for less than an hour of your 24-hour day! These policies don't offer coverage for the big ticket expenses. If you don't have a comprehensive health insurance policy, get one (see Chapter 17)!

Insuring packages in the mail

You buy a $40 gift for a friend, and when you go to the post office to ship it, the friendly postal clerk asks if you want to insure it. For a couple of bucks, you think, why not? The U.S. Postal Service may have a bad reputation for many reasons, but it rarely loses or damages things. Go spend your money on another gift instead!

Contact lens insurance

The things that people in this country come up with to waste money on just astound me. Contact lens insurance really does exist! The money goes to replace your contacts if you lose or tear them. Lenses are cheap. Don't waste your money on this kind of insurance.

Little stuff riders

Many policies that are worth buying, such as auto and disability insurance, have all sorts of add-on riders. These are extra bells and whistles that insurance agents and companies like to sell because of the high profit margin (for *them*). On auto insurance policies, for example, you can buy a rider for a few bucks per year that pays you $25 each time your car needs to be towed. Having your vehicle towed isn't going to bankrupt you, so it isn't worth insuring against. (Besides, what are you doing that your car is constantly being towed?)

Likewise, small insurance policies that are sold as add-ons to bigger insurance policies are usually not necessary and are overpriced. For example, you can buy some disability insurance policies with a small amount of life insurance added on. If you need life insurance, purchasing a sufficient amount in a separate policy is less costly.

Take the highest deductible you can afford

Most insurance policies have *deductibles* — the maximum amount you must pay in the event of a loss before your insurance coverage kicks in. On many policies, such as auto and homeowner's/renter's coverage, most folks opt for a $100 to $250 deductible.

Here are two benefits to taking a higher deductible:

✔ **You save premium dollars.** Year in and year out, you can enjoy the lower cost of an insurance policy with a high deductible. You may be able to shave 15 to 20 percent off the cost of your policy. Suppose, for example, that you can reduce the cost of your policy by $150 per year by raising your deductible from $250 to $1,000. That $750 worth of coverage is costing you $150 per year. Thus, you would need to have a claim of $1,000 or more every five years — highly unlikely — to come out ahead. If you are that accident-prone — guess what? — the insurance company will crank up your premiums.

✔ **You don't have the hassles of filing small claims.** If you have a $300 loss on a policy with a $100 deductible, you need to file a claim to get your $200 (the amount you're covered for after your deductible). Filing an insurance claim can take hours of time and can be an aggravating experience. In some cases, you may even have your claim denied after jumping through all the necessary hoops.

If you have low deductibles, you may file more claims (although this doesn't necessarily mean that you'll get more money). If you file more claims, you may be rewarded with jacked-up premiums — in addition to the headache of preparing those blasted forms! If you file too many claims, you may even have your coverage canceled!

Buy insurance to cover financial catastrophes

You should insure against what could be a huge financial loss for you. The price of insurance isn't cheap, but it is relatively small in comparison to the potential total loss. Many people make the mistake of not insuring against what could be a financial catastrophe.

The beauty of insurance is that it spreads risks over millions of other people. If your home burned to the ground, paying the rebuilding cost out of your own pocket probably would be a financial catastrophe. If you have insurance, the premiums paid in by you and all the other homeowners collectively can easily pay the bills.

Think for a moment about what your most valuable assets are. (No, it's not your dry wit or your charming personality.) Also consider potential large expenses.

✔ If you're still in your working years, your most valuable asset is probably your future earnings. If you were disabled and unable to work, what would you live on? That's why long-term disability insurance exists. If you have a family that is financially dependent on your earnings, how would your family manage financially if you died? Life insurance can fill the financial void left by your death.

✔ If you're a business owner, what would happen if you were sued for $1,000,000 for negligence in some work that you messed up? Liability insurance can bail you out.

✔ In this age of soaring medical costs, you can easily rack up a $100,000 hospital bill in short order. That's why you need major medical health insurance coverage. And, yet, a surprising number of people don't carry any health insurance, particularly those who work in small businesses. (See Chapter 17 for more on health insurance.)

Psychologically, buying insurance coverage for many of the little things that are more likely to occur is tempting. You don't want to feel like you're wasting your insurance dollars. You want to get some of your money back, darn it! You are more likely to get into a fender bender with your car or have a package lost in the mail than you are to lose your home to fire or suffer a long-term disability. But if the fender bender costs $500 (which you end up paying out of your pocket because you took my advice to take a high deductible), it isn't going to be a financial disaster. You probably won't be happy about having to pay for it, but you can and will.

If, on the other hand, you lose your ability to earn an income because of a disability or are sued for $1,000,000 but are not insured against such catastrophes, you will not only be extremely unhappy but you also face financial ruin. "Yes, but what are the odds," I hear people rationalize, "that I'll suffer a long-term disability or that I'll be sued for $1,000,000?" I agree that the odds are quite low. But the odds aren't as low as zero. The risk is there. The problem is that you just don't know what bad luck will befall you or when.

And don't make the mistake of thinking that you can figure the odds any better than the insurance companies can. The probability of your making a claim, large or small, is predicted with a great deal of accuracy by the insurance companies. That's why they employ armies of number-crunching actuaries to calculate the odds of bad things happening and the frequency of current policyholders making particular types of claims. The companies price their policies accordingly.

So buying or not buying insurance based on your perception of the likelihood of needing the coverage is just plain dumb. Insurance companies aren't stupid; in fact, they are ruthlessly smart! When insurance companies price policies, they look at a number of factors to determine the risk or likelihood of your filing a claim. Take the example of auto insurance. If you're a single male, age 20, living the fast life in a high-crime city, driving a macho, turbo-sports car, and having two speeding tickets in the past year, you're gonna pay a whole lot more than a couple in their 40s, living in a low-crime area, driving a four-door sedan, and having a clean driving record.

INVESTIGATE

Our misperceptions of risks

How high do you think are your risks of expiring prematurely if you're exposed to toxic wastes or pesticides or if you live in a dangerous area that has a high murder rate? Well, actually these risks are quite small when compared to the risks you're subjecting yourself to when you get behind the wheel of a car or light up yet another cigarette.

John Stossel, the crack ABC reporter, was kind enough to share with me the results of a study done for him by physicist Bernard Cohen who compared different risks. Cohen's study showed that our riskiest behaviors are smoking and driving. Smoking whacks an average of seven years off a person's life, whereas driving a car results in a bit more than half a year of life lost on average. Toxic waste shaves an average of one week off an American's life span.

Knowing what's risky and what isn't is part of what you need to know. Unfortunately, you can't buy a formal insurance policy to protect yourself against all of life's great dangers and risks. But that does not mean that you must face these dangers as a helpless victim. Simple changes in behavior can help you fight the odds.

Personal health habits are a good example. If you're overweight, eat fatty, high cholesterol foods, drink excessively, and don't exercise, you're asking for trouble, especially during post-middle age. Engage in these habits and you're dramatically increasing your risk of heart disease and cancer.

So does this mean that we should all eat bean sprouts, stay out of cars, never light up and cease being concerned about toxic waste? No. But understanding the consequences of your behaviors before you engage in them and prioritizing risks worth worrying about is important.

If you're reading this chapter, you obviously want to find out about insurance. My point is this: You can buy all the types of real insurance that I recommend in this book and still not be well-protected for the simple reason that you're overlooking uninsurable risks. But just because you can't buy formal insurance to protect against some risks doesn't mean that you can't drastically reduce your exposure to such risks through modifying your behavior.

Law II: Buy broad coverage

Another major mistake people make when buying insurance is purchasing coverage that is too narrow. The policies often seem like cheap ways to put their greatest fears to rest. For example, instead of buying life insurance, some folks buy flight insurance at an airport self-service kiosk. They seem to worry more about their mortality when getting on an airplane than they do when getting into a car. If they die on the flight, their beneficiaries collect. But if they die the next day in an auto accident or if they get some dreaded disease — which is statistically far more likely than going down in a jumbo jet — the beneficiaries don't collect anything from flight insurance.

The medical equivalent of flight insurance is cancer insurance. Older people, fearful of having their life savings depleted by a long battle with this deadly disease, are easy prey for unscrupulous insurance salespeople pitching this narrow insurance. If you get cancer, cancer insurance pays the bills. But what if you get heart disease, diabetes, AIDS, or some other disease? The cancer insurance doesn't pay these costs.

Our fears in life are natural and inescapable; they are also often arbitrary and irrational. Although we may not have control over the emotions that our fears invoke, we must often ignore those emotions in order to make rational insurance decisions. In other words, getting shaky in the knees and sweaty in the palms when boarding an airplane is okay, but letting your fear of flying cause you to make poor insurance decisions is not okay, especially when those decisions affect the lives of your loved ones.

You can't possibly predict what's going to happen to you. You want to get the broadest possible coverage that you can. Buy life insurance, not flight insurance. Buy major medical coverage, not cancer insurance.

Law III: Shop around and buy direct

The cost of insurance varies tremendously from insurer to insurer. Whether you're looking at auto, home, life, disability, or other types of coverage, some companies may be charging double or triple the rates that other companies are charging for the same coverage. The companies charging the higher rates may not be better about paying claims, however. You may even end up with the worst of both possible worlds — high prices and lousy service.

Most insurance is sold through agents and brokers who earn commissions based on what they sell. This, of course, tends to bias what they recommend that you buy. I see this bias in action all the time. A study done by Cummins and Weisbart and cited in Andrew Tobias's book *Invisible Bankers* confirms this bias: ". . . 48% of the time, an agent's decision on where to place a customer's business was based on which insurer paid the highest commission."

Not surprisingly, policies that pay agents the biggest commissions also tend to be more costly. In fact, insurance companies compete for the attention of agents by offering bigger commissions than other insurers. If you browse through magazines and other publications targeted to insurance agents (I'm sure you're anxious to do this), you see ads in which the very largest text is the commission percentage offered to agents who sell the advertiser's products.

Besides the attraction of policies that pay higher commissions, agents also get hooked, financially speaking, to companies whose policies they sell frequently. Once an agent has sold a certain amount of a company's insurance policies, he is rewarded with higher commission percentages on any future sales. Just as airlines bribe frequent fliers with mileage bonuses, insurers bribe agents with fatter commissions for their loyalty.

Shopping around is a challenge not only because most insurance is sold by agents working on commission but also because insurers set their rates in mysterious ways. Every company has a different way of analyzing how much of a risk you are; one company may offer low rates to me but not to you and vice versa.

Despite the obstacles, several strategies exist for obtaining low-cost, high-quality policies. Chapters 17 and 18 recommend how and where to get the best deals on specific types of policies. The following tips offer smart ways to shop for insurance.

Insurance without sales commissions

Your best bet for getting a good insurance value is to buy policies from the increasing number of companies that are selling their policies directly to the public and are cutting the insurance agent and the agent's accompanying commission out of the picture. Just as you can purchase no-load mutual funds directly from an investment company without paying any sales commission (refer to Chapter 11), you also can buy no-load insurance. Be sure to read Chapters 17 and 18 for more specifics on how to buy insurance directly from insurance companies.

Annuities, investment/insurance products traditionally sold through insurance agents, are also now available directly to the customer, without sales commission, through such no-load mutual fund companies as Vanguard and T. Rowe Price (refer to Chapter 12).

Legislation is currently before Congress aimed at repealing the insurance industry's federal antitrust exemption and allowing agents in all 50 states to compete on the pricing of the policies that they sell and to allow agents to rebate commissions to consumers. Don't hold your breath on this getting through any time soon — insurance companies and agents are a powerful lobbying force. Most people don't even know that the legislation is pending or how it can benefit them, but you can bet the insurance companies and agents are maneuvering stealthily to defeat it.

If you would like to see the insurance industry opened up to the same competitive forces as other industries (which would save us all big bucks), write a letter to your state insurance commissioner or congressperson today.

The straight scoop on commissions and how insurance is sold

The commission paid to an insurance agent is never disclosed through any of the documents or materials that you receive in the process of buying insurance. This information ought to be disclosed by insurers and agents, just as sales charges on mutual funds are disclosed through a prospectus.

The only way you can know what the commission is on a policy and how it compares with other policies is to ask the agent. Nothing is wrong or impolite about asking. It's your money, after all, that pays the commission. You need to know whether a particular policy is being pitched harder because of its higher commission.

Commissions are typically paid as a percentage of the first year's premium on the insurance policy. (Many policies pay smaller commissions on subsequent years' premiums.) On life and disability insurance policies, for example, a 50 percent commission on the first year's premium is not unusual. On life insurance policies that have a cash value, commissions of 80 to 100 percent of your first year's premium are possible. Commissions on health insurance are lower, but generally not as low as commissions on auto and homeowner's insurance.

Employer and other group plans

When you buy insurance as part of a larger group, you generally get a lower price because of the purchasing power or clout of the group. Most health and disability policies that you can access through your employer are less costly than equivalent policies that you can buy on your own.

Likewise, many occupations have professional associations through which you may be able to obtain lower cost policies. Not all associations offer better deals on insurance, so make sure to compare what they offer with other options available to you.

Insurance agents who want to sell you an individual policy can come up with 101 reasons why buying from them is preferable to buying through your employer or some other group. In most cases, agents' arguments for buying an individual policy from them include a lot of self-serving marketing hype. In some cases, agents tell outright lies (which are hard to detect if you're not insurance-savvy).

One valid issue agents will raise is that, if you leave your job, you'll lose your group coverage. Sometimes that may be true. If you know that you'll be leaving your job to become self-employed, securing an individual disability policy before you leave your job makes sense. However, your employer's health insurer may allow you to convert your health insurance policy into an individual one when you leave. And if you have no immediate plans to leave your job, why throw away money on an overpriced individual policy if you have access to low-cost, high-quality group coverage?

In the chapters that follow, you find out exactly what you need in the policies that you are looking for so that you can determine whether a group plan meets your needs. In almost all cases, group plans, especially through an employer, offer the necessary benefits. So as long as the group policy is cheaper than an identical policy you could buy as an individual, you'll save money buying through the group plan.

The financial health of your insurers

In addition to the price of a policy and the insurer's reputation and track record for paying claims, an insurer's financial health is an important consideration when you choose a company. If you faithfully pay your premium dollars year after year, you'll be more than a little bummed out if the insurer goes bankrupt right before you have a major claim.

Insurance companies can fail just like any other companies, and dozens do in a typical year. A number of organizations evaluate and rate, with some sort of letter grade, the financial viability and stability of insurance companies. The major rating agencies include A. M. Best, Moody's, Standard & Poor's, Duff & Phelps, and Weiss Research.

The rating agencies letter-grade system works just the way it does in high school: A is better than B or C. Each company uses a different scale. Some companies have as their highest rating AAA, and then AA, A, BBB, BB, and so on. Others use A, A-, B+, B, B-, and so on. Just as some teachers grade more easily, some firms, such as A. M. Best, have a reputation for giving out a greater number of high grades. Others, such as Weiss Research, are tough graders. Unlike in school, however, you want the tough critics when researching where to put your money and future security.

Just as it is a good idea to get more than one medical opinion, two or three financial ratings can give you a better sense of the safety of an insurance company. Stick with companies that are in the top two — or, at worst, three — levels on the different rating scales. The insurance companies recommended in the following chapters meet this criterion.

You can obtain current rating information about insurance companies, free of charge, by asking your agent for a listing of the current ratings. Ask the insurer itself if you are interested in a policy sold without the involvement of an agent.

Although the financial health of an insurance company is important, it's not as big a deal as some insurers (usually those with the highest ratings) and agents make it out to be. Just as financially unhealthy banks are taken over and merged into viable ones, sickly insurers usually follow a similar path under the direction of state insurance regulators.

In most insurance company failures, claims still get paid. The people who usually lose out are those who had money invested in life insurance or annuities with the failed insurer. Even then, you'll typically get back 80 or 90 cents on the dollar of your account value with the insurer, but you may have to wait years to get it.

One exception to the rule that group policies offer better value than individual policies is with life insurance. Group life insurance plans usually aren't cheaper than the best life insurance policies that you can buy individually. If the policies are competitively priced, however, group policies may have the attraction of convenience (ease of enrollment and avoidance of long-winded sales pitches from life insurance salespeople). Group life insurance policies that allow your enrollment without a medical evaluation will probably be more expensive because such plans attract more people with health problems who couldn't get coverage on their own. If you're in good health, you should definitely shop around for life insurance (see Chapter 17 for how).

Dealing with Insurance Problems

When you seek out insurance or have insurance policies, sooner or later you're bound to hit a roadblock. Although insurance problems can be among the more frustrating in life, in the sections ahead, I explain how to calmly and success-fully deal with the more common obstacles.

Help! I've been denied coverage!

Just as you can be turned down when you apply for a loan, you can also be turned down when applying for insurance. For medical, life, or disability insurance, a company may reject you if you have an existing medical problem (a preexisting condition) and are therefore more likely to file a claim. When it comes to insuring assets such as a home, you may have difficulty getting coverage if the property is deemed to be in a high risk area.

Here are some strategies to employ if you are denied coverage:

- ✔ **Ask the insurer why you were denied.** Perhaps the company made a mistake or misinterpreted some information that you provided in your application. If you are being denied coverage because of a medical condi-tion, see what information the company has on you and whether the information is accurate.

- ✔ **Request a copy of your medical information file.** Many people don't know that just as you have a credit report file that details your use (and misuse) of credit, you also have a medical information report. You can request a current copy of your medical information file by writing the Medical Information Bureau at P.O. Box 105, Essex Station, Boston, MA 02112. You can also call them at 617-426-3660. If a mistake is on your report, you have the right to request that it be fixed. As with changing your credit report, the burden is on you to prove that the information in your file is incorrect. This can be a major hassle — you may even need to contact physicians that you've seen in the past because their medical records could be the source of the incorrect information.

✔ **Shop other companies.** Just because one company denies you coverage doesn't mean that all insurance companies will. Some insurers better understand certain medical conditions and are more comfortable approving applicants with those conditions. Most insurers, however, charge a person with a blemished medical history a higher rate than a person with a perfect health record, but some companies penalize you less than others. That's why you must shop around even harder if you have a medical condition. An agent that sells policies from multiple insurers, called an *independent agent,* can be helpful because he or she can shop among a number of different companies.

✔ **Learn about state high-risk pools.** Check with your state department of insurance (see the government section of your local white pages phone directory) if you're turned down for health or property insurance. A number of states act as the insurer of last resort and provide insurance for those who can't get it from insurance companies. State high-risk pool coverage is usually bare bones, but it sure beats going without any coverage at all.

✔ **Check for coverage availability before you buy.** If you're considering buying a home, for example, and you can't get coverage, the insurance companies are trying to tell you something. What they are effectively saying is, "We think that property is so high risk, we're not willing to insure it even if you pay a high premium." (A few insurance companies in coastal Florida areas hard hit in recent years by hurricanes are actually paying existing policy holders to leave their companies. How's that for a sign that you live in a high-risk area?)

Help! My insurer is hassling me about paying a claim

In the event that you suffer a loss and file an insurance claim, you may hold the happy belief that your insurance company will cheerfully and expeditiously pay your claims. Given all the money that you've shelled out for coverage and all the hoops you jumped through to be approved for coverage in the first place, that's a reasonable expectation.

Insurance companies may refuse to pay you what you think you are owed for many reasons, however. In some cases, they may actually be right — your claim may not be covered under the terms of the policy. At a minimum, the insurer wants documentation and proof of your loss. Other people who have come before you have been known to cheat, so insurers aren't about to take your word for anything no matter how honest and ethical you are.

In other cases, though, you're right, and the insurance company is just jerking you around. Some companies view paying claims as an adversarial situation and take a "negotiate tough" stance. Thinking that all insurance companies are going to pay you a fair and reasonable amount unless you make your voice heard is a mistake.

The tips that I discuss in this section help you to ensure that you get paid everything your policy entitles you to.

Document your assets and case

When you're insuring assets, such as your home and its contents, having a record of what you own helps your case. A videotape is the most efficient record, but a handwritten list detailing your possessions works, too. Just remember to keep this record away from your home — if your home burns to the ground, you'll lose your documentation, too!

If you are robbed or are the victim of an accident, get the names, addresses, and phone numbers of witnesses. Take pictures of property damage and solicit estimates for the cost of repairing or replacing what's lost or damaged. File police reports if appropriate, if for no other reason than to bolster your documentation for the insurance claim.

The best offense is a good defense. If you've kept records of valuables and can document their cost, you should be in better shape.

Prepare your case

Filing a claim should be viewed the same way as preparing for a court trial or an IRS audit. Any information that you provide verbally or in writing can and will be used against you to deny your claim. First, you should understand whether the policy you bought covers your claim (this is why getting the broadest coverage possible helps). Unfortunately, the only way to find this out is by getting out the policy and reading it. Policies are hard to read because they use legal language in nonuser-friendly ways.

A possible alternative is to call the claims department and, *without* providing your name, ask a representative whether a particular loss (such as the one that you just suffered) is covered under its policy. You have no need to lie to the company, but you have no need to tell the representative who you are and that you're about to file a claim, either. Your call is informational so that you can understand what your policy covers. Some companies are not willing to provide very specific information, however, unless a specific case is cited.

After you initiate the claims process, keep records of all conversations and all copies of documents that you have given to the insurer's claims department. If you have problems down the road, this "evidence" may bail you out.

For property damage, you should get at least a couple of reputable contractors' estimates. Demonstrate to the insurance company that you're trying to shop for a low price, but don't agree to use a low-cost contractor without knowing that he or she can do quality work.

Remember, your claim is a negotiation

To get what you're owed on an insurance claim, you must approach most claims filings for what they are — a negotiation that is often not cooperative. And the bigger the claim, the more your insurer will play the part of adversary.

When I filed a homeowners' insurance claim after a winter storm significantly damaged my back yard, I was greeted on a weekday by a perky, smiley adjuster. Once the adjuster entered my yard and started to peruse the damage, her demeanor changed dramatically. She had a combative, hard-bargainer type attitude that I last witnessed during my days as a consultant when I worked on some labor-management negotiations.

While standing on my back porch a good distance away from the fences in my yard that had been blown over by wind and crushed by two large trees, the adjuster said that my insurer preferred to repair damaged fences rather than replace them. "With your deductible of $1,000, I doubt this will be worth filing a claim for," she said.

The fence that had blown over, she reasoned, could have new posts set in concrete. As we had already begun to clean up some of the damage for safety reasons, I presented to her some pictures of what the yard looked like right after the storm; she refused to take them. She took some measurements and said she'd have her settlement check to us in a couple of days. The settlement she faxed was for $1,119, no where near what it would cost me to fix the damage that was done.

Be persistent

If you take an insurance company's first offer and don't fight for what you're due, you could be leaving a lot of money on the table. To make my long fence-repair story somewhat shorter, after *five* rounds of haggling with the adjusters, supervisors, and finally managers, I was awarded payment to replace the fences and clean up most of the damage. Although the contractors I had contacted all recommended that the work be done this way, the insurance adjuster discredited their recommendations by saying, "Contractors try to jack up the price and recommended work once they know an insurer is involved."

My final total settlement came to $4,888, more than $3,700 higher than the insurer's first offer. Interestingly, my insurer backed off its preference for repairing the fence when the contractor's estimates for doing that work exceeded the cost of a new fence.

I was disappointed with the behavior of my insurance company. Having faithfully paid my premiums for years and having never filed a claim, I expected they
would be cooperative and not combative. Boy, was I naive. I knew from conversations with others that my homeowners' insurance company is not unusual in
its adversarial strategy, especially with larger claims. And to think that my
insurer has one of the "better" track records for paying claims!

Enlist support

If you do your homework and you're not making progress with the insurer's
adjuster, ask to speak with supervisors and managers. That's what I had to do
to get the additional $3,700 that was needed to get things back to where they
were before the storm.

The agent who sold you the policy may be helpful in preparing and filing the
claim. A good agent can help increase your chances of getting paid and getting
paid sooner. If you're having difficulty with a claim for a policy obtained through
your employer or other group, speak with the benefits department or a person
responsible for interacting with the insurer. These folks have a lot of clout
because of the potential threat to the agent and/or insurer of losing the entire
account.

For policies that you buy on your own, if you're having problems getting a fair
settlement from the insurer, try contacting the state department of insurance.
You can find the phone number in the state government white pages of your
phone book or possibly in your insurance policy.

Another option is to hire a public adjuster who, for a percentage of payment
(typically 5 to 10 percent), can negotiate with insurers on your behalf.

If all else fails and you have a major claim at stake, try contacting an attorney
who specializes in insurance matters. You can find these specialists in the
Yellow Pages of your phone directory under "Attorneys — Insurance Law."
Expect to pay around $150 per hour or so. Consider looking for a lawyer who is
willing to negotiate on your behalf, help draft letters, and so on, on an hourly
basis without filing a lawsuit. Your state department of insurance, the local bar
association, or other legal, accounting, or financial practitioners also may be
able to refer you to someone.

The possible headache in filing a claim is another reason to take the highest
insurance deductibles you're comfortable with. Remember, insurance is to
protect against large, not small, losses. With a high deductible and a small loss,
you'll save yourself some haggling.

Chapter 17

Insurance on You

· ·

In This Chapter

▶ Life insurance

▶ Disability insurance

▶ Health insurance

▶ Long-term care insurance

▶ Overlooked personal insurance

· ·

*M*ultiply your typical annual income by the number of remaining years you plan to work — you come up with a pretty big number, don't you? Didn't realize you were worth that much, did you? That dollar amount equals one of your most valuable assets — your ability to earn an income — and you probably need to protect it. You need to buy some insurance on you.

This chapter explains the ins and outs of buying insurance that protects your income: life insurance, in case of death, and disability insurance, in case of an accident or illness that prevents you from working. I tell you what you may want, what you want to avoid, and where you want to go looking for it.

In addition to protecting your income, you also need to insure against financially catastrophic expenses. I am not talking about December's credit card bill; you're on your own on that one. I am talking about the type of bills that are racked up from a major surgery and a six-week stay in the hospital. Medical expenses today can make even the most indulgent shopping mall spending spree look dirt-cheap. To protect yourself from potentially astronomical medical bills, you also need to buy some health insurance.

Life Insurance

You generally only need life insurance when other people are dependent on your income.

That means that a lot of people don't need life insurance to protect their incomes: single people, working couples who could maintain an acceptable lifestyle if one of the incomes were gone, independently wealthy people who don't need to work, and retired people who are no longer working and dependent on their retirement income.

But if people are in your life who are either fully or partly dependent on your paycheck (usually a spouse and/or children), you should buy life insurance, especially if you have major financial commitments such as mortgage or years of child rearing ahead. Considering life insurance if an extended family member is currently or likely to be dependent on your future income may also make sense.

Don't waste your money on life insurance for your children

You've surely heard of Gerber baby food. Well, the folks at Gerber knew that their brand name had clout with parents, so they sat around racking their brains about what other products they could pitch to parents.

So Gerber established a life insurance company that now has billions of dollars of life insurance in force. The only problem is that they specialize in selling life insurance policies on individuals who don't need it: children.

Gerber's "Grow-Up" policy provides $5,000 of life insurance for children. The marketing materials say, "Life insurance for the child you love . . . $1 a week at most ages. . . ."

Sounds like such a deal, but it's really a rip-off that contradicts the entire logic of life insurance. Unless your kid was the star of the *Home Alone* movies, you are not financially dependent on any of your children; your children are dependent on you! As any parent knows, kids cost a good deal of money — kids don't earn money!

And if a person does need life insurance coverage, of what use is a piddling $5,000 worth of

coverage?! And a buck a week is hardly a deal — a young adult could buy about ten times that amount of coverage ($50,000) for that cost!

Insurance agents love to prey on the emotional bond between parents and children. In one written sales pitch an agent made to one of my counseling clients, the agent said, ". . . as long as the policies remain in-force, your signature(s) will always be there as a reminder of your very thoughtful financial gift."

Agents also love to sell cash value life insurance on kids because such policies pay the agent a hefty commission (25 percent of all cash value policies sold are on children). Part of the supposed allure is that the huge premiums that you pump into such policies partly go into a savings account for the child's future. As you see later in this chapter, cash value life insurance is a costly life insurance and investment choice. If you want to secure your children's financial future, follow the advice in this book and pass this information on to your children. Don't waste money on life insurance on your kids — they don't need it.

How much do you need?

If you need life insurance, deciding how much to buy is as much a subjective thing as it is a quantitative decision. I've seen some worksheets that are incredibly long and tedious (some are worse than your tax returns). There's no need to get fancy. If you're like me, your eyes start to glaze over if you have more than 20 lines of calculations to complete. Figuring out how much life insurance you need doesn't have to be that complicated.

The main purpose of life insurance is to provide a lump sum payment that replaces the deceased person's income. The question you need to ask yourself is how many years of income do you want to replace? Table 17-1 provides a simple way to calculate how much life insurance you should consider purchasing. To replace a certain number of years of income, simply multiply the appropriate number in the table by the person's annual after-tax income.

Table 17-1	Life Insurance Need Calculation
Years of Income to Replace	*Multiply Annual After-Tax Income* by*
5	4.5
10	8.5
20	15
30	20

*You can roughly determine your annual after-tax income in one of two ways. You can get out last year's tax return (and form W-2) and calculate it by subtracting the federal, state, and Social Security taxes you paid from your gross employment income. Or you can estimate it by multiplying your gross income by 80 percent if you're a low-income earner, 70 percent if you're a moderate-income earner, or 60 percent if you're a high-income earner. (You need to replace only after-tax, not pre-tax, income because life insurance policy payouts are not taxed.)

Another way to determine the amount of life insurance to buy is to think about how much you will need to pay for major debts or expenditures, such as your mortgage, other loans, and college for your children. If, for example, you'd like your spouse to have enough of a life insurance death benefit to be able to pay off half of your mortgage and pay for half of your children's college education, then simply add half of your mortgage amount to half of their estimated college costs (refer to Chapter 14 for approximate numbers) and buy that amount of life insurance.

Social Security, if you're covered, can provide *survivors'* benefits to your spouse and children. However, if your surviving spouse earns more than about $20,000 per year, he or she is not going to get any coverage (so you can skip the rest of this section). If either you or your spouse anticipates earning less than $20,000 per year, however, you may want to factor this into how much life insurance to buy. Contact the Social Security Administration at 800-772-1213 and ask for form 7004, which gives you an estimate of your Social Security benefits.

The Social Security Administration can tell you how much your survivors will receive per month in the event of your death. Suppose that this benefit amounts to 40 percent of your current income. Then you need to purchase only approximately 60 percent (100 percent minus 40 percent) of the amount of life insurance that you calculated in Table 17-1.

Term versus cash value life insurance

In the next ten seconds, I'm going to tell you how you can save hours of time and thousands of dollars. Ready? *Buy term life insurance.* (The only exception is if you have a high net worth — a couple million bucks or more — in which case, you may want to consider other options. See the estate-planning section in Chapter 18.) If you've already figured out how much life insurance to purchase and this is all the advice you need to go ahead and buy it, you can skip the rest of this section (and go to the head of the class!).

The following information is for the rest of you who want all the details behind my recommendation for term insurance. Or maybe you've heard (and have already fallen prey to) the sales pitches from life insurance agents, most of whom love selling cash value life insurance because of the huge commissions it pays.

Cash value life insurance is the most oversold insurance and financial product in the history of the financial services industry. As you'll soon discover, cash value life insurance makes sense for only a very small percentage of people. You would think that the vast majority of life insurance that is bought by people like you — and therefore sold by agents — is term insurance. Wrong! The last numbers I saw showed that about 80 percent of life insurance that is sold is cash value because many people don't know any better. Don't make the same mistake.

Let me start with some background. Despite the variety of names that life insurance marketing departments have cooked up for policies, life insurance comes basically in two flavors:

- ✔ **Term insurance** is pure life insurance: You pay an annual premium for which you receive a predetermined amount of life insurance protection. If the insured person passes away, the beneficiaries collect; otherwise, the premium is gone. In this way, term life insurance is similar to auto or homeowner's insurance.

- ✔ **Cash value insurance.** All other life insurance policies (whole, universal, variable, and so on) combine life insurance with a supposed savings feature. Your premiums not only pay for life insurance, but some of your dollars are also credited to an account that grows in value over time, assuming you keep paying your premiums. On the surface, this sounds potentially attractive. People don't like to feel that all their premium dollars are getting tossed away.

But there's a very big catch. For the same amount of coverage (for example, for $100,000 of life insurance benefits), cash value policies cost you about eight times (800 percent) more than comparable term policies.

Agents know the buttons to push to get you interested in buying the wrong kind of life insurance. Here are typical arguments that they'll make for purchasing cash value polices, followed by the real truth.

"It's all paid up after x number of years. You don't want to be paying life insurance premiums for the rest of your life, do you?"

Agents pitching cash value life insurance show you all sorts of projections that imply that after the first 10 or 20 years of paying your premiums, you won't need to pay more premiums to keep the life insurance in force.

The only reason that you may be able to stop paying premiums is that you've poured too much extra money into the policy in the early years of payment. Remember that cash value life insurance costs eight times as much as term. Imagine that you're currently paying $500 a year for auto insurance and an insurance company comes along and offers you a policy for $4,000 per year. The representative tells you that after 10 years, you can stop paying and still keep your same coverage. I'm sure that you wouldn't fall for this sales tactic, but many people do when they buy cash value life insurance. You need to recognize that only by overcharging today can the insurer afford to continue your coverage in later years without a premium payment.

You also need to be wary of the projections because they often include unrealistic and lofty assumptions about the investment return that your cash balance can earn. When you stop paying into a cash value policy, the cost of each year's life insurance is deducted from the remaining cash value. If the rate of return on the cash balance is not high, the cash balance could begin sliding, and eventually you could receive notices saying that your policy needs more funding to keep the life insurance in place.

"You won't be able to afford term insurance when you're older."

As you get older, the cost of term insurance increases because the probability of your dying rises. But life insurance is not something you need all your life! It's typically bought in a person's younger years when financial commitments and obligations outweigh financial assets. Twenty or thirty years later, the reverse should be true.

If you retire 20 or 30 years from now, you probably won't need life insurance to protect your employment income because there won't be any to protect! You may have needed life insurance when you were raising a family and/or had a substantial mortgage you were responsible for, but by the time you retire, the kids should be out on their own (you hope!) and the mortgage paid down.

In the meantime, term insurance saves you a tremendous amount of money. For most people, it takes 20 to 30 years for the premium they are paying on a term insurance policy to finally catch up to (equal) the premium they've been paying all along on a comparable amount of cash value life insurance purchased today.

One exception to the preceding comment is the case of a small business owner who owns a business worth more than, say, one or two million dollars and who would not want his heirs to be forced to sell the business to pay estate taxes in the event of his death. (See "If you need cash value life insurance" later in this chapter.)

"You can borrow against the cash value at a low rate of interest."

Such a deal! It's your money in the policy, remember? If you deposited money in a savings or money market account, how would you like to pay for the privilege of borrowing your own money back? Borrowing on your cash value policy is not only expensive but also dangerous: You increase the chances of the policy exploding on you — leaving you with nothing to show for all the premiums to pay.

"Your cash value grows tax-deferred."

Ah, a glimmer of truth at last. The fact that the cash value portion of your policy grows without taxation until you withdraw it is true. But if you want tax-deferral of your investment balances, you should first be taking advantage of such savings plans as 401(k)s, 403(b)s, SEP-IRAs, and Keoghs (refer to Chapter 12) that give you an immediate tax deduction for your current contributions in addition to growth without taxation until withdrawal.

Money paid into a cash value life policy gives you *no* up-front tax deductions. If you've exhausted the tax-deductible plans, then variable annuities or a nondeductible individual retirement account (IRA) can provide tax-deferred compounding of your investment dollars (refer to Chapter 12) and access to better investment options.

Life insurance tends to be a mediocre investment. The insurance company quotes you an interest rate for the first year only. After that, the company pays you what it wants. If you don't like the future interest rates, you can be penalized for quitting the policy (see "How to get rid of cash value life insurance," later in this chapter). Would you ever invest your money in a bank account that quoted an interest rate for the first year only and then penalized you for moving your money within the next seven to ten years?

"It's forced savings."

Many agents argue that a cash value plan is better than nothing — at least it's forcing you to save. This is silly reasoning because so many people drop out of cash value life insurance policies after just a few years of paying into them.

If you like the idea of forced savings, you can accomplish it without using life insurance. Any of the retirement savings accounts mentioned in Chapter 12 can be set up for automatic monthly transfers. If your employer offers such a plan, it can deduct your contributions right out of your paycheck — and it doesn't shave a commission off the top! You can also set up monthly electronic transfers from your bank checking account to contribute into mutual funds (refer to Chapter 11).

"Life insurance is not part of your taxable estate."

If the ownership of a life insurance policy is properly structured, it's true that the death benefit is free of estate taxes. This part of the sales pitch is about the only sound reason that exists for buying cash value life insurance. Under current federal laws, a person can pass on $600,000 free of federal estate taxes. But even if you're one of the lucky, elite minority who can expect to pass away with such an estate, you have numerous other ways to reduce your taxable estate (see Chapter 18).

Summary

Cash value policies are aggressively pushed by insurance salespeople because of the high commissions that insurance companies pay them. Commissions on cash value life insurance range from 50 to 100 percent of your first year's premium. An insurance salesperson, therefore, can typically make *ten times more money* (yes, you read that right) selling you a cash value policy than he can selling you term insurance.

You are ultimately paying the high commissions that are built into these policies when you purchase cash value life insurance. As you can see in a policy's cash value table, you won't get back any of the money that you dump in the policy if you quit the policy in the first two to three years. The insurance company can't afford to give you any of your money back in those first few years because so much of it has been paid to the selling agent as commission. That's why these policies penalize you in the first seven to ten years for withdrawing your cash balance.

Cash value policies are also expensive ways to purchase life insurance. Because of the high cost of these policies relative to the cost of term, you are more likely to buy less life insurance coverage than you need — that's the sad part of the insurance industry's pushing of this stuff. *The vast majority of life insurance buyers need more protection than they can afford to buy with cash value coverage.*

Purchase low-cost term insurance and do your investing separately. Life insurance is rarely a permanent need; over time, you can gradually reduce the amount of term insurance that you carry as you accumulate more assets and savings.

Buying term insurance

Term insurance policies have several features to choose from. So that you can make an informed decision about purchasing term insurance, I briefly go over these features in this section.

How often your premium adjusts

As you get older, the risk of dying increases, so the cost of your insurance goes up. Term insurance can be purchased such that your premium adjusts (goes up) annually or every 5, 10, 15, or 20 years. The less frequently your premium adjusts, the higher the initial premium and its incremental increases will be.

The advantage of a premium that locks in for, say, 15 years is that you have the security of knowing how much you'll be paying each year for the next 15 years. You also don't need to go through medical evaluations as frequently to qualify for the lowest rate possible.

The disadvantage of a policy with a long-term rate lock is that you'll be paying more in the earlier years than you would on a policy that adjusts more frequently. In addition, you may want to change the amount of insurance you carry as your circumstances change, so you would be throwing money away if you dump a policy with a long-term premium guarantee before its rate is set to change.

Policies that adjust the premium every five to ten years offer a happy medium between price and predictability.

Guaranteed renewability

This feature guarantees that the policy cannot be canceled because of poor health; guaranteed renewability is standard practice on better policies. Do not buy a life insurance policy without this feature unless you're sure that your life insurance needs will disappear when the policy is up for renewal.

Where to buy term insurance

A number of sound ways are available to obtain high-quality, low-cost term insurance. If you choose to buy through a local agent — because you know her or because you'd prefer to buy from someone close to home — you should invest a few minutes of your time to get quotes from one or two of the following sources to get a sense of what's available in the insurance market. If nothing else, your familiarity with the market can prevent an agent from selling you an overpriced, high-commission policy.

Here are four sources for high-quality, low-cost term insurance:

- ✔ **USAA** sells low-cost term insurance direct to the public (800-531-8000).

- ✔ **Wholesale Insurance Network** is another good source for low-cost term insurance (800-808-5810). This organization is paid a marketing fee, which is basically a commission, from the companies whose insurance it sells.

- ✔ **Insurance agency quotation services** send you a handful of relatively user-friendly proposals from the highest-rated, lowest-cost companies available. Like other agencies, the services receive a commission if you buy a policy from them, which you're under no obligation to do. Unlike local insurance agents, they don't hound you (don't give them your phone number if you don't want to be called, however). They'll ask you your date of birth, whether you smoke, and how much coverage you'd like. The best quotation services in terms of customer service, pricing, and presentation of information are **SelectQuote** (800-343-1985) and **Direct Insurance Services** (800-622-3699).

How to get rid of cash value life insurance

If you were snookered into buying a cash value life insurance policy and want to get rid of it, go for it. *But don't cancel the coverage until you first secure new term coverage.* If you need life insurance, you don't want to leave open a period when you're not covered (Murphy's Law says *that's* when disaster will strike).

Cashing in a cash value life insurance policy has tax consequences. For most of these policies, you must pay tax on the amount you receive that is in excess of the premiums you paid over the life of the policy. Because some life insurance policies feature tax-deferred retirement savings, you may incur a 10-percent penalty on earnings withdrawn before age 59 $\frac{1}{2}$, just the way you would with an IRA. If you want to withdraw the cash balance in your life insurance policy, consider checking with the insurer or a tax advisor to clarify what the tax consequences may be.

You can avoid early withdrawal penalties and taxation on accumulated interest in a life insurance policy by doing a tax-free exchange into a no-load (commission-free) *variable annuity policy.* The no-load mutual fund company through which you buy the annuity takes care of transferring your existing balance. (Refer to Chapter 13 for more information about annuities.)

If you need cash value life insurance

Don't expect to get objective information on this important decision from anyone who sells cash value life insurance. Beware of insurance salespeople masquerading under the guise of self-anointed titles, such as estate planning specialists or financial planners.

As I discuss earlier in the chapter, purchasing cash value life insurance may make sense if you expect to have an estate tax problem. Read the section in Chapter 18 on estate planning *before* making any decisions. Cash value life insurance is just one of numerous ways to reduce your estate taxes.

Among the best places to shop for cash value life insurance policies are:

- ✔ **USAA** (800-531-8000)
- ✔ **Ameritas** (800-552-3553)
- ✔ **Wholesale Insurance Network** (800-808-5810)

If you want to obtain some cash value life insurance, avoid local insurance agents, especially while you're in the learning stage. Agents aren't as interested in educating as they are in selling (big surprise). Besides, the best cash value policies can be obtained free of most (or all) sales commissions if you buy from the preceding sources. The money saved on commissions is reflected in a much higher cash value for you — up to several thousand dollars' worth.

Disability Insurance

As with life insurance, the purpose of disability insurance is to protect your income. The only difference is that you're protecting the income for yourself (and perhaps also your dependents). If you're completely disabled, you still have living expenses, but you probably can't earn an income.

I'm talking here about long-term disabilities. If you throw out your back while reliving your athletic glory days with your aging adult body and wind up in bed for a couple of weeks, that won't be as much of a disaster to your finances as it is to your ego! What would be a financial disaster, however, is if you're disabled in such a way that you can't earn an income for several years.

Most large employers offer disability insurance to their employees. Many smaller company employees and all self-employed people are left to fend for themselves. As a result, many people don't have disability coverage. Being without disability insurance is a risky proposition, especially if, like most working people, you need your employment income to live on.

If you're married and your spouse earns a large enough income that you can make do without yours, then you may consider skipping disability coverage. The same is true if you've already got enough money accumulated for your future years (you're financially independent). Keep in mind, though, that your expenses may go up if you are disabled and require special care or medical attention.

For most people, dismissing the need for disability coverage is easy. The odds of suffering a long-term disability seem so remote — and they are. But if you meet up with bad luck, disability coverage can relieve you (and possibly your family) of a major financial burden.

Most disabilities are caused by medical problems, such as arthritis, heart conditions, hypertension, and back/spine or hip/leg impairments. Some of these ailments are caused by advancing age, but more than a third of disabilities are suffered by people under age 45. The vast majority of these medical problems cannot be predicted in advance, particularly those caused by accidents, which happen at random.

If you think that you have good disability coverage through government programs, you better think again:

- ✔ **Social Security disability.** Social Security pays long-term benefits only if you are not able to perform any substantial, gainful activity for more than a year or if your disability is expected to result in death. In fact, 70 percent of all applicants for Social Security disability benefits coverage are turned down. Furthermore, Social Security disability payments are quite low because they are intended to provide only for basic, subsistence-level living expenses.

- ✔ **Worker's compensation.** Worker's compensation, if you have such coverage through your employer, pays you if you're injured on the job but does not pay any benefits if you get disabled away from your job. You need coverage that kicks in regardless of where and how you are disabled.

- ✔ **State disability programs.** A few states have gotten into the disability insurance business, but the coverage is typically not extensive enough because benefits are paid over too short a period of time (rarely more than a year). State programs are also generally not good values because of the cost for the small amount of coverage they provide.

How much disability insurance do you need?

You need enough disability coverage to provide you with sufficient income to live on until other financial resources are available. If you don't have much saved in the way of financial assets and you would want to continue with the lifestyle supported by your current income, get enough disability coverage to replace your entire take-home (after-tax) monthly pay.

The benefits you purchase on a disability policy are quoted as dollars per month that you receive if disabled. So if your job provides you with a $2,000-per-month income after payment of taxes, then you ask for a policy that provides a $2,000-per-month benefit.

If you pay for your disability insurance, the benefits are tax-free (but hopefully you won't ever have to collect them). If your employer picks up the tab, your benefits are taxable, so you need a higher amount of benefits.

In addition to the monthly coverage amount, you also need to select the duration of time you want a policy to pay you benefits. You need a policy that pays benefits until an age at which you become financially self-sufficient. For most people, that's age 65 or so when their Social Security benefits kick in. If you anticipate continuing to be dependent on your employment income past your mid-60s, you may want to obtain disability coverage that pays you until a later age.

On the other hand, if you've crunched some numbers (refer to Chapter 8) and see that you expect to be financially independent by age 55, you can get a policy that pays benefits up to that age — it'll cost you less than one that pays benefits to you until age 65. If you're within five years of being financially independent or able to retire, five-year disability policies are available, too. You might also consider such short-term policies because you're sure that someone (for example, a family member) can support you financially over the long-term.

Other features you need in disability insurance

Disability insurance policies have many features that may be confusing to you. So that you can make an informed decision about purchasing disability insurance, I briefly go over these features.

- ✔ **Definition of disability.** An *own-occupation* disability policy provides benefit payments if you cannot perform the work you normally do. Some policies pay you only if you're unable to perform a job for which you are *reasonably trained*. Other policies revert to this definition after a few years of being own occupation.

  Own-occupation policies are the most expensive because there's a greater chance that the insurer will have to pay you. The extra cost may not be worth it for you unless you're in a high income or specialized occupation, and you'd have to take a big pay cut to do something else (and you wouldn't be happy about a reduced income and the required lifestyle changes).

- ✔ **Noncancelable and guaranteed renewable.** These features guarantee that your policy cannot be canceled because of poor health conditions. If you purchase a policy that requires periodic physical exams, you can lose your coverage just when you are most likely to need it.

✔ **Waiting period.** This is the "deductible" on disability insurance — the lag time between the onset of your disability and the time you begin collecting benefits. As with other types of insurance, you should take the highest deductible (longest waiting period) that your financial circumstances allow. This lag time significantly reduces the cost of the insurance and eliminates the hassle of filing a claim for a short-term disability. The minimum waiting period on most policies is 30 days, and the maximum can be up to 1 to 2 years. Try a waiting period of 3 to 6 months if you have sufficient emergency reserves.

✔ **Residual benefits.** This option pays you a partial benefit if you have a disability that prevents you from working full-time.

✔ **Cost-of-living adjustments (COLAs).** This feature automatically increases your benefit payment by a set percentage or in accordance with changes in inflation. The advantage of a COLA is that it retains the purchasing power of your benefits. A modest COLA, such as 4 percent, is worth having.

✔ **Future insurability.** A clause that many agents encourage you to buy, future insurability allows you, regardless of health, to buy additional coverage. For most people, paying for the privilege of buying more coverage later is not worth it because the income that you earn today fairly reflects your likely long-term earnings (except for cost-of-living increases). Disability insurance is sold only as a proportion of your income. Therefore, the only people who may benefit from the future insurability option are those whose income is artificially low now and who not only are confident of its rising significantly in the future but also need to protect it. (For example, you just got out of medical school and are earning a low salary while being enslaved as a resident.)

✔ **Insurer's financial stability.** As I discuss in Chapter 16, you should choose insurers that will be here tomorrow to pay your claim. But don't get too hung up on the safety of the company; benefits are paid even if the insurer fails because the state or another insurer almost always bails the insurer out.

Where to buy disability insurance

The best place to check for buying disability insurance is through your employer or professional association. Unless these groups have done a lousy job shopping for coverage, group plans offer better value than you can purchase on your own. Just make sure that the plan that's offered meets the specifications discussed in the preceding section.

Don't trust an insurance agent to be enthusiastic (or even honest) about the quality of a disability policy your employer or other group is offering. Agents have a huge conflict of interest when they criticize these options because your group insurance cuts them out of the picture.

Other "insurance" to protect your income

Life insurance and disability insurance replace your income if you die or suffer a disability. But you could also see your income reduced or completely eliminated if you lose your job. Although no formal insurance policy exists to protect you against the forces that can cause this to happen, you can do a couple of things to reduce your exposure to this risk.

Make sure that you have an emergency reserve of money that you can tap into if you lose your job. (Chapter 8 offers specific guidelines for deciding how much money is right for you.)

Another form of "insurance" is to continually attend to your skills and professional development. Not only does upgrading your education and skills ensure that you are employable if you have to hit the streets to look for a new job, but it may also help you keep your old one and earn a higher income.

If you need to purchase disability insurance on your own, check out the following for competitively priced policies:

- ✔ **Wholesale Insurance Network** (800-808-5810)

- ✔ **USAA** (800-531-8000)

- ✔ **Direct Insurance Services** (800-622-3699)

If you opt to purchase disability insurance through a local agent, tread carefully. Some agents try to load down a policy with all sorts of extra bells and whistles to pump up the premium and their own commission.

If you buy disability insurance through an agent, use a process called *list billing*. With list billing, you sign up with several others for coverage at the same time and are invoiced together for your coverage. It can knock up to 15 percent off an insurer's standard prices. Ask your insurance agent how this works.

Health Insurance

Everyone needs health insurance, but not everyone has it. Some people who can afford it choose not to buy it, believing that they're healthy and are not going to need it. Others who opt not to buy health insurance figure that if they ever really need it, they'll get care even if they can't pay. To a large extent, they're right. However, the care is usually a lot more expensive by the time they seek it (due to advanced illness, emergency room visits, and so on). People without health insurance generally put off getting more routine care, which can lead to small problems turning into big ones.

Choosing the best health plan

Before Medicare, the government-run insurance program for the elderly, kicks in at age 65, odds are you will obtain your health insurance through your employer. Be thankful if you do. Employer-provided coverage eliminates the headache of shopping for your own coverage and is usually cheaper than coverage bought on your own.

If you have options through your employer or need to hunt for a plan on your own, here are the major issues to consider when selecting among the health insurance offerings in the marketplace.

Major medical coverage

You need a plan that covers the *big* potential expenses: hospitalization, physician, and ancillary charges, such as X-ray and laboratory work. For women, if you're entering or already in your child-bearing years and may want to have children, make sure that your plan has maternity benefits.

Choice of health care providers

Increasing numbers of health insurance plans contract with specific health care providers, which restricts your choices. Health maintenance organizations (HMOs) and preferred provider organizations (PPOs) are the main plans that restrict your choices. They keep costs down because they negotiate lower rates with selected providers.

HMOs and PPOs are more similar than they are different. The main difference is that PPOs still pay the majority of your expenses if you use a provider outside their approved list. If you do this with an HMO, you typically won't be covered at all.

Health insurers: bigger is usually better

With health insurance plans, you should give preference to plans that insure large numbers of people and that have been around longer. Larger plans can negotiate better rates from providers, and older plans are more likely to be here tomorrow.

Many insurers operate in a bunch of different insurance businesses. You want those that are the biggest in the health insurance arena and are committed to the business. If your coverage is canceled, you might have to search for coverage that allows an existing medical problem. Other health insurers won't want to touch you. (Check if your state department of insurance offers a plan for people unable to get coverage.)

Nationally, Blue Cross, Blue Shield, and Kaiser Permanente are the older and larger health insurers.

Plans that allow you to use any health care provider you want are becoming less common and more expensive in most areas. If you have your heart set on particular physicians or hospitals, check which health insurance plans they accept as payment. If you can't use their services in the restricted-choice plans, ask yourself if the extra cost of the open-choice plan is worth being able to use their services. If you're interested in being able to use alternative types of medical professionals — that is, chiropractors, acupuncturists, and so on — also check to see if the plans that you're considering cover these services.

Don't be deterred from lower-cost HMO and PPO plans by stories of how hard getting an appointment with a doctor is or other logistical hassles. This can happen in plans with open choice, too — many doctors are always running late or are overbooked. It is also a myth that doctors who can't get patients on their own are the only ones who sign up with restricted-choice plans. Although HMO and PPO plans do offer less choice of providers, customer surveys show that customer satisfaction with these plans is as high as in plans that offer more choice.

Lifetime maximum benefits

Health insurance plans specify the maximum total benefits that they'll pay over the course of your time insured by their plan. Although a million dollars may be more money than you could ever imagine being spent on yourself, that's the minimally acceptable level of total benefits. With the cost of health care today, you can blow through that in short order if you develop major health problems. Ideally, choose a plan that has no maximum or that has a maximum of at least several million dollars.

Deductibles and copayments

To reduce your health insurance premiums, choose a plan with the highest deductible and copayment that you can afford. As with other insurance policies, the more you are willing to share in the payment of your claims, the less you will have to pay in premiums. Most policies have annual deductible options, such as $250, $500, $1,000, and so on, as well as copayment options, typically 20 percent or so.

When choosing a copayment percentage, don't let your imagination run wild and unnecessarily scare you. A 20 percent copayment does not mean that you would have to come up with $20,000 for a $100,000 claim. The insurance company almost always sets a maximum out-of-pocket limit on your annual copayments (usually around $1,000); the company will cover 100% of any medical expenses that go over that cap.

In plans provided by your employer, consider plans with low out-of-pocket expenses if you know you have health problems. Being part of a group, they won't increase your individual rates just because you're filing more claims.

Most HMO plans (that I discuss earlier in this chapter) don't have deductible and copayment options. Most just charge a nominal amount — $5 or $10 — for a physician's office visit.

Guaranteed renewable

You want a health insurance plan that keeps renewing your coverage without your needing to take more physical examinations to prove your continued good health.

Buying health insurance

You can buy many health plans through agents and some directly from the insurer. If it's sold both ways, you shouldn't have to pay any more to go through an agent.

If you're self-employed or work for a small employer that doesn't offer health insurance as a benefit, get proposals from Blue Cross, Blue Shield, Kaiser, or other large health insurers in your area. Also check with professional or other associations which you may belong to. A competent independent insurance agent who specializes in health insurance can help find insurers willing to offer you coverage.

Saving on your taxes when spending on health care

If you consistently have a lot of out-of-pocket medical expenses, check to see if your employer offers a flexible spending or health care reimbursement account. These accounts enable you to pay for uncovered medical expenses with pre-tax dollars. If, for example, you're in a combined 35% federal and state income tax bracket, these accounts allow you to pay for needed health care at a 35 percent discount. In addition to your out-of-pocket health care costs, these accounts can be used to pay for vision and dental care.

Be forewarned of some major stumbling blocks to saving through medical reimbursement accounts. First, you need to elect to save money from your paycheck prior to the beginning of each plan year. The only exceptions where you can start saving money during the plan year is at the time of a "life change" such as a family member's death, marriage, spouse job change, divorce, or birth of a child. You also need to use the money within the year saved because these accounts contain a "use or lose it" feature.

Another way that you may be able to save on taxes is if you have a substantial amount of health care expenditures in a year. You can deduct medical and dental expenses as an itemized deduction on Schedule A to the extent that they exceed 7.5% of your adjusted gross income (refer to Chapter 7). Unless you're a low income earner, you would need to have substantial expenses, usually caused by an accident or major illness, to take advantage of this tax break.

Health insurance agents have a conflict of interest common to all financial salespeople working on commission: The higher the premium plan they sell you, the bigger the commission they earn. So an agent may try to steer you into higher-cost plans and not suggest some of the strategies discussed in the previous section to reduce your cost of coverage.

If you're denied insurance

When you try to enroll with a particular health insurance plan, you may be turned down because of health problems you currently have or previously had. Your *medical information file* (the medical equivalent of a credit report) may contain information explaining why you were turned down. (Read the section in Chapter 16 to learn about steps you can take if you're denied coverage.)

Dealing with medical claims headaches

If you sign up for a health plan that has deductibles and copayments, be sure to review the benefits statements that your insurer sends you. Errors often pop up on these statements and in the claims filing process. Not surprisingly, the errors are rarely in your favor and usually at your expense.

Be sure that your insurer has kept accurate track of your contributions toward meeting your plan's annual deductible and maximum out-of-pocket charges. Also, don't pay any health care providers who send you bills until you've received proper notification from the insurance company detailing what you are obligated to pay those providers according to the terms of your plan. Because most insurance companies have negotiated discounted fee schedules with health care providers, the amount that a provider bills you is often higher than the amount they are legally due as per the terms of their contract with your insurer. Your insurer's benefit statement should detail what is the approved and negotiated rate.

And don't let providers try to bully you into paying them the difference between what they've billed you for and what the insurer says they are due. Providers are only due what discounted fees they've agreed to with your insurer.

Haggling with your health insurer is a real pain, and it usually happens after you have racked up significant medical expenses and when you are generally not feeling well. But if you don't stay on top of your insurer, you can end up paying thousands of dollars in overpayments.

If you're overwhelmed with an avalanche of claims and benefits statements, you might consider using a health insurance claims processing service. You can get a referral to firms in your area that are engaged in this line of work by contacting the National Association of Claims Assistance Professionals (800-660-0665).

If you have a so-called *preexisting condition* (current or prior medical problems), you have several options to pursue to secure health insurance:

- ✔ **Try health insurance plans that don't discriminate.** A few plans — typically Blue Cross, Blue Shield, and some HMO plans such as Kaiser Permanente — will sometimes take you regardless of your condition.

- ✔ **Find a job with an employer whose health insurer doesn't require a medical exam.** Of course, this shouldn't be your only reason for seeking new employment, but it can be an important factor. Likewise, if you're married, you may be able to get into an employer group plan if your spouse takes a new job.

- ✔ **Check to see if your state offers a plan.** A number of states maintain pools that insure people with pre-existing conditions who are unable to find coverage elsewhere. Try contacting your state's insurance department to see if your state offers such plans — you can find the phone number in the state government section of your phone book. I suppose, in a really drastic situation, if your state doesn't offer one of these plans, you could move to a nearby state that does.

Retiree medical care insurance

Medicare, the government-run health insurance plan for the elderly, is a two-part major medical plan. Enrollment in Part A (hospital expenses) is automatic. Part B, which covers physician and other charges including home health care coverage, is optional. Supplemental insurance policies may be of interest to you to help pay for those costs which Medicare doesn't.

Medigap insurance

Medigap coverage generally pays the deductibles and copayments that Medicare charges. For the first 60 days of a hospitalization, you'll pay $736 out of your own pocket. If you have an unusually long continuous hospitalization, you'll pay $184 per day for the 61st through 90th day, $368 per day for the 91st through 150th day; and all costs beyond 150 days. Clearly, if you stay in a hospital for many months, your out-of-pocket expenses could escalate. However, the longest hospitalizations tend to not last past a couple of months.

If the costs from a long hospital stay would be a financial catastrophe for you and if you're unable to pay for the deductibles and copayments because your income is low, Medicaid, the state-run medical insurance program for low-income people, may help pay your bills. Alternatively Medigap insurance can help close the gap.

Check with your physician(s) to see that he or she does not charge a fee higher than that listed on Medicare's fee schedule. If so, you should consider going to another physician if you can't afford the fee or want to save yourself some money. Medicare often pays only 80 percent of the physician charges that the program allows on its fee schedule. Some physicians charge higher fees than allowed by Medicare, others don't.

The biggest fear and reason that elderly people consider extra health insurance is that Medicare only pays for the first 100 days in a skilled nursing facility. Anything over that is your responsibility. But Medigap policies also don't address this issue.

Nursing-home insurance

Insurance agents, eager to earn a hefty commission from selling you a policy, will tell you that *nursing-home insurance* is the solution to your concerns about an extended stay in a nursing home. Don't get your hopes up. Policies are complicated and filled with all sorts of exclusions and limitations. On top of all that, they're expensive, too.

The decision to purchase nursing-home insurance is a trade-off. Do you want to pay thousands of dollars annually from age 60 onward to guard against the possibility of a long-term nursing-home stay? If you live into or past your mid-80s, you could pay more than $50,000 to $100,000+ on a nursing-home policy (not to mention the lost investment earnings on these insurance premiums).

If you end up in a nursing home for years on end, you might come out ahead financially if you bought nursing-home insurance. The majority of people are in homes less than a year, though, because they either pass away or move out.

Medicare pays for the bulk of the first 100 days' cost of nursing home stays as long as certain conditions are satisfied. First, the nursing home stay must follow, within 30 days, a hospitalization, and the nursing home stay must be for the same medical condition that caused the hospitalization. Once discharged from a nursing home, you can qualify for an additional 100-day benefit period if you have not been hospitalized or in a nursing home the prior 60 days.

If you have relatives or a spouse who would probably care for you in the event of a major illness, you should definitely *not* waste your money on nursing-home insurance. I would also bypass this coverage if you have and don't mind using retirement assets to help pay nursing home costs.

Even if you do deplete your assets, remember that you do have a back-up: *Medicaid* (state-provided medical insurance) can pick up the cost if you can't. You should, however, be aware of a number of potential drawbacks to getting coverage for nursing home stays under Medicaid:

- ✔ **What medical conditions warrant coverage is up to your state.** With the budget noose tightening more in some states, some are disallowing certain types of coverage: for example, mental problems for elderly people who are otherwise in good physical health.

- ✔ **Medicaid patients are at the bottom of the priority list.** Most nursing homes are interested in the bottom line, so those patients who bring in the least revenue — namely Medicaid patients — get lowest priority on nursing home waiting lists.

- ✔ **Some nursing homes don't take Medicaid patients.** Check with homes in your area where you could envision being happy and see if they accept Medicaid.

- ✔ **The states might squeeze Medicaid further.** The federal government finances part of Medicaid, and the federal trend these days is to give states blocks of money and let them decide what they want to do with it. In such an environment, more states might restrict Medicaid access.

If you're concerned about having your stash of money wiped out by an extended nursing home stay and you've always dreamed of passing money onto family or a favorite charity, you could start giving it away while you're still healthy. (If you're already in poor health, legal experts can do Medicaid planning, which is strategizing to preserve your assets and keep them away from being used to pay nursing home costs.)

If you want to retain and protect your assets and it gives you peace of mind to know that a long-term nursing-home stay is covered, consider buying nursing home insurance. But do your homework. Comparison shop policies and be sure to buy a policy that pays until your passing. A year's worth or even a few years of benefits won't protect your assets if your stay lasts longer. Also be sure to get a policy that adjusts the daily benefit amount for increases in the cost of living. Watch out for policies that restrict benefits to limited types of facilities and settings. Get a policy that covers needed care in your home or other settings if you don't need to be in a high-cost nursing home and which does not require prior hospitalization for benefits to kick in.

You might also consider retirement communities if you're willing to live as a younger retiree in such a setting. After paying an entrance fee, you would pay a monthly fee, which usually covers your rent, care, and meals. Be sure that any such facility you're considering guarantees care for life and accepts Medicaid in case you run out of assets.

The Most Overlooked Form of Insurance

You buy health insurance to cover large medical expenses, disability insurance to replace your income in the event of a long-term disability, and perhaps life insurance to provide money to those dependent on your income in the event of your death. Many people buy all the right kinds of personal insurance, spending a small fortune over the course of their lives in the process. Yet they overlook the obvious, virtually free protection: taking care of themselves.

If you work all day at a desk and use many of life's modern conveniences, you could end up being the Great American Couch Potato. Odds are that you've heard of most of these forms of "life insurance," but if you're still on the couch, it apparently didn't sink in.

So, for you sofa spuds, I review these seven healthful tips:

- ✔ Don't smoke.
- ✔ Drink alcohol in moderation, if you are going to drink at all.
- ✔ Get plenty of rest.
- ✔ Exercise regularly.
- ✔ Eat healthfully (refer to Chapter 6 for diet tips that improve your health and save you money).
- ✔ Get regular health care checkups to detect medical, dental, and vision problems.
- ✔ Take time to smell the roses.

Chapter 18

Insuring Your Assets

● ●

In This Chapter

▶ Homeowner's/renter's insurance

▶ Automobile insurance

▶ Planning your estate

● ●

*I*n Chapter 17, I discuss the importance of protecting your future income from the possibilities of death, disability, or large, unexpected medical expenses. But you also need to insure major assets that you have acquired in the past: your home, your car, your personal property.

You need to protect some of these assets for two reasons:

✔ **Your assets are valuable.** If you were to suffer a loss, replacing the assets with money out of your own pocket could be a financial catastrophe.

✔ **For liability purposes.** This reason is less well-known. If someone were injured or killed in your home or because of your car, a lawsuit could be even more financially devastating than an outright loss of the offending asset.

Homeowner's/Renter's Insurance

When you buy a home, most lenders require that you purchase homeowner's insurance. But even if they don't, you are wise to do so because your home and the personal property within it are worth a great deal and would cost a bundle to replace.

As a renter, damage to the building in which you live is not your financial concern, but you still have personal property that you may want to protect. And there's also the possibility, albeit remote, that you could be sued by someone who is injured in your apartment.

When shopping for a homeowner's or renter's policy, you should consider the important features that I cover in this section.

Dwelling coverage: the cost to rebuild

Neither the purchase price nor the size of your mortgage has anything to do with how much *dwelling coverage* you need. Ask yourself how much you would have to spend to *rebuild* your home if you lost it completely in a fire, an attack of locusts, or whatever. The cost to rebuild should be based on the size (square footage) of your home.

If you're a renter, rejoice that you don't need this coverage. If you're a condominium owner, check whether the coverage that the condo association has bought for the entire building is sufficient.

Be sure that your homeowner's policy includes a *guaranteed replacement cost* provision. This nifty little feature ensures that the insurance company will rebuild the home even if the cost of construction is more than the policy coverage. If the insurance company underestimates your dwelling coverage, then *it* has to make up the difference.

Just to make your life more complicated, insurers define guaranteed replacement cost differently. Some companies pay for the full replacement cost of the home, no matter how much it ends up costing. Other insurers set limits. For example, the company may only pay up to 25 percent more than the dwelling coverage on your policy. Ask your insurer how it defines guaranteed replacement cost.

If you have an older property that has many costly-to-replace features that do not meet building codes, consider buying a rider that pays for code upgrades. This covers the cost of rebuilding your home to comply with building codes that are more stringent today than when your home was built. Ask your insurance company what your basic policy covers and what it doesn't cover. Some companies include a certain amount (for example, 10 percent of your dwelling coverage) for code upgrades in the base policy.

Personal property coverage

On a homeowner's policy, the amount of personal property coverage is typically derived from the amount of dwelling coverage you carry. Generally, you get personal property coverage of 50 to 75 percent of the dwelling coverage. This is usually more than enough.

I am not a fan of riders that you can buy to cover jewelry, computers, furs, and other somewhat costly items that may not be fully covered by typical homeowners policies. Ask yourself if your out-of-pocket expense from the loss of such items would constitute a financial catastrophe. Unless you have tens of thousands of dollars worth of jewelry or computer equipment, for example, I'd skip such riders.

Some policies come with *replacement cost guarantees,* which pay you for the cost to replace an item. This payment can be considerably more than what a used item was worth before it was damaged or stolen. If this feature is not part of the standard policy sold by your insurer, you may want to purchase it as a rider, if available.

As a renter or condominium owner, you need to choose a dollar amount of the personal property that you want covered. Tally it up instead of guessing — the total cost of replacing all of your personal property may surprise you.

Make a list — or even better, take pictures or make a video — of your belongings with an estimate of what they're worth. Keep this list updated; you need it if you have to file a claim. Keeping receipts for major purchases may also help your case. No matter how you document your belongings, don't forget to keep the documentation somewhere besides your home — otherwise, it could be destroyed along with the rest of your house in a fire or other disaster.

Liability insurance

Liability insurance protects you financially against lawsuits arising from bad things that happen to others on your property. At a minimum, you want enough insurance to cover your financial assets — covering two times your assets is better. Buying extra coverage is inexpensive and well worth the cost.

The probabilities of being sued are low, but if you *are* sued and lose, you could owe big bucks. If you have substantial assets to protect, you might consider an umbrella or excess liability policy (which I discuss later in this chapter).

Liability protection is one of the side benefits of purchasing a renter's policy — you protect your personal property as well as insure against lawsuits. (But don't be reckless with your banana peels now that you have liability insurance!)

Flood and earthquake insurance

As I discuss in Chapter 16, you want to purchase the broadest possible coverage when buying any type of insurance. The problem with homeowner's insurance is that it is not broad enough — it doesn't typically cover losses due to earthquakes and floods. You must buy such disaster coverage piecemeal.

If an earthquake or flood strikes your area and your home is destroyed, you would be out tens, if not hundreds, of thousands of dollars without proper coverage. Yet, many people don't carry these important coverages, often due to misconceptions:

✔ **"Not in my neighborhood."** Many people mistakenly believe that earthquakes occur only in California. I wish this were true for those of you who live in the other 49 states, but it's not. In fact, one of the strongest earthquakes in the last century happened in the Midwest, and known (though not very active) fault lines lie along the East coast. The cost of earthquake coverage is based on insurance companies' assessment of the risk of your area and property type, so you shouldn't decide whether to buy insurance based on how small you think the risk is. The risk is already built into the price.

An estimated 20,000 communities around the country face potential flood damage. Like earthquakes, floods are not a covered risk in standard homeowner's policies, so you need to purchase a flood insurance rider. Check with your current homeowner's insurer or with those recommended in this chapter. The federal government flood insurance program (800-638-6620) can provide background information on the types of policies available through private insurance companies.

✔ **"The government will bail me out."** Not true. The vast majority of government financial assistance is through low-interest loans. Loans, unfortunately, need to be repaid, and the money comes out of your pocket.

✔ **"In a major disaster, insurers would go bankrupt anyway."** This is highly unlikely given the reserves that insurers are required to keep and the fact that the insurance companies *reinsure* — that is, they buy insurance to back up the policies they write.

The only people who might consider not buying earthquake or flood coverage are people who have little equity in their property and who are willing to walk away from the property and the mortgage in the event of a major quake or flood. Keep in mind that doing so damages your credit report because you will have essentially defaulted on your loan.

You may be able to pay for much of the cost of earthquake or flood insurance by raising the deductibles on the main part of your homeowner's/renter's insurance and other insurance policies, such as those for autos. You can more easily afford the smaller claims, not the big ones. If you think flood or earthquake insurance is too costly, compare those costs with what you will incur to completely replace your home and personal property. Buy this insurance if you live in an area that has a chance of being affected by these catastrophes. To help keep the cost of earthquake insurance down, consider taking a 10 percent deductible. Most insurers offer deductibles of 5 or 10 percent of the cost to rebuild your home. Ten percent of the rebuilding cost is a good chunk of money. But what you want to insure against is losing the other 90 percent.

Deductibles

As I discuss in Chapter 16, you're better off with the highest deductibles you're comfortable with. You'll save on insurance premiums year after year, and you won't have to go through the hassle of filing small claims. The point of insurance is to protect against catastrophic losses, not the little losses.

Special discounts

You may qualify for special discounts. Companies and agents that sell homeowner's and renter's insurance don't always check to see if you're eligible for discounts. After all, the more you spend on policy premiums, the more money they make! If your property has a security system, if you are older, or if you have other policies with the same insurer, you may qualify for a lower rate. Don't forget to ask.

Where to buy homeowner's/renter's insurance

Each insurance company prices its homeowner's and renter's policies based on its own criteria. So the lowest-cost company for my property might not be so for yours. You have to shop around at several companies to find the best rates. The following is a list of companies that historically offer lower-cost policies for most people and that have good track records with customer satisfaction and payment of claims:

- ✔ **Allstate.** Check your local phone directory for agents who sell.
- ✔ **Erie Insurance.** Does business primarily in the Midwest and Mid-Atlantic. Check your local phone directory for agents who sell.
- ✔ **GEICO.** Call the company (800-841-3000).
- ✔ **Liberty Mutual.** Check your local phone directory for agents who sell.
- ✔ **Nationwide Mutual.** Check your local phone directory for agents who sell.
- ✔ **State Farm.** Check your local phone directory for agents who sell.
- ✔ **USAA.** Available to military officers and their family members. Call the company for specifics to see if you might qualify (800-531-8080).

Don't worry that some of these companies require you to call an 800 number for a price quote. This doesn't mean they are unreachable. This process saves you money because these insurers don't have to pay commissions to local agents hawking their policies. These companies have local claims representatives to help you if and when you do have a claim.

You may have access to more specific information for your state. Some state insurance departments, which you can locate through the state government listings in your phone book, conduct surveys of insurers' prices and tabulate complaints received.

A number of the previously named companies sell other types of insurance (for example, life insurance) that are not as competitively priced. Be sure to check out the relevant sections in this book for the best places to buy these other coverages if you need them.

Auto Insurance

Over the course of your life, you'll probably spend tens of thousands of dollars on auto insurance. Much of the money that people spend on auto insurance is wasted because their insurance money is not spent where it is most needed. In other cases, it is simply wasted. You should look for the following important features when searching for an auto insurance policy.

Bodily injury/property damage liability

As with homeowner's liability insurance, auto liability insurance provides insurance against lawsuits. Especially in a car, accidents happen. Make sure that you have enough bodily injury liability insurance to cover your assets. (Coverage of double your assets is preferable.)

If you are just beginning to accumulate assets, do not mistakenly assume that you do not need any liability protection. Many states require a minimum amount — insurers should be able to fill you in on the details for your state. Also, don't forget that your future earnings, which are an "asset," can be garnisheed in a lawsuit.

Property damage liability insurance covers damage done by your car to other people's cars and property. The amount of property damage liability coverage in an auto insurance policy is usually determined as a consequence of the bodily injury amount selected. $50,000 is a good minimum to shoot for.

Uninsured or underinsured motorist liability

If you are in an accident with another motorist and he doesn't carry his own liability protection or doesn't carry enough, *uninsured or underinsured motorist liability coverage* allows you to collect for lost wages, medical expenses, and pain and suffering incurred in the accident.

If you already have a comprehensive major medical plan and long-term disability insurance, then uninsured or underinsured motorist liability coverage is largely redundant; you only give up the ability to collect for general pain and suffering if you drop this coverage. But note that this coverage also insures passengers in your car who may lack adequate medical and disability coverage.

To provide a death benefit to those financially dependent on you in the event of a fatal auto accident, buy term life insurance (refer to Chapter 17).

Coping with teen drivers

If you have a teenage driver in your household, in addition to worrying a lot more, you are going to be spending a lot more on auto insurance. Try to keep your teenager out of your car as long as possible: It's the best advice I can offer.

If you're foolish enough to allow your teenager to drive (just kidding), you can take a number of steps to keep from spending all of your take-home pay on auto insurance bills. First, if you have more than one car in your household, don't let your teenager drive the more expensive one(s).

Second, make sure that your teen does well in school. Some insurers offer discounts if your child is a high-academic achiever and has successfully completed a nonrequired driver's education class.

And finally, have your teenager share in the costs of using the car. If you pay all the insurance, gas, oil changing, and maintenance bills, your teenager won't value the privilege of using your "free" car.

Deductibles

To keep your auto insurance premiums down and to eliminate the need to file small claims, take the highest deductibles you are comfortable with (most people should consider $500 to $1,000). On an auto policy, two deductibles exist: *Collision* and *Comprehensive*. Collision applies to claims arising from collisions (note that you can bypass collision coverage when you rent a car if you have collision coverage on your own policy). Comprehensive applies to other claims for damages not caused by collision (for example, a window broken by vandals).

As your car ages and is worth less, you can eventually eliminate your comprehensive and collision coverages altogether. The point at which you do this is up to you. Remember that the purpose of insurance is to compensate you for losses that are financially catastrophic to you. For some people, this amount may be as high as $5,000 or more — others would choose $1,000 as their threshold point. But most insurance companies won't pay more than the book value of your car, regardless of what it costs to repair or replace it.

Special discounts

You may be eligible for special discounts on auto insurance. Don't forget to tell your agent or insurer if your car has a security alarm, air bags, or antilock brakes. If you're older or have other policies or cars insured with the same insurer, you may also qualify for discounts. And make sure that you're being given appropriate "good driver" discounts if you've been accident- and ticket-free in recent years.

And here's another idea. *Before* you buy your next car, call your insurer and ask for insurance quotes for the different models that you're considering. The cost of insuring a car should factor into your decision as to which car you buy because the insurance costs will be a major portion of your car's ongoing operating expenses. And different insurers have differing pricing systems for particular car models.

Little stuff coverage to skip

Auto insurers have dreamed up all sorts of riders, such as towing and rental car reimbursement, that cover small-dollar items that usually aren't worth insuring. On the surface, these riders appear to be inexpensive. But the riders are expensive given the little that you'd collect from a claim plus the hassle of filing.

Riders that waive the deductible under certain circumstances make no sense, either. The point of the deductible is to reduce your policy cost and the hassle of filing small claims. *Medical payments coverage* typically pays a few thousand dollars for medical expenses. If you and your passengers carry major medical insurance coverage, this rider isn't really necessary. Besides, a few thousand dollars of medical coverage doesn't protect you against catastrophic expenses.

Overlooked auto insurance: safe driving

A gunman walks into a fast food restaurant and murders several people waiting in line. A pipe bomb explodes in a crowded park and kills a person. An airplane crashes into the sea and a couple hundred people die.

Such tragic events are well-covered by our media, but the number of deaths that make the front pages of our newspapers pales in comparison to the approximately 40,000 people who die on America's roads every year.

I am not arguing that our national media should start reporting every automobile fatality. Even 24 hours of daily CNN coverage could probably not keep up with all the accidents on our roads. But the real story with auto fatalities lies not in the who, what, and where of specific accidents; the real story with auto fatalities is in the why. When

we ask that question, we see how many of them are preventable.

No matter what kind of car you drive, you can and should drive safely. Stay within the speed limits and don't drive while intoxicated, tired, or in adverse weather conditions. And wear your seat belt! A U.S. Department of Transportation study found that 60 percent of auto passengers killed were not wearing their seat belts.

You can also greatly reduce your risk of dying in an accident by driving a safe car. You don't need to spend buckets of money to get a car with airbags; reinforced sides, and front and rear-impact resistance; and good visibility. *Consumer Reports'* annual auto buying guide has lots of good information on individual car model safety.

Where to buy auto insurance

You can use the same list presented earlier in this chapter for homeowner's insurers to obtain quotes for auto insurance. In addition, if you live in the great state of California, consider checking with Mercury Insurance (check your local phone directory for agents who sell).

Umbrella Insurance

Umbrella or excess liability insurance is additional liability insurance that is added on top of the liability protection on your home and car(s). If you are fairly affluent and have, for example, $700,000 in assets, you can buy a one-million-dollar umbrella liability policy for around $200 per year to add to the $300,000 liability that you have on your home and car. This is a small cost for big protection. Each year, thousands of people suffer lawsuits of more than one million dollars related to their cars and homes.

Umbrella or excess liability insurance is generally sold in increments of one million dollars. So how do you decide how much you need if you have a lot of assets? As I've said with other insurance coverages, you should have at least enough liability insurance to protect your assets and preferably enough to cover twice the value of those assets.

Purchasing umbrella or excess liability insurance through your existing homeowner's or auto insurance company is usually necessary.

Investment insurance

Insurance companies do not sell policies that protect the value of your investments. But you can shield your portfolio from many of the dangers of a fickle market. It's called diversification.

If all of your money is invested in bank accounts or bonds, you're exposed to the risks of inflation, which can erode the purchasing power of your money. Conversely, if the bulk of your money is invested in one high risk stock, your financial future could go up in smoke if that stock explodes.

Chapter 10 discusses the benefits of diversification and how to choose investments that do well under different conditions. Chapter 11 discusses how mutual funds are powerful investment vehicles that make diversification easy and cost-effective.

Estate Planning

Estate planning is the process of preparing what is to happen to your assets after you die. Thinking about this in the context of insurance may seem a bit odd. But the time and cost of various estate-planning maneuvers is really nothing more than buying insurance: You are insuring that, after you die, everything will be taken care of as you wish and that taxes will be minimized. Thinking about it in this way can help you to better evaluate whether or not certain options make sense at particular points in your life.

Depending upon your circumstances, you may eventually want to contact an attorney who specializes in estate-planning matters. However, educating yourself first about the different options is worth a little bit of your time. More than a few attorneys have their own agendas (increased fees) about what you should do, so be careful. And most of the estate-planning strategies that you're likely to benefit from do not require hiring an attorney.

Wills, living wills, and medical powers of attorney

If you have children who are minors (dependent), a *will* is a necessity: A will names the guardian to whom you entrust your children if both you and your spouse die. If you and your spouse both die without a will (called *intestate*), the state (courts and social-service agencies) decides who will raise your children. Therefore, even if you cannot decide at this time who would raise your children, you should *at least* appoint a trusted guardian who could decide for you.

If you don't have kids, a will still makes good sense: It gives instructions on how to handle and distribute all your worldly possessions. If you die without a will, your state decides how to distribute your money and other property, according to state law. Therefore, your friends, more-distant relatives, and favorite charities will probably receive nothing. If you have no living relatives, your money could go to the state government!

And without a will, your heirs are legally powerless, and the state may appoint an administrator to supervise the distribution of your assets at a fee of around 5 percent of your estate. A bond typically must also be posted at a cost of several hundred dollars.

Living wills and a medical power of attorney are useful additions to a standard will. A *living will* tells your doctor what, if any, life-support measures you would accept or would not accept. A *medical power of attorney* grants authority to someone you trust to make decisions with a physician regarding your medical care options.

The simplest and least costly way to prepare a will, a living will, and a medical power of attorney is to use one of the high-quality, user-friendly software packages that I recommend in Chapter 21. Be sure to give copies of these documents to the guardians and executors named in the documents.

You don't need an attorney to make a legal will. Most attorneys, in fact, prepare wills and living trusts using software packages! What makes a will *valid* is that it is witnessed by three people.

If doing it all yourself seems overwhelming, another option (besides hiring an attorney) is to use a paralegal typing service to help you prepare the documents. The National Association for Independent Paralegals (707-935-7951) can provide you with some names of paralegals in your area. These services generally charge 50 percent or less of what an attorney charges.

Probate and living trusts

Because of our quirky legal system, even if you have a will, some or all of your assets must go through a court process known as probate. *Probate* is the legal process for administering and implementing the directions in a will. Property and assets that are owned in joint tenancy or inside retirement accounts, such as IRAs or 401(k)s, generally pass to heirs without having to go through probate. Most other assets pass through probate.

A *living trust* effectively transfers assets into a trust. You control those assets and can revoke the trust whenever you desire. The advantage of a living trust is that upon your death, assets can pass directly to your beneficiaries without going through probate. Probate can be a lengthy, expensive hassle for your heirs — with legal fees tallying around 5 to 7 percent of the value of the estate. In addition, your assets become a matter of public record as a result of probate.

Living trusts are likely to be of greatest value to people who meet the following criteria:

- ✔ Age 60 and older
- ✔ Single
- ✔ Assets worth more than $100,000 that must pass through probate (including real estate, nonretirement accounts, and small business)

As with a will, you do *not* need an attorney to establish a legal and valid living trust. (See the software recommendations in Chapter 21 and consider paralegal services that I mention in the previous section on wills.) Attorney fees to establish a living trust can range from $700 to $2,000. A competent attorney who charges reasonable fees is of greatest value to people with large estates (greater than $600,000) who do not have the time, desire, and expertise to maximize the value derived from estate planning.

Note: Living trusts keep assets out of probate but have nothing to do with minimizing estate or inheritance taxes.

Estate planning to minimize estate taxes

Under current tax laws, an individual can pass $600,000 to beneficiaries without federal estate taxes. Whether or not you will have an estate tax "problem" is dependent on several issues.

First and most important is how much of your assets you will use up during your life. This depends on how much your assets grow over time, as well as how rapidly you spend money. During retirement, you will (hopefully) be spending your money.

 I've seen too many affluent individuals worrying about estate taxes on their money throughout their retirements. If your intention is to leave your money to your children, grandchildren, or a charity, why not start giving while you're still alive so that you can enjoy the act? You can give $10,000 annually to each of your beneficiaries, *tax-free.* By giving away money, you reduce your estate and, therefore, the estate taxes owed on it.

In addition to gifting, a number of trusts allow you to minimize estate taxes. For example, if you're married, both you and your spouse can each pass on up to $600,000 to your heirs (for a total of $1,200,000), free of federal estate taxes. This can be accomplished by your each establishing a *bypass trust.* Upon the death of the first spouse, assets held in his or her name would go into the bypass trust, which effectively removes those assets from the remaining spouses' taxable estate.

Buying cash value life insurance is another estate planning tool but one which, unfortunately, is overused. People who sell cash value insurance — that is, insurance salespeople and others masquerading as financial planners — too often advocate life insurance as the one and only way to reduce estate taxes. Most other methods are superior in most cases because they don't require wasting money on life insurance.

Small-business owners whose businesses are worth one million dollars or more may want to consider cash value life insurance under specialized circumstances. If you lack the necessary additional assets to pay expected estate taxes and you don't want your beneficiaries to be forced to sell the business, you can buy cash value life insurance to pay expected estate taxes.

If you want to learn more about how to reduce your estate (and other) taxes, pick up a copy of *Taxes For Dummies* (IDG Books Worldwide, Inc.).

Part V
The Part of Tens

The 5th Wave — By Rich Tennant

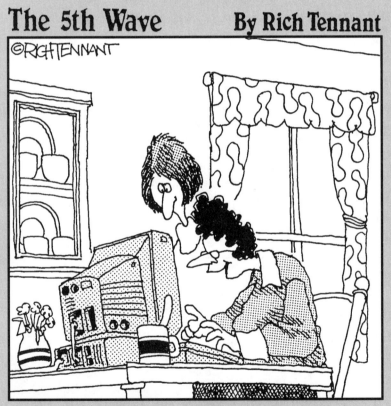

"IT'S REALLY QUITE AN ENTERTAINING PIECE OF SOFTWARE. THERE'S ROLLER COASTER ACTION, SUSPENSE AND DRAMA, WHERE SKILL AND STRATEGY ARE MATCHED AGAINST WINNING AND LOSING. AND I THOUGHT MANAGING OUR BUDGET WOULD BE DULL."

In this part . . .

Y ou encounter what might be called a diverse and valuable hodge-podge. Here you'll find the choicest information, ranging from financial strategies for ten life changes to the best financial software packages. Here you'll also find the all-important "Ten Questions to Ask Financial Advisers Before You Hire Them," which may save you a lot of heartache and money.

Why "tens"? Why not?

Chapter 19

Ten Questions to Ask Financial Advisors
Before You Hire Them

....

Don't consider hiring a financial advisor until you have read the rest of this book. If you're not educated about personal finance, how can you possibly evaluate the competence of someone you might hire to help you make important financial decisions?

I firmly believe that you are your own best financial advisor. However, I know that some people don't want to make financial decisions without getting assistance. Perhaps you're busy, or you simply can't stand making money decisions.

But recognize that when you hire a financial advisor, you have a lot at stake. Besides the cost of his services, which generally don't come cheaply, you're placing a lot of trust in the advisor's recommendations. The more you know, the better the advisor you'll end up working with and the fewer services you'll need to buy.

These ten questions get to the core of an advisor's competence and professional integrity. Get answers to these questions *before* you decide to hire a financial advisor.

What percentage of your income comes from fees paid by your clients versus commissions from the products that you sell?

Asking this question first may save you the trouble and time of asking the next nine. The right answer is, "100 percent of my income comes from fees paid by clients." Anything less than 100 percent means the person you're speaking with is a salesperson with a vested interest in recommending certain strategies and product purchases.

Sadly, more than a few "financial advisors" don't tell the truth. In an undercover investigation done by *Money* magazine, nearly a third of advisors who claimed they were fee-only turned out to be brokers who sold investment and insurance products on a commission-basis. How can you ferret these people out?

All advisors who provide investment advice must register with the U.S. Securities and Exchange Commission (SEC). They must file Form ADV, otherwise known as the Uniform Application for Investment Advisor Registration. This lengthy document asks for very specific information from investment advisors, such as

- A breakdown of where their income comes from
- Relationships and affiliations with other companies
- Each advisor's educational and employment history
- The types of securities the firm recommends
- The firm's fee schedule

In short, Form ADV provides — in black and white — answers to all the questions. In a pitch over the phone or in marketing materials sent in the mail, a planner is much more likely to gloss over or avoid certain issues. Although an advisor can lie to the SEC on Form ADV (it has happened on numerous occasions), an advisor will likely be more truthful on this form than in her own marketing to you.

You can ask the advisor to send you a copy of the Form ADV. You can also check to see that the advisor is registered and whether he or she has a track record of problems by calling the SEC at 800-732-0330 (or write them at 450 Fifth St. NW, Washington, D.C. 20549). You might also check with the department in your state that oversees investment advisors (all states have one except Colorado, Iowa, Ohio, and Wyoming).

What percentage of fees paid by your clients are for ongoing money management versus hourly financial planning?

The answer to how the advisor is paid provides a big clue as to whether the planner has an agenda to convince you to hire him to manage your money. If what you want are objective and specific financial planning recommendations, you should seek advisors who derive their income from hourly fees. Many counselors and advisors call themselves "fee-based," which usually means they make their living managing money for a percentage.

Some advisors do not tell you the truth. Reviewing the advisor's Form ADV generally helps you get closer to the truth. Also be aware that some advisors have been known to operate two separate companies. One company claims to give advice on a fee-basis. However, the other (generally hidden) company sells products or manages money.

If you want a money manager, you can hire the best quite inexpensively through a mutual fund or, if you have substantial assets, you can hire an established money manager (refer to Chapter 11).

What is your hourly fee?

Rates, as with legal and tax advisors, vary all over the map. I've seen and heard of fees as low as $50 per hour all the way to several hundred dollars per hour. If you shop around, you can find terrific planners who charge around $100 per hour and who work faster than a snail's pace.

Because good planners spend a reasonable portion of their time researching and running their business, don't assume they're getting rich at your expense at this rate. Running a business is costly, but you shouldn't pay hundreds of dollars per hour unless you're wealthy and want an advisor who works only with people like you. Also, be aware that a number of planners who manage money or sell products charge very high hourly rates because they don't really want to work with people on an hourly fee basis.

Do you also perform tax or legal services?

Be wary of someone who claims to be an expert beyond one area. The tax, legal, and financial fields are vast in and of themselves and are difficult for even the best and brightest advisor to cover simultaneously. One exception is the accountant who also performs some basic financial planning by the hour. Likewise, a good financial advisor should have a good grounding in tax and legal issues that relate to your personal finances. Larger firms may have specialists available in different areas.

What work and educational experience qualifies you to be a financial planner?

There's no one right answer here. Ideally, a planner should have experience in the business or financial services field. Some say to look for planners with at least five or ten years experience. I've always wondered how planners earn a living their first five or ten years if folks won't hire them until they reach these benchmarks?! A good planner should also be good with numbers, speak in plain English, and have good interpersonal skills.

Education is sort of like food. Too little leaves you hungry. Too much might leave you feeling stuffed and uncomfortable. And less of high quality is better than a lot of low quality.

Don't place too much value on the CFP (certified financial planner) degree. Most advisors with this "credential," which can be earned by taking a self-study course at home, sell investment products.

Because investing decisions are a critical part of financial planning, take note of the fact that the most common designations of educational training among professional money managers are MBA (master of business administration) and CFA (chartered financial analyst). And some tax advisors who work on an hourly basis have earned the "Personal Financial Specialist" credential. Refer to Chapter 3 for a complete explanation of the financial planning industry.

Have you ever sold limited partnerships? Options? Futures? Commodities?

The correct answers here are *no, no, no, no.* If you don't know what these disasters are, refer to Chapter 10. Also, be wary of any financial advisor who once dealt in these areas but claims to have seen the light and reformed his ways.

Professionals with poor judgment may not repeat the same mistakes, but they're more likely to make some new ones at your expense. My experience is that even advisors who have "reformed" are unlikely to be working by the hour. Most work on commission or want to manage your money for a hefty fee.

Do you carry liability insurance?

You wouldn't (or shouldn't) let contractors into your home to do work without knowing they have insurance to cover any mistakes they make should they cause your home to look like the one in the movie *The Money Pit.* Likewise, you should insist on hiring a planner who carries protection in case she makes a major mistake for which she is liable. Make sure that she carries enough coverage given what she is helping you with.

Some counselors may be surprised by this question or may think you're a problem customer looking for a lawsuit. On the other hand, accidents happen; that's why insurance exists. So if the planner doesn't have liability insurance, she missed one of the fundamental concepts of planning: Insure against risk. Don't you make the same mistake by hiring her.

Can you provide references of clients with needs similar to mine?

Take the time to ask other people who have used the planner what the planner did for them. Inquire what the advisor's greatest strengths and weaknesses are. You can learn a bit about the planner's track record as well as style. And because you want to have as productive a relationship as possible with your planner, the more you learn about the planner, the easier it will be for you to hit the ground running if you hire him.

Some financial advisors offer a "free" introductory consultation. If this is offered to allow you to check out the advisor and it makes you feel more comfortable about hiring that planner, fair enough. But be careful: most "free" consultations are offered by planners who work on commission or who will try to sell you ongoing money management services. So the "free" consultation ends up being a big sales pitch for certain products or services offered through the advisor.

The fact that a planner doesn't offer a "free" consultation may be a good sign. Counselors who work strictly by the hour and are busy can't afford to burn an hour of their time for an in-person "free" session. They also need to be careful of folks seeking "free" advice. Such advisors usually are willing to spend some time on the phone answering background questions. They should also be able to send background materials by mail and provide references if you ask.

Will you provide specific strategies and product recommendations that I can implement on my own if I choose?

This is an important question. Some advisors may indicate that you can hire them by the hour. But then they provide only generic advice without many specifics. Even worse is the troubling trend among planners who *double dip* — they charge an hourly fee to make you feel like you're not working with a salesperson. Then they try selling commission-based products. Also be aware that some advisors say you can choose to implement their recommendations on your own, but then recommend financial products that carry commissions.

How is implementation handled?

Ideally, find an advisor who lets you choose whether or not you can hire him to help with implementation after the recommendations have been presented to you. If you know that you will follow through on the advice and can do so without further discussions and questions, don't buy the planner's time to implement.

On the other hand, if you hired the counselor in the first place because you lack the time, desire, and/or expertise to manage your financial life, building implementation into the planning work makes good sense. If you're the type of person who needs to tie a string around a finger to remember to do something but then forgets why the string is there, pay for the necessary hand-holding.

Chapter 20

Eric's Tips for Ten Life Changes

M any of life's changes come unexpectedly, like earthquakes. Others we can see coming when they are still far off on the horizon, like a big storm moving in off the ocean.

Ideally it shouldn't matter. Whether a life change is predictable or not, our ability to navigate successfully through its challenges and to adjust quickly to its new circumstances depends largely on our degree of preparedness.

Perhaps you find my comparison of life changes to earthquakes and storms to be a bit negative. After all, some of the changes I discuss in this chapter should be occasions for joy, and here I am comparing them to natural disasters. But realize that what one defines as a "disaster" has everything to do with his or her preparedness. To the person who has stored no emergency rations in his basement, the big snow storm that has trapped him in his home could mean a disaster. But to the prepared person with plenty of food and water, that same storm could mean a vacation from work and a relaxing week in the midst of a winter wonderland.

Before I discuss critical financial issues for you to deal with before and during major life changes, here are some general tips that apply to all life changes:

- ✔ **Stay in financial shape.** An athlete is best able to withstand physical adversities during competition by training and eating well. Likewise, the more sound your finances are to begin with, the better able you'll be to deal with life changes.

- ✔ **Changes requires change.** Even if your financial house is in order, a major life change — birth of a child, buying a home, starting a business, getting a divorce, retiring — should prompt you to review your personal financial strategies. Why? Because life changes often affect your income, spending, need for insurance, and ability to accept financial risk.

- ✔ **Make changes sooner rather than later.** Being human, most of us procrastinate. But with a major life change on the horizon, procrastination could be costly. You (and your family) might overspend and accumulate high-cost debts, lack proper insurance coverage, or take other unnecessary risks. Early preparation can save you from these pitfalls.

✔ **Control stress and your emotions.** Life changes often are accompanied by stress and other emotional upheavals. Not only taking action but also doing so fully informed is vital during this period. Educating yourself is key, and you may want to hire experts to help (refer to Chapter 3). Avoid hiring advisors at this time if you can. Abdicating decisions and responsibilities to advisors can be dangerous; the advisors may not have your best interests at heart, and they can't fully understand and appreciate your needs as well as you can.

Here, then, are the major life changes that you may have to deal with at some point in your life. I hope and wish you more of the good changes than the bad.

Starting Out: Your First Job

If you've just graduated from college or some other program, or are otherwise entering the workforce, your increased income and reduction in educational expenses is usually a welcome relief. You would think then that more young adults wouldn't have financial trouble and challenges. But they do, largely because of poor financial habits picked up at home or from the world at large. Here's how to get on the path to financial success:

✔ **Don't abuse credit.** The use and abuse of credit can cause financial pain and hardship well into adult life. You'd like furniture, a new television, and lots of fun vacations: All these things cost money. To get off on the right financial foot, young workers should not get in the habit of making purchases on credit cards that they can't pay for in full when the bill arrives in the mail. The simple solution if you overspend and run up outstanding credit card balances: don't carry a credit card. Cash and checks worked fine for decades before credit cards arrived on the scene. If you need the convenience of making purchases with a piece of plastic instead of cash or checks, get a debit card (refer to Chapter 5).

✔ **Get in the saving and investing habit.** If you hope to someday own a home and cease full-time work, you'll need to save over many years. Thinking about a home purchase or retirement is usually not in the active thought patterns of first time job seekers. I'm often asked, "At what age should a person start saving?" To me, that's similar to asking at what age you start brushing your teeth. Well, when you have teeth to brush! So I say, you should start saving and investing money from your first paycheck. Try starting to save 5 percent and then eventually 10 percent of every paycheck. If you're having trouble saving money, track your spending and make cutbacks as needed (refer to Chapters 4 and 6).

Ideally, your savings should be directed into retirement accounts (refer to Chapter 8) that offer tax benefits. You might also want to accumulate down payment money for purchase of a home.

✔ **Get insured.** Many people starting out are able to rationalize themselves out of buying insurance. When you're young and healthy, it's hard to imagine life otherwise. Many twentysomethings give little thought to the potential for health care expenses. But because accidents and unexpected illnesses can strike at any age, forgoing coverage can be financially devastating. Buying disability coverage, which replaces income lost to a long-term disability, in a first full-time job with more limited benefits is wise as well. And as you begin to build your assets, consider making out a will to insure that your assets go where you want in the event of your death.

✔ **Continue your education.** Once you're out in the work force, you (like many other people) may realize how little you've learned in formal schooling that can be used in the real world and, conversely, how much you need to learn (like personal financial management) that school never taught you. Read, learn, and continue to grow. Continuing education will help you with your career and to enjoy the world around you.

Changing Jobs or Careers

During your adult life, you will almost surely change jobs — perhaps as often as several times a decade. I hope that most of the time you'll be changing by your own choice. But let's face it: Job security is not what it use to be. Corporate downsizing has made victims of even the most talented workers.

Always be prepared for a job change. No matter how happy you are in your current job, knowing that your world won't fall apart if you are not working tomorrow will give you an added sense of security and encourage an openness to possibility. Whether it's a job change by choice or necessity, the following financial maneuvers will ease the transition:

✔ **Structure your finances to afford an income dip.** Spending less than you earn always makes good financial sense, but if you're coming up to a possible job change, this is even more important, particularly if you are entering a new field or starting your own company and you expect a short-term income dip. Many people view a lifestyle of thriftiness as restrictive, but ultimately those thrifty habits can give you *more* freedom to do what you want to do. Be sure to keep your emergency reserve fund always full (refer to Chapter 8).

✔ **If you're relocating, evaluate the total financial picture.** At some point in your career, you may have the option of relocating. But, don't call the moving company until you understand the financial consequences of such a move. You can't simply compare salaries and benefits between the two jobs. Also compare the cost of living between the two areas: that includes housing, commuting, state income and property taxes, food, utilities, and all the other major expenditure categories that I discuss in Chapter 4.

If you lose your job, batten down the hatches. Normally, when you lose your job through no choice of your own, you get little advance warning. That does not mean, however, that you can't do anything financially. Evaluating and slashing your current level of spending may be necessary. Everything should be fair game, from how much you spend on housing to how often you eat out to where you do your grocery shopping. Avoid at all costs the temptation to maintain your level of spending by accumulating consumer debt.

✔ **Track your job search expenses for tax purposes.** If you are looking around for a new job in your current (or recently current) field of work, your job search expenses are tax-deductible. For example, if you are a black-jack dealer in Las Vegas but are looking to work the craps tables in Reno, then keep all the receipts for those craps table training classes, the phone calls to the Reno casinos, the printing and mailing of resumes, and the travel costs for your big interview at Harrah's. Even if you don't get the job, you can deduct all those expenses.

Remember, however, if you are moving into a new career, your job search expenses are not tax-deductible. If you're tired of the Las Vegas glitter and are thinking, for some silly reason, about moving to New York City and becoming a commodities trader, you won't get any tax breaks. You may think that you haven't left the gambling profession, but the IRS looks at that as a career change.

Getting Married

If you're ready to tie the knot with the one you love, congratulations! I hope that you'll have a long, healthy, and happy life together. In addition to the emotional and moral commitments that you and your spouse make to one another, you'll probably be merging many of your financial decisions and resources. It would be highly unusual that you and your spouse have identical money personalities; after all, opposites often attract. Even if you are in complete agreement about your financial goals and strategies, managing as two is different than one.

✔ **Take a compatibility test.** Because so many marriages end in failure and some that stay together probably shouldn't, a good way to minimize your chances for heartache is to ensure you know what you're getting yourself into. Too many couples never discuss their goals and plans before marriage; failing to do so breaks up way too many of these marriages. Finances are just one of many issues to discuss: others include expectations for having and raising children, dealing with in-laws, career goals, and so on. Ministers, priests, and rabbis sometimes offer premarital counseling to surface issues and differences. Don't let the euphoria of short-term romance blind you to important issues vital to the long-term health of your marriage.

✔ **Consider taxes.** Some couples are depressed to learn that their joint income tax bill will be higher, perhaps significantly higher, once married. More than a few couples actually allow their joint tax burdens to influence when and even if they marry. You're more likely to be hit with a higher combined tax bill when married if both you and your partner earn above average incomes and/or are high-income earners. The only way to know what will happen to your tax bill is to get out a tax return and plug in the relevant numbers and see what the IRS will do to you after you're married. If you're flexible in terms of the timing of your wedding and a late-in-the-year wedding will cause you to pay much more in taxes, consider waiting until early the following year.

✔ **Discuss and set joint goals.** Once you are married, you and your spouse should set aside time once a year or every few years to discuss personal and financial goals for the years ahead. If for no other reason, talking about where you want to go will ensure that you're not rowing your financial boat in opposite directions.

✔ **Separate but equal or jointly managed?** Some couples choose to keep separate financial accounts, whereas others pool resources. Philosophically, I like the idea of pooling better. After all, marriage is a partnership and shouldn't be a "his" versus "hers" affair. In some marriages, however, spouses choose to keep some money separate, particularly for spending purposes so that they don't feel the scrutiny of a spouse with different spending preferences. Spouses who have been through divorce(s) may choose to keep the assets they bring into the new marriage separate in order to earmark and protect their assets in the event they divorce again. As long as you're jointly accomplishing what you need to, some separation of money is okay. But for the health of your marriage, don't hide money from one another, and, if you're the higher-income spouse, don't try to assume power and control over your joint income.

✔ **Coordinate and maximize employer benefits.** If one or both of you have access to a package of employee benefits through an employer, both of you should understand how best to make use of those benefits. Coordinating and using the best that each package has to offer is like giving yourselves a pay raise. For example, if you both have access to health insurance, compare which of you has better benefits. Likewise, one of you may have a better retirement savings plan — one which matches and offers superior investments options. Unless you can afford to save the maximum through both your plans, saving more in the better plan will increase your combined assets. (**Note:** if you're concerned about what happens if you save more in one of your retirement plans and then divorce, in most states that money is considered part of your joint assets and can be divided equally.)

✔ **Discuss life and disability insurance needs.** If you and your spouse can make do without each other's income, you might not need any income protecting insurance. However, if, like many husbands and wives, both spouses depend upon each other's incomes, or if one spouse depends fully or partly on the other's income, you might each need to have long-term disability and term life insurance policies (refer to Chapter 17).

✔ **Update your wills.** When you marry, you should update your wills. If you haven't gotten around to making a will, having a will is potentially more valuable when you're married, especially if you want to leave money to others in addition to your spouse, or if you have children for whom you should name a guardian. Refer to Chapter 17 for more information on wills.

✔ **Reconsider beneficiaries on investment and life insurance.** With retirement accounts and life insurance policies, you name beneficiaries to whom the money or value in those accounts will go in the event of your passing. When you marry, you will probably want to rethink those beneficiaries.

Starting a Small Business

Many people aspire to be their own bosses, but far fewer people actually leave their jobs in order to achieve that dream. Psychologically and financially, giving up the apparent security of a job with benefits and a built-in network of co-workers is difficult for most people. Going into small business is not for everyone, but don't let inertia be the pin that deflates your dream. Here are some tips to help get you started and increase your chances for long-term success:

✔ **Prepare to ditch your job.** If you spend all or nearly all that you earn while employed and haven't banked a war chest, you're going to feel financially dependent on your paycheck. Many people in such a situation will never leave their jobs behind to pursue their entrepreneurial dreams. Live as spartan a lifestyle as you can while you are employed so that you maximize your ability to save money; you will simultaneously be developing thrifty habits that will help you weather the reduced income and increased expenditure period that comes with most small business start-ups. You might also consider easing into your small business if you can by working at it part-time in the beginning, with or without cutting back on your normal job.

✔ **Develop a business plan.** If you research and think through your business idea, you'll not only reduce the likelihood of your business failing and increase its success if it thrives, but you'll also feel more comfortable taking the entrepreneurial plunge. A good business plan should be a blueprint for how you expect to build the business. It should describe in detail the business idea, the marketplace you'll be competing in, your marketing plans, and expected revenue and expenses.

✔ **Replace your insurance coverage.** Before you finally decide to leave your job, set the wheels in motion to get proper insurance coverage. With health insurance, employers allow you to continue your existing coverage (at your own expense) for 18 months. Thanks to a new provision in the 1996 health care reform bill, effective July, 1, 1997, individuals with existing health problems are enabled to purchase an individual policy at the same price that a healthy individual can. With disability insurance, securing coverage before you leave your job is best so that you have income to qualify for coverage. If you have life insurance through your employer, you should secure new individual coverage as soon as you know you're going to leave your job (refer to Chapter 17 for more details).

✔ **Establish a retirement savings plan.** Once your business is up and making a profit, consider establishing a retirement savings plan such as a SEP-IRA or Keogh. As I explain in Chapter 12, such plans allow you to shelter up to 20 percent of your business income from federal and state taxation. When you're your own boss and don't have an employee benefits department to help look out for you, no one but you is going to be concerned about your financial future.

Buying a Home

Most Americans end up buying a home. To be a financial success, you need not own a home, but home ownership, if done right, certainly offers financial rewards. Over the course of your adult life, the real estate that you own should appreciate in value. Additionally, someday you should have your mortgage paid off, which will greatly reduce your housing costs. As a renter, on the other hand, your full housing costs will increase over time because of inflation.

If you're considering buying a home:

✔ **Get your overall finances in order.** Before you consider buying a home, you need to analyze your current budget, your ability to afford debt, and your future financial goals. Make sure that your expected housing expenses still allow you to save properly for retirement and other long or short-term objectives. Don't buy a home based upon what lenders are willing to lend. Read and digest the relevant portions of this book to get your financial house in order before you buy.

✔ **Determine if now's the time.** Especially if you're a first-time home buyer, buying if you don't see yourself staying put 3 to 5 years rarely makes financial sense. Buying and selling a home gobbles up a good deal of money in transaction costs — you'll be lucky to recoup all those costs even within a five year period. Also, if your income is likely to drop or you have other pressing goals, such as starting a business, you might wait to buy.

To learn more about buying a home, be sure to read Chapter 15.

Having Children

If you thought being a responsible adult, holding down a job, paying your bills on time, and preparing for your financial future was tough, wait 'til you add kids to the equation. Most parents find that, with kids in the family, the already precious commodities of time and money become even more precious — sometimes even extinct. The more efficiently you learn how to manage your time and money, the better able you will be to have a sane, happy, and financially successfully life as a parent.

Here are some key things to recognize and to do both before and after you begin your family:

- **Set your priorities: You can't do it all and have it all.** As with many other financial decisions, starting or expanding a family requires that you financially plan ahead. Set your priorities and structure your finances and living situation accordingly. Is it more important to have a bigger home in a nice community, or would you rather have less pressure to work and spend more time with your family? Keep in mind that a less hectic work life not only gives you more free time but also often reduces your cost of living by decreasing meals out, dry cleaning, day care expenses, and so on.

- **Take a hard look at your budget.** If you've had a hard time living within your means before children, then you definitely should take an honest look at how your income and spending will change after your family grows. In addition to diaper changes and less sleep at night, children mean increased spending. At a minimum, expenditures for food and clothing will increase. But you're also likely to spend more on housing, insurance, day care, and education. On top of that, if you want to play an active role in raising your children, working at a full-time job won't be possible. So while you consider the added expenses, you may also need to factor in a decrease in income.

  No simple rules of thumb exist for estimating how children will affect your household's income and expenses. On the income side, figure out how much you'll want to cut back on work. On the expense side, government statistics show that the average household with school-age children spends about 20 percent more than those without. A more scientific approach would be you for you to go through your budget category by category and estimate how kids will change your spending (use the worksheets in Chapter 4).

- **Boost insurance coverages *before* getting pregnant.** Before you try to have a baby, be sure that your health insurance plan offers maternity benefits (ask about waiting periods that may exclude coverage for a pregnancy within the first year or so of the insurance). With disability insurance, pregnancy is considered a pre-existing condition so a woman lacking such coverage should secure it before getting pregnant. And most families-to-be should buy life insurance. Buying life insurance *after* the bundle of joy comes home from the hospital is a risky proposition — if Mom or Dad develops a health problem, she or he could be denied coverage. Also consider buying life insurance for a stay-at-home parent. Even though that parent is not bringing in income, if he or she were to pass away, hiring assistance could cripple the family budget.

✔ **Check maternity leave with your employers.** Many larger employers offer some sort of maternity leave for women and, in rare but thankfully increasing cases, for men. At some employers, the leaves are paid and with others they're not. Understand the options and the financial ramifications before you consider the leave and ideally before you get pregnant. If you're concerned about damaging your career if you tell your employer that you may want such a leave, simply ask your benefits departments for the current booklets that explain all the company's benefits.

✔ **Update your will.** If you had a will before starting a family, you'll need to do a new one. If you don't have a will, make one now. With children in the picture, you must name a guardian in your will who will be responsible for raising your children should you and your spouse both pass away. Although choosing a guardian is a daunting decision, even more frightful is the thought of letting local courts decide who would raise your children.

✔ **Get the baby enrolled in your health plan.** Once he or she is welcomed into this world, get your newborn enrolled on your health insurance plan. Most insurers give you about a month or so to enroll — do so as soon as you can. New parents tend to forget to do things amidst the whirlwind of time-consuming parenting responsibilities. Also get junior a Social Security number. It comes in handy for many occasions, but you'll especially want and need it when you to file your next income tax return. Without a Social Security number, you can't claim your child as a dependent and be entitled to that nice tax break.

✔ **Understand child care tax benefits.** For every one of your children with an official Social Security number, you get a $2,550 deduction from your income taxes (tax year 1996). So if you're in the 28 percent federal tax bracket, each child saves you a cool $714 in federal taxes. That should certainly motivate you to take the two minutes to apply for your kid's Social Security number!

If you and your spouse are both working full or part time and you have children under the age of 13, you can also claim a tax credit for child care expenses. Or, you may work for one of the increasing numbers of employers who offer flexible benefit or spending plans. These plans allow you to put money away from your paycheck on a pre-tax basis, up to $5,000 per year, which you can then use to pay for child care expenses. For many parents, especially those in higher income tax brackets, these plans can save a lot of taxes. Keep in mind, however, that if you take advantage of one of these plans, you cannot also claim the child care tax credit mentioned above, and you must deplete the entire account every tax year or you forfeit any money not used.

✔ **Ignore saving in custodial accounts.** New parents often feel the weight of new responsibilities on their shoulders. One common concern is how to sock away enough money to pay for the ever rising cost of a college education. If you start saving money in your child's name in a so-called custodial account, however, you might not only be harming your child's future ability to qualify for financial aid but you might also be missing out on the tax benefits that come with investing elsewhere. Refer to Chapter 14 to learn why.

✔ **Don't indulge the children.** Toys, art classes, sports, field trips, and the like can rack up big bills, especially if not controlled. Some parents exercise little control over children's programs. Most parents don't set guidelines or limits on extracurricular activities. Many are putting their children's desires ahead of all other financial needs and goals. Others are mindlessly following the example of the family that lives next door. Introspective parents have shared with me that they feel some insecurity about providing the best for their children. The parents (and kids) that seem happiest and most financially successful are those who clearly distinguish between material luxuries and family necessities.

As children get older and become indoctrinated into the world of shopping, all sorts of other purchases come into play. Consider giving your kids a weekly allowance and letting them learn how to spend and manage it. And when they're old enough, having your kids get a part-time job helps teach financial responsibility as well.

Caring for Aging Parents

There comes a time for many of us when we reverse roles with our parents. Instead of being the one who is cared for, you become the caregiver or the caretaker. As your parents age, they may need help with a variety of issues and living tasks. Although it's unlikely that you'll have the time or ability to perform all these functions yourself, you may well end up being the coordinator of service providers who can.

Here are some things to do when caring for aging parents:

✔ **Take some time off.** Caring for an aging parent, particularly one who is having health problems, can be time consuming and emotionally draining. If you were already juggling the responsibilities of a job, marriage, and parenthood before your parents needed help, you now may well feel completely overwhelmed. Do yourself and your parents a favor and use some vacation time to help get things in order. Although not the kind of vacation you probably envisioned, the time should reduce your stress and help you get more on top of things.

✔ **Get help where possible.** In most communities, a variety of nonprofit organizations offer information and sometimes even counseling to families grappling with caring for the elderly parents. You might best find your way to such resources through your state's department of insurance as well as recommendations from local hospitals and doctors. You'll especially want to get assistance and information if your parent(s) may need some sort of home care, nursing home care, or assisted living arrangement.

✔ **Get involved in their health care.** Your aging parents may already have a lot on their minds or simply may not be able to coordinate and manage all the health care providers giving them medications and advice. Try, as best you can, to be their advocate. Speak with their doctor(s) to understand their current medical condition and need for various medications and to help coordinate care givers. Visit nursing homes and speak with prospective care providers.

✔ **Understand tax breaks.** If you are financially supporting your parents, you may be eligible for a number of tax credits and deductions for elder care. Some employer's flexible benefit plans, for example, allow you to put away money on a pre-tax basis to pay for the care of your parents. Also explore the dependent care tax credit, which you can take on your federal income tax Form 1040. And if you provide half or more of the support costs for your parent(s), you may be able to claim them as dependents on your tax return.

✔ **Discuss getting the estate in order.** Parents don't like talking and thinking about their demise and usually feel awkward discussing it with their children. But opening a dialogue between you and your folks about such issues can be healthy in many ways. Discussing wills, living wills, living trusts, and estate planning strategies (refer to Chapter 18) can not only make you aware of your folks' situation but can also improve their plans to both their benefit and yours.

Getting a Divorce

Sadly, half of all marriages end in divorce. In most marriages destined to split up, there are early warning signs that both parties recognize; sometimes, however, one spouse surprises the other with an unexpected request for divorce.

Whether planned or unexpected, here are some key things to consider when getting a divorce:

✔ **Question the divorce.** Some say that divorcing in America is too easy, and I tend to agree. Although some couples are indeed better off to part their ways, others give up too easily, thinking that the grass is greener elsewhere only to later discover that all lawns have weeds and crab grass. Just as with a lawn that isn't watered and fertilized, relationships can wither without nurturing.

Money and disagreements over money are certainly a contributing factor to marital unhappiness. Unfortunately, in many relationships, money is wielded as power by the spouse who earns more of it. Try talking things over, perhaps with a marital counselor; invest in making your relationship stronger, and reap the dividends for years to come.

✔ **Separate your emotions from the financial issues.** Separating your feelings from your finances is easier said than done, but extremely important nonetheless. Feelings of revenge may be common in some divorces but they will probably only help to ensure that the attorneys get rich at your expense as the two of you butt heads. If you really want a divorce, work at doing it efficiently and harmoniously so that you can get on with your life.

✔ **Detail resources and priorities.** Draw up a list of all the assets and liabilities that you and your spouse have. Be sure that you're getting the financial facts including investment account records and statements. Once you know the whole picture, begin to think about what is and is not important to you financially and otherwise.

✔ **Educate yourself about personal finance and legal issues.** Divorce sometimes forces nonfinancially oriented spouses to get a crash course in personal finance at a difficult emotional time. Hopefully, this book can help educate your financially. In terms of the legal issues of divorce, visit a bookstore and pick up a good legal guide or two about divorce.

✔ **Choose advisors carefully.** Odds are that you will retain the services of one or more specialists to assist you with the myriad issues, negotiations, and concerns of your divorce. Legal, tax, and financial advisors can help, but recognize their limitations and conflicts of interest. Attorneys, unfortunately, have the conflict of benefiting financially the more complicated things become and the more you haggle with your spouse. Don't use your divorce attorney for financial or tax advice — your lawyer probably knows no more than you do in these areas. Also, realize that you don't need an attorney to get divorced. As for choosing tax and financial advisors, if you think you need that type of help, refer to Chapters 7 and 19 for how to find good advisors.

✔ **Analyze your spending needs.** When you're going back to being single, while your "household" expenses will surely be less, you'll probably be making do with less income. Many divorcees find themselves financially squeezed in the early years following a divorce. In addition to helping you to adjust to a new budget, analyzing your spending needs pre-divorce will help you negotiate a fairer settlement with your spouse.

✔ **Review needed changes to insurance.** If you are covered under your spouse's employer insurance plans for any type of insurance, be sure to set the wheels in motion to get those coverages replaced (refer to Chapter 17). If you or your children will still be financially dependent upon your spouse post-divorce, be sure that the divorce agreement mandates life insurance coverage. And you should re-do your will (refer to Chapter 18).

✔ **Redo your retirement plan.** With changes to your income, expenses, assets, liabilities, and future needs, your retirement savings plan will surely need an overhaul after a divorce. Refer to Chapter 8 for a reorientation.

Receiving a Windfall

Whether through inheritance, stock options, small business success, or lottery winnings, you may receive a financial windfall at some point in your life. Like many who are totally unprepared psychologically and organizationally for their sudden good fortune, you may well find that a flood of money can create more problems than it solves. If you're saying, "I should have such problems," fair enough. Who wouldn't rather be rich than poor?

Here are a few tips to help you make your windfall the financially pleasant experience that it should be:

✔ **Take the time to educate yourself.** If you've never had to deal with significant wealth, there's no reason that I'd expect you to know how to handle it. Don't rush and pressure yourself to get it invested as soon as possible. Leaving the money where it is or stashing it in one of the higher yielding money market funds recommended in Chapter 13 is a far better short-term solution than piling into investments that you don't understand and haven't taken the time to research.

✔ **Beware the sharks.** You may begin to wonder if someone has posted your net worth, address, and home telephone number in the local newspaper and on the Internet. Brokers and financial advisors may flood you with marketing materials, telephone solicitations, and lunch date requests. Most of these folks who pursue you are doing so for a reason: They want to convert your money into their income either by selling you investment and other financial products or by managing your money. Stay away from these sharks, educate yourself, and take charge of your own financial moves. Decide on your own terms whom to hire and seek them out. Most of the best advisors that I know don't have the time or philosophical orientation to chase after prospective clients.

✔ **Recognize the emotional side of coming into a lot of money.** One of the side effects of accumulating wealth quickly is that you may have feelings of guilt or otherwise be unhappy, especially if you expected money to solve your problems. Getting a big inheritance from your folks may make you feel guilty if you didn't invest in your relationship with them and now, with their passing, you regret how you interacted with them. As another example, if you poured endless hours into a business venture that finally paid off, all that money sitting in your investment accounts may leave you with a hollow feeling if you divorced and lost friends through neglecting your relationships.

✔ **Pay down debts.** One of the simplest and best investments you can make if you come into wealth is to pay off your debts. I had a counseling client come to me who was frustrated because he didn't know how to invest several million dollars he had. Partly because he had worked so hard in his business to build his wealth, he was worried about losing money on investments. He had a decent-size home mortgage at 8 percent interest, which made complete sense for him to pay off. Money is generally borrowed to allow us to buy things that we otherwise couldn't buy in one fell swoop. When you have plenty of money at hand, getting rid of debts is an especially good move.

✔ **Diversify.** To protect your wealth, don't keep it all in one pot. Mutual funds (refer to Chapter 11) are an ideally diversified, professionally managed investment vehicle to consider. And if you want your money to continue growing, consider the wealth-building investments — stock mutual funds, real estate, and small business options — I discuss in Part III of this book.

✔ **Make use of the opportunity.** Most people spend their whole lives working for a paycheck in order to pay a never ending stream of monthly bills. Although I'm not advocating a hedonistic lifestyle, why not take some extra time to travel, spend time with your family, and do the hobbies you've long been putting off? And how about trying a new career that you'd find more fulfilling and that might make the world a better place? Most people never have the flexibility to choose how they spend their time. If you do, don't waste it.

Retiring

If you've spent the bulk of your adult life working, retiring can be a challenging life transition. Most Americans have an idealized vision of how wonderful a retired life would be. No more irritating bosses and pressure of work deadlines. Unlimited time to travel, play sports, and lead the good life. Sounds good, huh? Well, the reality for most Americans is far different, especially for those who don't plan ahead financially and otherwise.

Here are some tips to help you through retirement:

✔ **Plan both financially and personally.** Leaving a full-time job and career behind creates even bigger challenges — what to do with all your free-time — the opposite problem new parents have. You can get too much of a good thing, which is why planning for your time and activities in retirement is even more important than planning financially. If your focus during your working years is solely on your career and saving money, you may lack interests, friends, and the ability to know how to spend money once you do retire.

✔ **Take stock of your resources.** Many people worry and wonder if they have sufficient assets to cut back on work or retire completely, yet they haven't crunched any numbers to see where they stand. Sometimes in life, ignorance can be blissful, but this is a case where ignorance might cause you to misunderstand how little or much you really have accumulated for retirement versus what you need. Start by reading the relevant portions of Chapter 8 and obtaining some of the recommended work booklets and software that can help you with retirement planning.

✔ **Reevaluate your insurance needs.** During your working years, you carried disability and perhaps some life insurance to protect you and your dependents should you not be able to earn an income. If you have sufficient assets to retire, you won't need to retain insurance to protect your employment income any longer. On the other hand, as your assets have grown over the years, you may be underinsured with regards to liability insurance (refer to Chapter 18).

✔ **Decide on health care/living options.** Medical expenses in your retirement years, particularly the cost of nursing home care, can be daunting. Which course of action you take — supplemental insurance, buying into a retirement community, or not doing anything — depends upon your financial and personal situation. Early preparation increases your options. If you wait until you have major health problems, it may be too late to choose certain paths. Refer to Chapter 17 for more details.

✔ **Decide on what to do with your retirement plan money.** When you're set to retire, you may have to elect what to do with your retirement plan money and which of your employer's pension options you'd like. If you have money in a retirement savings plan, many employers will offer you the option of leaving the money in the plan rather than rolling it over into your own retirement account. Brokers and financial advisors clearly prefer that you do the latter since it means more money for them. Read Part III of this book to learn about investing and evaluating the quality of your employer's retirement plan investment options.

✔ **Pick a pension option.** Selecting a pension option (plans that pay a monthly benefit during retirement) is similar to choosing a good investment — each pension option carries different risks, benefits and tax consequences. Pensions are structured by actuaries based on reasonable life expectancies. The younger the age when you start collecting your pension, the less you'll get per month. Check to see if the amount of your monthly pension stops increasing past a certain starting age. You obviously wouldn't want to delay access to your pension benefits past that age because you will receive no reward for waiting any longer, and you'll collect the benefit for fewer months.

If you know that you have a health problem that shortens your life expectancy, drawing your pension sooner is usually to your benefit. If you plan to continue working in some capacity and earning a decent income once you leave your employer, waiting for higher pension benefits when you'll be in a lower tax bracket is probably wise.

As for your other choices that affect what pension amount your surviving spouse receives should you die first, at one end of the spectrum you have the risky single life option, which pays benefits until you pass away and provides no benefits thereafter for your spouse. This option maximizes your monthly take while you are alive. Only consider this option if your spouse could do without this income. The least risky option and thus least financially rewarding while the pensioner is still living is the *100 percent joint and survivor option,* which pays your survivor the same amount that you received while still alive. The other joint and survivor options fall somewhere in between these two extremes and generally make sense for most couples who desire decent pensions early in retirement but want a reasonable amount to continue should the pensioner die before his or her spouse.

✔ **Get your estate in order.** Confronting one's mortality is never a joy, but when you're considering retiring or are retired, getting your estate in order makes all the more sense. Learn about wills and trusts that might benefit you and your heirs. Also consider gifting if you have more than you need. You can't take it with you, and if you are worried about estate taxes, gifting money yearly to your heirs will reduce your taxable estate.

Chapter 21

Ten Tips for Using Your Computer for Your Personal Finances

● ●

*S*oon everybody is going to own a computer. And every business is soon to have an online site. So shouldn't you just buy a bunch of software and load it onto a personal computer and join up with everyone else in the cyber-universe?

The short answer is no.

Although a computer may be able to assist you with your personal finances, it's simply one of many tools. Computers are really best at performing routine tasks faster: processing lots of bills or performing many calculations.

Computers aren't smart, and computers and all the accompanying paraphernalia certainly aren't cheap. And never assume that, just because you're accessing something financial through your computer, the information you're accessing is any good or that it's even information at all.

You can access three major repositories of personal finance stuff through your computer. Although the lines are sometimes a bit blurry among these three categories, they are roughly defined as software, commercial online services, and the Internet.

- ✔ *Software* is a computer program, typically packaged in a box about as big as a hardcover book such as *War and Peace* and sold at a retail store (although my technogeek friends tell me that more and more software will be sold online). Most of the mass-marketed financial software packages sell for under $100. If you've ever used a word processing program, such as Word or WordPerfect, or a spreadsheet program such as Lotus or Excel, then you've used software.

- ✔ *Commercial online services* can be accessed through your computer via a modem. America Online and CompuServe are the two biggest such services. For a monthly fee of around $10, such services offer you around 5 hours per month (additional hours can be had for additional fees) to access their information online.

✔ The Internet is a vast ocean of stuff that can generally be accessed via a modem, which allows your computer to talk with other computers over phone lines. To access the Internet, you need some sort of Web browser, which the previously mentioned commercial online services provide or which you can obtain through an Internet service provider. Most of the financial stuff on the Internet is supplied by companies marketing their wares and, hence, is available for free.

Note: My recommendations for the *best* personal finance software packages and online sites appear in **bold** type throughout this chapter. I mention the runners-up if they make sense for certain types of situations, but they are not highlighted in bold. Unless otherwise stated, you can purchase the recommended software packages through most software sellers. To access the online sites, here are some useful phone numbers: America Online 800-827-6364; CompuServe 800-848-8990; Prodigy 800-PRODIGY (800-776-3449).

Focus on software

Although the number of personal finance software packages and online sites is mushrooming rapidly, quality is having a hard time keeping up, especially among the free Internet sites. Most of the best of what is financially out there for your computer falls into the software category.

✔ Good software can guide you to better organization and management of your personal finances.

✔ Good software can help you complete mundane tasks or complex calculations more quickly and easily and provide basic advice in unfamiliar territory.

✔ Good software can make you feel in control of your life.

Mediocre and bad software can make you feel stupid, however, or, at the very least, it make you want to tear your hair out. Lousy packages usually end up in the software graveyard.

Having reviewed many of the packages available, I can assure you that, if you are having a hard time with some of the programs out there (even sometimes the more useful ones), you are not at fault. Too many packages assume that you already know things such as your tax rate, your mortgage options, and the difference between stock and bond mutual funds. Much of what's out there isn't user-friendly and is too technically oriented. Some of it is even flawed in its financial accuracy.

A good software package, like a good tax or financial advisor, should be your partner in helping you better manage your finances. It should simply and concisely explain financial terminology and provide a road map to help you make decisions by offering choices and recommendations so that you can "play" with alternatives before following a particular course of action.

With increasing regularity, financial software packages are being designed to do more than one task or to address more than one area of personal finances. But no package covers the whole range of issues in your financial life.

Tread carefully on the Web

"Go surfing!"

"Cool!"

No, you're not eavesdropping on a Southern California beach conversation. To hear promoters of and companies with sites on the globe's largest computer network known as the Internet, you may think that the Internet is not only a hip place to be but The Place to Be.

I'm increasingly asked questions like, "How do I research investments through the Internet?" or, "How can I use the Internet to manage my personal finances?"

My answer — "very carefully."

Like information from any medium, you have to sift out the good from the bad. If you blindly navigate on the Internet and naively think that what's out there is useful "information," "research," or "objective advice," you may be in for a rude awakening.

Most personal finance sites on the Internet are free, which — guess what — means that these sites are basically advertising or are dominated and driven by advertising. If you're looking for written material by unbiased experts or journalists — well — you don't have much to pick from.

Consider the source

The Internet Report, recently published by the investment banking firm Morgan Stanley, cites a short list of the "coolest finance" sites. On the list is the site of banking giant Bank of America (B of A). As it's been a long time since I was in junior high school, I'm not quite sure what cool means anymore. If cool can be used to describe a well-organized and graphically pleasing web site, then I guess I could say that B of A's site is cool.

However, if you are looking for sound information and advice, then B of A's site is decidedly "uncool." It steers you in a financial direction that benefits, not surprisingly, the bank and not you. For example, in the At Home section, users are asked to plug in their gross monthly income and down payment, which then is used to spit out the supposed amount that one can "afford" to spend on a home. No mention is given to other financial goals and concerns — such as saving for retirement — that affect one's ability to spend a particular amount of money on a home.

In the Credit Cards and Loans area, consider this advice: "Maybe you *can* have it now. When you don't have the cash on hand for important purchases, Bank of America can help you borrow what you need. From a new car, to that vacation you've been longing for, to new kitchen appliances, you can make these dreams real now." Click on a button on the bottom of this screen — and presto, you're on your way to racking up credit card and auto debt. Why bother practicing delayed gratification, living within your means, or buying something used if getting a loan is "easy" and comes with "special privileges"?

Watch out for "sponsored" content

Another problem to watch out for on Internet sites is "sponsored" content, a euphemism for advertising under the guise of editorial content. Often buried in small print in an obscure part of the Web page or site, you'll usually find a disclaimer or note saying that an article is sponsored by (in other words, paid advertising by) the "author."

For example, The Mutual Fund Home Page states that its "primary purpose is to provide viewers with an independent guide that contains information and articles they can't get anywhere else." The "content" of the site suggests otherwise. In the Expert's Corner, viewers are treated to material reprinted from a newsletter that advocates frequent trading in and out of mutual funds to time market moves. Turns out that the "article" is "sponsored by the featured expert": In other words, it's a paid advertisement. (The track record of the newsletter's past recommendations, which isn't discussed, is poor.)

Financial planning or financial selling?

I also suggest skipping virtually all the financial planning advice offered by financial service companies with financial products to sell. Such companies cannot take the necessary objective, holistic view required to render useful advice. Investment companies, for example, will prod you into establishing college savings accounts with them without pointing out the benefits of funding your employer's retirement savings plan instead or the deleterious effect that college accounts have on your child's ability to qualify for financial aid (refer to Chapter 14 for more details).

For example, Fidelity Investments has an Internet site, which has a good deal of material on its mutual funds. The site's college planning advice is off the mark as it urges parents to put money in a custodial account in the child's name. Ignored is the fact that this will undermine your child's ability to qualify for financial aid and that you're likely best off funding your employer's retirement plan. If you did that, though, you couldn't set up a Fidelity College Savings Plan account, which this area prods you to do.

Short-term thinking and hot-tip touting

Many financial Internet sites provide real time stock quotes as a hook to some site that is cluttered with advertising. My experience working with individual investors is that the more short-term they think, the worse they do, and checking your portfolio during the trading day certainly promotes short-termism. Some of these sites charge a nominal monthly fee and in return also throw in largely worthless content.

And finally, beware of tips offered around the electronic water cooler — message boards. As in the real world, chatting with strangers and exchanging ideas is fine. However, if you don't know the identity and competence of message board posters or chat room participants, why would you follow their financial advice or stock tips? Getting ideas from various sources is okay, but educate yourself and do your homework before making personal financial decisions.

If you want to best manage your personal finances and learn more, remember that there's a grain of truth in the old expression, "You get what you pay for." Free information on the Internet, especially that which is provided by companies in the financial services industry, is largely self-serving. Stick with information providers who have proven themselves in the printed world or who don't have anything to sell, except objective information and advice. Where appropriate in this chapter, I recommend useful Internet sites that meet these criteria.

Pay your bills and track your money

Every month, you write out by hand a bunch of checks to the same organizations and people you wrote checks to last month and the month before that. Checkbook software automates the process of paying your bills. When you have to make your monthly payment to the phone company, for example, your monthly check, already made payable to the phone company, pops up on-screen at your command. All you have to do is fill in the new amount that you have to pay. And your check gets printed on your computer's printer. (For a small monthly fee, you can even pay your bills electronically, completely eliminating the process of writing and mailing in checks.) What's even better is that the program automatically tracks your check writing and prepares reports that detail your spending by category — so that you can get a handle on where the fat is in your budget.

Using checkbook software to plan for life changes

One thing is certain about life: It changes — marriage, buying a home, family expansion, starting a business, divorce, retirement, or death of a spouse. As I highlight in Chapter 20, although some life events bring joy and others sorrow, all bring financial change. If you don't manage this change, it may end up managing and ruling you.

I've witnessed the best of savers turn into deficit financiers due to the financial upheaval and shock waves from a major life event — even those events that were anticipated. One of the useful things that you can do with a checkbook software program is to use it to plan ahead for life changes.

For example, if you'd like to take the entrepreneurial plunge and leave your full-time job, you should know if you can afford to do that and what impact changed expenses and income would have on your ability to save money. Wannabe parents, likewise, should consider how increased expenses and a likely reduction in income would affect their monthly budget.

The checkbook software programs come with suggested categories for tallying your expenses — such as housing, clothing, auto, cable TV, furniture, insurance, telephone, other utilities, education, and so on. Useful for planning for change, the better programs which I recommend in this chapter also allow you to create your own categories. You can adjust and create new spending and income categories to match your personal financial situation. For

example, if you're planning on having a baby, the program allows you to create a new major category *baby,* and then subcategories within it: diapers, clothing, childcare, baby equipment, and so on. Before Junior arrives, you can plug in estimated spending numbers and compare the income and expense numbers to the ones in your current expense report without the baby expenditures.

Going through this exercise is a great way to estimate what impact a child or other significant life change will have on your financial situation. I advised some nervous expectant parents to use their existing checkbook software as they were wondering what financial impact having a baby would have on their household finances. Their findings: Given their expected spending, the parents would go from saving 12 percent of their annual incomes to spending 5 percent more than they earned. But the lower income spouse was also surprised to see that, by working half-time rather than full-time, the couple's net savings would actually increase thanks largely to lower taxes, child-care, and work-related expenses.

As you plan for your next life change, remember software's limitations. It can't factor in the nonfinancial considerations such as how you feel about working more or less because of a life change. Software may also mistakenly give you the illusion of control. Those expectant parents that I told you about earlier learned that they were having three new additions to their family and not just one!

✔ **Quicken** (available in Windows, DOS, and Macintosh versions) is an easy-to-use checkbook software program. In addition to offering the printed checks and electronic bill-payment features, Quicken is a financial organizer. The program also allows you to track your investments and other assets and your loans and other financial liabilities.

> ✔ Although many small-business owners have used Quicken for their accounting needs, **QuickBooks** (available in Windows, DOS, and Macintosh versions) is a useful, straightforward software package specifically designed for keeping track of a small business's finances.

> ✔ In addition to Quicken, Microsoft's Money and Kiplinger's Simply Money programs are good programs that I've reviewed.

One drawback of using all of the above programs to track your spending is that each only captures what is entered. So the amount and spending category of your individual credit card and cash purchases, which for most people are substantial, are omitted unless you enter such data (or get a credit card from the software company, which allows you to download your credit card transactions using a modem).

Plan for retirement

Retirement planning software helps you to plan for retirement by crunching the numbers for you. But it can also teach you how particular changes — such as your investment returns, rate of inflation, or your savings rate — can affect when, and in what style, you can retire. The biggest time savings aspect of retirement planning software is that it lets you more quickly play with and see the consequences of changing the assumptions.

Some of the major investment companies that I profile in Part III of this book are the sources for some high-quality, low-cost retirement planning software.

Here are some good retirement planning programs to consider:

> ✔ **Vanguard's Retirement Planner** can be purchased only through Vanguard (800-876-1840) and sells for $15.

> ✔ **Quicken Financial Planner** (Windows only) is available through software retailers.

Quicken and some of the other checkbook packages that I recommend earlier in this chapter have retirement-planning calculators that do a decent job in giving you a sense of where you stand with saving and planning for retirement. If you're a Macintosh user, Quicken for Macintosh is a good option.

If you're already in retirement or near retirement, check out the **Vanguard Retirement Manager** (Windows or Mac). It's available only through Vanguard at 800-950-1971.

Prepare your taxes

Tax preparation software can save you time and money. Unlike most other personal finance software, this type of software is relatively easy to learn because you just have to enter data that the program specifically asks for. The program then plugs the data into the appropriate tax form. Good tax preparation software contains all the forms needed to file your return. This feature reduces your chances having to run to the post office for specialized forms that you didn't realize you'd need until April 14th.

Among the better tax preparation programs I've reviewed are **TurboTax** (Windows and DOS versions), **MacInTax** (Macintosh version), and **Kiplinger Taxcut** (for Windows, DOS, and Macintosh). These programs are easy to use. They "interview" you to gather the necessary information and select the appropriate forms based on your responses. More experienced taxpayers can bypass the interview and jump directly to the forms they know they need to complete. These programs also help flag overlooked deductions and identify other tax-reducing strategies.

In addition to the federal tax packages, tax-preparation programs are available for state income taxes, too. Many state tax forms are fairly easy to complete because they are based on information from your federal form. If that's your situation, you may just skip buying the state income tax preparation packages and prepare the state return by hand.

If you're mainly after tax forms, you can download all sorts of tax forms without charge through a government Web site (http://www.ustreas.gov). You can also get these forms through the major commercial online services, such as America Online and CompuServe.

Research investments

When you research investments with your computer, if you so desire, you can bypass the software and online worlds and not be at all left behind. Why? Well, much of what's out there is either watered down versions of better printed publications, not very good, or geared for professional investors.

If you are an investing and mutual fund novice, you probably won't succeed using the major mutual fund software programs in the marketplace published by Morningstar, Value Line, and a few other companies. None of the programs offer enough guidance on mutual fund basics, such as how to analyze annual operating expense ratios, the merits of no-load versus load funds, how to construct a portfolio, and how to allocate assets. And they're not cheap. The best program — Morningstar's *Principia Plus* — costs several hundred dollars.

The main problem with Morningstar's Principia Plus, as with other mutual fund software, is the lack of guidance and advice. Morningstar's *Ascent,* which is aimed at the nonexpert investor, does provide more background for the novice but it's superficial.

Much of the best information in the commercial online world is geared toward investing in individual stocks. So if you have given up on being the next Warren Buffett and use mutual funds, the online world will be of limited use to you.

The major commercial online services — which are set up to charge for information — offer a number of helpful resources for an individual stock investor.

The advantage of going online isn't that you profit from getting news sooner or from tapping into the latest predictions of yet more gurus, but that you can access useful resources quicker and cheaper than you could before (that is, if your modem is speedy and you know where to look). Rather than schlepping off to the library and fighting over the favorite investing reference manuals, ponying up hundreds of dollars to buy print versions for your own use, or slogging through voice mail hell when you call government agencies, you can access a variety of materials with your computer. You can also usually pay for just what you need.

For a concise financial summary of an individual company that comes with links to the company's Web site, SEC filings, and a Web search for references, check out Hoover's Company Profiles on America Online. Because of these connections, Hoover's is a good starting point for researching individual companies.

Also on American Online (AOL), the Disclosure site supplies information from SEC filings and other sources on public companies. Like Hoover's, Disclosure is a useful place to start if you have particular stocks already in mind and want to learn more about the companies' businesses and financials. Disclosure holds your hand through the process of navigating and understanding the various documents. To sidestep the commercial online service's charges, you can access Securities and Exchange Commission (SEC) documents directly via the SEC's Internet site (`http://www.sec.gov/index.html`) but be aware that navigating this site takes patience. All public corporations, as well as mutual funds, file with the agency.

Morningstar's AOL site gives access to their individual stock and mutual fund reports. The reports are free, but they are watered down versions of the company's comprehensive software and paper products. Its mutual fund reports lack analyst commentary, risk analysis, investment style data, comprehensive portfolio analysis, tax analysis, and other useful features found in its print and software products. If you want to buy Morningstar's unabridged fund reports online, you can do so for $5 apiece at the Web site (`http://www.investools.com/`) or via CompuServe.

Fools and their money . . .

In addition to research tools and publications, the online world is also home to pundits attempting to pick the next Microsoft or claiming to have a trading system to beat the market.

Although virtually unknown two years back when they had a few dozen subscribers to their printed stock-picking newsletter, AOL's Motley Fools have promoted themselves to prominence by flogging the market-beating returns of their Fool Portfolio. The chief Fools are David and Tom Gardner, who also now oversee AOL sites on such disparate topics as sports, movies, and contemporary culture.

The Gardners claim that with minutes of effort, novices can easily earn 25 to 35 percent per year investing in individual stocks and can handily beat mutual funds. But as is the case in the careers of so many stock-picking pundits, the Fools' rapid ascent to visibility in early 1996 has since been followed by less than stellar returns.

Two stocks, Iomega and America Online, which were entirely responsible for the Fool portfolio's short-term market-beating returns, were knocked down by more than 65 percent from their early 1996 peaks. Like investors who started following the prognostications of Elaine Garzarelli (refer to Chapter 9) after her market beating performance during the crash of 1987, Fools-come-lately are licking their wounds.

The Fools also post the returns of two other model portfolios; both have underperformed the market averages. Thus, although the Fools love to point out that the majority of mutual funds lag market averages, the same can be said for their own portfolios. Like many other newsletters, the Fools also use trading methods developed by looking at historic data to claim propriety to market-beating trading systems. In their Investing for Growth area, they make it seem as if they've actually been using this system since

1980 to generate 26+ percent annual returns. In the first full quarter after this system was published in a book last year, their model portfolio plunged more than 25 percent while the stock market rose.

The Fools attribute the uniqueness of their investment philosophy to the phenomenon of electronic message boards. The theory behind these message boards is certainly admirable: Thousands of citizen investors are given a place to exchange hot new stock tips before the big guys on Wall Street even know what's going on. Although it's an appealing idea, the reality is uglier. Message boards are a Never-Never Land of accountability; identities, agendas, and the competence of message writers are usually a mystery. Any postings of true substance are buried in an avalanche of hype: owners of a given stock are cheerleading, and anyone with a dissenting viewpoint is often torn to shreds.

Other print newsletters, most with mediocre to dismal historic performance, are putting their wares online as well. Just as you shouldn't invest in a mutual fund without first examining its actual track record and that of its manager, do the same before following the advice of stock-picking pundits online. Mark Hulbert, who tracks the performance of investment newsletters, is just beginning to track online-only newsletters, but if their records parallel those of their printed brethren, you're best skipping the lot. After adjusting for risk, not a single print investment newsletter over the past 15 years has beaten the stock market averages (refer to Chapter 9).

If you decide to become a cyber-stock picker and take on the risks of individual stock-picking, remember the old expression about the parting of fools and their money. Do your homework and research *before* you buy and don't buy a stock based on a pundit's opinion.

Of the three major commercial online services, Prodigy has the least to offer but still has some unique and useful features. The Strategic Investor is my favorite area on Prodigy. Like Hoover's, it provides a good overview of a company but it goes further by providing historic financials compared with industry norms. You can also use the service, which costs $14.95 per month, to screen for stocks that meet particular selection criteria such as low price-earnings ratios and high growth rates.

Although I've always been leery of financial service company "educational" materials because of bias and self-serving advice, some companies have done a worthy job. The investor-friendly, penny-pinching Vanguard Group of mutual funds has an online university on AOL as well as at Vanguard's internet site (http://www.vanguard.com) where investors can learn the basics of fund investing. Additionally, investors in Vanguard's funds can access up-to-date personal account information through Vanguard's Internet site.

Tracking your investment returns often not worth the headache

Accurately tracking the return on your investments can be an extremely complicated, tedious, and time-consuming task — exactly the type of chore that computers were designed to relieve us of. Although one would think that a number of excellent investment tracking software packages would be on the market today, I feel that such available packages are . . . well . . . complicated, tedious, and time-consuming. At this point anyway, these programs are often not any more efficient than the old-fashioned method of pencil, paper, and a calculator.

My big gripe with the investment tracking software programs is that most of them don't allow you to determine your investment's total return. And the few programs that do require lots of time to get to that point. Your effective or *internal rate of return* (IRR), which compares your original amounts invested to the current market value, is the best way to measure the success of your investments over time. Two of the packages that I discuss earlier in the chapter, Microsoft Money and Quicken, calculate IRR, but most other software packages that I have reviewed do not.

Most of the other packages calculate your *cost basis,* which is your original investment plus reinvested dividends and capital gains, for which you would have already paid taxes in a nonretirement account. When you sell a nonretirement account investment, you need to know the cost basis for tax purposes (refer to Chapter 7). Cost basis reports make your returns look less generous because reinvested distributions increase your original investment and seemingly reduce your returns. I know from direct experience that investors often look at the cost basis reports — which are sometimes misleadingly named "investment performance" or "investment analysis" — and assume that it is telling them what their total investment returns are. Using software for cost basis calculations is generally not worthwhile because most investment companies provide cost basis information for you upon request or when you sell an investment.

If you want to analyze your historic returns, you'll need to gather up all your old account statements (if you can find them) and enter in every investment you made as well as all re-investments of dividends, interest, and capital gains distributions.

If you are a buy-and-hold mutual fund investor, investment tracking software has limited benefit given the time required to enter your data. Mutual funds and many other published resources tell you what the funds' total return was for the past year so you don't need to enter every dividend and capital gain distribution for yourself.

As for calculating the return of your overall portfolio with the old-fashioned method of paper and pencil mentioned above, simply weight the return of each investment by the portion of your portfolio invested in it. For example, with a simple portfolio equally divided between two investments, which returned 10 percent and 20 percent respectively, your overall portfolio return would be 15 percent.

Investment tracking software can be more useful for stock traders. In my experience, stock traders don't usually track their overall returns. If they actually used one of these programs, they could at least see how all their trading is depressing their returns. (I've never worked with a stock picker who went through this exercise with me and beat the market indexes over the long term.)

One of the greatest benefits of these packages is that using them can help get you organized. If you enter your investments into the package, they can help you make sure you don't lose track of your holdings. Of course, if your home burns to the ground and you don't have a back-up copy of your files or software, you'll have to start from scratch. (At least, I hope, you've got home/renter's insurance!)

Trading online

If you've done your investing homework, trading securities online may save you money and perhaps some time. For years, discount brokers (which I discuss in Chapter 9) had been heralded as the low cost source for trading. Now, online brokers such as eTrade (800-786-2575; America Online, Keyword: ETRADE; CompuServe, GO ETRADE; http://www.etrade.com), Charles Schwab's eSchwab service (800-eSchwab; http://www.schwab.com) and Jack White (800-323-3263; http://pawws.com/jwc) have set a new lower cost standard.

eTrade, in fact, has built its securities brokerage business around online trading. Without the overhead of branch offices, and by accepting and processing trades by computer, eTrade keeps its costs and brokerage charges to a minimum. Cut rate electronic brokerage firms like eTrade are for people who want to direct their own financial affairs and don't want or need to work with a personal broker. However, eTrade has limited products and services. For example, it does not offer many of the best mutual funds. And, my own experience with reaching live people at eTrade was trying. When I first called eTrade's customer service line, I hung up after 26 minutes on hold. The second time, a customer service representative answered the line after 23 minutes. At least, they're getting better.

You can also trade online using investment software, some of which also allows you to do investment research. These packages are offered through a specific investment company, and your choice of the investment company is the major difference among the recommended packages. (For more information on deciding which investment firms you'd like to work with, refer to Chapter 11.) An added benefit of investing through this type of software is the 10 percent discount on transaction fees for trades placed through your computer.

Among the packages that allow you to access your account information and place trades with some of the best firms recommended in this book are Charles Schwab & Company's **StreetSmart**, a Windows-based software program that you can purchased only through Charles Schwab, either by calling 800-334-4455 or visiting one of the company's branch offices. StreetSmart costs $40. Jack White's ComputerPATH program costs $30 and can be ordered by calling Jack White & Company at 800-753-1700.

Investment tracking and trading software can be helpful, but it can also encourage people to trade more than they should. Following investments on a daily basis encourages you to think short term. Remember that the best investments are bought and held for the long haul (see Part III for more information).

If you are attracted to using the software merely for the 10 percent trading discount, then don't bother: Place your trades through Fidelity or Schwab by using a touch-tone telephone and get your 10 percent discount without spending your time and money on computer programs.

Reading and searching periodicals

The AOL Company News and the CompuServe News sites provide recent news from the major wire services. Prodigy has Dow Jones News Retrieval, but it only covers the past 21 days. All the services can search for information on specific subjects, but be forewarned that you'll probably get way more information than is relevant to you.

For access to print publications online, the AOL Financial Newsstand has current issues of major business magazines and a host of major newspapers and other magazines. The CompuServe Business Database Plus is even more extensive: It contains five years of articles from 750 publications including industry and specialized business newsletters. The cost for this service is $.25 per minute and $1.50 per downloaded article.

Many business and financial publications are going online to offer investors current news and financial market data. *The Wall Street Journal* offers an online personalized edition of the paper (`http://update.wsj.com`). You can tailor the content to meet your specific needs. The cost is $49.95 per year ($29.95 if you're an existing *Journal* subscriber).

Also offering value for the money and an intelligent news search engine is EyeQ (`http://www.datatimes.com`). Be careful though not to run up a hefty bill — the service costs $39 per month, $0.20 per minute connected, and $2.95 per article retrieved.

Preparing legal documents

Just as you can prepare a tax return with the advice of a software program, you can also prepare common legal documents. This type of software may save you from the often-difficult task of finding a competent and affordable attorney.

Using legal software is generally preferable to using fill-in-the-blank documents. Software has the built-in virtues of directing and limiting your choices and keeping you from making common mistakes. Quality software also incorporates the knowledge and insights of the legal eagles who developed the software. And it can save you money.

If your situation isn't unusual, legal software may work well for you. As to the legality of documents that you create with legal software, remember that a will, for example, is made legal and valid by your witnesses; the fact that an attorney prepares the document is *not* what makes it legal.

An excellent package for preparing your own will is **WillMaker** (available in Windows, DOS, and Macintosh versions), published by Nolo Press, a name synonymous with high quality and user-friendliness in the legal publishing world. In addition to allowing you to prepare wills, WillMaker can also help you prepare a *living will* and medical power of attorney (refer to Chapter 18).

Nolo's Living Trust software (available in Windows and Macintosh versions) allows you to create a living trust that serves to keep property out of probate in the event of your death (refer to Chapter 18). Like wills, living trusts are fairly standard legal documents that you can properly create with the guidance of a top-notch software package. The Living Trust package also advises you to seek professional guidance for your situation, if necessary.

Index

• A •

AARP (American Association of Retired Persons), 320
accounts
  balanced mutual funds, 242
  bank savings, 254–255
  bond mutual funds, 241
  credit union savings, 254–255
  custodial, 270
  GICs (guaranteed-investment contracts), 241–242
  managed, 177
  money market, 186–187, 241
  retirement, 229–250
  savings, 186–187, 241
  stock mutual funds, 242
  tax-reduction, 132–133
  transaction/checking, 186
  wrap, 177
accumulation phase, annuities, 236
addictions, spending, 59, 106
adult education classes, unethical practices, 52
ADV Form, 380
advisors, 33–52
  See also financial advisors
  associations, 51
  bank specialists, 41
  CFP (certified financial planner), 34–38
  commission sales, 40
  commission-based, 45–46
  conflicts of interest, 36, 40–43
  credentials, 35, 37
  double-dipping, 40
  employer retirement plan recommendations, 41–42
  fee-based, 38, 46
  fee-only, 38
  financial consultants, 34
  financial product commissions, 46
  hiring, 33–52
  hourly based, 47
  investment churning, 40
  investment follow-through, 49
  legal service selling, 43
  locating, 38–43, 50–51
  mediation assistance, 49
  objective voice, 49
  ongoing money-management service selling, 42
  oversight agencies, 39, 380
  percentage of assets under management, 46
  personal referrals, 50
  priority setting, 48
  problem/goal identification, 48
  real estate investments, 42
  regulatory problems, 39
  research resources, 48
  RIAs (registered investment advisors), 39
  unethical practices, 51–52
AFBA Industrial Bank, 100
agents
  buyer's brokers, 310
  home sale, 320–321
  insurance commission scheme, 335
  real estate, 307–313
aggressive growth stocks, 34
aging parents, care of, 394–395
AICPA (American Institute of Certified Public Accountants), 51
Allen, John, 15
Allstate, 369
alternative minimum tax, 111
America Online, 401–402
  ETRADE keyword, 412
  investment research, 409–410
  reading/searching online periodicals, 413–414
American Advantage, 100

American Arbitration Association, 180
American Stock Exchange, 189
Ameritas, 352
AMT (alternative minimum tax), 111
analysis, spending, 61–68
annual reports, 220
annuities, 35, 203–204, 239, 267
  accumulation phase, 236
  insurance, 334
  retirement accounts, 236–237
  tax-sheltered 403(b) plans, 231
application fees, mortgages, 297
appraisals, mortgages fees, 297
arbitration, 180
ARM (adjustable-rate mortgage), 290–292,
  298–301
Ascent program, 409
asset allocation
  investments, 260
  investment diversification, 169–170
  long-term, 171–172
assets, 24–25, 78,
  insuring, 365–376
associations, financial planner referrals, 51
audits
  performance records/expenses, mutual
    funds, 206
  tax, 128–130
auto insurance, 370–373
automobiles
  leasing vs buying, 96–97
  multiple-car families, 98
  operation costs, 97
  paying cash, 97
  registration fees, 119
  regular unleaded gas, 98
  researching before purchase, 96
  servicing considerations, 98
  spending reduction strategies, 95–98
  vs commuter passes, 98

• *B* •

bad debt, 21–24, 69
balanced mutual funds, 210, 242
bank accounts, savings investments,
  254–255
Bank of America Web site, 403–404
bankruptcies
  attorney conflict-of interest, 81
  bank charge-offs, 79
  benefits, 77
  CCCS (Consumer Credit Counseling
    Services), 79–81
  Chapter 13, 79
  Chapter 7, 79
  discharged debts, 77
  drawbacks, 77–79
  filing, 76–81
  limited partnerships, 15
  secured credit cards, 78
  statistics, 11
  untouchable assets, 78
banks, 41, 79
Barrons, financial planner association
  cautions, 39
Bogle, John, 221
bond mutual funds, 209, 241, 260–265
bonds, 187–188
  maturity, 209
  tax reduction strategies, 114–115
  tax-free, 238
brand names, 87
broker-dealer networks, 175
brokers
  buyer's, real estate, 310
  discount, 173–174
  mortgages, 302–303
  suing, 180
  savings, 91
budgeting, 91
business, saving to buy, 135–136
buyer's brokers, real estate, 310
buying vs renting (real estate)
  affordability, 283–285
  expense comparisons, 285–287

long-term rental cost, 287–288
mortgage borrowing ability, 284–285
renting advantages, 282
timeline, 282

calculations
disability insurance, 353–354
life insurance need, 345
net worth, 25–27
retirement, 140
savings analysis, 28–29
callable bonds, 188
cancer insurance, 333
capital gains, 219, 227
car loans, overspending, 58
career counseling, tax reduction strategies,
120–121
cash value life insurance, 17, 136
borrowing against, 70
cashing in, 351
vs term insurance, 346–350
catastrophe insurance, 330–331
CCCS (Consumer Credit Counseling
Services), 79–81
CDs (certificates of deposit), 188, 265–266
CFP (certified financial planner), 34–38
CFP (College for Financial Planning), 37
CFP Board of Standards, CFP (certified
financial planner) credentials, 37
CFP, National Endowment for Financial
Education, 39
Chapter 13 bankruptcy, 79
Chapter 7 bankruptcy, 79
charge cards, vs credit card, 75
charge-offs, 79
charitable contributions, tax reduction
strategies, 119
Charles Schwab & Company, 222
debit cards, 74
self-employment retirement investment
options, 245
checkbook balancing, 67
checkbook software, 405–407

children
educational expense saving, 136
financial strategies, 392–394
overspending on health/well-being, 60
clothing, spending reduction strategies, 99
COLA adjustments, disability insurance, 355
cold calling, 51–52
collectibles, 204
College for Financial Planning (CFP), 37
college, cost estimates, 276–277
commercial online services, 401–402
commission sales, financial advisors, 40
commission-free (no load) mutual fund
companies, 173
commissions
financial product, 46
impact on human behavior, 175
insurance, 335
investment mistake, 157
components of total return, 227
CompuServe, 401
GO ETRADE keyword, 412
reading/searching online periodicals,
413–414
computers, spending analysis software,
66–67
computers, using for finances, 401–414
condominiums, 305
conflicts of interest
financial advisors, 36, 40–43
investment salespeople, 175–177
consumer as consumption machine, 56
Consumer Reports, financial advisor hiring
pitfalls, 36
contact lens insurance, 329
Continental Airlines card, 100
contingency-fee basis, 180
cooperatives, 305
corporation, described, 123
cost basis, 411
cost of funds, 11th district, 300
costs, mutual funds, 206, 214–217
CPAs (certified public accountants), 127–128
credentials, financial advisors, 35–38

credit
  access to, 56–57
  resisting, 75
credit cards
  access to, 56–57
  credit limit reduction, 75
  debt load formula, 23
  grace period, 11, 23
  interest accumulation, 11
  interest rates, 72–73
  minimum monthly payment pitfalls, 57
  no-fee, 100
  overspending, 57
  paying off debt, 252
  playing the float, 23
  reducing number carried, 75
  secured, 78
  vs charge card, 75
credit disability insurance, 328
credit life insurance, 328
credit limit, reducing, 75
credit repair firms, 84
credit reports
  correcting mistakes, 83–84
  mortgages fees, 297
credit unions, savings investments, 254–255
custodial accounts, educational expenses,
    270, 272–273

DA (Debtors Anonymous), 81–82
daily hospitalization insurance, 329
Davis, Leona, 80
debt
  bankruptcy filing reduction, 76–81
  charge-offs, 79
  consumer vs mortgage, 118–119
  DA (Debtors Anonymous), 81–82
  decreasing, 71–76
  discharged, 77
  good vs bad, 21–24, 69
  investment mistake, 156
  living within your means, 86
  paying off credit cards, 252
  reducing with savings, 69

debit cards, 73–76
debt repayment, spending reduction
    strategies, 99–100
debt-and-spend cycle, ending, 81–82
deductibles, insurance, 329–330
deductions
  auto registration fees, 119
  charitable contributions, 119
  expenses, 119
  itemized, 116–117
  limitations on, 120
  miscellaneous expenses, 120–121
  real estate purchases, 117
  self-employment expenses, 121–124
  shifting/bunching, 118
  standard, 116
  state income taxes, 119
  state insurance, 119
  trading consumer debt for mortgage debt,
      118–119
defined-benefit plans, 144–145, 235
defined-contribution plans, 145
dental insurance, 328
derivatives, 163
Dickson, Joel M., 18
Direct Insurance Services, 351
Direct Marketing Association, Mail
    Preference Service, 75
directories, fund, 225–226
disability insurance, 352–356
discount brokers, 173–174
Discover Card, 100
distributions, tax effects, 253–254
diversification, 158, 206
  asset-allocation, 169–170
  investment, 168–172
dividend reinvestment plans, 194
dividends, 227
divorce, financial strategies, 395–397
do-it-yourself, financial management, 44
dollar-cost averaging, investments, 167
do-nothing approach, financial management,
    44
Donovan, Nancy (teacher), 12
double-dipping, 40
Drexel Burnham, 185

• E •

EAs (enrolled agents), 127
education, teaching personal finance, 12
educational expenses, 269–280
  borrowing vs saving, 276
  children's saving, 136
  college costs, 276–277
  custodial account pitfalls, 270
  FAF (Financial Aid Form), 271
  FAFSA (Free Application for Federal
      Student Aid), 271
  financial aid system, 270–274
  financial needs analysis, 271
  good/bad investments, 278–280
  grants, 270–271, 274–276
  investments, 269–280
  loans, 274–276
  needs-based financial aid, 271
  no-load mutual funds, 278
  Parent Loans for Undergraduate Students
      (PLUS), 275
  paying for, 274–278
  prepaid tuition plans, 279
  savings goals, 277–278
  scholarships, 274–276
  Subsidized Stafford Loans, 275
  taking care of self first, 270
  tax reduction strategies, 120
  Unsubsidized Stafford Loans, 275
efficient market, 197
emergency reserve savings, 133–135,
    254–258
employer-sponsored retirement plans,
    230–232
entertainment, spending reduction
    strategies, 101
equity funds, 210
equity, real estate, 195
Erie Insurance, 369
escrow fees, real estate, 316
estate planning, 374–376
estate planning specialists, 45
eTrade, Web site address, 412–413
evaluations, bad reviewers, 224
exchanges, stock, 189

expenses, tax reduction strategies, 119
extended warranty/repair plans, 327–328
EyeQ search engine, 414

• F •

401(k) plans, 144, 149, 230
403(b) plans, 231, 249–250
457 plans, 232
FAF (Financial Aid Form), 271
FAFSA (Free Application for Federal Student
    Aid), 271
Family Pharmaceuticals of America, 104
family, borrowing from, 70
FDIC (Federal Deposit Insurance
    Corporation), 186
FDIC insurance, CDs, 266
Federal Student Financial Aid Information
    Center, 275
federally tax-free only money market funds,
    258
federal-tax-free-only bond funds, 265
fee-based financial advisors, 38, 46
feel good overspending syndrome, 59
fee-only financial advisors, 38
fees
  commissions, 157
  escrow, 316
  management, 157
  mortgages, 297
Fidelity Advisor funds, 222
Fidelity Investments, 146, 221–222
  debit cards, 74
  self-employment retirement investment
      options, 245
  Web site, 404–405
finances, using personal computer, 401–404
financial advisors
  See also advisors
  client references, 382–383
  commission rates, 379–380
  Form ADV, 380
  hiring truths/consequences, 33–52
  hourly fees, 381
  implementation of advice, 383
  liability insurance, 382

financial advisors (*continued*)
money-management fees, 380–381
publishing/advising conflicts, 14–15
questions for, 379–384
strategies/product recommendations, 383
tax/legal services, 381
work/educational experience, 381–382
financial aid system
custodial accounts treatment, 272–273
educational expenses, 270–274
FAF (Financial Aid Form), 271
FAFSA (Free Application for Federal
Student Aid), 271
financial needs analysis, 271
home equity treatment, 273
needs-based financial aid, 271
reform needs, 274
retirement accounts treatment, 272
financial assets, described, 24–25
financial catastrophe insurance, 330–331
financial consultants, 34, 45, 175
financial goals, ignoring when buying goods/
services, 59–60
financial health, 21–32
bad debt described, 22
good vs bad debt, 21–24
measuring, 21–32
net worth, 24–28
financial illiteracy, 10–20
finance plan, 19–20
good/bad investment writers, 16–17
home-taught money-management habits,
13–14
investment publisher ethics, 17–19
media as watchdog, 15
predictive advice, 15–16
publication advertising dependency, 18
publishing/advising conflicts, 14–19
rising above, 10–19
school subjects, 12
statistics, 11
traps, 1–3
financial liabilities, 25

financial management
commission-based planners, 45–46
do-it-yourself, 44
do-nothing approach, 44
hourly based advisors, 47
options, 43–47
percentage of assets under management
advisors, 46
financial needs analysis, 271
financial planners (*see also* advisors,
financial advisors), 175
financial product commissions, 46
financial service representatives, 45
financial strategies for life changes
aging parents care, 394–395
birth of children, 392–394
changing jobs/careers, 387–388
first job, 386–387
home purchase, 391
marital status change, 388–390, 395–397
retirement, 398–400
small business start up, 390–391
windfall, 397–398
first job, financial strategy, 386–387
fixed-rate mortgages, 289–292, 296–298
float, credit card, 23
food
eating out, 92
spending reduction strategies, 90–92
vegetarian diet savings, 92
wholesale superstore savings, 90–91
Forbes magazine, wrap account concerns,
177
Ford Card, 100
Form ADV (Uniform Application for Investment Advisor Registration), 380
formulas
ARM (adjustable-rate mortgage), 299–300
debt load, 23–24
net worth, 24
free seminars, unethical practice, 52
friends, borrowing from, 70
fund family reputation, mutual fund
selection, 218
fund manager, mutual fund selection, 218

funds
  bad tracking sources, 224
  balanced, 210
  bond, 209, 260–265
  capital gains, 227–228
  Charles Schwab & Company, 222
  directories, 225–226
  dividends, 227
  equity, 210
  Fidelity Advisor, 222
  following/selling, 228
  global, 211–212, 225
  hybrid, 209–210
  index, 212–213
  international, 211–212
  Jack White & Company, 223
  money market mutual, 114–115, 208–209,
    255–258
  mutual, 115
  no transaction fee, 222
  risk-adjusted performance, 225
  sector, 213
  share price changes, 228
  socially responsible, 214
  specialty, 213
  stock, 210, 266–267
  total return, 227
  tracking rankings/performance, 223–228
  types, 208–214
  U.S., 211–212
  underperform the market, 212
  understanding performance, 226–228
  worldwide, 225
funds of funds, 211

gambling
  vs investments, 163–164
  vs stock market, 191
Garzarelli, Elaine, 182
GEICO, 369
Gerber "Grow-Up" insurance, 344
gifts, spending reduction strategies, 100–101
Giszczak, Helen, 15

Givens, Charles, 14–16
Glassman, James, 138
global categories, 225
global funds, 211–212
GM Card, 100
goal-oriented savings, 131–152
  big-ticket items, 137
  business start-up, 135–136
  children's educational expenses, 136
  common dreams, 131
  competing goal strategies, 133
  emergency reserves, 133–135
  home purchases, 135–136
  prioritizing, 132–133
  retirement planning, 137–152
goals, mutual fund selection, 219–220
good debt
  acceptable levels, 24
  described, 23, 69
  vs bad, 21–24
grants, educational expenses, 270–271,
    274–276
Greenberg, Herb, 183
group insurance, 335–336
growth stocks, 210
gurus
  investment mistake, 159
  investments, 178–183
  publishing/advising conflicts, 14–15

H&R Block, tax preparers, 126–127
hair care, spending reduction strategies, 102
hard sell, 49
health clubs, spending reduction strategies,
    102
health insurance, 356–363
  buying guidelines, 359–360
  claim assistance, 360
  copayments, 358–359
  coverage denied, 360–361
  deductibles, 358–359
  guaranteed renewable, 359
  lifetime maximum benefits, 358

health insurance *(continued)*
  major medical coverage, 357
  medical information file, 360
  Medigap, 361–362
  nursing-home, 362–363
  preexisting conditions, 361
  provider choices, 357–358
  retiree medical care, 361–363
Help-U-Sell, 321
historic performance, mutual fund selection, 217–218
HMO (health maintenance organizations), 357
home equity, borrowing against, 70
home warranty plans, 328
homeowner expenses, saving, 94–95
homeowner/renter insurance, 365–370
  deductibles, 368
  dwelling coverage, 366
  flood/earthquake, 367–368
  liability, 367
  personal property, 366–367
  purchasing guidelines, 369
  special discounts, 369
homes
  buying vs renting, 93
  goal savings, 135–136
  homeowner expenses, 94–95
  mortgage refinancing, 95
  property-tax assessment appeal, 95
  purchasing, 391
  renting out a room, 95
  second, 199–200
  selling, 320–322
  spending reduction strategies, 93–95
  utility cost reductions, 95
hourly based advisors, 47
House Ways and Means Committee, tax preparers, 108
HSH Associates, 302
Hulbert, Mark, 179–181
hybrid loan, mortgages, 292
hybrid mutual funds, 209–210

• I •

IAFP (International Association of Financial Planners), 39
ICFP (Institute of Certified Financial Planners), 39
icons, used in book, 6
income
  investment, 113–116
  shifting, 113
  tax reduction strategies, 112–124
  taxable, 111–112
income tax, *see* taxes
income tax rates, 110–111
index funds, 212–213
individual stocks, 191–192, 194
inflation-indexed Treasury bonds, 262
information, bad tracking sources, 224
inspections, real estate, 315
insurance, 325–376
  add-on riders, 329
  annuities, 334
  asset, 365–376
  auto, 370–373
  basics, 325–342
  broad coverage, 332–333
  buying direct, 333–337
  buying guidelines, 326–337
  buying without paying commissions, 334
  cancer, 333
  cash value life, 17, 70, 136, 204, 351
  claim payment hassles, 338–341
  commission agents, 326
  commissions, 335
  contact lens, 329
  coverage denied, 337–338
  credit disability, 328
  credit life, 328
  daily hospitalization, 329
  deductible limits, 329–330
  deductibles, 104–105
  dental, 328
  disability, 352–356
  earthquake, 367–368
  employee overload, 326

employer provided, 335–336
estate planning, 374–376
extended warranty/repair plans, 327–328
financial catastrophes, 330–331
flood, 367–368
Gerber "Grow-Up" policy, 344
group policies, 335–336
health, 356–363
home warranty plans, 328
homeowner liability, 367
homeowner/renter, 365–370
informed purchases, 20
insurers' financial health, 336
intelligence questionnaire, 31–32
investment, 373
life, 343–352
mailed packages, 329
McCarran-Ferguson Act of 1945, 326
Medicaid, 362
Medigap, 361–362
National Insurance Consumer
    Organization, 325
nursing-home, 362–363
overview, 325–326
PMI (private mortgage insurance), 293
professional liability, 123
property damage liability, 370
quotation services, 351
rating agencies, 336
retiree medical care, 361–363
risk misperceptions, 332
shopping for, 333–337
small potato policies, 327
Social Security survivors' benefits,
    345–346
spending reduction strategies, 104–105
state disability programs, 353
term, 17, 350–351
term vs cash value, 17, 346–350
title, 316
troubleshooting problems, 337–342
types, 343–364
umbrella, 373
universal life, 204
variable annuity policy, 351

variable life, 204
whole life, 204
worker's compensation, 353
insurance brokers, 45
interest rates
    credit cards, 72–73
    mortgages, 296
international
    funds, 211–212
    stocks, 190
Internet, personal finance Web sites,
    403–405
investment distributions, 253
investment expenses, tax reduction
    strategies, 121
investment firms, 172–178
    broker-dealer networks, 175
    choosing, 173–174
    discount brokers, 173–174
    financial consultants, 175
    financial planners, 175
    no load (commission-free) mutual fund
        companies, 173
    places to avoid, 174–178
    types, 173–174
investment income, tax reduction strategies,
    113–116
investment insurance, 373
investment vehicles
    annuities, 203–204
    bonds, 187–188
    cash value life insurance, 204
    CDs (certificates of deposit), 188
    collectibles, 204
    money market accounts, 186–187
    precious metals, 203
    real estate, 195–200
    REITs (real estate investment trusts), 197
    savings accounts, 186–187
    small business, 200–202
    stocks, 189–195
    transaction/checking accounts, 186
investments, 155–184
    annuities, 239, 267
    asset allocation, 260

investments *(continued)*
  bank accounts, 254–255
  bond funds, 260–265
  brokerage research, 178
  cash-value insurance, 17
  CDs (certificates of deposit), 265–266
  commissions impact on human behavior, 175
  credit unions, 254–255
  diversification, 158, 168–172
  dollar-cost averaging, 167
  educational expenses, 269–280
  federally tax-free only money market funds, 258
  federal-tax-free-only bond funds, 265
  firms, 172–178
  goal setting, 159–160
  gurus, 178–183
  inflation-indexed Treasury bonds, 262
  intermediate, 259
  investment mistakes described, 155–159
  lending, 161–162
  limited partnerships (LPs), 16, 239
  long-term, 258–268
  long-term asset-allocation, 171–172
  low-risk/high-return, 168
  managed accounts, 177
  middle-of-the-road type, 172
  money market mutual funds, 255–258
  mutual funds, 205–228
  newsletters, 179–181
  online trading, 412–413
  outside retirement accounts, 250–268
  ownership, 162–163
  predictors, 178–183
  real estate, 42, 267, 281–322
  research software, 408–411
  retirement, 144
  retirement accounts, 229–250
  returns, 164–165
  rights/wrongs questionnaire, 30–31
  risks, 166–168
  salespeople's conflicts of interest, 175–177
  savings, 20
  selling for debt reduction, 70
  short-term, 259

small-business, 42, 268
state-and-federal-tax-free bond funds, 263–265
state-federal-tax-free money market funds, 257–258
stock funds, 266–267
suing brokers, 180
tax effects, 253–254
taxable bond funds, 260–261
taxable money market funds, 257
tax-free bonds, 238
tax-friendly, 115
U.S. Treasury bond funds, 261–263
U.S. Treasury money market funds, 257
vehicles, 185–204
vs gambling, 163–164
wrap accounts, 177
IRAs (individual retirement accounts), 29, 134, 235–236
IRR (internal rate of return), 411
IRS (Internal Revenue Service), tax forms and publications, 109, 125
itemized deductions, 116–117

Jack White & Company, 223, 245–246
Jackson Hewitt, tax preparers, 126–127
Jaffe, Charles, 37
job expenses, tax reduction strategies, 121
job search, tax reduction strategies, 120–121
job/career changes, financial success path, 387–388
Johnson, Edward C. II, 221
Johnson, Edward C. III, 221
junk mail, removing name from mailing lists, 75

Keogh plans, 112, 234–235
Kiplinger Taxcut software, 126, 408

• L •

latest/greatest overspending syndrome, 59
legal services, trusts, 43
lender fees, mortgages, 297
lenders, mortgages, 301–303
lending investments, 161–162
liabilities, described, 25
Liberty Mutual, 369
life insurance, 343–352
lifetime cap, ARM (adjustable-rate mortgage), 292
limited partnerships (LPs), 15–16, 198–199, 239
Living Trust program, 414
living trusts, 375
living wills, 374–375
living within your means, described, 55–56
loads, mutual fund cost, 215–216
loans
  educational expenses, 274–276
  friends/family, 70
  negative amortization, 301
long-term investments, 258–268

• M •

MacInTax program, 126, 408
mailed packages, insuring, 329
mailing lists, removing name from, 75
major medical coverage, health insurance, 357
Malkiel, Burton, 193
managed accounts, 42, 177
management fees, investment mistake, 157
marginal income tax rate, 110–111
marital status, financial success path, 388–390, 395–397
market capitalization, stocks, 189
market index, relevant, 218
marriages, divorce statistics, 11
MasterCard, debit cards, 74
maturity, of bonds, 209
McCarran-Ferguson Act of 1945, 326
media, 15–16
Medicaid insurance, 362
medical care, spending reduction strategies, 103–104
medical information file, 360
medical powers of attorney, 374–375
Medigap insurance, 361–362
Microsoft Money program, 407
Milken, Michael, 188
mistakes, investment, 155–159
MLS (multiple listing service), 321
money, 51–68, 70, 91, 239–246
money market accounts, 186–187, 241
money market funds, 114–115, 208–209
money market mutual funds, 255–258
Money/Vanguard, investment quiz statistics, 11
money-management, home-taught habits, 13–14
money-purchase pension plans, Keoghs, 234
Morgensen, Gretchen, 38
Morningstar, Principia Plus, 408–409
Morningstar, Web site address, 225, 409
mortgage broker, 302–303
mortgages
  15 vs 30 year terms, 294–295
  adjustment period/frequency, ARM, 300
  ARM (adjustable-rate), 290–292, 298–301
  brokers, 302–303
  fixed-rate, 289–292, 296–298
  formulas, ARM, 299–300
  hybrid loan, 292
  interest rate, 296
  lender fees, 297
  life insurance, 318–319
  lifetime cap (ARM), 292
  locating lenders, 301–303
  low-down payments, 293
  lying to qualify, 305
  negative amortization, 301
  PMI (private mortgage insurance), 293
  points, 296
  pre-approval, 303–305
  prepayment penalties, 298
  rate caps, ARM, 300–301
  refinancing, 95, 317–318
  reverse, 319–320
  start (initial) rate, ARM, 298–299
  term considerations, 292–295

Mutual Fund Home Page, 404
mutual fund industry, 207
mutual funds, 205–228
  balanced, 242
  benefits, 205–207
  best funds, 220–223
  bond, 241
  capital gains, 219
  costs, 215–217
  Fidelity Investments, 221–222
  money market, 255–258
  no-load, 259
  operating expense ratios, 217
  poor performers, 213
  prospectuses, 220
  safety of investments, 207
  selecting the best, 214–220
  stock, 242
  tax reduction strategies, 115
  tracking rankings/performance, 223–228
  tracking sources, bad, 224
  Vanguard Group, 220–221
  vs individual stock investments, 191–195
Myers, Dr. David, 61, 68

NAPFA (National Association of Personal
  Financial Advisors), 51
NASD (National Association of Securities
  Dealers), 248
NASDAQ, 189
National Association of Claims Assistance
  Professionals, 360
National Association of Enrolled Agents, 127
National Association of Independent
  Paralegals, 81
National Cancer Institute, 106
National Clearinghouse for Alcohol and
  Drug Information, 106
National Drug Abuse Information and
  Treatment Hotline, 106
National Endowment for Financial
  Education, 39

National Insurance Consumer Organization,
  325
National Opinion Research Center, 61
Nationwide Mutual, 369
needs-based financial aid, educational
  expenses, 271
negative amortization, mortgages, 301
net worth, 24–28
  assets, 24–25
  calculation sheet, 25–27
  described, 71
  formula, 24
  insurance intelligence questionnaire, 31–32
  investment rights/wrongs questionnaire,
    30–31
  liabilities, 25
  results interpretation, 27–28
  savings analysis, 28–29
New York Stock Exchange, 189
New York Times (The), "Gaming on Wall
  Street" article, 191
newsletters, investment, 179–181
Newsweek magazine, 36, 87
no load (commission-free) mutual fund
  companies, 173
no transaction fee funds, 222
no-fee credit cards, 100
no-load mutual funds, 206, 216, 259, 278
noncancelable, disability insurance, 354
nondeductible IRA contribution, 235
non-diversification, investment mistake, 158
nursing-home insurance, 362–363

Office on Smoking and Health at the Centers
  for Disease Control, 106
online services, 401–402, 409–410
online trading, 412–413
operating expenses, mutual funds, 216–217
options, 163
overspending, 56–61
ownership investments, 162–163
own-occupation policy, disability insurance,
  354

• P •

paired plans, Keoghs, 235
parents, aging, 394–395
partnerships, limited, 15
peer pressure, overspending, 59
pensions, retirement, 144–145
performance
  records, mutual funds, 206
  tracking fund, 223–228
  understanding mutual funds, 226–228
periodicals, reading/searching online,
    413–414
personal business, spending reduction
    strategies, 103
personal care, spending reduction
    strategies, 102–103
phone bills, spending reduction strategies,
    94
phone numbers
  AARP (American Association of Retired
    Persons), 320
  AFBA Industrial Bank, 100
  America Online, 402
  American Advantage, 100
  American Arbitration Association, 180
  Ameritas, 352
  Charles Schwab & Co, 74, 276
  CompuServe, 402
  Continental, 100
  Direct Insurance Services, 351, 356
  Discover Card, 100
  eTrade, 412
  Family Pharmaceuticals of America, 104
  Federal Student Financial Aid Information
    Center, 275
  Fidelity Investments, 74, 146, 245, 256
  Ford Card, 100
  GEICO, 369
  GM Card, 100
  Help-U-Sell, 321
  HSH Associates, 302
  IRS, 109, 125
  Jack White, 246
  Ken Scholen (*Your New Retirement Nest
    Egg*), 320

  MCI, 94
  National Association of Claims Assistance
    Professionals, 360
  National Association of Enrolled Agents,
    127
  National Association of Independent
    Paralegals, 81
  National Cancer Institute, 106
  National Clearinghouse for Alcohol and
    Drug Information, 106
  National Drug Abuse Information and
    Treatment Hotline, 106
  Office on Smoking and Health at the CDC,
    106
  PriceCostco, 90
  Prodigy, 402
  Retired Persons Services, Inc, 104
  Schwab, 256
  SEC (Securities and Exchange
    Commission), 380
  SelectQuote, 351
  Social Security Administration, 144, 346
  Sprint, 94
  T. Rowe Price, 146, 267
  TRW, 303
  United Mileage Plus, 100
  USAA Federal Savings, 100, 257, 351, 369
  Value Line Investment Survey, 195
  Vanguard, 244, 256, 267, 407
  Wholesale Insurance Network, 351
PLUS (Parent Loans for Undergraduate
    Students), 275
PMI (private mortgage insurance), 293
points, mortgages, 296
PPO (preferred provider organizations), 357
precious metals, 203
predictive advice, 15–16
predictors, investments, 178–183
preexisting conditions, 361
prepaid tuition plans, 279
preparers, tax, 126–128
PriceCostco, 90
price-earnings ratio, stocks, 189
Princeton Survey Research Associates,
    investment basics test, 11
principal, described, 161

Principia Plus program, 408–409
private pension plans, pitfalls, 233
probates, 375
processing fees, mortgages, 297
Prodigy, 402, 411
products, brand name cost considerations, 87
professional liability insurance, 123
profit-sharing plans, Keoghs, 234
property damage liability insurance, 370
property-tax assessments, appealing, 95
prospectus, mutual funds, 34, 220
publications
  A Random Walk Down Wall Street, 193
  advertising dependency, 18
  Barrons, 39
  Boston Globe, 37
  Complete Car Cost Guide (The), 96
  Consumer Federation of America, 308
  Consumer Reports, 36
  Consumer Reports Buying Guide, 96
  Diet for a New America, 92
  Eat for Life, 92
  Forbes magazine, 108, 177
  Gaming on Wall Street, 191
  Garzarelli Edge (The), 182
  Home Made Money, 320
  How to File for Bankruptcy, 81
  Hulbert's Financial Digest, 179–181
  Internet Report, 403
  Invisible Bankers (The), 326, 333
  IRS, 125
  Morningstar, 225
  Mutual Funds For Dummies, 223
  New York Times (The), 103, 191
  Newsweek, 36, 87, 103
  Pursuit of Happiness: Who Is Happy and Why (The), 61
  Ranking Mutual Funds on an After Tax Basis, 218
  Residential Property Acquisition Handbook, 308
  San Francisco Chronicle, 183
  spending reduction strategies, 103
  Surgeon General's Report on Nutrition and Health (The), 92

Tax Guide for Small Businesses, 125
Taxes For Dummies, 125
Value Line, 225
Value Line Investment Survey, 195
Wall Street Journal, 141
"We Can Beat the Market" unrealistic promises, 16
Wealth Without Risk, 14
Your Federal Income Tax, 125
Your New Retirement Nest Egg, 320
publicly held companies, stock issues, 189
publishers, publishing ethics, 17–19

• *Q* •

questionnaires, 30–32
QuickBooks software, 407
Quicken software, 406–407
Quinn, Jane Bryant, 36
quotation services, insurance, 351

• *R* •

rate caps, ARM (adjustable-rate mortgage), 300–301
real estate, 267, 281–322
  affordability, 283–284
  agents, 307–313
  ARM (adjustable-rate mortgage), 290–292, 298–301
  bad investments, 198–200
  buyer's brokers, 310
  buying vs renting, 281–288
  condominiums, 305
  cooperatives, 305
  equity, 195
  escrow fees, 316
  fixed-rate mortgages, 289–292, 296–298
  for sale by owner, 306
  home sale, 320–322
  informed purchases, 20
  inspections, 315
  investment advantages, 196–197
  investment options, 197–198
  limited partnerships, 198–199

locating, 305–307
long-term rental costs, 287–288
mortgage borrowing ability, 284–285
mortgage life insurance, 318–319
mortgage refinancing, 317–318
mortgages, 289–305
negotiating for, 313–314
pricing research, 307
REITs (real estate investment trusts), 197
rent vs buy expense comparisons, 285–287
reverse mortgage, 319–320
second homes, 199–200
tax reduction strategies, 115–117
time shares, 199
timeline, 282
title insurance, 316
townhomes, 305
vs stocks, 198
real estate agents, 307–313
Reed, John T., 79, 308
REITs (real estate investment trusts), 197
relevant market index, 218
rent, spending reduction strategies, 93
renter's insurance, 365–370
renting, 281–288
rent-to-own, 88
residual benefits, disability insurance, 355
Retired Persons Services, Inc (AARP), 104
retiree medical care insurance, 361–363
retirement, 112–113, 139–145, 398–400, 407
retirement accounts, 229–250
  401(k) plans, 230
  403(b) plans, 231, 249–250
  457 plans, 232
  advantages, 132–133, 229
  annuities, 236–239
  balanced mutual funds, 242
  bond mutual funds, 241
  borrowing against, 70
  contribution prioritizing, 240
  early withdrawal penalties, 134
  employer investment option constraints, 240–243
  employer-sponsored plans, 230–232
  employing-company stocks, 242–243
  GICs (guaranteed-investment contracts), 241–242
  inappropriate investments, 238–239
  IRAs (individual retirement accounts), 235–236
  Keoghs, 234–235
  limited partnerships, 239
  long-term asset-allocation, 171–172
  money allocation, 239–246
  money markets, 241
  objections to, 150–152
  private pension plan pitfalls, 233
  savings, 241
  savings goal, 137-152
  self-employment, 123, 232–235
  self-employment plan money allocation, 243–246
  SEP-IRAs, 233
  setting up, 240
  spousal IRA, 235
  stock mutual funds, 242
  tax-free bonds, 238
  tax-sheltered, 113–116
  transferring, 246–249
Retirement Manager program, 407
Retirement Planner program, 407
retirement plans. See retirement accounts
returns, investments, 164–165
reverse mortgage, 319–320
RIAs (registered investment advisors), 39
riders, insurance add-ons, 329
risk ignorance, investment mistake, 157
risk level, mutual fund benefits, 207
risk-adjusted performance, 225
risk-adjusted returns, 181
risks, 166–168, 332
Robbins, John, 92
rooms, renting, 95

• S •

sales loads, mutual funds, 215
sales solicitations, investment mistake, 156
salespeople, mutual fund benefits, 207
Sam's Club, 98

savings accounts, 186–187, 241
  analysis, 28–29
  college costs, 277–278
  emergency reserves, 133–135
  goals, 131–152
  investing, 20, 254–258
  prioritizing goals, 132–133
  reducing debt with, 70–71
  retirement plans, 137–152, 144
  saving too much/spending too little, 138
  statistics, 11
  vs money market funds, 208–209
Scheiber, Anne, 138
scholarships, educational expenses,
    274–276
Scholen, Ken, 320
school subjects, lobbying for personal
    finance, 12
SEC (Securities and Exchange Commission),
    34, 39, 173, 248, 409
second homes, real estate investment,
    199–200
sector funds, 213
secured credit cards, 78
SelectQuote, 351
self-employment
  data tracking, 124
  money allocation, 243–246
  retirement plans, 232–235
  tax reduction strategies, 121–124
self-perpetuating consultants, 43
selling your house, 320
Senate Finance Committee, tax preparers,
    108
SEP-IRA (simplified employee pension
    individual retirement account), 122, 233
share price vs distribution, 227
Shaw, George Bernard, 36
shelter, 93–95
Shoven, John D., 18
Simon, William E, 107
Simply Money program, 407
small business
  financial success path, 390–391
  investment vehicles, 200–202
  investments, 268
Social Security, 141–144, 345–346, 353

Social Security integration, Keogh plans, 234
socially responsible funds, 214
software
  checkbook, 405–407
  investment research, 408–411
  investment return tracking, 411–412
  legal document preparation, 414
  personal finance, 401–403
  retirement planning, 407
  spending analysis, 66–67
  tax information organization, 117
  tax preparation, 126, 408
soothsayers, investment mistake, 159
sources, debit cards, 74
specialty funds, 213
speculation, 163
spending, 20, 85–106
spending analysis, 61–68
spousal IRA, 235
standard deductions, 116
State Farm Insurance, 369
state-and-federal-tax-free bond funds,
    263–265
state-federal-tax-free money market funds,
    257–258
statistics, financial illiteracy, 11
stock brokers, 45, 207
stock mutual funds, 210, 242, 266–267
stocks, 189–195
  aggressive growth, 34
  employment company, 242–243
  exchanges, 189
  individual investment, 191–195
  international, 190
  investment mistake, 158–159
  market capitalization, 189
  mutual funds vs individual investments,
    191–195
  price-earnings ratio, 189
  publicly held companies, 189
  vs legalized gambling, 191
  vs real estate, 198
Stossel, John, 332
strategies, spending reduction, 89–106
StreetSmart program, 413
Subsidized Stafford Loans, 275
suits, brokers, 180

• T •

T. Rowe Price, 146
T. Rowe Price's Spectrum funds, 212
tax attorneys, 128
tax forms Web site, 408
tax system, understanding, 108–112
taxable bond funds, 260–261
taxable money market funds, 257
Taxcut program, 408
taxes
  1040-ES, 109
  alternative minimum tax, 111
  audits, 128–130
  CPAs (certified public accountants),
    127–128
  deduction strategies, 116–124
  distributions, 253–254
  do-it-yourself preparation, 124–126
  EAs (enrolled agents), 127
  employment income reductions, 112–113
  estate planning, 376
  ignoring consequences, 159
  income shifting, 113
  investment effects, 253–254
  investment income, 113–116
  IRS publications, 125
  marginal income tax rate, 110–111
  mutual funds, 218–219
  nondeductible IRA contribution, 235
  preparation software, 126, 408
  preparation/planning options, 124–128
  preparers, 126–128
  spending reduction strategies, 105
  system overview, 108–112
  tax attorneys, 128
  taxable income defined, 111–112
  tax-friendly investments, 114–116
  total, 109
  W-4 form, 109
tax-free bonds, 238
tax-reduction accounts, 132–133
tax-sheltered
  annuities, 403(b) plans, 231
  retirement accounts, 113–116
telemarketing, investment mistake, 156

telephones, spending reduction strategies,
  94
tens
  life changing tips, 385–400
  questions for financial advisors, 379–384
  tips for using your computer for your
    personal finances, 401–414
  top market underperformers, 213
term insurance
  purchasing, 350–351
  vs cash value insurance, 17, 346–350
time shares, real estate investment, 199
title insurance, real estate, 316
Tobias, Andrew, 326, 333
top producers, real estate agents, 312
total cost, vs monthly payments, 75
total return, mutual funds, 11, 227
total tax, 109
townhomes, 305
trading online, 412–413
transaction/checking accounts, 186
transportation, spending reduction
  strategies, 95–98
Treasury bonds, buying direct, 262
Triple Check, tax preparers, 126–127
troubleshooting, insurance problems,
  337–342
trusts, 43, 197
TRW, 303
TurboTax program, 126, 408
types of funds, 208–214

• U •

U.S. Treasury bond funds, 261–263
U.S. Treasury money market funds, 257
umbrella insurance, 373
unethical practices, 51–52
uninsured/underinsured motorist insurance,
  370
United Mileage Plus, 100
universal life insurance, 204
unreimbursed job expenses, tax reduction
  strategies, 121
Unsubsidized Stafford Loans, 275
USAA Federal Savings, 100, 351, 369
utility costs, spending reduction strategies,
  95

• *V* •

vacations, spending reduction strategies, 101–102
value stocks, 210
Vanguard Group, 213, 220–221, 244, 411
Vanguard's Star and Life strategy funds, 212
variable life insurance, 204
vehicles, investment, 185–204
vesting schedules, Keogh plans, 234
VISA, debit cards, 74

• *W* •

W-4 form, acquiring, 109
waiting periods, disability insurance, 355
Wall Street Journal (The), Web site address, 414
Web sites
  eSchwab service, 412
  eTrade, 412
  EyeQ search engine, 414
  Fidelity Investments, 404–405
  IRS, 408
  Jack White, 412
  Morningstar, 409
  Mutual Fund Home Page, 404
  personal finance, 403–405
  SEC (Securities and Exchange Commission), 409
  sponsored content, 404
  tax forms, 408
  Vanguard, 411
  Wall Street Journal (The), 414
whole life insurance, 204
Wholesale Insurance Network, 351
WillMaker program, 414
Winchester Mystery House, 107
Winchester, Sarah, 107
windfalls, financial strategies for, 397–398
worker's compensation, 353
worldwide categories, 225
worldwide funds, 211–212
wrap accounts, 42, 177

IDG BOOKS WORLDWIDE REGISTRATION CARD

RETURN THIS REGISTRATION CARD FOR FREE CATALOG

Title of this book: **Personal Finance For Dummies®, 2E**

My overall rating of this book: ❑ Very good [1] ❑ Good [2] ❑ Satisfactory [3] ❑ Fair [4] ❑ Poor [5]

How I first heard about this book:

❑ Found in bookstore; name: [6]   ❑ Book review: [7]

❑ Advertisement: [8]   ❑ Catalog: [9]

❑ Word of mouth; heard about book from friend, co-worker, etc.: [10]   ❑ Other: [11]

What I liked most about this book:

_____

_____

What I would change, add, delete, etc., in future editions of this book:

_____

_____

Other comments:

_____

Number of computer books I purchase in a year: ❑ 1 [12] ❑ 2-5 [13] ❑ 6-10 [14] ❑ More than 10 [15]

I would characterize my computer skills as: ❑ Beginner [16] ❑ Intermediate [17] ❑ Advanced [18] ❑ Professional [19]

I use ❑ DOS [20] ❑ Windows [21] ❑ OS/2 [22] ❑ Unix [23] ❑ Macintosh [24] ❑ Other: [25]_____
                                                                                    (please specify)

I would be interested in new books on the following subjects:
(please check all that apply, and use the spaces provided to identify specific software)

❑ Word processing: [26]   ❑ Spreadsheets: [27]

❑ Data bases: [28]   ❑ Desktop publishing: [29]

❑ File Utilities: [30]   ❑ Money management: [31]

❑ Networking: [32]   ❑ Programming languages: [33]

❑ Other: [34]

I use a PC at (please check all that apply): ❑ home [35] ❑ work [36] ❑ school [37] ❑ other: [38] _____

The disks I prefer to use are ❑ 5.25 [39] ❑ 3.5 [40] ❑ other: [41]_____

I have a CD ROM: ❑ yes [42]   ❑ no [43]

I plan to buy or upgrade computer hardware this year: ❑ yes [44]   ❑ no [45]

I plan to buy or upgrade computer software this year: ❑ yes [46]   ❑ no [47]

Name: _____ Business title: [48] _____ Type of Business: [49]

Address (❑ home [50] ❑ work [51]/Company name: _____)

Street/Suite# _____

City [52]/State [53]/Zipcode [54]: _____ Country [55] _____

❑ **I liked this book!** You may quote me by name in future
IDG Books Worldwide promotional materials.

My daytime phone number is _____

IDG BOOKS

®

THE WORLD OF COMPUTER KNOWLEDGE

☐ # YES!

Please keep me informed about IDG's World of Computer Knowledge.
Send me the latest IDG Books catalog.

COMPUTER
BOOK SERIES
FROM IDG

NO POSTAGE
NECESSARY
IF MAILED
IN THE
UNITED STATES

BUSINESS REPLY MAIL
FIRST CLASS MAIL   PERMIT NO. 2605   FOSTER CITY, CALIFORNIA

IDG Books Worldwide
919 E Hillsdale Blvd, STE 400
Foster City, CA 94404-9691